朗文
外研社
新概念英语

NEW CONCEPT ENGLISH

New Edition 新 版

Fluency in English
流利英语

4

亚历山大（**L. G. ALEXANDER**）何其莘 著

外语教学与研究出版社

PEARSON LONGMAN

京权图字：01-2004-4975

图书在版编目（CIP）数据

朗文·外研社新概念英语：新版.4 ／（英）亚历山大（L. G. Alexander），何其莘著. ——
北京 ：外语教学与研究出版社，1997.10（2019.4 重印）
ISBN 978-7-5600-1349-7

Ⅰ．①朗… Ⅱ．①亚… ②何… Ⅲ．①英语－自学参考资料 Ⅳ．①H31

中国版本图书馆 CIP 数据核字（2017）第 118482 号

出 版 人　蔡剑峰
出版发行　外语教学与研究出版社
社　　址　北京市西三环北路 19 号（100089）
网　　址　http://www.fltrp.com
印　　刷　唐山市润丰印务有限公司
开　　本　787×1092　1/16
印　　张　19.75
版　　次　1997 年 10 月第 1 版 2019 年 4 月第 75 次印刷
印　　数　1606000 — 1656000 册
书　　号　ISBN 978-7-5600-1349-7
定　　价　29.90 元

购书咨询：（010）88819926　电子邮箱：club@fltrp.com
外研书店：https://waiyants.tmall.com
凡印刷、装订质量问题，请联系我社印制部
联系电话：（010）61207896　电子邮箱：zhijian@fltrp.com
凡侵权、盗版书籍线索，请联系我社法律事务部
举报电话：（010）88817519　电子邮箱：banquan@fltrp.com
物料号：113490101

朗文　新概念英语（新版）
外研社

NEW CONCEPT ENGLISH (*New Edition*)
FLUENCY IN ENGLISH *Students' Book* 流利英语　学生用书4

English edition © L. G. Alexander 1967
Original English material © Addison Wesley Longman Ltd. 1997
This revised edition of New Concept English with the addition of Chinese material is
published by arrangement with Addison Wesley Longman Limited, London and
Longman Asia Limited, Hong Kong.

Licensed for sale in the mainland territory of the People's Republic of China only

This simplified Chinese characters edition first published
in 1997 jointly by Foreign Language Teaching and Research Press
and Longman Asia Ltd.

双语版出版人：沈维贤
合作出版人：李朋义
合作编著者：亚历山大（L. G. Alexander），何其莘
策划编辑：赵嘉文，蔡女良
责任编辑：（朗文）王德厚，梅丹心；（外研社）孙蓓，任小玫
封面设计：梁若基

外语教学与研究出版社
朗文出版亚洲有限公司　联合出版

What's new in this edition?

This is the only new edition ever to be undertaken since *NCE* was originally published. The classic course continues to provide a complete and well-tried system for learning English, enabling students to reach their maximum potential in the four primary skills of understanding, speaking, reading and writing. The sound basic principles which made *NCE* a world-famous course have been retained. However, the following important features have been introduced in the new edition:

- All topical references in the texts and exercises have been brought up to date.
- All outdated texts have been completely replaced and accompanied by new exercises and new artwork.
- The original methodology has been modified to improve communication skills, with active training in listening comprehension right from the very first lesson.
- Drills and written exercises, previously published separately as supplementary materials, have been incorporated into the main coursebooks.
- The following features have been added to help Chinese learners of English:
  Bi-lingual vocabulary lists; notes in Chinese on texts and exercises and suggested translations of the texts.
- The pages have been enlarged and, where possible, are self-contained, so that lessons are easy to conduct.

本版本有什么新内容？

本版是《新概念英语》首次出版以来第一次推出的新版本 。这套经典教材一如既往地向读者提供一个完整的 、经过实践检验的英语学习体系, 使学生有可能在英语的 4 项基本技能——理解 、口语 、阅读和写作——方面最大限度地发挥自己的潜能。新版本保留了《新概念英语》得以成为世界闻名英语教程的一整套基本原则, 同时又包含了以下重要特色:

- 所有课文和练习中有关时事的内容都已更新 。
- 所有过时的课文都已更换, 由新课文和配套的新练习、新插图取代 。
- 原有的教学法经过调整, 以利于提高学生的交际能力 。从第一课开始就安排了有效的听力训练 。
- 教材更简洁精练, 过去作为补充材料单独出版的句型训练和笔头练习均已取消, 其精华纳入主干教程 。
- 为了帮助中国的英语学习者, 新版增加了英汉对照词汇表、课文注释、简短的练习讲解和课文的参考译文 。
- 版面加大, 在可能情况下, 每课书相对独立, 以方便课堂教学 。

ACKNOWLEDGEMENTS

We are grateful to the following for permission to reproduce copyright material:
George Allen & Unwin Ltd for material from *Science Makes Sense* by Ritchie Calder, *Portraits from Memory* by Bertrand Russell; Associated Iliffe Press Ltd for material from 'The Past Life of the Earth' by Errol White published in Discovery (Discovery is now incorporated with *Science Journal*); The Barrie Group of Publishers (Barrie Books Ltd) for material from *Finding Fossil Man* by Robin Place; the author for material from 'Non-Auditory Effects of Noise' by D. E. Broadbent, M.A. published in *Science Survey*, 2nd Edn; the author and Chatto & Windus Ltd for material from *Elephants* by Richard Carrington; the Proprietors of *The Week-End Telegraph* for material from 'The Great Escape' by Nigel Buxton published in issue 11 June 1965 and 'Are There Strangers in Space' by Anthony Michaelis published in issue 13 August 1965; Dennis Dobson, Publishers from material from *The Pegasus Book of Inventors* by Egon Larsen; the author from material from 'The Stuff of Dreams' by Dr. Christopher Evans, published in *The Listener*, 8 December 1966; *Pieces of Mind* by C. E. M. Joad Faber & Faber Ltd and Doubleday & Company, Inc. for material from *The Snake* by John Crompton, Copyright © 1963 by John Crompton (published in the U.S.A. under the title *Snake Lore*); the author for material from 'Virtue and a Fast Gun' by Carl Foreman, published in *The Observer*, 10 October 1965; the author's agents for material from 'Exploring the Sea-Floor' by Dr. T. F. Gaskell, published in *Science Survey*, 2nd Edn; the author's agents for material from 'Television and Education' by Grace Wyndham Goldie, published in *The Listener*, 16 April 1964; Victor Gollancz Ltd for material from *Matterhorn Man* by Walter Unsworth; Granada TV Networks Ltd for an extract from the transcript of 'The Search for Earth's Minerals' By Dr. T. F. Gaskell which was transmitted by Granada TV in their Schools programme *Discovery* and subsequently published by Methuen & Co. Ltd in 1961 for Granada TV Networks Ltd. Robert Hale Ltd for material from *Spies in Britain* by Bernard Newman; Hamish Hamilton Ltd and Harper & Row, Publishers for material from *Man, the Unknown* by Alexis Carrel; George G. Harrap & Co. Ltd for material from *The Origin of Things* by Julius E. Lips; Heinemann Educational Books Ltd and the University of Washington Press for material from *Of Men and Galaxies* by Fred Hoyle; the author's agents for material from *Window in the Sea* by Ralph Nading Hill; the author for material from 'Galileo Reborn' by Michael A. Hoskin published in *The Listener*, 27 February 1964; the author for material from 'Out of the Air' by Fielden Hughes published in *The Listener*, 12 November 1964; Michael Joseph Ltd for material from *A Countryman's Creed* by Sir William Beach Thomas; Le Carré Productions Ltd for material from *What Every Writer Wants* by John le Carré published in *Harper's Magazine*, November 1965; Longmans, Green & Co. Ltd and David McKay Company, Inc. for material from *The Status Seekers* by Vance Packard; Longmans, Green & Co. Ltd and St. Martin's Press, Inc. for material from *The Backward Society* by Raymond Frost; Macgibbon & Kee Ltd for material from *The Habit of Loving* by Doris Lessing; the author for material from 'Seeing Hands' by Eric de Mauny, published in *The Listener*, 13 August 1964; the author for material from 'The Sculptor Speaks' by Henry Moore, published originally in *The Listener*, 25 February 1965; Frederick Muller Ltd for material from *The Earth Beneath Us* by H. H. Swinnerton; Odhams Books Ltd for material from *Painting as a Pastime* by Winston S. Churchill; the author for material from *Journey Through Adolescence* by Doris Odlum, published by Delisle Ltd; Oliver & Boyd Ltd for material from *Our Friends the Spiders* by T. H. Gillespie; the Estate of the late George Orwell for material from *This Sporting Spirit* by George Orwell; Penguin Books Ltd for material from *The Consumer Society and the Law* by Gordon Barrie and Aubrey L. Diamond, *The Personality of Man*

by G. N. M. Tyrrell, and *Patients and Doctors* by Kenneth Walker; Routledge & Kegan Paul Ltd for material from *The Social Function of Science* by J. D. Bernal; Routledge & Kegan Paul Ltd and Houghton Mifflin Company for material from *Patterns of Culture* by Ruth Benedict; the author for material from *The Raising of the Vasa* by Roy Saunders published by Oldbourne Press; Ward Lock & Co. Ltd for material from *Curiosities of Animal Life* by Maurice Burton; and George Weidenfeld & Nicolson Ltd and The New American Library, Inc. for material from *The Process of Ageing* by Dr. Alex Comfort, Copyright © 1961, 1964 by Alex Comfort; © The Economist, London (24 May 1997) for material from *Trading standards*; Susan J. LeClair, Director, Editorial Service for material from *2 silicon valley* in *US News & World Report*; Florence Eichin, Permissions, Viking Inc. for material from *The Butterfly Effect* in *Chaos* by James Gleick; Oxford UK for material from *Water and the Traveller* by Richard Dawood; Lynne Sellers, Investors Chronicles for material from *Planning a Share Portfolio*.

We have been unable to trace the copyright owner in 'Space Odyssey' from a journal called '7 Days', Feb 19, 1989 and 'Waves' from World Magazine and would welcome any information that would enable us to do so.

We are grateful to the following for permission to use the photographs throughout the book:
Aerofilms Library – Lesson 16; BP – Lesson 13; Camera Press Limited – Lesson 2; J. Allan Cash – Lessons 36B, 47; Douglas Dalton: Natural History Photo Agency – Lesson 23; Fox Photos Ltd. – Lessons 37, 46; I. C. I. – Lesson 15; Keystone Press Agency – Lesson 31; Malawi High Commission – Lesson 36A; Mansell Collection – Lesson 30; Novosti Press Agency – Lesson 4; PAF International – Lesson 18; Paramount – Lesson 39; Paul Popper – Lessons 7, 17, 20, 29, 41, 43, 44; Radio Times Hulton Picture Library – Lessons 1, 9, 26; Royal Astronomical Society – Lesson 32; Russell Preece – Lesson 12; Science Museum – Lesson 42A; Sjöhistoriska Museet – Lesson 27; Swiss National Tourist Office – Lesson 3; United States Information Services – Lessons 19, 22, 25; Vu Picture Agency – Lesson 33; Science Photo Library – Lessons 10, 14, 19, 48; Sygma – Lessons 6, 22, 35; Robertlam Photo Agency – Lesson 28; David Kirby – Lesson 12.

CONTENTS 目录

To the teacher and student

Towards fluency

The student who has successfully completed an intermediate course in English often has good reason to feel disheartened when he embarks on an advanced course. The reason for this is not so much that he has at his command only a fairly limited vocabulary, but that he is suddenly thrust into the world of ideas. The biggest barrier, particularly with younger students, is not language as such, but mental maturity. An advanced course necessarily presupposes a degree of mental maturity and fairly wide general knowledge which many students do not possess. In oral work, the student is expected to take part in discussions on argumentative topics covering a wide range of subjects. As far as writing is concerned, it is not enough to be able to write narrative or descriptive compositions in simple, correct English. The student must pay close attention to form and content; he must express difficult ideas and know how to handle facts and opinions. Where before his précis work consisted largely in reproducing the main sequence of events in a piece of narrative, he now has to summarize difficult passages of factual, argumentative and reflective prose. In addition to this, he frequently has to work under pressure, particularly if he is preparing for an examination. Because the syllabus is loaded, the teacher is obliged to assume that his students have, by now, grasped the fundamentals of grammar. He therefore spends little, if any, time on it, even though he knows how much his students require further practice.

The answer to these problems is again to be found in the use of carefully selected passages which can be used as multi-purpose texts to continue the student's training in the four skills, understanding, speaking, reading and writing. At this level, the texts should be selected from the work of a wide variety of authors, so that the student can become familiar with different styles of writing. The passages should be graded in terms of length, complexity and intellectual content to introduce the student gradually to the world of ideas.

About this course

Basic aims

1   To provide a comprehensive course for adult or secondary students who have completed an intermediate course. The course contains enough material for one or two years' work, depending on the amount of time allotted to it. The student will receive most of his training in the classroom and will be required to do some extra work in his own time.

2   To introduce the student gradually to the world of ideas and to make him familiar with a wide range of different styles of writing. The passages are graded not only from the point of view of language, but in terms of length and intellectual content as well.

3   To continue the student's training in the four skills: *understanding, speaking, reading* and *writing* — in that order. In this respect, the course sets out to do two things: to provide material which will be suitable for aural/oral practice and which can also be used to train the student systematically to write English at a difficult level. The passages will be used to develop a maturity of approach as well as to provide a stimulating basis for discussion and study.

4   To provide the student with a book which will enable him to *use* the language.

5   To provide the teacher with material which will enable him to conduct each lesson with a minimum of preparation.

6   To enable the teacher and the student to work entirely from a single volume without the need for additional 'practice books'.

For whom the course is intended

This course should be found suitable for:

1   Adult or secondary students who have completed *Practice and Progress* and *Developing Skills*, or who have completed any other intermediate course.

2   Schools and Language Institutes where 'wastage' caused by irregular attendance is a problem.

3   Advanced students who wish to study on their own.

How much knowledge has been assumed?

The material in *Developing Skills*, the intermediate course which precedes this one, has been designed to 'overlap' this course. Students who have completed it will have no difficulty whatever in continuing where they left off.

Students who have learnt English from other courses and who now wish to continue their studies with this course should have a fair working knowledge of the items listed below.

Assumed knowledge

Listening comprehension and speaking

1   The ability to understand English dealing with everyday subjects and spoken at normal speed.

2   The ability to answer questions which require short or extended answers.

3   The ability to ask questions to elicit short or extended answers.

4   The ability to use orally a large number of elementary sentence patterns.

5   The ability to reproduce orally the substance of a passage of English after having heard it several times and read it.

6   The ability to conduct a simple conversation on everyday subjects (e.g. expressing preferences; polite interchange; careers; travel; common experiences, etc.)

7   The ability to give a short talk (prepared or unprepared) lasting up to four minutes on everyday subjects.

Reading

1   The ability to read a passage of English aloud. The student should have a fair grasp of the *rhythm* of the language (stress and intonation) even if he is unable to pronounce unfamiliar words correctly.

2   Students should have a passive vocabulary range of around 3,000 words and should be able to read works of fiction and non-fiction to this level.

Writing

1   *Word order*

The ability to write simple, compound and complex sentences. The ability to join simple sentences using conjunctions to form compound and complex sentences. A sound command of the *word order* in an English sentence.

2   *Comprehension*

The ability to cope with reading comprehension exercises to the level of the Cambridge First Certificate or any equivalent examination.

3   *Vocabulary*

The ability to deduce the meaning of words and phrases from a context and to explain them by means of other words and phrases.

4   *Summary writing*

The ability to reconstruct the main sequence of events in a piece of narrative prose (e.g. describing actions or experiences). This presupposes that the student is capable of the following:

a   Reading, understanding and carrying out instructions.

b   Extracting specific information to write a list of *points* in note form outlining the main sequence of events in a piece of narrative prose.

c Connecting these points to form simple, compound and complex sentences and arranging them logically to write a well-constructed paragraph in a set number of words.

5 *Composition*
The ability to write a narrative or descriptive composition of about 300 words. This presupposes that the student is capable of the following:

a Making a short plan (i.e. listing a few ideas in note form).
b Connecting the ideas to write a composition of about three or four paragraphs. The composition should contain an Introduction, Development and Conclusion.

6 *Letter writing*
The ability to write a short personal letter of about 100 words. This presupposes that the student is familiar with correct layout (heading, salutation, subscription).

Command of language
1 *Grammar (Key structures)*
The course presupposes that the student has had a fair amount of practice in using tenses, articles and prepositions. It is clearly recognized, however, that further practice is required.

2 *Usage (Special difficulties)*
The student should be familiar with common phrasal verbs, certain words which are often confused or misused, and a limited number of idiomatic expressions.

A description of the course

The course consists of the following:

- One textbook (to be used by teachers and students)
- A set of cassettes, on which the multi-purpose texts have been recorded.

General arrangement of material
The course falls into two parts each of which is preceded by a searching test. The first part aims to teach English at the pre-advanced level: it ensures that there will be a smooth transition between intermediate and advanced levels. The second part aims to teach English at the advanced level.

Each part consists of three units and each unit comprises eight passages, making a total of forty-eight passages in all. As the course progresses, the passages become longer and more complex. Each unit is preceded by Instructions to the Student.

The passages are multi-purpose texts. Each passage will be used to train the student in the following: aural comprehension; oral practice; reading aloud; oral composition; extended oral exercises; dictation; comprehension; vocabulary; sentence and paragraph structure; summary; composition; grammar and usage.

Instructions to the student

The instructions which precede each Unit should be read carefully. They deal only with the difficulties presented by the central exercises in each Unit: Sentence structure; The paragraph; Summary; Composition, etc. The successful completion of this course depends entirely on the student's ability to carry out the instructions given. Worked examples have not been provided; what the student has to do should be abundantly clear without the aid of examples. The exercises that follow each passage should be done *in the order in which they have been presented*.

Introductory tests

The test which precedes Part 1 will enable the student to tell if he is ready for this course. The test leading to Part 2 is so designed that the student will not be expected to make too sudden a jump between one year's work and the next. It will provide a clear indication of how much the student has assimilated.

The passages

The passages have been drawn from the work of a wide variety of modern authors and are extremely varied in style and subject matter. Some of the passages are broadcast talks and will be suitable for oral work. The approximate length of the passages in each unit is as follows:

Unit 1: 250-300 words.
Unit 2: 250-300 words.
Unit 3: 300-350 words.
Unit 4: 350-400 words.
Unit 5: 400-500 words.
Unit 6: 550-700 words.

Oral exercises

Oral exercises are not included in the book itself and must be supplied by the teacher. They may be along the lines suggested in the section on *How to use this course*.

Comprehension questions

The questions in Part 1 are straightforward; in Part 2, they are more searching.

Vocabulary

The student will be required to write sentences using words and phrases derived from the passage.

Summary writing and composition

The work that will be done in summary and composition has been carefully graded and controlled by means of a series of progressive exercises which gradually become more difficult as the Course proceeds.

The treatment of these two exercises is based on the principle that summary-writing is the exact counterpart of composition, the former being largely a matter of *analysis*; the latter of synthesis. For instance, when setting out to write a summary, the student must be able to understand a passage, break it down into its component parts, and reconstruct the original 'plan' of the piece in note form before writing his own version. Essay writing requires the reverse procedure, for the student sets out with a subject which has to be developed first in note form and ultimately written out in continuous prose. Accordingly, the exercises will aim at training the student in these two processes and will run exactly parallel. In Part 1 many of the exercises are based directly on material contained in the passages. The student will therefore be able to correct his own work simply by referring to the passage after he has finished an exercise.

Key structures and Special difficulties

All the exercises on Key structures (Essential grammar) and Special difficulties (Usage) are derived from each passage. No use has been made of grammatical terminology, all difficulties being presented as sentence pattern. Where explanations are necessary, this has been done by relating one pattern to another.

Practice work in the Key structures consists largely of exercises in recall, particular attention being paid to the use of verbs, prepositions, articles and the position of adverbs. The student will again be able to correct a great deal of his own work by referring to the passage after he has completed an exercise.

The exercises on Special difficulties deal entirely with problems concerning usage: vocabulary, phrasal verbs and idiomatic expressions. Many of these are deliberately repetitive, the aim being to eliminate common recurring errors.

Multiple choice questions

Multiple choice is a *testing* device, not a *teaching* device. Its purpose here is to train students for the kind of objective testing which is usual in public examinations. Multiple choice exercises cover the following: reading comprehension, structure and vocabulary.

How to use this course

TEACHERS! PLEASE READ THIS INTRODUCTION CAREFULLY!

Allocation of time

Ideally, two classroom lessons of approximately 50 minutes each should be spent on each text. The first lesson should be devoted to Guided and free conversation; the second to Composition and language study. This means that there is enough material in this book for 120 lessons. However, you may choose to spend only one classroom lesson on each text — in which case, every lesson may be devoted to Guided conversation and a selection of exercises may be set as homework. Your first task is to decide how much time you have in your programme in relation to the material available in the course.

The suggestions given below outline the basic steps in each lesson. You may decide to follow them closely, adapt them to suit your style of teaching, or reject them altogether — BUT PLEASE READ THEM FIRST!

Lesson 1: Guided and free conversation

Books Required:
Fluency in English (for teachers and students)

The stages of the Lesson

1 Listening comprehension	about 15 minutes
2 Question and answer practice	about 10 minutes
3 Oral reconstruction of the text	about 10-20 minutes
4 Topics for discussion	about 10-20 minutes

Let's see what each step involves:

1 Listening comprehension (about 15 minutes)

There are eight recommended steps for presenting each text which will train students to understand spoken English. The steps are as follows:
a Introduce the topic
b Understand the situation
c Listening objective
d Play the tape or read the text
e Answer the question
f Intensive reading
g Play the tape or read the text again
h Read aloud

Every one of these steps must be very brief:

a Introduce the topic

The teacher introduces the topic with a few words, so the student clearly understands what's going on and is not obliged to guess. English should be used entirely as far as possible. For example (Text 1):

Today we'll listen to a text about pre-historic people.

b Understand the situation

The students are asked to look at the photograph to see if they can understand what is going on in the text. The teacher may ask a few questions in English to help the students understand the photo. For example (Text 1):

Look at the photo and tell me what you can see.

What were these tools used for?

c Listening objective

The teacher gives the students 'a listening objective', by setting them a question they will try to find the answer to. This means, the students will listen to the text *actively* rather than *passively*.

For example (Text 1):

Listen to the story, then tell me: Why are legends handed down by story-tellers useful?

The Coursebook always provides a question of this kind.

d Play the tape or read the text

The teacher plays the tape or reads the text just once while the students simply listen without interruption. They should try to 'hear' the answer to the question given in *c* above.

e Answer the question

Now the teacher asks the question (*c* above) again and the students try to answer it: 'Now you've heard the story, why are legends handed down by story-tellers useful?' Don't let students shout out the answer. Train them to raise their hands if they think they know the answer. Get one student to answer, then ask the others, 'How many of you agree with him/her?' 'Put up your hands if you agree with him/her.' 'You don't agree (to another student), so what do you think the answer is?' 'How many of you agree with him/her? Put up your hands.' This keeps the students guessing and involves *the whole class*. Students should be trained to listen right from the start without 'preparation' or 'translation'. They will soon get used to the sound of English and to understanding the meaning of what they hear.

f Intensive reading

Now the teacher plays the tape or reads the text again, pausing after every sentence to check the students understand. This is an extremely important part of the lesson as the students must fully understand the text at the end of the presentation. Rather than give direct explanations, try to get as much information as possible from the students (think of it as 'a corkscrew operation'!). Explanations should be given entirely in English, but don't carry direct-method teaching to absurd lengths. Use gesture and mime where possible. If some of your students still don't understand, ask the best students in the class for a 'confirmatory translation' of a particular word or phrase for the benefit of other students who haven't grasped the meaning. Remember, if you don't translate a particular difficulty, then someone in the class will. However, translation should always be regarded as a last resort.

g Play the tape or read the text again

Play the tape or read the text again right through without interruption. This time, the students will understand it without difficulty because of the careful explanation you provided in *f* above.

h Read aloud

Ask a few students to read the text aloud, taking turns round the class. You will be able to tell from this how well particular students can pronounce correctly the English they have already heard.

This preparation should not take more than about fifteen minutes. DON'T SPEND TOO MUCH TIME ON ANY ONE ACTIVITY!

Students working at home on their own should listen to the recording of each text as often as is necessary for them to become thoroughly familiar with it.

2 Question and answer practice (about 10 minutes)

Once the text has been presented, proceed with question and answer practice. This is in two parts:

a The teacher asks a variety of questions and the students answer them

b The students ask a variety of questions

a The teacher asks a variety of questions and the students answer them

The questions you ask should be highly varied (including both yes/no questions and Wh-questions). They should be asked rapidly round the class and the students should be trained to answer naturally (i.e. don't insist on complete answers where they would not normally be given in the course of ordinary conversation). The essence of this exercise is *pace*, so it's better to get the students to answer individually rather than in chorus. Here, for example are a few questions which relate to Text 1:

TEACHER: How long ago did people first learn to write?
Was it two thousand years ago?
What's the situation regarding writing in some parts of the world today?

b The students ask a variety of questions

In order to prevent incorrect forms like *Where he went?*, students are trained to ask two questions at a time. The first of these is a yes/no question and the second a Wh-question. For example:

TEACHER: Ask me if people first learned to write 5,000 years ago.
STUDENT: Did people first learn to write 5,000 years ago?
TEACHER: How long ago ...?
STUDENT: How long ago did people first learn to write? (Not *How long ago people first learned to write?* or *How long ago people first write?*)

3 Oral resconstruction of the text (about 10-20 minutes)

This is an optional exercise. You can skip it and go straight on to Topics for discussion, or spend a little time on oral reconstruction before going on to Topics for discussion. The section consists of numbered notes which form a summary of the text. Write notes on the blackboard (or have them written up and covered before the lesson begins) and ask individual students round the class to tell you the story. This gives students semi-prepared practice in speaking without interruption. Point out only the main errors made *after* students finish speaking. Don't constantly interrupt them!

Here, for example, are some notes which relate to part of Text 1:

1. Read — 5,000 — Near East — people — write.
2. Some parts of the world — people — now — write.
3. Can preserve history — sagas legends — generation.
4. Useful — migrations — people long ago — none could write.
5. Anthropologists wondered — ancestors Polynesia — came from.
6. Sagas — Indonesia — 2,000 years ago.

4 Topics for discussion (about 10 minutes)

The final part of the Guided conversation lessons should be devoted to free conversation. Students should be invited to 'have a go' at expressing their own ideas, no matter how many mistakes they make. The topics become progressively harder *within* each lesson and one or all of them may be attempted. Individual students should be invited to make one or two statements about the topics. As conversational skill develops, you may occasionally arrange to spend more time on free conversation (completely omitting, for example, 'Oral reconstruction of the text'). Here, for example, are a few topics suggested by Text 1:

a Exchange information about local history and pre-history: tell us what you know.
b Exchange information about the migration of people in ancient and modern time: tell us what you know.
c Is migration more difficult now than it used to be in the past? Why/ Why not?

Lesson 2: Composition and language study

As has already been indicated, this entire lesson may be omitted and a selection of written exercises may, instead, be set as homework. If this approach is adopted, then the Summary and Composition exercises *must always be set*. Needless to say, more satisfactory results will be obtained where a complete classroom lesson can be devoted to written exercises.

Book required: *Fluency in English* (for teachers and students)

The exercises may be tackled in the order in which they are given. While the students are writing, you may go round the class helping individuals. Exercises not completed in class time may be set as homework. The written exercises become more demanding and time-consuming as the student progresses through the course. However, it is not necessary to complete every single exercise.

Dictations

Depending on the amount of time available, dictations should be given frequently. A few sentences taken from a passage the students have already studied may be dictated. The students may correct their own work by comparing their version with the passage. Dictation is an excellent exercise in syntax, spelling, and listening comprehension.

Multiple choice exercises

Multiple choice exercises provide extra practice in reading comprehension, structure and vocabulary.

Homework

The written exercises become more demanding and time-consuming as the student progresses through the course. At a later stage, exercises which have not been completed in class may be set as homework.

致教师和学生

达到流利程度

　　成功地学完中级教程的学生进而学习高级教程时，有时会感到信心不足，产生这种感觉是有理由的。出现这种情况的主要原因不是因为学生掌握的词汇量有限，而是因为他突然被抛入思想的海洋。最大的障碍不是语言问题，而是心理状况尚不成熟，对于年轻的学生来说尤其如此。一本高级教程有必要要求使用者在心理上达到某种成熟程度，并具有比较广泛的基础知识，而这些是我们不少学生所不具备的。在口语方面，要求学生能就有争议的广泛题材进行讨论。在写作方面，能简单正确地写出叙述性和描写性的作文是不够的，还要注意文章的形式和内容，要能表达复杂的思想，学会处理素材和观点。在中级水平阶段，学生主要是把一篇叙事文的主要事件改写一下，而现在则要对难度大的说理性、辩论性和随感性的文章进行概括。不仅如此，学生还常常在学习上有一种压力，尤其是如果他正在准备考试的时候。按教学大纲规定，教师应认定学生已基本上掌握了语法知识。因此，即使学生需要进一步的语法练习，教师也不能在这上面花费更多的时间。

　　要解决这些问题，仍需认真学习精选出来的可作多功能课文的教材，继续对学生进行理解、口语、阅读和写作 4 项技能的训练。在这个阶段，各篇课文应选自各种流派的作家的作品，以使学生熟悉各种不同的文体。各篇课文应按长度、难度和知识内容循序渐进地予以安排，逐渐把学生引入一个充满各种不同思想的世界。

关于本教材的说明

基本目的

1　　为完成中级教程的成年人或中学生提供一本综合性的教材。这本教材中的内容足够一或两个学年使用,而这取决于可供使用的时间。学生主要在课堂上接受训练,在课下仅做一点额外的作业。

2　　逐渐将学生引入一个充满各种不同思想的世界,并使他们熟悉各种不同的文体。课文的排列不仅考虑到了语言的因素,同时也顾及了长度和知识内容。

3　　继续训练学生 4 项技能：理解、口语、阅读、写作——按此顺序进行训练。从这方面来讲,这本教材准备做两件事：为听／说练习提供适合的材料,同时,这些材料也可用于系统地训练学生掌握更高水平的写作能力。这些课文不仅可以用来促进交际方法上的成熟,同时可以为讨论和研究提供一个极好的基础。

4　　为学生提供一本令他能够**使用语言**的教材。

5　　为教师提供一本只需很少的备课时间即可登台讲授的教材。

6　　为教师和学生提供一本单卷本的教材,而不必增加各种"练习手册"。

适用对象

本教材应适用于：

1　　已经学完《实践与进步》和《培养技能》或任何中级教程的成年人或中学生。

2　　那些由于学生上课出勤率不高而造成严重"损失"的中学和语言学校。

3　　愿意自学高级教程的学生。

应具备的知识范围

本教材的前一册是中级水平综合教材《培养技能》,其内容编排与本册有所重叠。学完前一册的学生接着学本册,不会有什么困难。

学完其他教程而想接着学本册教材的学生应对下列语言知识具备较好的基础。

应有的知识

听力理解和口语

1　　能听懂以正常语速讲述的、有关日常话题的英文。

2　　能就所提问题给出简短或较长的回答。

3　　能提出问题以要求对方给出简短或较长的回答。

4　　能口头使用大量的基本句型。

5　　对一篇英语课文在听几遍和读一篇后,能口头复述其大意。

6　　能就日常话题（如：表示倾向性、友好地交换意见、职业、旅游、共同的经历,等等）进行对话。

7　　能就日常话题发表长达 4 分钟的简短的讲话（经过准备的或未经准备的）。

阅读

1   能大声朗读英语课文。即使不熟悉的单词读不准，也应能掌握好语言的**节奏**（重音和语调）。

2   应具有 3,000 单词的认知词汇，并能读懂相应程度的小说类和非小说类作品。

写作

1   语序

能写出简单句、并列句和复合句。能用连词连接简单句，以组成并列句和复合句。能很好地掌握英语句子中的**语序**。

2   理解

能完成"剑桥初级证书"或与其水平相当的测试中的阅读理解练习题。

3   词汇

能够从上下文中推断词和短语的意思，并用其他词和短语对其进行解释。

4   摘要写作

能够按一篇叙述性文章中事件发生的先后顺序把它重写出来（如：讲述活动和经历）。这就意味着学生要有以下能力：

a   阅读、理解和按指令去做的能力。

b   选取具体的信息，用要点的形式列出一篇叙述性文章中事件发生的先后顺序的能力。

c   将这些要点扩展成简单句、并列句和复合句，并按逻辑思维的顺序排列起来，组成一个有特定字数的、结构完整的段落的能力。

5   作文

能够写出 300 个词左右的叙述性或描写性文章。这就意味着学生应有以下能力：

a   制定简短的计划（如：用要点形式列出要表达的思想）。

b   将这些思想扩展成 3 至 4 个段落的文章。文章应有开头、展开部分和结论。

6   书信写作

能够写大约 100 个词左右的简短私人信件。这就意味着学生应熟悉私人信件的格式（信头、问候语、署名）。

对语言的掌握程度

1   语法（关键句型）

学习本书的先决条件是学生必须在运用动词时态、冠词和介词方面有过一定的训练。但应清楚地认识到，对学生进一步的训练仍是必要的。

2   惯用法（难点）

学生应熟悉常用的短语动词、部分容易混淆和错用的词以及少量的习惯用语。

教材内容

本书由以下各部分组成：

• 课本一册（供教师和学生使用）
• 一组录有多功能课文的盒式磁带

材料的总体编排

本教材分为两大部分,每部分之前都有一个摸底测验。第 1 部分为高级以下水平,目的是保证从中级水平到高级水平的顺利转换。第 2 部分为高级英语。

每一部分又分为 3 个单元,每单元有 8 篇课文,因此,全书共有 48 课。课文逐渐变长,难度逐渐加大。每一单元之前都有"学生须知"。

每篇课文均为多功能课文,可用来对学生进行下列方面的训练:听力理解、口头练习、朗读、口头作文、口头发挥练习、听写、理解、词汇、句子和段落结构、摘要写作、作文、语法和惯用法。

学生须知

应该认真阅读每一个单元前的"学生须知"。它们仅涉及每一单元的主要练习可能带来的一些难点,如:句型结构、段落、摘要、作文等。学生能否学好这本教材,完全取决于学生是否能按须知去做。这册书没有提供实例示范,但是,即使没有例子学生应该如何来做也是非常清楚的。每课后面的练习应按书上排列的顺序来做。

介绍性测试

第 1 部分前的测试可以使学生了解自己的水平,看看自己是否有能力开始这册书的学习。第 2 部分前的测试是为过渡而设计的,使学生不致从学习的第 1 年突然跳到第 2 年。它可以清楚地告诉学生他已经掌握了多少知识。

课文

课文选自多种多样的现代作家的作品,体裁和题材都很不相同。有些是广播讲话,适于进行口头练习。各单元中课文的长度大致如下:

第 1 单元: 250 - 300 个词;
第 2 单元: 250 - 300 个词;
第 3 单元: 300 - 350 个词;
第 4 单元: 350 - 400 个词;
第 5 单元: 400 - 500 个词;
第 6 单元: 550 - 700 个词。

口头练习

本书没有编排口头练习,需要教师自己去补充。可按"本教材使用说明"中的有关原则自行编写。

理解问题

第 1 部分的问题比较直截了当,第 2 部分的问题则比较深入。

词汇

要求学生用课文中的词和词组来造句。

摘要写作和作文

摘要写作和作文练习都是按由浅到深的方式仔细安排的,练习随着课程进展变得越来越难。

这两种练习的安排原则是：摘要写作与作文互为补充；摘要写作是一种分析和分解，而作文则是一种综合。比如说，为了写一篇摘要，学生首先需要理解课文，把它分解成几个组成部分，重新用要点的形式组成文章原来的梗概，然后才能写出它的摘要。而作文恰恰是一个相反的过程。学生开始有一个题目，然后进行构思并用要点的形式记录下来，最后写出连贯的文章。因此，目的在于训练学生适应这两个程序的练习是平行安排的。在第 1 部分，许多练习是直接以课文为基础的，学生在做完练习后可以对照课文自己来纠正写作中的错误。

关键句型和难点

关键句型（基本语法）和难点（惯用法）的所有练习都是根据课文中出现的语言现象编写的。语法术语一概弃之不用。所有难点都以句型的形式出现。在必须进行解释的地方，则通过把一个句型与另一个句型进行比较的方式来作说明。

关键句型的练习以复习为主，主要集中在动词的使用、介词、冠词和副词的位置。学生在完成练习之后，可以对照课文自己来纠正错误。

难点部分的所有练习都与用法有关：词汇、短语动词和习惯用法。其中的许多练习特意安排有一定的重复，目的是消除经常出现的错误。

多项选择练习

多项选择练习是一种**测试**手段，而不是一种**教学**手段。其目的是为了培养学生应付公共测试中常见的客观试题的能力。多项选择题包含以下方面的练习：阅读理解、结构和词汇。

本教材使用说明

请各位老师仔细阅读本说明！

时间分配

理想的安排是，每篇课文用两个课时，每课时约 50 分钟。第 1 课时用于教师引导下的会话和自由会话，第 2 课时用于作文和语言学习。这样，本书内容足够 120 个课时使用。但是，每篇课文也可只用 1 个课时——在这种情况下，上课时间便完全用于教师引导下的对话，而选一部分练习作为课外作业。教师的首要任务是根据教学大纲规定的课时数确定自己的教学内容。

下列建议简要地说明了每课书的讲授步骤。你可以遵照执行，可以加以修订以适应你的教学方法，也可以拒之不用——不过，请你先读一下本说明。

第 1 课时：教师引导下的会话

所需书目

《流利英语》 （师生均用此书）

讲课步骤

1 听力训练   约 15 分钟
2 问答练习   约 10 分钟
3 复述课文   约 10 - 20 分钟
4 专题讨论   约 10 - 20 分钟

现把这 4 个步骤分别说明如下：

1 听力训练（大约 15 分钟）

我们推荐介绍课文的 8 个步骤，以训练学生听懂英语口语的能力。步骤如下：
a 介绍题目
b 了解情景
c 听力训练目标
d 播放录音或朗读课文
e 回答问题
f 精读
g 再次播放录音或朗读课文
h 大声朗读

每一个步骤都必须简洁：

a　　介绍题目

教师用几句话介绍题目，这样学生就能清楚课文讲的是什么，而不需要去猜测。只要有可能应完全使用英语。以第 1 课为例：

Today we'll listen to a text about pre-historic people.

（今天我们要听一篇课文，讲的是史前的人类。）

b　　了解情景

要求学生看照片，以便检查学生是否了解课文中所发生的事情。教师可以用英语向学生提几个问题，以帮助学生理解照片的内容。以第 1 课为例：

Look at the photo and tell me what you can see.

（看照片，然后告诉我你看到了什么。）

What were these tools used for ?

（这些工具当时是用来做什么的？）

c　　听力训练目标

通过给学生提个问题，让他们去寻找答案，教师为学生确立一个"听力训练目标"。这就意味着学生会**积极地**而不是**消极地**去听课文录音。

以第 1 课为例：

Listen to the story, then tell me : why are legends handed down by story-tellers useful ?

（听故事，然后告诉我：为什么讲故事的人流传下来的传说很有用？）

教材中总是提供这样的一个问题。

d　　播放录音或朗读课文

教师只播放录音或朗读课文一次，学生不停顿地静听一遍课文。他们应试图听出 c 项中所列问题的答案。

e　　回答问题

现在教师再一次问第 3 步骤（即上述 c 项）中的问题，让学生试着回答："现在你听了这个故事，为什么讲故事的人流传下来的传说很有用？"训练学生不要集体回答。如果他们认为自己知道答案，请他们举手。问一个学生，然后问其他人："你们中有多少人同意他／她的回答？""如果你们同意，请举手。""〔对另一个学生〕如果你不同意，那么你认为答案是什么？""你们中有多少人同意他／她的回答？请举手。"这样就能让学生不断地猜测，而且把**全班学生**都调动起来。从一开始就要训练学生不做任何准备地去听，也不通过翻译。他们很快会适应英语的语音，并理解他们所听到的内容。

f　　精读

现在教师重放录音或重读课文，每句话后停顿，以检查学生是否理解。这是课堂教学中非常重要的一个环节，因为在介绍课文结束时，学生应该彻底理解课文。教师不要直接讲解，而应尽量从学生那里获取信息（可以把这种方法看作是"用螺丝起子拔瓶塞的行动计划"）。讲解全部要用英文，但不要把直接教学法用到一种近乎荒唐的程度。在可能的情况下，使用手势和模拟动作。如果班上的一些学生仍无法理解，教师应该请班上学得最好的学生给出一个单词或词组的译文，以照顾尚未理解词义的学生。请记住，如果你不把一个难点译成中文，班上的其他人会这样做的。但是，翻译始终应被看成是最后一着。

g　　再次播放录音或朗读课文

不停顿地再次播放录音或朗读课文，因为有了 f 项中的精心解释，这次学生会很容易听懂。

h　大声朗读

在班上轮流让学生大声朗读课文。从朗读中你可以看出不同的学生是否能够准确地读出他们听过的英语。

介绍课文不应超过 15 分钟左右的时间。

不要在任何一项活动中花费太多的时间!

在家里自学的学生应根据自己的需要尽可能多听课文录音, 以便完全熟悉课文。

2　问答练习（大约 10 分钟）

在介绍完课文之后, 开始问答练习。这个练习分为两部分:

a　教师提出多种多样的问题, 学生回答

b　学生提出多种多样的问题

a　教师提出多种多样的问题, 学生回答

你提的问题必须形式多样（包括一般疑问句和用 Wh- 开头的疑问句）。提问的速度要快, 全班每个人都应问到。应训练学生作出自然的回答（例如, 在日常对话中常不用完整的句子的地方, 就不要坚持要求用完整的句子来回答问题）。这项练习的关键是**速度**, 因此, 最好让学生单个回答, 而不要集体回答。这里是有关第 1 课的几个问题:

教师：How long ago did people first learn to write?（人们在多久以前开始学写字?）

　　　Was it two thousand years ago?（是两千年以前吗?）

　　　What's the situation regarding writing in some parts of the world today?（如今在世界某些地方写字的情况如何?）

b　学生提出多种多样的问题

为了避免诸如 *Where he went?* 这种不正确的形式, 要训练学生每次提两个问题。如今第 1 个是一般疑问句, 第 2 个是 Wh- 开头的疑问句。例如:

教师：Ask me if people first learned to write 5,000 years ago.（问我人们是否是在 5,000 年前开始学写字的。）

学生：Did people first learn to write 5,000 years ago?（人们是在 5,000 年前开始学写字的吗?）

教师：How long ago...?（多久以前……?）

学生：How long ago did people first learn to write?（人们在多久以前开始学写字的?）　（而不是 *How long ago people first learned to write?* 或 *How long ago people first write?*）

3　复述课文（大约 10-20 分钟）

这部分可以省略, 可以跳过这一项直接进入专题讨论, 或者用很少的时间来复述课文, 然后开始专题讨论。这部分包括一些有编号的要点, 由这些要点组成课文的摘要。把要点写到黑板上（或课前写到黑板上, 并把它们遮挡起来）, 然后让全班学生逐个为你复述故事。这种练习可以使学生在半准备状态下不停顿地进行口语练习。在学生讲完**之后**, 可以指出学生复述过程中出现的主要语言错误。不要经常打断学生。

下面是与第 1 课有关的要点:

1　　Read — 5,000 — Near East — people — write.

2　　Some parts of the world — people — now — write.

3　　Can preserve history — sagas legends — generation.

4　　Useful — migrations — people long ago — none could write.

5   Anthropologists wondered — ancestors Polynesia — came from.

6   Sagas — Indonesia — 2,000 years ago.

4   专题讨论（大约 10 分钟）

在教师引导下的会话课上，最后一部分时间应用于自由会话。应给学生机会试着表达自己的思想，不论他们会在表达时出现多少语言错误。在每一课中，讨论题会变得越来越复杂，可以讨论其中的一个，也可以讨论所有题目。应该请学生就题目讲一两句话。随着学生会话能力的加强，你可以偶尔在自由会话这部分多用一些时间（比如说，可省略诸如"复述课文"这样的练习）。

以下是第 1 课中建议的一些会话题目：

a   Exchange information about local history and pre-history: tell us what you know.（就地方史和史前交换信息：告诉我们你掌握的信息。）

b   Exchange information about the migration of people in ancient and modern time: tell us what you know.（就古代和现代人迁居的情况交换信息：告诉我们你掌握的信息。）

c   Is migration more difficult now than it used to be in the past? Why/Why not?（现代迁居是否比以前更困难了？为什么？）

第 2 课时：作文和语言学习

如上所述，第 2 课时可以完全不上，而将这一部分笔头练习作为课外作业。如采取这种教学方法，在课外作业中必须布置摘要写作与作文练习。当然，如果用一整个课时做笔头练习，效果肯定会更好。

所需书目
《流利英语》（师生均用此书）

笔头练习要按练习编排的顺序进行。在学生做练习时，教师可以在课堂上来回走动，进行个别辅导。课堂上未做完的练习，可留作课外作业。随着学习的不断深入，笔头练习会越来越难，越来越费时间。但并不要求每题必做。

听写

如果时间允许，应经常做听写练习。可以从学生已学过的课文中抽出几个句子做听写练习。学生可参照原文，自行批改。听写是句法、拼写和听力方面极好的一项训练。

多项选择练习

多项选择练习在阅读理解、结构和词汇方面提供额外的训练。

课外作业

随着学习的不断深入，笔头作业会越来越难，越来越费时间。学到后面阶段，凡在课堂上完不成的作业可留作课外作业。

IF YOU CAN DO THIS TEST GO ON TO PART 1

Read the following passage carefully, then do the exercises below:

The boy put on his goggles, fitted them tight, tested the vacuum. His hands were shaking. Then he chose the biggest stone he could carry and slipped over the edge of the rock until half of him was in the cool, enclosing water and half in the hot sun. He looked up once at the empty sky, filled his lungs once, twice, and then sank fast to the bottom with the stone. He let it go and began to count. He took the edges of the hole in
5 his hands and drew himself into it, wriggling his shoulders in sideways as he remembered he must, kicking himself along with his feet.

Soon he was clear inside. He was in a small rock-bound hole filled with yellowish-grey water. The water was pushing him up against the roof. The roof was sharp and pained his back. He pulled himself along with his hands — fast, fast — and used his legs as levers. His head knocked against something; a sharp
10 pain dizzied him. Fifty, fifty-one, fifty-two ... He was without light, and the water seemed to press upon him with the weight of rock. Seventy-one, seventy-two ... There was no strain on his lungs. He felt like an inflated balloon, his lungs were so light and easy, but his head was pulsing.

He was being continually pressed against the sharp roof, which felt slimy as well as sharp. Again he thought of octopuses, and wondered if the tunnel might be filled with weed that could tangle him. He gave
15 himself a panicky, convulsive kick forward, ducked his head, and swam. His feet and hands moved freely, as if in open water. The hole must have widened out. He thought he must be swimming fast, and he was frightened of banging his head if the tunnel narrowed.

A hundred, a hundred and one ... The water paled. Victory filled him. His lungs were beginning to hurt. A few more strokes and he would be out. He was counting wildly; he said a hundred and fifteen, and then, a
20 long time later, a hundred and fifteen again. The water was a clear jewel-green all around him. Then he saw, above his head, a crack running up through the rock. Sunlight was falling through it, showing the clean dark rock of the tunnel, a single mussel shell, and darkness ahead.

He was at the end of what he could do. He looked up at the crack as if it were filled with air and not water, as if he could put his mouth to it to draw in air. A hundred and fifteen, he heard himself say inside
25 his head — but he had said that long ago. He must go on into the blackness ahead, or he would drown. His head was swelling, his lungs cracking. A hundred and fifteen, a hundred and fifteen pounded through his head, and he feebly clutched at rocks in the dark, pulling himself forward, leaving the brief space of sunlit water behind. He felt he was dying. He was no longer quite conscious. He struggled on in the darkness between lapses into unconsciousness. An immense, swelling pain filled his head, and then the darkness
30 cracked with an explosion of green light. His hands, groping forward, met nothing, and his feet, kicking back, propelled him out into the open sea.

DORIS LESSING *Through the Tunnel* from *The Habit of Loving*

1

Comprehension

Give short answers to these questions in your own words as far as possible. Use one complete sentence for each answer.

1 Why was the boy able to get to the sea bed quickly?
2 Why did the boy find it difficult to swim after he was inside the tunnel?
3 Why did the boy get into a panic as he swam through the tunnel?

Vocabulary

Explain the meaning of the following words and phrases as they are used in the passage: goggles (1.1); filled his lungs (1.3); wriggling (1.5); as levers (1.9); dizzied (1.10); inflated (1.11); slimy (1.13).

Summary writing

In not more than 80 words write an account of the boy's experiences under the sea as described in lines 18-31 ('A hundred ... the open sea.') Use your own words as far as possible. Do not include anything that is not in the last two paragraphs.

Composition

Write a composition of about 300 words on one of the following subjects:

1 The most frightening experience I have ever had.
2 A holiday by the sea.
3 Dangerous sports.

Part 1

Unit 1

INSTRUCTIONS TO THE STUDENT

Content

This unit consists of eight passages followed by exercises on Comprehension, Vocabulary, Sentence structure, Key structures, Special difficulties and Multiple choice questions.

Aim

To provide practice in the writing of complex sentences.

How to work

1 Read each passage carefully two or three times.
2 Answer the questions in the order in which they are given.

Sentence structure

All the exercises given under this heading are based directly on the passage. You may correct your own answers to some of the questions by referring to the passage immediately after you have completed the exercises. The following types of exercise have been given:

1 Joining simple statements to make complex statements.
2 Supplying conjunctions (joining words) to make complex statements.
3 Completing sentences taken from the passage in any way you wish.
4 Writing sentences related to the subject matter of the passage.

Lesson 1　Finding fossil man　发现化石人

First listen and then answer the following question.

听录音, 然后回答以下问题。

Why are legends handed down by storytellers useful?

We can read of things that happened 5,000 years ago in the Near East, where people first learned to write. But there are some parts of the world where even now people cannot write. The only way that they can preserve their history is to recount it as sagas—legends handed down from one generation of storytellers to another. These legends are useful because they can tell us something about migrations of people who lived

5　long ago, but none could write down what they did. Anthropologists wondered where the remote ancestors of the Polynesian peoples now living in the Pacific Islands came from. The sagas of these people explain that some of them came from Indonesia about 2,000 years ago.

But the first people who were like ourselves lived so long ago that even their sagas, if they had any, are forgotten. So archaeologists have neither history nor legends to help them to find out where the first 'modern

10　men' came from.

Fortunately, however, ancient men made tools of stone, especially flint, because this is easier to shape than other kinds. They may also have used wood and skins, but these have rotted away. Stone does not decay, and so the tools of long ago have remained when even the bones of the men who made them have disappeared without trace.

ROBIN PLACE　*Finding fossil man*

Polished axeheads found at Seamers Moor in Yorkshire

5

Unit 1   Lesson 1

New words and expressions 生词和短语

fossil man (title) /'fɒsəl-'mæn/ 化石人

recount (1.3) /rɪ'kaʊnt/ v. 叙述

saga (1.3) /'sɑːgə/ n. 英雄故事

legend (1.3) /'ledʒənd/ n. 传说，传奇

migration (1.4) /maɪ'greɪʃən/ n. 迁移，移居

anthropologist (1.5) /ˌænθrə'pɒlədʒɪst/ n. 人类学家

ancestor (1.5) /'ænsestə/ n. 祖先

Polynesian (1.6) /ˌpɒlɪ'niːzɪən/ adj. 波利尼西亚（中太平洋群岛之一）的

Indonesia (1.7) /ˌɪndə'niːzɪə/ n. 印度尼西亚

archaeologist (1.9) /ˌɑːki'ɒlədʒɪst/ n. 考古学家

flint (1.11) /flɪnt/ n. 燧石

rot (1.12) /rɒt/ v. 烂掉

Notes on the text 课文注释

1   read of, 读到, 和 read about 是相同的意思 。

2   the first people, 原始人 。

3   when even the bones of the men who made them have disappeared without trace, 这个以 when 引导的状语从句表示让步的意思, 而 when 可以译成"虽然", "尽管" 。

参考译文

　　我们从书籍中可以读到 5000 年前近东发生的事情, 那里的人最早学会了写字 。但直到现在, 世界上仍然有些地方, 人们还不会书写 。他们保存历史的唯一办法是将历史当作传说讲述, 由讲述人一代接一代地将史实描述为传奇故事口传下来 。这些传说是很有用的, 因为它们能告诉我们以往人们迁居的情况 。但是, 没有人能把他们当时做的事情记载下来 。人类学家过去不清楚如今生活在太平洋诸岛上的波利尼西亚人的祖先来自何方, 当地人的传说却告诉了人们: 其中有一部分是在约 2000 年前从印度尼西亚迁来的 。

　　但是, 和我们相似的原始人生活的年代太久远了, 有关他们的传说即使有如今也失传了 。所以, 考古学家们既缺乏历史记载, 又无口头传说来帮助他们弄清最早的"现代人"是从哪里来的 。

　　然而, 幸运的是, 远古人用石头制作了工具, 特别是用燧石, 因为燧石较之其他石头更易成形 。他们也可能用过木头和兽皮, 但这类东西早已腐烂殆尽 。石头是不会腐烂的 。因此, 尽管制造这些工具的人的骨头早已荡然无存, 但远古时代的石头工具却保存了下来 。

Comprehension 理解

Give short answers to these questions in your own words as far as possible. Use one complete sentence for each answer.

1   How can anthropologists learn about the history of ancient peoples who have not left written records?

2   Why did ancient men prefer to use flint for making tools?

Vocabulary 词汇

Refer to the text to see how the following words have been used, then write sentences of your own using these words: preserve (1.3); recount (1.3); migrations (1.4); anthropologists (1.5); remote (1.5); decay (1.13); without trace (1.14).

Sentence structure 句子结构

A Combine the following statements to make complete sentences. Add conjunctions and relative pronouns of your own and omit the words or phrases in italics. Do not refer to the passage until you have finished the exercise:

1 These legends are useful. They can tell us something about migrations of people. *These people* lived long ago. None could write down what they did. (ll.4-5)

2 The first people who were like ourselves lived long ago. Even their sagas, if they had any, are forgotten. (ll.8-9)

3 Archaeologists have *no* history to help them to find out where the first 'modern men' came from. *Archaeologists have no* legends *to help them to find out where the first modern men came from.* (ll.9-10)

4 Fortunately, however, ancient men made tools of stone, especially flint. This is easier to shape than other kinds. (ll.11-12)

5 They may also have used wood and skins. These have rotted away. (l.12)

B Write a sentence to describe the work of an archaeologist.

C Write three short sentences on the history of early man using the following words in each sentence:
1 written records
2 sagas
3 stone tools

Key structures 关键句型

A Compare these two sentences:

Instead of saying:

The only way that they can preserve their history is to recount it as sagas—*legends which have been handed down* from one generation of storytellers to another.

We can say:

The only way that they can preserve their history is to recount it as sagas—*legends handed down* from one generation of storytellers to another. (ll.2-4)

Write sentences using the following phrases:

tools made of stone; legends recorded; remains found.

B Note the use of *tell* in this sentence:

They can *tell us* something about migrations of people. (ll.4-5)

Supply the correct form of *say* or *tell* in these sentences:

1 What did he _____ to you?
2 He _____ everybody that he had been ill.
3 Did you _____ that you have written a novel?
4 I can't _____ you about it now.

C Note the use of *where ... from* in this sentence:

Anthropologists wondered *where* the remote ancestors of the Polynesian peoples came *from*. (ll.5-6)

Write two sentences using the same construction with the verbs *get* and *buy*.

D   Compare these two sentences:

Instead of saying:

So archaeologists have neither history nor legends to *help them to find* out where the first 'modern men' came from. (ll.9-10)

We can say:

So archaeologists have neither history nor legends to *help them find out* where the first 'modern men' came from.

Write two sentences using these expressions: help me to lift; helped me make.

E   Supply the word *the* where necessary in this paragraph. Do not refer to the passage until you have finished the exercise:

Fortunately, however, _____ ancient men made _____ tools of _____ stone, especially _____ flint, because this is easier to shape than _____ other kinds. They may also have used _____ wood and _____ skins, but these have rotted away. _____ stone does not decay, and so _____ tools of long ago have remained when even _____ bones of _____ men who made them have disappeared without trace. (ll.11-14)

F   Compare these two sentences:

Instead of saying:

It is possible that they used wood and skins, but these have rotted away.

We can say:

They may have used wood and skins, but these have rotted away. (l.12)

Write these sentences again using the construction with *may have*.

1   It is possible that your mother called when you were out.

2   It is possible that you left your umbrella in the waiting room.

3   It is possible that he changed his mind.

Special difficulties 难点

A   Study the following pairs of words and then write sentences of your own to bring out the difference.

1   parts (l.2) — places

Ancient rock paintings have been found in many parts of Spain and Portugal.

Of all the wonderful places in Italy, Florence and Venice are the two that most tourists wish to see.

2   history (l.3) — story

We often know little about the history of our own times.

Climb into bed and I'll read you a bedtime story.

(Please note: a story is an account, often fictional, of what happened in someone's experience; history is a factual account of past public or universal events)

3   wonder (l.5) — wander

I wonder if we've made a mistake here.

I love wandering around second-hand bookshops.

4   like (l.8) — as

There's no one like you.

Please do as I say.

5   find out (l.9) — find

What we have to do now is find out why the accident happened.

I'm sure I've already paid this bill, but I can't find the receipt.

6   ancient (l.11) — old

Property developers often have little regard for ancient/old buildings. (old in terms of time; ancient = old in terms of history)

World leaders are often old men.

Mr. Briggs is an old friend of mine. (= one I have known for a long time)

7   tool (l.11) — instrument

We need some basic tools like a hammer and a screwdriver.

A dentist's instruments need to be constantly sterilized.

8   stone (l.11) — rock

The old church is full of beautiful stone sculptures.

Rocks had fallen from above, making the roads impassable.

9   skin (l.12) — leather

I've such a bad skin, I'm always coming out in spots.

Shoes made of real leather have become so expensive.

B   Study the use of *happen* in these sentences:

We can read of things that *happened* 5,000 years ago ... (l.1)

He *happened* to be an archaeologist.

It *happened* that he knew the answer.

Complete the following sentences:

1   Do you happen _____ ?

2   It so happens that _____ .

3   Can you tell me what _____ ?

Multiple choice questions 选择题

Choose the correct answers to the following questions.

Comprehension 理解

1 In illiterate societies, story-telling is a way of _____ .

   (*a*) teaching people how to write

   (*b*) allowing us to find out about things that happened 5,000 years ago

   (*c*) passing knowledge of the past from one generation to another

   (*d*) preserving sagas recounted by story-tellers

2 It is extremely likely that ancient people _____ .

   (*a*) moved from one place to another

   (*b*) came from Indonesia

   (*c*) have left us information about their migrations

   (*d*) preserved their sagas and legends

3 Anthropologists have been curious about _____ .

   (*a*) how Indonesia came to be inhabited

   (*b*) how the Polynesian islands came to be inhabited

   (*c*) why the Polynesian people travelled from Indonesia

   (*d*) how the sagas told by ancient people were written

4 Though wood and skins rot away, anthropologists can learn a great deal from _____ .

(a) materials that are easy to shape

(b) the bones of men who made tools

(c) stones that do not decay

(d) ancient tools made of stone

Structure 句型

5 In some parts of the world people are still _____ to write. (ll.1-2)

(a) incapable   (b) impotent   (c) enable   (d) unable

6 They can preserve their history _____ down legends. (l.3)

(a) by hand   (b) by handing   (c) to hand   (d) in hand

7 The _____ why these legends are useful is that they tell us about migrations. (l.4)

(a) cause   (b) effect   (c) why   (d) reason

8 There weren't _____ of them who could write down what they did. (l.5)

(a) any   (b) none   (c) no one   (d) no

Vocabulary 词汇

9 The only way they can preserve their history is to _____ stories. (ll.2-3)

(a) tell   (b) make   (c) say   (d) recount

10 The people who lived long ago could not _____ their history. (l.5)

(a) make   (b) know   (c) record   (d) note

11 Some sagas tell us about the _____ of Polynesian peoples. (ll.6-7)

(a) origin   (b) ancestors   (c) explanation   (d) legend

12 Tools made of stone, especially flint, were made by _____ . (l.11)

(a) old men   (b) men who lived long ago

(c) men of old   (d) past men

Lesson 2   Spare that spider   不要伤害蜘蛛

First listen and then answer the following question.

听录音,然后回答以下问题 。

How much of each year do spiders spend killing insects?

Why, you may wonder, should spiders be our friends? Because they destroy so many insects, and insects
include some of the greatest enemies of the human race. Insects would make it impossible for us to live in
the world; they would devour all our crops and kill our flocks and herds, if it were not for the protection we
get from insect-eating animals. We owe a lot to the birds and beasts who eat insects but all of them put
5 together kill only a fraction of the number destroyed by spiders. Moreover, unlike some of the other insect
eaters, spiders never do the least harm to us or our belongings.

How many spiders are engaged in this work on our behalf? One authority on spiders made a census of the
spiders in a grass field in the south of England, and he estimated that there were more than 2,250,000 in one
acre; that is something like 6,000,000 spiders of different kinds on a football pitch. Spiders are busy for at
least half the year in killing insects. It is impossible to make more than the wildest guess at how many they
kill, but they are hungry creatures, not content with only three meals a day. It has been estimated that the
weight of all the insects destroyed by spiders in Britain in one year would be greater than the total weight of
15 all the human beings in the country.

Spiders are not insects, as many people think, nor even nearly related to them. One can tell the difference
almost at a glance, for a spider always has eight legs and an insect never more than six.

How many spiders are engaged in this work on our behalf? One authority on spiders made a census of the
10 spiders in a grass field in the south of England, and he estimated that there were more than 2,250,000 in one
acre; that is something like 6,000,000 spiders of different kinds on a football pitch. Spiders are busy for at
least half the year in killing insects. It is impossible to make more than the wildest guess at how many they
kill, but they are hungry creatures, not content with only three meals a day. It has been estimated that the
weight of all the insects destroyed by spiders in Britain in one year would be greater than the total weight of
15 all the human beings in the country.

T. H. GILLESPIE *Spare that spider* from *The Listener*

A spider destroys a grasshopper

New words and expressions 生词和短语

beast (l.4) /biːst/ *n.* 野兽

census (l.9) /'sensəs/ *n.* 统计数字

acre (l.11) /'eɪkə/ *n.* 英亩

content (l.13) /kən'tent/ *adj.* 满足的

Notes on the text 课文注释

1   you may wonder 是这个疑问句的插入语。

2   if it were not for the protection we get from insect-eating animals, 这是一个非真实条件状语从句, were 表示虚拟语气。

3   almost at a glance, 几乎一眼（就能看出）。

参考译文

你可能会觉得奇怪, 蜘蛛怎么会是我们的朋友呢? 因为它们能消灭那么多的昆虫, 其中包括一些人类的大敌。要不是人类受一些食虫动物的保护, 昆虫就会使我们无法在地球上生活下去, 昆虫会吞食我们的全部庄稼, 杀死我们成群的牛羊。我们要十分感谢那些吃昆虫的鸟和兽, 然而把它们所杀死的昆虫全部加在一起也只相当于蜘蛛所消灭的一小部分。此外, 蜘蛛不同于其他食虫动物, 它们丝毫不危害我们和我们的财物。

许多人认为蜘蛛是昆虫, 但它们不是昆虫, 甚至与昆虫毫无关系。人们几乎一眼就看出二者的差异, 因为蜘蛛都是 8 条腿, 而昆虫的腿从不超过 6 条。

有多少蜘蛛在为我们效力呢? 一位研究蜘蛛的权威对英国南部一块草坪上的蜘蛛作了一次调查。他估计每英亩草坪里有 225 万多只蜘蛛。这就是说, 在一个足球场上约有 600 万只不同种类的蜘蛛。蜘蛛至少有半年时间忙于吃昆虫。它们一年中消灭了多少昆虫, 我们简直无法猜测, 它们是吃不饱的动物, 不满意一日三餐。据估计, 在英国蜘蛛一年里所消灭昆虫的重量超过了这个国家人口的总重量。

Comprehension 理解

Give short answers to these questions in your own words as far as possible. Use one complete sentence for each answer.

1   Why have we reason to be grateful to insect-eating animals?

2   How can we tell the difference between a spider and an insect?

3   What do you understand by the statement 'One authority on spiders made a census of the spiders in a grass field ...'? (ll.9-10)

Vocabulary 词汇

Refer to the text to see how the following words have been used, then write sentences of your own using these words: destroy (l.1); devour (l.3); fraction (l.5); belongings (l.6); estimated (l.10).

Sentence structure 句子结构

A   Combine the following sentences to make one complex statement out of each group. Make any changes you think necessary, but do not alter the sense of the original. Do not refer to the passage until you have finished the exercise:

1   Moreover, spiders are unlike some of the other insect eaters. They never do the least harm to us or our belongings. (ll.5-6)

2 Spiders are not insects. They are not even nearly related to them. Many people think they are. (l.7)

3 One can tell the difference almost at a glance. A spider has eight legs. An insect never has more than six. (ll.7-8)

4 How many do they kill? It is impossible to make more than the wildest guess at this. They are hungry creatures. They are not content with only three meals a day. (ll.12-13)

B Complete the following sentences in any way you wish. Then compare what you have written with the sentences in the passage:

1 Why, you may wonder, should spiders be our friends? Because _____ . (ll.1-2)

2 We owe a lot to birds and beasts who _____ . (ll.4-5)

3 One authority on spiders _____ . (ll.9-10)

4 It has been estimated that _____ . (ll.13-15)

C Write three sentences saying why you like or dislike spiders.

Key structures 关键句型

A Compare these two sentences:

Instead of saying: *I wonder why* spiders are our friends.

We can say: *Why ... should spiders be* our friends? (l.1)

Write these sentences again using the construction with *should* in place of the phrases in italics:

1 *I wonder why he is* so disappointed.

2 *I wonder why you are* so unwilling to change your mind.

3 *I wonder why there are* so many traffic accidents.

B Note the form of the verb *be* in this sentence:

They would devour all our crops if it *were* not for the protection we get from insect-eating animals. (ll.3-4)

Supply the correct form of *be* in these sentences:

1 I certainly wouldn't buy that car if I (be) in your position.

2 Do you think you would buy it if it (be) cheaper?

3 If I (be) made such an offer I would certainly accept it.

C Supply *a, an* and *the* where necessary in the spaces below. Do not refer to the passage until you have finished the exercise:

_____ spiders are not _____ insects, as _____ many people think, nor even nearly related to them. One can tell _____ difference almost at _____ glance for _____ spider always has eight legs and _____ insect never more than six.

　　How many spiders are engaged in this work on our behalf? One authority on _____ spiders made _____ census of _____ spiders in _____ grass field in _____ south of _____ England, and he estimated that there were more than 2,250,000 in _____ acre; that is something like 6,000,000 spiders of different kinds on _____ football pitch. (ll.7-11)

Special difficulties 难点

A   Study the following pairs of words and then write sentences of your own to bring out the difference:

1   all ... together (ll.4-5) — altogether

Let's sing it again. All together now!

As far as I am concerned, Frank's proposal is altogether nonsensical.

2   other (l.5) — else

One of these blouses has buttons; the other hasn't.

We need one more helper. Can you find anyone else?

3   the least (l.6) — the last

He passed all his exams without seeming to make even the least effort.

She wouldn't marry him even if he was the last man on the planet.

4   harm (l.6) — hurt

Fertilizers have done a lot of harm to the soil. The bad effects will last a long time.

I banged my arm against the door and hurt myself. My arm still hurts. It's very painful.

5   glance (l.8) — glimpse

Would you mind having a glance at my essay before I hand it in?

I caught a glimpse of him as he walked past my window.

6   work (l.9) — job

I'm looking for work as a journalist.

Have you been doing all this work on your own?

I'd like a job in TV. Are there any jobs in TV?

7   estimated (l.10) — calculated

I estimate there must be at least eight hundred names on the list.

We've calculated the cost of a new office and it's more than we can afford.

B   Which verbs could be used in place of *get* in these sentences:

1   They would devour all our crops and kill our flocks and herds, if it were not for the protection we *get* from insect-eating animals. (ll.2-4)

2   I *got* this hat at the shop on the corner.

3   Will you *get* that book for me please? It's on the shelf.

4   I *got* a letter from my brother yesterday.

5   I'm sorry, I didn't *get* that remark.

6   I didn't laugh because I didn't *get* the joke.

C   Note the use of *tell* in this sentence:

One can *tell the difference* almost at a glance. (ll.7-8)

Supply the correct form of *say* or *tell* in these sentences:

1   Will you please _____ me the time?

2   I'm not very good at _____ stories.

3   You must _____ your prayers and go to bed.

4   Please _____ nothing more about it.

5   I can _____ you something about it.

6   We _____ goodbye and left.

7   I want you to _____ the truth.

D   Note the use of *make* in this sentence:

One authority on spiders *made a census*. (ll.9-10)

Supply the correct form of *make* or *do* in the following sentences:

1   I _____ a number of proposals, none of which was accepted.

2   I'll _____ the washing up.

3   Will you help me to _____ this crossword puzzle?

4   You've _____ quite a few mistakes.

5   I've _____ an appointment for you for next week.

6   They _____ an announcement about it on the radio.

7   I'll _____ my best to help you.

E   Write sentences using the following phrases with *at*:

at a glance (l.8); at least (ll.11-12); at any rate; at a loss; at sight; at a time.

Multiple choice questions 选择题

Choose the correct answers to the following questions.

Comprehension 理解

1 Spiders are our friends because they _____ .

(*a*) are beneficial insects

(*b*) destroy insects without hurting us in any way

(*c*) protect insect-eating animals

(*d*) include some of the greatest enemies of the human race

2 Birds and beasts _____ .

(*a*) eat as many insects as spiders

(*b*) eat more insects than spiders

(*c*) can't compare with spiders as destroyers of insects

(*d*) destroy a larger fraction of insects than spiders

3 If spiders were insects, they would _____ .

(*a*) have eight legs

(*b*) have six legs

(*c*) be able to fly

(*d*) not destroy their own kind

4 Spiders are active in killing insects _____ .

(*a*) all the time

(*b*) for most of the year

(*c*) in the summer months

(*d*) for a minimum of six months of each year

Structure 句型

5 It would _____ impossible for us to live in this world if insects had no enemies. (ll.2-3)

(*a*) make it   (*b*) stay   (*c*) be   (*d*) have it

Unit 1 Lesson 2

6 We owe _____ to the birds and beasts who eat insects. (1.4)

(*a*) a great deal   (*b*) a lot of   (*c*) a great many   (*d*) much of

7 How many spiders are involved _____ this work on our behalf? (1.9)

(*a*) at   (*b*) for   (*c*) in   (*d*) to

8 There are many different _____ spiders. (1.11)

(*a*) sorts of   (*b*) kind of   (*c*) type of   (*d*) kinds

Vocabulary 词汇

9 Spiders _____ insects. (ll.3-4)

(*a*) defend us from   (*b*) guard   (*c*) protect   (*d*) insure us against

10 You can see at a glance that spiders are not _____ insects. (1.7)

(*a*) similar   (*b*) like to   (*c*) as   (*d*) the same as

11 Spiders are creatures with large _____ . (1.13)

(*a*) hunger   (*b*) appetites   (*c*) desires   (*d*) eating

12 Spiders like to eat more than _____ a day. (1.13)

(*a*) three   (*b*) three time   (*c*) three times   (*d*) threes

Lesson 3　Matterhorn man　马特山区人

🖭 **First listen and then answer the following question.**

听录音，然后回答以下问题。

What was the main objective of early mountain climbers?

Modern alpinists try to climb mountains by a route which will give them good sport, and the more difficult it is, the more highly it is regarded. In the pioneering days, however, this was not the case at all. The early climbers were looking for the easiest way to the top, because the summit was the prize they sought, especially if it had never been attained before. It is true that during their explorations they often faced
5　difficulties and dangers of the most perilous nature, equipped in a manner which would make a modern climber shudder at the thought, but they did not go out of their way to court such excitement. They had a single aim, a solitary goal—the top!

It is hard for us to realize nowadays how difficult it was for the pioneers. Except for one or two places such as Zermatt and Chamonix, which had rapidly become popular, Alpine villages tended to be impov-
10　erished settlements cut off from civilization by the high mountains. Such inns as there were were generally dirty and flea-ridden; the food simply local cheese accompanied by bread often twelve months old, all washed down with coarse wine. Often a valley boasted no inn at all, and climbers found shelter wherever they could—sometimes with the local priest (who was usually as poor as his parishioners), sometimes with shepherds or cheese-makers. Invariably the background was the same: dirt and poverty, and very uncom-
15　fortable. For men accustomed to eating seven-course dinners and sleeping between fine linen sheets at home, the change to the Alps must have been very hard indeed.

WALTER UNSWORTH *Matterhorn Man*

Bergdorf, a mountain village in Switzerland

New words and expressions 生词和短语

Matterhorn (title) /'mætəhɔːn/ *n.* 马特峰（阿尔卑斯山脉山峰之一，在意大利和瑞士边境）

alpinist (l.1) /'ælpɪnɪst/ *n.* 登山运动员

pioneer (l.2) /ˌpaɪə'nɪə/ *v.* 开辟，倡导；*n.* 先锋，开辟者

summit (l.3) /'sʌmɪt/ *n.* 顶峰

attain (l.4) /ə'teɪn/ *v.* 到达

perilous (l.5) /'perɪləs/ *adj.* 危险的

shudder (l.5) /'ʃʌdə/ *v.* 不寒而栗

court (l.6) /kɔːt/ *v.* 追求

solitary (l.6) /'sɒlɪtəri/ *adj.* 唯一的

impoverish (ll.9-10) /ɪm'pɒvərɪʃ/ *v.* 使贫困

Alpine (l.9) /'ælpaɪn/ *adj.* 阿尔卑斯山的

flea-ridden (l.11) /'fliːˌrɪdn/ *adj.* 布满跳蚤的

coarse (l.12) /kɔːs/ *adj.* 粗劣的

boast (l.12) /bəʊst/ *v.* 自恃有

parishioner (l.13) /pə'rɪʃənə/ *n.* 教区居民

shepherd (l.14) /'ʃepəd/ *n.* 牧羊人

linen (l.15) /'lɪnɪn/ *n.* 亚麻布

the Alps (l.16) /ælps/ *n.* 阿尔卑斯山脉

Notes on the text 课文注释

1　in the pioneering days, 在初创时期，这里指登山运动的初创期。

2　equipped in a manner which would make a modern climber shudder at the thought, 他们的装备如此简陋，足以使现代登山者一想起来就胆战心惊。at the thought, 一想到（他们的装备），英文中省略了 of the manner。

3　go out of one's way, 特地，不怕麻烦。

4　cut off ... from ..., 把 …… 与 …… 隔绝。

5　such inns as there were, 那里有的小客栈, as there were 用来修饰 inns, 作定语。

6　the food simply local cheese, 在 food 后面省略了 was。

参考译文

　　现代登山运动员总想找一条能够给他们带来运动乐趣的路线来攀登山峰。他们认为，道路愈艰险愈带劲儿。然而，在登山运动的初期，全然不是这种情况。早期登山者所寻找的是通往山顶的最方便的途径，因为顶峰——特别是前人未曾到过的顶峰——才是他们寻求的目标。确实，在探险中他们经常遇到惊心动魄的困难和危险，而他们装备之简陋足以使现代登山者一想起来就胆战心惊。但是，他们并非故意寻求这种刺激，他们只有一个目的，唯一的目标——顶峰!

　　我们今天很难想象昔日的登山先驱们是多么艰苦。除了采尔马特和夏蒙尼等一两个很快出了名的地方外，阿尔卑斯山山区的小村几乎全是高山环抱、与世隔绝的穷乡僻壤。那里的小客栈一般都很肮脏，而且跳蚤猖獗。食物是当地的干酪和通常存放了一年之久的面包，人们就着劣质酒吞下这种食物。山谷里常常没有小客栈，登山者只好随遇而安。有时同当地牧师（他通常和他的教民一样穷）住在一起，有时同牧羊人或制乳酪的人住在一起。无论住在哪儿，情况都一样: 肮脏、贫穷，极其不舒适。对于过惯了一顿饭吃 7 道菜、睡亚麻细布床单的人来说，变换一下生活环境来到阿尔卑斯山山区，那一定是很艰难的。

Comprehension 理解

Give short answers to these questions in your own words as far as possible. Use one complete sentence for each answer.

1　In what way does the modern climber's attitude towards mountains differ from that of the pioneer?

2　Name three factors which made most Alpine villages inhospitable places.

Vocabulary 词汇

Refer to the text to see how the following words have been used, then write sentences of your own using these words: route (l.1); regarded (l.2); summit (l.3); sought (l.3); faced (l.4); perilous (l.5); shudder (l.5); court (l.6); solitary (l.6); coarse (l.12); boasted (l.12); invariably (l.14).

Sentence structure 句子结构

A   Combine the following statements to make complete sentences. Add conjunctions of your own and omit the words or phrases in italics. Do not refer to the passage until you have finished the exercise:

1   It is true that during their explorations they often faced difficulties. *They often faced* dangers of the most perilous nature. *They were* equipped in a manner which would make a modern climber shudder at the thought. They did not go out of their way to court such excitement. (ll.4-6)

2   One or two places such as Zermatt and Chamonix had rapidly become popular. Alpine villages tended to be impoverished settlements. *They were* cut off from civilization by high mountains. (ll.8-10)

3   Often a valley boasted no inn at all. Climbers found shelter wherever they could. *They* sometimes *found shelter* with the local priest. (*He* was usually as poor as his parishioners.) *They* sometimes *found shelter* with shepherds or cheese-makers. (ll.12-14)

B   Write three sentences saying why you like or dislike mountaineering.

Key structures 关键句型

A   Study the form of these sentences:
The more difficult it is, *the more highly* it is regarded. (ll.1-2)
The quicker you work, *the sooner* you will finish.
Write sentences using the following words:

1   The more _____ the less _____ .
2   The more _____ the worse _____ .
3   The sooner _____ the better _____ .

B   Give the correct form of the verbs in parentheses in the paragraph below. Do not refer to the passage until you have finished the exercise:

Modern alpinists try to climb mountains by a route which will give them good sport, and the more difficult it is, the more highly it is regarded. In the pioneering days, however, this _____ (be) not the case at all. The early climbers _____ (look) for the easiest way to the top because the summit _____ (be) the prize they _____ (seek), especially if it _____ (never attain) before. It is true that during their explorations they often _____ (face) difficulties and dangers of the most perilous nature, equipped in a manner which _____ (make) a modern climber shudder at the thought, but they _____ (not go) out of their way to court such excitement. They _____ (have) a single aim, a solitary goal — the top! (ll.1-7)

C   Note the position of the word *often* in these sentences:

They *often* faced difficulties and dangers. (ll.4-5)

The food (was) simply local cheese accompanied by bread (which was) *often* twelve months old. (ll.11-12)

Often a valley boasted no inn at all. (l.12)

In the following sentences, the word *often* can be placed in two or more different positions. Indicate the correct positions in each sentence:

1   I am in such a hurry, I don't have time for breakfast.

2   We buy things we don't really need.

3   He is sent abroad by his firm.

D   Compare these two sentences:

It is hard for us to realize ... how difficult it was ... (l.8)

It is hard to realize how difficult it was.

Complete the following sentences:

1   It was impossible for them _____ .

2   It is difficult _____ .

3   It is easy for you _____ .

E   Note the use of *such* in these two sentences:

They did not go out of their way to court *such* excitement. (l.6)

Such inns as there were were generally dirty. (ll.10-11)

Write sentences using the following phrases:

such requests; such freedom; such difficulty; such films.

F   Note the form of the verb in italics:

For men accustomed to *eating* seven-course dinners ... (l.15)

Complete the following using a verb after each phrase:

1   I am used to _____ .

2   Do you object to my _____ ?

3   I am looking forward to _____ .

Special difficulties 难点

A   Study the following pairs of words and then write sentences of your own to bring out the difference.

1   case (l.2) — situation

Do you know the date of the last recorded case of smallpox?

The waiter brought me the bill and I didn't have enough money. I'd never been in such a situation before.

2   especially (ll.3-4) — specially

I think you'll find this article especially interesting.

I've had this area specially designed as a herb garden.

3   realize (l.8) — understand

I hope you realize that you're making a big mistake.

I don't think I understand the meaning of the sentence.

4   except for (1.8) — except

   Except for one old lady, the bus was empty.

   You can have any of the cakes except this one.

5   coarse (1.12) — course

   He wore an old jacket made of coarse cloth.

   In a French household, soup is generally the first course of the main meal of the day.

6   home (1.16) — house

   When I'm abroad, my thoughts are never far from home.

   They live in a large house.

B   Explain the meaning of the phrases in italics:

1   They did not go *out of their way* to court such excitement. (1.6)

2   Please ask him to get *out of the way*; I can't get past.

3   We bought a beautiful *out-of-the-way* cottage, miles from anywhere.

4   Please move that table. Can't you see it's *in the way*?

5   I'll call in and see you *on my way* home from work.

6   We must do this exercise *in the way* we have been taught.

Multiple choice questions 选择题

Choose the correct answers to the following questions.

Comprehension 理解

1 Modern climbers differ from their predecessors because they _____ .

   (*a*) like to find the easiest way to the top of a mountain

   (*b*) like sport

   (*c*) prefer difficult climbs to easy ones

   (*d*) always follow a particular route

2 It is probably true to say that modern climbers _____ .

   (*a*) enjoy testing themselves on difficult climbs

   (*b*) avoid dangerous situations

   (*c*) are not as well equipped as earlier climbers

   (*d*) are only interested in getting to the top of a mountain

3 The pioneers had a hard time because _____ .

   (*a*) Zermatt and Chamonix had rapidly become popular

   (*b*) Alpine villages were primitive

   (*c*) the mountains were extremely high

   (*d*) there wasn't anything to eat

4 It is probably true to say that early climbers _____ .

   (*a*) had seven-course dinners when they were climbing

   (*b*) didn't mind uncomfortable conditions

   (*c*) always found accommodation with the local priest

   (*d*) enjoyed a higher standard of living back home

Unit 1 Lesson 3

Structure 句型

5 Earlier climbers liked summits _____ had never been climbed before. (ll.2-4)

   (*a*) which   (*b*) which they   (*c*) that they   (*d*) unless they

6 _____ single aim was getting to the top. (ll.6-7)

   (*a*) They're   (*b*) There   (*c*) Their   (*d*) Theirs

7 _____ Zermatt and Chamonix, most places were unknown. (ll.8-9)

   (*a*) Except   (*b*) Unless   (*c*) Without   (*d*) Apart from

8 _____ were generally dirty and flea-ridden. (ll.10-11)

   (*a*) The few inns that existed   (*b*) Inns like this

   (*c*) Such inns   (*d*) Few inns

Vocabulary 词汇

9 In the pioneering days this was not the _____ at all. (l.2)

   (*a*) condition   (*b*) situation   (*c*) history   (*d*) event

10 They often faced difficulties of the most _____ nature. (ll.4-5)

   (*a*) dangerous   (*b*) dreadful   (*c*) extreme   (*d*) pitiful

11 – all washed down with _____ wine. (l.12)

   (*a*) course   (*b*) sour   (*c*) rough   (*d*) new

12 Often a valley _____ no inn at all. (l.12)

   (*a*) was proud of   (*b*) advertised   (*c*) showed   (*d*) possessed

Lesson 4 　Seeing hands 　能看见东西的手

First listen and then answer the following question.

听录音，然后回答以下问题 。

How did Vera discover she had this gift of second sight?

Several cases have been reported in Russia recently of people who can read and detect colours with their fingers, and even see through solid doors and walls. One case concerns an eleven-year-old schoolgirl, Vera Petrova, who has normal vision but who can also perceive things with different parts of her skin, and through solid walls. This ability was first noticed by her father. One day she came into his office and happened to put
5　her hands on the door of a locked safe. Suddenly she asked her father why he kept so many old newspapers locked away there, and even described the way they were done up in bundles.

　　Vera's curious talent was brought to the notice of a scientific research institute in the town of Ulyanovsk, near where she lives, and in April she was given a series of tests by a special commission of the Ministry of Health of the Russian Federal Republic. During these tests she was able to read a newspaper through an
10　opaque screen and, stranger still, by moving her elbow over a child's game of Lotto she was able to describe the figures and colours printed on it; and, in another instance, wearing stockings and slippers, to make out with her foot the outlines and colours of a picture hidden under a carpet. Other experiments showed that her knees and shoulders had a similar sensitivity. During all these tests Vera was blindfold; and, indeed, except when blindfold she lacked the ability to perceive things with her skin. It was also found that although she
15　could perceive things with her fingers this ability ceased the moment her hands were wet.

ERIC DE MAUNY *Seeing hands* from *The Listener*

Another Russian girl, Rosa Kuleshova, reads blindfold.

New words and expressions 生词和短语

solid (1.2) /'sɒlɪd/ *adj.* 坚实的

safe (1.5) /seɪf/ *n.* 保险柜

Ulyanovsk (1.7) /uːˈljɑːnɔːfsk/ *n.* 乌里扬诺夫斯克

commission (1.8) /kəˈmɪʃən/ *n.* 委员会

opaque (1.10) /əʊˈpeɪk/ *adj.* 不透明的

lotto (1.10) /'lɒtəʊ/ *n.* 一种有编号的纸牌

slipper (1.11) /'slɪpə/ *n.* 拖鞋

blindfold (1.13) /'blaɪndfəʊld/ *adj. & adv.* 被蒙上眼睛的（地）

Notes on the text 课文注释

1　of people who can read ..., 这个定语从句用来修饰主语 cases, 由于太长, 因此被移至谓语之后 。

2　through solid walls 与 with different parts of her skin 并列, 作 perceive 的状语 。

3　lock something away, 把……锁起来 。

4　do up, 捆, 包 。

5　bring ... to the notice of, 引起某人注意 。

6　except when blindfold, 其中 when 之后省略了 she was 。

7　the moment her hands were wet, 这是一个时间状语从句, the moment 有 "一 …… 就 ……" 的意思 。

参考译文

　　俄罗斯最近报道了几个事例, 有人能用手指看书识字和辨认颜色, 甚至能透过厚实的门和墙看到东西 。其中有一例谈到有一个名叫维拉 · 彼托洛娃的 11 岁女学生 。她的视力与常人一样, 但她还能用皮肤的不同部位辨认东西, 甚至看穿坚实的墙壁 。是她父亲首先发现她这一功能的 。一天, 维拉走进父亲的办公室, 偶然把手放在一个锁着的保险柜的门上, 她突然问父亲为什么把这么多的旧报纸锁在柜子里, 还说了报纸捆扎的情况 。

　　维拉的特异功能引起了她家附近乌里扬诺夫斯克城一个科研单位的注意 。4月里, 俄罗斯卫生部的一个特别委员会对她进行了一系列的测试 。在这些测试中, 她能隔着不透明的屏幕读报纸 。更为奇怪的是, 她把肘部在儿童玩的 "罗托" 纸牌上移动一下, 便能说出印在纸牌上的数字和颜色 。还有一次, 她穿着长筒袜子和拖鞋, 能用脚识别出藏在地毯下面的一幅画的轮廓和颜色 。其他实验表明, 她的膝盖和双肩有类似的感觉能力 。在所有这些实验中, 维拉的双眼都是蒙着的 。如果不蒙上双眼她的皮肤就不再具有识别物体的能力 。这是千真万确的 。同时还发现, 尽管她能用手指识别东西, 但她的手一旦弄湿, 这种功能便会立即消失 。

Comprehension 理解

Give short answers to these questions in your own words as far as possibe. Use one complete sentence for each answer.

1　How did Vera's father accidentally discover that his daughter possessed unusual powers of perception?

2　Under what conditions was Vera incapable of perceiving objects with her skin?

3　Under what conditions did Vera lose the ability to perceive objects with her fingers?

Vocabulary 词汇

Refer to the text to see how the following words have been used, then write sentences of your own using these words: several (1.1); detect (1.1); vision (1.3); perceive (1.3); curious (1.7); series (1.8); outlines (1.12); a similar (1.13); ceased (1.15).

Sentence structure 句子结构

A   Supply the missing words in the following sentences. Do not refer to the passage until you have finished the exercise:

1   Several cases have been reported in Russia recently of people _____ can read _____ detect colours with their fingers, _____ even see through solid doors and walls. One case concerns an eleven-year-old schoolgirl, Vera Petrova, _____ has normal vision _____ _____ can also perceive things with different parts of her skin, _____ through solid walls. (ll.1-4)

2   It was also found that _____ she could perceive things with her fingers, this ability ceased _____ _____ her hands were wet. (ll.14-15)

B   Complete these sentences in any way you wish. Then compare what you have written with the sentences in the passage:

1   One day she came into his office and _____ . (ll.4-5)
2   Suddenly she asked her father why _____ . (ll.5-6)
3   Vera's curious talent was _____ . (l.7)
4   During these tests she _____ . (l.9)
5   It was also found that _____ . (ll.14-15)

C   Write three sentences describing Vera's unusual abilities.

Key structures 关键句型

A   Supply the correct form of the verbs in parentheses. Do not refer to the passage until you have finished the exercise:

1   Several cases _____ (report) in Russia recently of people who can read and detect colours with their fingers. (ll.1-2)

2   This ability first _____ (notice) by her father. (l.4)

3   Vera's curious talent _____ (bring) to the notice of a scientific research institute in the town of Ulyanovsk, near where she lives, and in April she _____ (give) a series of tests by a special commission of the Ministry of Health of the Russian Federal Republic. (ll.7-9)

4   It also _____ (find) that although she _____ (can) perceive things with her fingers, this ability _____ (cease) the moment her hands _____ (be) wet. (ll.14-15)

B   Compare the word order in these two sentences:

Why did he keep so many old newspapers locked away there?

She asked her father *why he kept* so many old newspapers locked away there. (ll.5-6)

Write these sentences again, beginning each one with the words *I asked him*:

1   When did he buy that car?
2   Where did he find that book?
3   Why did he send a fax?
4   How did he know I was here?
5   Which one did he like best?

C   Note the form of the verb in italics in this sentence:

By *moving* her elbow over a child's game of Lotto she was able to describe the figures and colours printed on it. (ll.10-11)

Supply the correct form of the verbs in parentheses:

1   He can walk for miles without _____ (get) tired.

2   On _____ (arrive) at the station, I went and bought a ticket.

3   While _____ (try) to climb over that wall, he fell down and broke his leg.

4   You will never succeed in _____ (persuade) me to come with you.

D   Compare these two sentences:

Instead of saying: She *was able to describe* the colours and figures printed on it. (ll.9-10)

We can say: She *succeeded in describing* the colours and figures printed on it.

Supply *could* or *was able to* in the following sentences:

1   I _____ easily swim across this river if I wanted to.

2   He _____ run a mile in five minutes when he was younger.

3   Amundsen _____ reach the South Pole before Scott.

4   I rang up several times before I _____ contact him.

5   I _____ get these tickets because I was willing to stand in the queue for several hours.

Special difficulties 难点

A   Study the following pairs of words and then write sentences of your own to bring out the difference.

1   normal (l.3) — ordinary

I'm not looking for anything fancy, just a normal kettle.

I'm just an ordinary person.

2   skin (l.3) — complexion

I got so sunburnt that my skin is peeling.

Drinking a lot of water is good for the complexion.

3   noticed (l.4) — remarked

I've noticed that there are more butterflies this year.

'You're looking very well!' she remarked.

4   office (l.4) — study

Reuters is a big news agency with offices all over the world.

I'll have a bigger study in my new apartment.

5   game (l.10) — toy

Let's play a game of hide-and-seek.

Alice got a new toy for her birthday.

6   lack (l.14) — need

His real problem is that he lacks confidence.

We need an hour to get to the airport.

7   wet (l.15) — damp

Don't sit on that bench. The paint is still wet.

You shouldn't wear that shirt if it's still damp.

B   Explain the expressions in italics:

1   The newspapers were *done up* in bundles. (l.6)

2   It's too late to save him now. He's *done for*.

3   She'll never go back to her husband. She's *done with* him for good.

4   This room looks lovely now that we've *done it up*.

5   I wouldn't trust him if I were you. He once *did me out of* a lot of money.

C   Explain the word *figure* in these sentences:

1   By moving her elbow over a child's game of Lotto she was able to describe the *figures* and colours printed on it. (ll.10-11)

2   I could make out the *figure* of a man on the bridge.

3   She has such a beautiful *figure*, she could make a living as a model, I'm sure.

D   Explain the expressions with *make* in these sentences:

1   She was able to *make out* with her foot the outlines and colours of a picture. (ll.10-12)

2   The thief *made off* with quite a lot of money.

3   He's a strange fellow. I just can't *make him out*.

4   Before he died, he *made over* all his money to his wife.

5   Are you any good at *making up* stories for children?

Multiple choice questions 选择题

Choose the correct answers to the following questions.

Comprehension 理解

1   Solid doors and walls are _____ .

   (*a*) no obstacle for people who can read and detect colours with their fingers

   (*b*) invisible to people who can read and detect colours with their fingers

   (*c*) transparent to people who can read and detect colours with their fingers

   (*d*) concerned in cases reported in Russia recently

2   Vera Petrova's father _____ .

   (*a*) had always known his daughter had this talent

   (*b*) found that his daughter could perceive things with different parts of her skin

   (*c*) discovered his daughter's gift by accident

   (*d*) described the way newspapers were done up in bundles

3   The scientific research institute in the town of Ulyanovsk _____ .

   (*a*) made Vera read a newspaper

   (*b*) arranged that Vera should undergo a number of experiments

   (*c*) tested Vera thoroughly

   (*d*) set up a game of Lotto with Vera

4   Which one of these statements is true?

   (*a*) Vera couldn't always perceive things with her skin.

   (*b*) Vera was occasionally blindfold when she did the tests.

   (*c*) Vera's hands had to be wet before she could perceive things through her skin.

   (*d*) Vera's knees didn't have the same sensitivity as her fingers.

Structure 句型

5 Several cases have been reported in Russia recently of people _____ can read ... (l.1)

    (*a*) whom   (*b*) that   (*c*) which   (*d*) they

6 One day she came into his office and put her hands on the door of the safe _____ . (l.5)

    (*a*) as it happened   (*b*) by chance   (*c*) perhaps   (*d*) intentionally

7 _____ these tests were being conducted, she was able to read a newspaper. (l.9)

    (*a*) During   (*b*) On occasion   (*c*) While   (*d*) As if

8 Vera couldn't 'see' with her skin _____ she was blindfold. (ll.13-14)

    (*a*) only   (*b*) except   (*c*) as if   (*d*) unless

Vocabulary 词汇

9 This ability was first _____ by her father. (l.4)

    (*a*) observed   (*b*) remarked   (*c*) regarded   (*d*) acknowledged

10 Vera's curious talent was brought to the _____ of a research institute. (l.7)

    (*a*) attention   (*b*) observation   (*c*) regard   (*d*) care

11 – wearing stockings and slippers, she was able to _____ colours with her foot. (ll.11-12)

    (*a*) draw   (*b*) see   (*c*) understand   (*d*) watch

12 This ability _____ the moment her hands were wet. (l.15)

    (*a*) continued   (*b*) renewed   (*c*) increased   (*d*) stopped

Lesson 5　Youth　青年

First listen and then answer the following question.

听录音，然后回答以下问题 。

How does the writer like to treat young people?

People are always talking about 'the problem of youth'. If there is one—which I take leave to doubt—then it is older people who create it, not the young themselves. Let us get down to fundamentals and agree that the young are after all human beings—people just like their elders. There is only one difference between an old man and a young one: the young man has a glorious future before him and the old one has a splendid future
5　behind him: and maybe that is where the rub is.

　　When I was a teenager, I felt that I was just young and uncertain—that I was a new boy in a huge school, and I would have been very pleased to be regarded as something so interesting as a problem. For one thing, being a problem gives you a certain identity, and that is one of the things the young are busily engaged in seeking.
10　　I find young people exciting. They have an air of freedom, and they have not a dreary commitment to mean ambitions or love of comfort. They are not anxious social climbers, and they have no devotion to material things. All this seems to me to link them with life, and the origins of things. It's as if they were, in some sense, cosmic beings in violent and lovely contrast with us suburban creatures. All that is in my mind when I meet a young person. He may be conceited, ill-mannered, presumptuous or fatuous, but I do not turn
15　for protection to dreary clichés about respect for elders—as if mere age were a reason for respect. I accept that we are equals, and I will argue with him, as an equal, if I think he is wrong.

FIELDEN HUGHES from *Out of the Air, The Listener*

A group of young people

29

Unit 1   Lesson 5

New words and expressions 生词和短语

leave (l.1) /liːv/ *n.* 允许

fundamentals (l.2) /ˌfʌndəˈmentlz/ *n.* 基本原则

glorious (l.4) /ˈɡlɔːrɪəs/ *adj.* 光辉灿烂的

splendid (l.4) /ˈsplendɪd/ *adj.* 灿烂的

rub (l.5) /rʌb/ *n.* 难题

identity (l.8) /aɪˈdentɪti/ *n.* 身份

dreary (l.10) /ˈdrɪəri/ *adj.* 沉闷的

commitment (l.10) /kəˈmɪtmənt/ *n.* 信奉

mean (l.11) /miːn/ *adj.* 吝啬的, 小气的

social climber (l.11) /ˌsəʊʃəl-ˈklaɪmə/ 追求更
高社会地位的人, 向上爬的人

devotion (l.11) /dɪˈvəʊʃən/ *n.* 热爱

cosmic (l.13) /ˈkɒzmɪk/ *adj.* 宇宙的

suburban (l.13) /səˈbɜːbən/ *adj.* 见识不广的, 偏狭
的

conceited (l.14) /kənˈsiːtɪd/ *adj.* 自高自大的

presumptuous (l.14) /prɪˈzʌmptʃʊəs/ *adj.* 自以为是
的, 放肆的

fatuous (l.14) /ˈfætʃʊəs/ *adj.* 愚蠢的

cliché (l.15) /ˈkliːʃeɪ/ *n.* 陈词滥调

Notes on the text 课文注释

1   which I take leave to doubt, 这是一个插入成分, 用两个破折号与句子的主要部分分开。take leave to do sth.
是 "擅自做", "冒昧去做" 的意思。

2   get down to, 认真处理, 认真研究。

3   ... that is where the rub is. There's the rub. = That's the problem. 这就是问题所在。

4   for one thing, 首先。

5   air of freedom, 无拘无束。

6   in some sense, 在某种意义上。

7   turn to ... for ..., 为 …… 而求助于 …… 。

参考译文

　　人们总是在谈论 "青年问题"。如果这个问题存在的话——请允许我对此持怀疑态度——那么, 这个问题
是由老年人而不是青年人造成的。让我们来认真研究一些基本事实: 承认青年人和他们的长辈一样也是人。老
年人和青年人只有一个区别: 青年人有光辉灿烂的前景, 而老年人的辉煌已成为过去。问题的症结恐怕就在
这里。

　　我十几岁时, 总感到自己年轻, 有些事情拿不准——我是一所大学校里的一名新生, 如果我当时真的被看成
像一个问题那样有趣, 我会感到很得意的。因为这至少使我得到了某种承认, 这正是年轻人所热衷追求的。

　　我觉得年轻人令人振奋, 无拘无束。他们既不追逐卑鄙的名利, 也不贪图生活的舒适。他们不热衷于向上
爬, 也不一味追求物质享受。在我看来, 所有这些使他们与生命和万物之源联系在了一起。从某种意义上讲, 他
们似乎是宇宙人, 同我们这些凡夫俗子形成了强烈而鲜明的对照。每逢我遇到年轻人, 脑子里就想到这些。年
轻人也许狂妄自负, 举止无理, 傲慢放肆, 愚昧无知, 但我不会用应当尊重长者这一套陈词滥调来为我自己辩护,
似乎年长就是受人尊敬的理由。我认为我和他们是平等的。如果我认为他们错了, 我就以平等的身份和他们争
个明白。

Comprehension 理解

Give short answers to these questions in your own words as far as possible. Use one complete sentence for
each answer.

1   What, according to the writer, is the one difference between an old man and a young one?

2   Why would the writer have been pleased to have been regarded as a problem when he was young?

3   Name three qualities in young people which the author particularly admires.

Vocabulary 词汇

Refer to the text to see how the following words have been used, then write sentences of your own using these words: create (l.2); teenager (l.6); devotion (l.11); link (l.12); origins (l.12); dreary (l.15).

Sentence structure 句子结构

A Complete the following sentences in any way you wish. Then compare what you have written with the sentences in the passage:

1 There is only one difference between an old man and a young one: _____ . (ll.3-4)
2 When I was a teenager, I _____ . (l.6)
3 I find young people exciting. They _____ . (l.10)

B Combine the following statements to make complete sentences. Add conjunctions of your own and omit the words in italics. Do not refer to the passage until you have finished the exercise.

1 If there is one, I take leave to doubt *it*. It is older people who create it. *It is* not the young themselves. (ll.1-2)
2 They are not anxious social climbers. They have no devotion to material things. (ll.11-12)

C Write three statements which an adult might make to criticize adolescents.

D Write three statements which an adolescent might make to criticize adults.

Key structures 关键句型

A Compare these two sentences:

People *are always talking* about 'the problem of youth'. (l.1)

Whenever I meet him, he *always talks* about his personal problems.

The first sentence describes something that happens *all the time*; the second sentence describes something that happens *frequently*.

Write similar pairs of sentences using the following verbs: change; make; tell; ask.

B Compare these two sentences:

It is older people who create it, not *the young* themselves. (l.2)

There is only one difference between an old man and *a young one*. (ll.3-4)

Write similar pairs of sentences using the following words: the rich, a rich man; the sick, a sick man; the blind, a blind man; the dead, a dead man.

C Compare these two sentences:

Instead of saying: I would have been very pleased *if anyone regarded me* as a problem.

We can say: I would have been very pleased *to be regarded* as a problem. (l.7)

Write these sentences again using this construction with *to be* in place of the phrases in italics:

1 You would not like *it if you were accused* of theft.
2 I was astonished *when they told me* that all the tickets had been sold out.
3 I expect *they will inform me* about it tomorrow.

Unit 1 Lesson 5

D Compare these two sentences:

Instead of saying: *To be* a problem gives you a certain identity.

We can say: *Being* a problem gives you a certain identity ... (1.8)

Rewrite these sentences changing the form of the verbs in italics:

1 It is not very pleasant *to have* to write so many letters.

2 *To expect* others to help you and then not *to help* them in return is hardly commendable.

3 It is very enjoyable *to teach* young children.

E Note the construction in italics:

That is one of the things the young *are* busily *engaged in seeking*. (ll.8-9)

Write sentences using the same construction with the following verbs: delight; interest; persist; believe.

F Compare these two sentences:

Instead of saying: They have *no* devotion to material things. (ll.11-12)

We can say: They *haven't any* devotion to material things.

Write these sentences again using *not ... any* in place of *no*.

1 He doesn't know. There's no point in asking him.

2 You'll pass your driving test if you make no mistakes.

3 I have no faith in him.

Special difficulties 难点

A Study the following pairs of words and then write sentences of your own to bring out the difference.

1 older (1.2) — elder

I know both buildings are very old, but which one is older?

My elder brother is a doctor.

2 agree (1.2) — accept

They invited me to their wedding and I've agreed to go. (*agree to do* something)

She offered me some clothes her children had grown out of and I accepted them. (*accept* + object = take what is offered)

But *agree* and *accept* are interchangeable in the text, as in these sentences:

I don't agree with your opinion/accept your opinion of the youth of this country. I agree/I accept that this is a difficult matter.

3 between (1.3) — among

It's hard to choose between these two pictures. I like them both.

There are quite a few talented artists among the people I know.

4 please (1.7) — beg

It pleases me to say you've got the job.

I begged the traffic-cop not to book me for speeding and he just laughed.

5 regard (1.7) — look at

I don't regard a degree as a meal ticket for life.

Just look at those children picking apples.

6 interesting (1.7) — interested

I found his talk very interesting.

I got interested in stamp collecting when I was a child.

7   exciting (l.10) — excited

There are some exciting items in the current fashion show.

We got excited when we thought we had won the lottery.

8   reason (l.15) — cause

What was the reason for the delay?

The doctor recorded the cause of death as heart failure.

B   Note this phrase with *get:*

Let us *get down to* fundamentals. (l.2)

Explain these expressions with *get*:

1   The children are very quiet. I wonder what they're *getting up to*.

2   I can't see how we can *get round* this difficulty.

3   I've been abroad three times this year. I *get about* quite a bit.

4   Hasn't she *got over* her illness yet?

5   Don't think you'll *get off* so lightly if you're caught.

6   It's your turn to do the washing up and it's no use your trying to *get out of* it.

C   Note the phrase in italics:

He may be *ill-mannered*. (l.14)

Write sentences using the following adjectives:

ill-advised; ill-protected; ill-tempered; ill-fated; ill-used; ill-bred; ill-natured.

Multiple choice questions 选择题

Choose the correct answers to the following questions.

Comprehension 理解

1   What's the main difference between young people and old people?

(*a*) Old people think of the young as 'a problem'.

(*b*) Old people create this 'problem' of age difference.

(*c*) Old people have a past; young people have a future.

(*d*) Old people and young people forget they are all human beings.

2   One of the things young people want to do is to _____ .

(*a*) find out who they are

(*b*) make sure they become 'a problem'

(*c*) feel uncertain about themselves

(*d*) feel they are in a huge school

3   According to the writer, young people _____ .

(*a*) are conceited, ill-mannered or fatuous

(*b*) don't see life in the same way their elders do

(*c*) don't have any ambitions

(*d*) come from another planet

4 The writer doesn't believe that _____ .

   (*a*) people automatically deserve respect because they are old

   (*b*) young people and old people are equals

   (*c*) you should argue with young people if they are wrong

   (*d*) young people have any faults

Structure 句型

5 The problem, if there is one, _____ by older people. (l.2)

   (*a*) created   (*b*) is created   (*c*) creates   (*d*) is creating

6 For one thing, if you _____ a problem, you have a certain identity. (ll. 7-8)

   (*a*) were   (*b*) being   (*c*) had   (*d*) are

7 _____ to be linked with life, and the origin of things. (l.12)

   (*a*) They seem   (*b*) It seems   (*c*) This seems   (*d*) What seems

8 It is _____ they are conceited and ill-mannered. (l.14)

   (*a*) necessary   (*b*) permissible   (*c*) possible   (*d*) likely

Vocabulary 词汇

9 Let us get down to _____ . (l.2)

   (*a*) what is needed   (*b*) basics   (*c*) the end   (*d*) the bottom

10 Perhaps that's where the _____ is. (l.5)

   (*a*) wound   (*b*) problem   (*c*) hurt   (*d*) injury

11 Identity is one of the things in life the young are busy _____ . (ll.8-9)

   (*a*) looking at   (*b*) looking to   (*c*) looking over   (*d*) looking for

12 That's what I _____ when I meet a young person. (ll.13-14)

   (*a*) am annoyed with   (*b*) care about

   (*c*) object to   (*d*) think about

Lesson 6   The sporting spirit   体育的精神

🎙️ **First listen and then answer the following question.**
听录音, 然后回答以下问题 。
How does the writer describe sport at the international level?

I am always amazed when I hear people saying that sport creates goodwill between the nations, and that if only the common peoples of the world could meet one another at football or cricket, they would have no inclination to meet on the battlefield. Even if one didn't know from concrete examples (the 1936 Olympic Games, for instance) that international sporting contests lead to orgies of hatred, one could deduce it from
5   general principles.

    Nearly all the sports practised nowadays are competitive. You play to win, and the game has little meaning unless you do your utmost to win. On the village green, where you pick up sides and no feeling of local patriotism is involved, it is possible to play simply for the fun and exercise: but as soon as the question of prestige arises, as soon as you feel that you and some larger unit will be disgraced if you lose, the most
10   savage combative instincts are aroused. Anyone who has played even in a school football match knows this. At the international level, sport is frankly mimic warfare. But the significant thing is not the behaviour of the players but the attitude of the spectators; and, behind the spectators, of the nations who work themselves into furies over these absurd contests, and seriously believe—at any rate for short periods—that running, jumping and kicking a ball are tests of national virtue.

GEORGE ORWELL *The sporting spirit*

New words and expressions 生词和短语

goodwill (1.1) /'gʊdwɪl/ *n.* 友好
cricket (1.2) /'krɪkɪt/ *n.* 板球
inclination (1.3) /ˌɪnklɪ'neɪʃən/ *n.* 意愿
contest (1.4) /'kɒntest/ *n.* 比赛
orgy (1.4) /'ɔːdʒi/ *n.* 无节制, 放荡
deduce (1.4) /dɪ'djuːs/ *v.* 推断
competitive (1.6) /kəm'petɪtɪv/ *adj.* 竞争性的

patriotism (1.8) /'pætriətɪzəm/ *n.* 地方观念, 爱国主义
disgrace (1.9) /dɪs'greɪs/ *v.* 使丢脸
savage (1.10) /'sævɪdʒ/ *adj.* 野性的
combative (1.10) /'kɒmbətɪv/ *adj.* 好斗的
mimic warfare (1.11) /'mɪmɪk-'wɔːfeə/ 模拟战争
behaviour (1.11) /bɪ'heɪvjə/ *n.* 行动, 举止
absurd (1.13) /əb'sɜːd/ *adj.* 荒唐的

Notes on the text 课文注释

1   if only the common peoples of the world ..., 这里 if only 引导的一个非真实条件句, if only 作 "要是……就好了" 讲 。
2   have no inclination to do, 无意做……, 不想做…… 。
3   deduce ... from ..., 从 …… 推断出 …… 。
4   You play to win. 句中的 you 是泛指人, 可译作 "人们" 。
5   pick up, 随意挑选 。
6   and, behind the spectators, of the nations, 在 of the nations 前面省略了 the attitude 。

35

East Midlands 'PIX'

参考译文

　　当我听人们说体育运动可创造国家之间的友谊，还说各国民众若在足球场或板球场上交锋，就不愿在战场上残杀的时候，我总是惊愕不已。一个人即使不能从具体的事例（例如 1936 年的奥林匹克运动会）了解到国际运动比赛会导致疯狂的仇恨，也可以从常理中推断出结论。

　　现在开展的体育运动几乎都是竞争性的。参加比赛就是为了取胜。如果不拚命去赢，比赛就没有什么意义了。在乡间的草坪上，当你随意组成两个队，并且不涉及任何地方情绪时，那才有可能是单纯为了娱乐和锻炼而进行比赛。可是一旦涉及到荣誉问题，一旦你想到你和某一团体会因你输了而丢脸时，那么最野蛮的争斗天性便会被激发起来。即使是仅仅参加过学校足球赛的人也有这种体会。在国际比赛中，体育简直是一场模拟战争。但是，要紧的还不是运动员的行为，而是观众的态度，以及观众身后各个国家的态度。面对着这些荒唐的比赛，参赛的各个国家会如痴如狂，甚至煞有介事地相信——至少在短期内如此——跑跑、跳跳、踢踢球是对一个民族品德素质的检验。

Comprehension 理解

Give short answers to these questions in your own words as far as possible. Use one complete sentence for each answer.

1　Why, according to the author, do international sporting contests lead to orgies of hatred?

2　What, according to the author, do spectators believe when they watch international sporting contests?

Vocabulary 词汇

A　Refer to the text to see how the following words have been used, then write sentences of your own using these words: amazed (l.1); goodwill (l.1); inclination (l.3); deduce (l.4); utmost (l.7); prestige (l.9); disgraced (l.9); significant (l.11).

B　Explain the following phrases as they have been used in the passage: pick up sides (l.7); local patriotism (ll.7-8); the most savage combative instincts are aroused (ll.9-10); frankly mimic warfare (l.11); absurd contests (l.13).

Sentence structure 句子结构

A Supply the missing words in the following paragraph. Do not refer to the passage until you have finished the exercise:

You play to win, _____ the game has little meaning _____ you do your utmost to win. On the village green, _____ you pick up sides _____ no feeling of local patriotism is involved, it is possible to play simply for the fun and exercise; but _____ the question of local prestige arises, _____ you feel that you and some larger unit will be disgraced _____ you lose, the most savage combative instincts are aroused. Anyone _____ has played even in a school football match knows this. (ll.6-10)

B Combine the following sentences to make one complete statement. Make any changes you think necessary, but do not change the sense of the original. Refer to the passage when you have finished the exercise:

The significant thing is not the behaviour of the players. It is the attitude of the spectators. Behind the spectators, it is the attitude of the nations. They work themselves up into furies over these absurd contests. Running, jumping and kicking a ball are tests of national virtue. They seriously believe this—at any rate for short periods. (ll.11-13)

C Complete the following sentences in any way you wish. Then compare what you have written with the sentences in the passage:

1 I am always amazed when _____ . (l.1)
2 Nearly all the sports practised _____ . (l.6)

D State in a single sentence what you think the author believes about competitive sports.

Key structures 关键句型

A Study the form of the verbs after *if* in these sentences:

If only the common peoples of the world *could meet* one another at football or cricket, they *would have* no inclination to meet on the battlefield. (ll.1-3)

If one didn't know from concrete examples that international sporting contests lead to orgies of hatred, one *could deduce* it from general principles. (ll.3-5)

Some larger unit *will be disgraced if you lose*. (l.9)

Complete the following in any way you wish:

1 If you play a game to win _____ .
2 If only we could afford to _____ .
3 You could learn to play golf if you _____ .
4 You won't find it difficult if you _____ .

B Note carefully the form of the verbs after the phrase *as soon as* in this sentence:

As soon as the question of prestige *arises, as soon as* you *feel* that you and some larger unit will be disgraced, the most savage combative instincts *are aroused*. (ll.8-10)

Supply the correct form of the verbs in parentheses in these sentences:

1 If he _____ (make) any trouble, he will be asked to leave the meeting.
2 You will feel much better when you _____ (stop) smoking.
3 As soon as he _____ (arrive) in New York, he will send me a fax.
4 You can wait here until the rain _____ (stop).
5 When you _____ (move) to your new house, you will be far more comfortable than you are now.

Unit 1   Lesson 6

C   Supply the missing words in the following paragraph. Do not refer to the passage until you have finished the exercise:

Anyone who has played even _____ a school football match knows this. _____ the international level, sport is frankly mimic warfare. But the significant thing is not the behaviour _____ the players but the attitude _____ the spectators: and, _____ the spectators, _____ the nations who work themselves _____ furies _____ these absurd contests. (ll.10-13)

Special difficulties 难点

A   Study the following pairs of words and then write sentences of your own to bring out the difference.

1   hear (l.1) — listen
The walls of this house are so thin, you can hear the neighbours cough next door.
I often listen to music.

2   even (l.3) — still
Mr. Wilks is not only working at the age of 95; he's even running a company.
Though he's 95, Mr. Wilks still plays bowls.

3   lead (l.4) — guide
Walking just in front, and pausing to check everyone was following, the young man led them to the market place. (i.e. He went in front)
The doorman drew a quick sketch map to guide us through the narrow streets. (i.e. to show the way)

4   principle (l.5) — principal
A good principle is not to borrow money you can't repay.
He has just been appointed principal of the college.

5   practise (l.6) — practice
I practise lifting every day.
Your tennis will improve with practice.
However, in American English, both the noun and the verb are spelt *practice*.

6   win (l.6) — beat
Tottenham won the Cup Final.
Tottenham beat Liverpool in the Cup Final.

7   lose (l.9) — loose
Try not to lose your ticket.
The handle on this suitcase is very loose.

8   arise (l.10) — arouse
A serious problem has arisen which will take time to solve.
His behaviour was arousing the interest of his neighbours.

9   level (l.11) — flat
Inflation had dropped to its lowest level in five years.
It is much easier to walk on the flat.

B   Explain the meaning of the word *peoples* in this sentence:
If only the common *peoples* of the world could meet. (ll.1-2)
Write two sentences using the words *people* and *peoples*.

C Compare these two expressions:

Instead of saying: The Olympic Games that were held in 1936 ...

We can say: The 1936 Olympic Games ... (ll.3-4)

What can we say in place of the phrases in italics?

1   I shall catch the *train that leaves at four o'clock*.

2   I have a copy of the *edition that was published in 1937*.

3   *The Education Act of 1944* aimed at providing equal opportunities for every child in the country.

4   *The revolution of 1917* had important consequences.

D Compare these two sentences:

One could deduce it from general principles. (ll.4-5)

You play to win, and the game has little meaning unless *you* do your utmost to win. (ll.6-7)

Write two sentences using the words *one* and *you* in the ways shown above.

E Explain the words and phrases in italics:

1   It is possible to play simply *for the fun* and exercise. (l.8)

2   There was a lot of *fun* and laughter at the party.

3   He didn't mean any harm; it was all *in good fun*.

4   He's upset because everyone *made fun of* him.

Multiple choice questions 选择题

Choose the correct answers to the following questions.

Comprehension 理解

1 The writer questions the assumption that _____ .

(*a*) people enjoy sport

(*b*) there are general principles governing sport

(*c*) sport makes war less likely

(*d*) sport is enjoyed by common people

2 According to the writer, the only purpose of competitive games is _____ .

(*a*) beating your opponent

(*b*) getting plenty of exercises

(*c*) having fun

(*d*) doing your best

3 A competitive sportsman is likely to feel _____ if he loses.

(*a*) patriotism

(*b*) savage

(*c*) shame

(*d*) even more competitive

4 At the international level _____ .

(*a*) the players are at war with each other

(*b*) the spectators take part in the sporting contests

(*c*) nations appear to be at war with one another

(*d*) sport brings out the best qualities in a nation

Unit 1　Lesson 6

Structure 句型

5　If only _____ possible for the common peoples to meet each other. (ll.1-2)

 (*a*) it would be　　(*b*) it could be　　(*c*) it were　　(*d*) it might be

6　You play _____ win. (1.6)

 (*a*) in order to　　(*b*) in order that　　(*c*) so that　　(*d*) for

7　The village green is the _____ you pick sides. (1.7)

 (*a*) the place　　(*b*) the time　　(*c*) the reason　　(*d*) the cause

8　_____ the question of national prestige arises ... (ll.8-9)

 (*a*) The moment　　(*b*) Just　　(*c*) As long as　　(*d*) Providing

Vocabulary 词汇

9　If we could meet at football, we would have no _____ to meet on the battlefield. (ll.1-2)

 (*a*) bent　　(*b*) feeling　　(*c*) opportunity　　(*d*) desire

10　You could _____ from general principles that international sporting contests lead to orgies of hatred. (ll.4-5)

 (*a*) include　　(*b*) conclude　　(*c*) exclude　　(*d*) delude

11　If you lose, the _____ combative instincts are aroused. (ll.9-10)

 (*a*) wildest　　(*b*) most serious　　(*c*) most frightening　　(*d*) most dangerous

12　The _____ thing is not the behaviour of the players ... (ll.11-12)

 (*a*) important　　(*b*) unusual　　(*c*) signal　　(*d*) obvious

Lesson 7   Bats   蝙蝠

First listen and then answer the following question.

听录音，然后回答以下问题 。

In what way does echo-location in bats play a utilitarian role?

Not all sounds made by animals serve as language, and we have only to turn to that extraordinary discovery of echo-location in bats to see a case in which the voice plays a strictly utilitarian role.

To get a full appreciation of what this means we must turn first to some recent human inventions. Everyone knows that if he shouts in the vicinity of a wall or a mountainside, an echo will come back. The further off this solid obstruction, the longer time will elapse for the return of the echo. A sound made by tapping on the hull of a ship will be reflected from the sea bottom, and by measuring the time interval between the taps and the receipt of the echoes, the depth of the sea at that point can be calculated. So was born the echo-sounding apparatus, now in general use in ships. Every solid object will reflect a sound, varying according to the size and nature of the object. A shoal of fish will do this. So it is a comparatively simple step from locating the sea bottom to locating a shoal of fish. With experience, and with improved apparatus, it is now possible not only to locate a shoal but to tell if it is herring, cod, or other well-known fish, by the pattern of its echo.

It has been found that certain bats emit squeaks and by receiving the echoes, they can locate and steer clear of obstacles—or locate flying insects on which they feed. This echo-location in bats is often compared with radar, the principle of which is similar.

MAURICE BURTON *Curiosities of animal life*

Echo-location in bats is often compared with radar.

New words and expressions 生词和短语

bat (1.2) /bæt/ n. 蝙蝠

strictly (1.2) /'strɪktli/ adv. 明确地

utilitarian (1.2) /juːˌtɪlɪ'teərɪən/ adj. 实用的

appreciation (1.3) /əˌpriːʃi'eɪʃən/ n. 理解

obstruction (1.5) /əb'strʌkʃən/ n. 障碍物

elapse (1.5) /ɪ'læps/ v. 消逝

hull (1.6) /hʌl/ n. 船体

interval (1.6) /'ɪntəvəl/ n. 间隔

receipt (1.7) /rɪ'siːt/ n. 收到

apparatus (1.8) /ˌæpə'reɪtəs/ n. 仪器

shoal (1.9) /ʃəʊl/ n. 鱼群

herring (1.11) /'herɪŋ/ n. 鲱鱼

cod (1.11) /kɒd/ n. 鳕鱼

squeak (1.13) /skwiːk/ n. 尖叫声

Notes on the text 课文注释

1 Not all sounds made by animals serve as language, 动物发出的声音不全是作语言交际。此句采用了部分否定, 即不是否定所有的动物, 而只是一部分。serve as, 作……之用。

2 turn to, 求助于。

3 play a role in, 在……方面起作用。

4 in the vicinity of, 在……的附近。

5 So was born the echo-sounding apparatus, 这样就诞生了回声探测仪。这是一个倒装句, 主要是为了避免因主语过长而使全句失去平衡, 同时也为了使 apparatus 的定语 now in general use in ships 紧挨着名词。in general use, 普遍使用。

6 steer clear of, 避开。

参考译文

　　动物发出的声音不都是用作语言交际。我们只要看一看蝙蝠回声定位这一极不寻常的发现, 就可以探究一下声音在什么情况下有绝对的实用价值。

　　要透彻理解这句话的意义, 我们应先回顾一下人类最近的几项发明。大家都知道, 在墙壁或山腰附近发出喊声, 就会听到回声。固体障碍物越远, 回声返回所用时间就越长。敲打船体所发出的声音会从海底传回来, 测出回声间隔的时间, 便可算出该处海洋的深度。这样就产生了目前各种船舶上普遍应用的回声探测仪。任何固体都反射声音, 反射的声音因物体的大小和性质的不同而不同。鱼群也反射声音。从测定海深到测定鱼群, 这一进展比较容易。借助经验和改进了的仪器, 不仅能够确定鱼群的位置, 而且可以根据鱼群回声的特点分辨出是鲱鱼、鳕鱼, 还是人们所熟悉的其他鱼。

　　人们发现, 某些蝙蝠能发出尖叫声, 并能通过回声来确定并躲开障碍物, 或找到它们赖以为生的昆虫。蝙蝠的这种回声定位常常可与雷达相比较, 其原理是相似的。

Comprehension 理解

Give short answers to these questions in your own words as far as possible. Use one complete sentence for each answer.

1 How is the echo-location principle applied to measure the depth of the sea?

2 Why do the sounds reflected by solid objects vary?

3 What use do bats make of the principle of echo-location?

Vocabulary 词汇

Refer to the text to see how the following words have been used, then write sentences of your own using these words: strictly utilitarian (l.2); vicinity (l.4); elapse (l.5); tapping (l.5); apparatus (l.8); shoal (l.9); comparatively (l.9); emit (l.13); steer clear (ll.13-14).

Sentence structure 句子结构

A Combine the following sentences to make one complex statement out of each group. Make any changes you think necessary, but do not alter the sense of the original. Refer to the passage when you have finished the exercise:

1 Not all sounds made by animals serve as language. We have only to turn to that extraordinary discovery of echo-location in bats. We can see a case in which the voice plays a strictly utilitarian role. (ll.1-2)
2 A sound can be made by tapping on the hull of a ship. It will be reflected from the sea bottom. We can measure the time interval between the taps and the receipt of the echoes. The depth of the sea at that point can be calculated. (ll.5-7)
3 Every solid object will reflect a sound. This varies according to the size and nature of the object. (ll.8-9)
4 With experience, and with improved apparatus, it is now possible to locate a shoal. It is possible to tell if it is herring, cod, or other well-known fish, by the pattern of its echo. (ll.10-12)
5 A few years ago it was found that certain bats emit squeaks.
They received echoes. They could locate obstacles.
They could steer clear of obstacles. They could locate flying insects on which they feed. (ll.13-14)

B Without referring to the passage write three sentences indicating three different uses of the principle of echo-location.

Key structures 关键句型

A Compare these two sentences:
Instead of saying: *If we wish to get* a full appreciation of what this means we must turn first to some recent human inventions.
We can say: *To get* a full appreciation of what this means we must turn first to some recent human inventions. (l.3)
Complete the following sentences:
1 To understand _____ .
2 To enjoy _____ .
3 To succeed _____ .

B Supply *a, an* or *the* where necessary in the following paragraph. Do not refer to the passage until you have finished the exercise:
Everyone knows that if he shouts in _____ vicinity of _____ wall or _____ mountainside, _____ echo will come back. _____ further off this solid obstruction, _____ longer time will elapse for _____ return of _____ echo. _____ sound made by tapping on _____ hull of _____ ship will be reflected from _____ sea bottom, and by measuring _____ time interval between _____ taps and _____ receipt of _____ echoes _____ depth of _____ sea at that point can be calculated. So was born _____ echo-sounding apparatus, now in _____ general use in _____ ships.

Every solid object will reflect _____ sound, varying according to _____ size and _____ nature of _____ object. _____ shoal of _____ fish will do this. So it is _____ comparatively simple step from locating _____ sea bottom to locating _____ shoal of _____ fish. (ll.3-10)

C   Study the form of the verbs in italics in these sentences:

A sound made by *tapping* on the hull of a ship will be reflected from the sea bottom, and by *measuring* the time interval between the taps and the receipt of the echoes, the depth of the sea at that point can be calculated. (ll.5-7)

It has been found that certain bats emit squeaks and by *receiving* the echoes they can locate ... obstacles. (ll.13-14)

Write three sentences in the same way using *by* followed by the *-ing* form of a verb.

D   Note that the verb *compared* is followed by *with* in this sentence: Echo-location in bats is ... *compared with* radar ... (ll.14-15)

Supply *with, for,* or *to* in the following sentences:

1   I have been corresponding _____ him for many years.
2   He was arrested and charged _____ murder.
3   How much do you charge _____ this service?
4   I can't provide you _____ all the things you need.
5   We have provided _____ every emergency.
6   Did you apply _____ that job?
7   If you want a loan you should apply _____ the bank.
8   He's much too quick for me. I just can't compete _____ him.

Special difficulties 难点

A   Study the following pairs of words and then write sentences of your own to bring out the difference.

1   sound (l.1) — echo (l.2)
    Don't make a sound, any of you!
    The echo of the gunfire died away, and the valley was quiet again.
2   discovery (l.1) — invention (l.3)
    The discovery of oil in Alaska was a boon to the economy.
    The invention of personal computers was a very important event in the second half of the twentieth century.
3   appreciation (l.3) — estimation
    He lacks a realistic appreciation of the situation.
    In my estimation, you'll need twelve rolls of wallpaper.
4   obstruction (l.5) — obstacle (l.14)
    There's an obstruction in the fuel pipe.
    Fear of change is the greatest single obstacle to progress.
5   steer (l.13) — drive
    The captain steered his ship into the harbour.
    It's quite possible to drive from Geneva to London in a day.

B   Supply the missing words in these sentences:

1   Not all the sounds made _____ animals serve as language. (l.1)
2   This camera was made _____ Japan.
3   Glass is made _____ sand and lime.
4   This watch is made _____ gold.

C   Explain the word *experience* in these sentences:

1   With *experience* it is now possible not only to locate a shoal but to tell if it is herring, cod, or other well-known fish. (ll.10-11)

2   He is a very *experienced* surgeon.

3   It was one of the strangest *experiences* I have ever had.

D   What does the phrase *to tell if* mean in this sentence:

It is now possible *to tell if* it is herring, cod, or other well-known fish. (ll.10-11)

Write two sentences using *to tell if*.

E   Note the spelling of *echoes* (l.12). Write the plural of the following words: potato, piano, tomato, solo.

Multiple choice questions 选择题

Choose the correct answers to the following questions.

Comprehension 理解

1   What happens if you shout on a mountainside?

(*a*) You will be able to measure distance.

(*b*) Nothing.

(*c*) It will take a long time for an echo to come back.

(*d*) You will hear an echo.

2   You can measure the depth of the sea by _____ .

(*a*) shouting so you get back an echo

(*b*) tapping on the hull of a ship

(*c*) working out how long it takes to get an echo from the sea bottom

(*d*) calculating the reflection

3   The echo-location principle means you can even _____ .

(*a*) locate and distinguish different species of fish

(*b*) hear a fish's echo

(*c*) improve the apparatus now in use

(*d*) easily catch different species of fish

4   Bats use echo-location to _____ .

(*a*) see where they're going

(*b*) avoid bumping into things

(*c*) avoid flying insects

(*d*) emit squeaks

Structure 句型

5   Not _____ sound made by animals serves as language. (l.1)

(*a*) every   (*b*) each   (*c*) the whole   (*d*) the entire

6   We have only to turn to that extraordinary discovery of echo-location in bats to see a case _____ the voice plays a strictly utilitarian role. (ll.1-2)

(*a*) which   (*b*) where   (*c*) when   (*d*) why

Unit 1 Lesson 7

7 _____ he shout in the vicinity of a wall, an echo will come back. (1.4)

    (*a*) Should   (*b*) If   (*c*) When   (*d*) Though

8 _____ the echo-sounding apparatus was born. (ll.7-8)

    (*a*) Such   (*b*) The way   (*c*) That's how   (*d*) Like this

Vocabulary 词汇

9 The voice plays a strictly _____ role. (1.2)

    (*a*) secondary   (*b*) important   (*c*) usual   (*d*) practical

10 A sound made by _____ the hull of a ship ... (ll.5-6)

    (*a*) hitting   (*b*) knocking   (*c*) beating   (*d*) bashing

11 The sound varies _____ the size and nature of the object. (ll.8-9)

    (*a*) depending on   (*b*) relating to   (*c*) influencing   (*d*) by

12 A _____ of fish will do this. (1.9)

    (*a*) class   (*b*) herd   (*c*) school   (*d*) flock

Lesson 8　Trading standards　贸易标准

📼 **First listen and then answer the following question.**
听录音，然后回答以下问题。
What makes trading between rich countries difficult?

Chickens slaughtered in the United States, claim officials in Brussels, are not fit to grace European tables. No, say the Americans: our fowl are fine, we simply clean them in a different way. These days, it is differences in national regulations, far more than tariffs, that put sand in the wheels of trade between rich countries. It is not just farmers who are complaining. An electric razor that meets the European Union's safety standards
5　must be approved by American testers before it can be sold in the United States, and an American-made dialysis machine needs the EU's okay before it hits the market in Europe.

As it happens, a razor that is safe in Europe is unlikely to electrocute Americans. So, ask businesses on both sides of the Atlantic, why have two lots of tests where one would do? Politicians agree, in principle, so America and the EU have been trying to reach a deal which would eliminate the need to double-test many
10　products. They hope to finish in time for a trade summit between America and the EU on May 28th. Although negotiators are optimistic, the details are complex enough that they may be hard-pressed to get a deal at all.

Why? One difficulty is to construct the agreements. The Americans would happily reach one accord on standards for medical devices and then hammer out different pacts covering, say, electronic goods and drug
15　manufacturing. The EU—following fine continental traditions—wants agreement on general principles, which could be applied to many types of products and perhaps extended to other countries.

From: *The Economist,* May 24th, 1997

An electric razor that meets the European Union's safety standards must be
approved by American testers before it can be sold in the United States.

New words and expressions 生词和短语

slaughter (l.1) /'slɔːtə/ v. 屠宰

fit (l.1) /fɪt/ adj. 适合

grace (l.1) /greɪs/ v. 给……增光

tariff (l.3) /'tærɪf/ n. 关税

standard (l.4) /'stændəd/ n. 标准

dialysis (l.6) /daɪ'ælɪsɪs/ n. 分离, 分解; 透析, 渗析

electrocute (l.7) /ɪ'lektrəkjuːt/ v. 使触电身亡

eliminate (l.9) /ɪ'lɪmɪneɪt/ v. 消灭

accord (l.13) /ə'kɔːd/ n. 协议

device (l.14) /dɪ'vaɪs/ n. 仪器, 器械

hammer out (l.14) /'hæmə-ˌaʊt/ 推敲

pact (l.14) /pækt/ n. 合同, 条约, 公约

Notes on the text 课文注释

1   Chickens slaughtered in ... to grace European tables. 在这句话中引用了布鲁塞尔官员的评论, 却没有放在引号之中。这种方式常用于报刊文章, 对读者的直接影响更大。在 claim officials in Brussels 中, 动词 claim 置于名词之前。

2   it is differences in national regulations ... between rich countries, 是各国管理条例上的差异, 而不是关税阻碍了发达国家之间的贸易。这是一个 it 引导的强调句。put sand in the wheels of, 阻碍, 阻挠。

3   So, ask businesses on both sides of the Atlantic, why have two lots of tests where one would do? 这是另一个没有引号的直接引语的例子。注意 why have two ... do 中的语序, 这是非常口语化的直接引语的语序。

参考译文

布鲁塞尔的官员说, 在美国屠宰的鸡不适于用来装点欧洲的餐桌。不, 美国人说, 我们的家禽很好, 只是我们使用了另一种清洗方式。当前, 是各国管理条例上的差异, 而不是关税阻碍了发达国家之间的贸易。并不仅仅是农民在抱怨。一把符合欧盟安全标准的电动剃须刀必须得到美国检测人员的认可, 方可在美国市场上销售; 而美国制造的透析仪也要得到欧盟的首肯才能进入欧洲市场。

碰巧在欧洲使用安全的剃须刀不大可能使美国人触电身亡, 因此, 大西洋两岸的企业都在问, 当一套测试可以解决问题时, 为什么需要两套? 政治家在原则上同意了, 因此, 美国和欧盟一直在寻求达成协议, 以便为许多产品取消双重检查。他们希望尽早达成协议, 为 5 月 28 日举行的美国和欧盟贸易的最高级会议作准备。虽然谈判代表持乐观态度, 但协议细节如此复杂, 他们所面临的困难很可能使他们根本无法取得一致。

为什么呢? 困难之一是起草这些协议。美国人很愿意先就医疗器械的标准达成一个协议, 然后推敲出不同的合同, 用以涵盖——比如说——电子产品和药品的生产。欧盟遵循优良的大陆传统, 则希望就普遍的原则取得一致, 而这些原则适用于许多不同产品, 同时可能延伸到其他国家。

Comprehension 理解

Give short answers to these questions in your own words as far as possible. Use one complete sentence for each answer.

1   What does this phrase mean: ... put sand in the wheels of trade between rich countries. (l.3)

2   What point is made about European-approved electric razors compared with American dialysis machines?

3   Why will the Americans and Europeans be 'hard-pressed to get a deal'? (ll.11-12)

Vocabulary 词汇

Give another word or phrase to replace these words as they are used in the passage: slaughtered (l.1); grace European tables (l.1); the EU's okay (l.6); hits (l.6); eliminate the need (l.9); summit (l.10); complex (l.11); they may be hard-pressed (l.11); construct (l.13); accord (l.13); hammer out (l.14); products (l.16).

Sentence structure 句子结构

A   Combine the following sentences to make one complex statement out of each group. Make any changes you think necessary but do not alter the sense of the original. Refer to the passage when you have finished the exercise:

1   Chickens have been slaughtered in the United States. They are not fit to grace European tables. Officials in Brussels claim this. (l.1)

2   An electric razor meets the European Union's safety standards. It must be approved by American tests. Only then can it be sold in the United States. An American-made dialysis machine needs the EU's okay. Only then can it be sold in Europe. (ll.4-6)

3   Politicians agree in principle. America and the EU have been trying to reach a deal. This would eliminate the need to double test many products. (ll.8-10)

4   Negotiators are optimistic. The details are complex. They may be hard-pressed to get a deal at all. (ll.11-12)

5   The EU follows fine continental traditions. It wants agreement on general principles. They could be applied to many types of products. Perhaps they could be extended to other countries as well. (ll.15-16)

B   What, in your opinion, is the author's main argument in this text?

Key structures 关键句型

A   Write these sentences again changing the position of the words or phrases in italics. Do not refer to the passage until you have finished the exercise:

1   *Before it can be sold in the United States*, an electric razor that meets the European Union's safety standards must be approved by American testers. (ll.4-5)

2   A razor that is safe in Europe is unlikely to electrocute Americans, as *it happens*. (l.7)

3   The details are complex enough that they may be hard-pressed to get a deal at all, *although negotiators are optimistic*. (ll.11-12)

B   Replace the words in italics with suitable alternatives:

1   Our fowl are fine, we simply clean them *in a different way*. (l.2)

2   It is not *just* farmers *who* are complaining. (ll.3-4)

3   They hope to finish *in time for* a trade summit between America and the EU on May 28th. (l.10)

C   Supply the missing words and explain their use, then refer to the passage.

1   No, ... the Americans: our fowl are fine. (l.2)

2   The Americans would happily reach one accord on standards for medical devices and then hammer out different pacts covering, ... , electronic goods and drug manufacturing. (ll.13-15)

D   Supply the missing words, then refer to the passage.

1   It is not just farmers ... are complaining. (ll.3-4)

2   An electric razor ... meets the European Union's safety standards must be approved by American testers. (ll.4-5)

3   As it happens, a razor ... is safe is unlikely to electrocute Americans. (l.7)

4   America and the EU have been trying to reach a deal ... would eliminate the need to double-test. (l.9)

5   The EU wants agreement on general principles ... could be applied to many types of products. (ll.15-16)

Special difficulties 难点

A Note this use of *way:*

We simply clean them in a different *way*. (l.2)

Explain the meaning of these phrases with *way* in these sentences:

1 We simply clean them *in a different way.*

2 I think they went *this way.*

3 I bought an evening paper *on my way* home.

4 *In a way,* I think you may be right.

5 Could you move that step-ladder please? It's *in my way.*

B Note this use of the verb *sell.*

An electric razor must be approved by American testers before it can be *sold* in the US. (ll.4-5)

Explain the various uses of sell and sale in these sentences:

1 The house next door has been *sold.*

2 The flat upstairs is *for sale.*

3 I bought this coat quite cheaply *in the sales.*

4 I've been asking for a reasonable amount for my car, but it's still *unsold.*

C Note the use of *in time* in this sentence:

They hope to finish *in time* for a trade summit. (l.10)

Explain these phrases with *time*:

1 I was *on time* for my appointment with my dentist.

2 In *times* like these people become cautious about spending money.

3 I'm glad I didn't live in the middle ages. In *those times* people died young.

4 Fortunately, I was *just in time* to catch the last train home.

5 I missed the celebrations in Hong Kong. I was in Singapore *at the time.*

Multiple choice questions 选择题

Choose the correct answers to the following questions.

Comprehension 理解

1 Which one of these statements is true?

   (*a*) American farmers are the only ones who are complaining about trading standards.

   (*b*) Problems with trading standards don't affect only American farmers.

   (*c*) Europe is happy to import American poultry.

   (*d*) There is general agreement about regulations for world trade.

2 An electric razor made in the EU can only be sold in the US _____.

   (*a*) if it conforms with European required standards

   (*b*) when it is safe to use

   (*c*) when it has hit the markets in Europe

   (*d*) after it has been given approval by US authorities

3 Business people on both sides of the Atlantic _____ .

(*a*) question whether two sets of tests are necessary

(*b*) think the present situation is satisfactory

(*c*) have agreed to abandon two sets of tests

(*d*) have set up a single test which has everyone's approval

4 The main difference between the two sides is that _____ .

(*a*) it's difficult to construct agreements

(*b*) one side wants a general agreement and the other wants lots of separate ones

(*c*) neither of them can agree about electronic goods and drug manufacturing

(*d*) the EU follows fine continental traditions

Structure 句型

5 American farmers can't export chickens to Europe _____ differences in national regulations. (l.1)

(*a*) through   (*b*) according to   (*c*) in respect of   (*d*) because of

6 An electric razor from the EU _____ sold in the US unless it meets US standards. (ll.4-5)

(*a*) oughtn't to be   (*b*) can't be   (*c*) shouldn't be   (*d*) doesn't have to be

7 America and the EU _____ to reach a deal. (l.9)

(*a*) are still trying   (*b*) always try   (*c*) tried   (*d*) were trying

8 The details are _____ that they may be hard-pressed to get a deal. (ll.11-12)

(*a*) so complex   (*b*) enough complex   (*c*) such complexity   (*d*) too complex

Vocabulary 词汇

9 There are many differences in national _____ . (ll.2-3)

(*a*) laws   (*b*) rules   (*c*) commands   (*d*) orders

10 An electric razor that _____ Europe must be approved by American testers. (ll.4-5)

(*a*) fits   (*b*) matches   (*c*) is suitable for   (*d*) likes

11 America and the EU have been trying to get _____ double tests. (l.9)

(*a*) away from   (*b*) rid of   (*c*) out of   (*d*) lost in

12 Although negotiators are _____ ... (l.11)

(*a*) clear-sighted   (*b*) uncertain   (*c*) hopeful   (*d*) enthusiastic

Unit 2

Content

This unit consists of eight passages followed by exercises on Comprehension, Vocabulary, The paragraph, Key structures, Special difficulties and Multiple choice questions.

Aim

To provide practice in paragraph construction.

How to work

1 Read each passage carefully two or three times.
2 Answer the questions in the order in which they are given.

The paragraph

All the exercises given under this heading are based directly on the passage. You may correct your own answers to some of the questions by referring to the passage immediately after you have completed the exercises. The following types of exercise have been given :

1 Selecting a suitable title for the passage.
2 Selecting a statement which best expresses the main idea of a paragraph.
3 Expressing the main idea of a paragraph in a sentence.
4 Rearranging sentences taken from the passage so as to make up a complex paragraph.

Lesson 9　Royal espionage　王室谍报活动

听录音，然后回答以下问题 。

What important thing did King Alfred learn when he penetrated the Danish camp of Guthrum?

Alfred the Great acted as his own spy, visiting Danish camps disguised as a minstrel. In those days wandering minstrels were welcome everywhere. They were not fighting men, and their harp was their passport. Alfred had learned many of their ballads in his youth, and could vary his programme with acrobatic tricks and simple conjuring.

5　　While Alfred's little army slowly began to gather at Athelney, the king himself set out to penetrate the camp of Guthrum, the commander of the Danish invaders. These had settled down for the winter at Chippenham: thither Alfred went. He noticed at once that discipline was slack: the Danes had the self-confidence of conquerors, and their security precautions were casual. They lived well, on the proceeds of raids on neighbouring regions. There they collected women as well as food and drink, and a life of ease had
10　made them soft.

　　Alfred stayed in the camp a week before he returned to Athelney. The force there assembled was trivial compared with the Danish horde. But Alfred had deduced that the Danes were no longer fit for prolonged battle: and that their commissariat had no organization, but depended on irregular raids.

　　So, faced with the Danish advance, Alfred did not risk open battle but harried the enemy. He was constantly
15　on the move, drawing the Danes after him. His patrols halted the raiding parties: hunger assailed the Danish army. Now Alfred began a long series of skirmishes—and within a month the Danes had surrendered. The episode could reasonably serve as a unique epic of royal espionage!

BERNARD NEWMAN *Spies in Britain*

Alfred, disguised as a harpist, in the camp of the Danes

53

Unit 2　Lesson 9

New words and expressions 生词和短语

espionage (title) /ˈespɪənɑːʒ/ *n.* 间谍活动

Alfred (1.1) /ˈælfrɪd/ 阿尔弗雷德（849-899），
　　公元 871-899 年间任英国国王

Danish (1.1) /ˈdeɪnɪʃ/ *adj.* 丹麦的, 丹麦人的, 丹麦
　　语的

minstrel (1.1) /ˈmɪnstrəl/ *n.* 中世纪的吟游歌手

wandering (1.1) /ˈwɒndərɪŋ/ *adj.* 漫游的

harp (1.2) /hɑːp/ *n.* 竖琴

ballad (1.3) /ˈbæləd/ *n.* 民歌

acrobatic (1.3) /ˌækrəˈbætɪk/ *adj.* 杂技的

conjuring (1.4) /ˈkʌndʒərɪŋ/ *n.* 魔术

Athelney (1.5) /ˈæθəlni/ *n.* 阿塞尔纳（英国一个小岛）

Chippenham (1.7) /ˈtʃɪpənəm/ *n.* 奇彭纳姆（英国一城市）

thither (1.7) /ˈðɪðə/ *adv.* 向那里

Dane (1.7) /deɪn/ *n.* 丹麦人

slack (1.7) /slæk/ *adj.* 涣散的

conqueror (1.8) /ˈkɒŋkərə/ *n.* 征服者

casual (1.8) /ˈkæʒuəl/ *adj.* 马虎的, 随便的

precaution (1.8) /prɪˈkɔːʃən/ *n.* 预防, 警惕

proceeds (1.8) /ˈprəʊsiːdz/ *n.* 所得

assemble (1.11) /əˈsembəl/ *v.* 集合

trivial (1.11) /ˈtrɪvɪəl/ *adj.* 微不足道的

prolonged (1.12) /prəˈlɒŋd/ *adj.* 持久的

commissariat (1.13) /ˌkɒmɪˈseərɪət/ *n.* 军粮供应

harry (1.14) /ˈhæri/ *v.* 骚扰

assail (1.15) /əˈseɪl/ *v.* 袭击

skirmish (1.16) /ˈskɜːmɪʃ/ *n.* 小规模战斗

episode (1.17) /ˈepɪsəʊd/ *n.* 一个事件, 片断

epic (1.17) /ˈepɪk/ *n.* 史诗

Notes on the text 课文注释

1　settle down, 驻扎 。

2　They lived well, on the proceeds of raids ..., 他们的生活舒适, 靠袭击（周围地区）掠夺得到的财物为生 。
　　live on, 靠……为生 。

3　be fit for, 适宜于 …… 。

参考译文

　　阿尔弗雷德大帝曾亲自充当间谍 。他扮作吟游歌手到丹麦军队的营地里侦察 。当时, 浪迹天涯的吟游歌手到处受到欢迎, 他们不是作战人员, 竖琴就是他们的通行证 。阿尔弗雷德年轻时学过许多民歌, 并能穿插演一些杂技和小魔术使自己的节目多样化 。

　　当阿尔弗雷德人数不多的军队开始在阿塞尔纳慢慢集结时, 他亲自潜入丹麦侵略军司令官古瑟罗姆的营地 。丹麦军已在奇彭纳姆扎下营准备过冬, 阿尔弗雷德便来到此地 。他马上发现丹麦军纪律松弛, 他们以征服者自居, 安全措施马马虎虎 。他们靠掠夺附近地区的财物过着舒适的生活 。他们不仅搜刮吃的喝的, 而且抢掠妇女, 安逸的生活已使丹麦军队变得软弱无力 。

　　阿尔弗雷德在敌营呆了一个星期后, 回到了阿塞尔纳 。他集结在那里的军队和丹麦大军相比是微不足道的 。然而, 阿尔弗雷德断定, 丹麦人已不再适应持久的战争, 他们的军需供应处于无组织状态, 只是靠临时抢夺来维持 。

　　因此, 面对丹麦人的进攻, 阿尔弗雷德没有贸然同敌人进行正面作战, 而是采用骚扰敌人的战术 。他的部队不停地移动, 牵着敌人的鼻子, 让他们跟着他跑 。他派出巡逻队阻止敌人抢劫, 因而饥饿威胁着丹麦军队 。这时, 阿尔弗雷德发起一连串小规模的进攻, 结果不出一个月, 丹麦人就投降了 。这一幕历史可以说是王室谍报活动中最精彩的篇章 。

Comprehension 理解

Give short answers to these questions in your own words as far as possible. Use one complete sentence for each answer.

1   Give two reasons why it was easy for Alfred the Great to penetrate the Danish camp.

2   Explain briefly how Alfred defeated the Danes.

Vocabulary 词汇

Refer to the text to see how the following words have been used, then write sentences of your own using these words: disguised (l.1); thither (l.7); slack (l.7); security precautions (l.8); proceeds (l.8); trivial (l.11); harried (l.14); assailed (l.15); skirmishes (l.16); unique (l.17).

The paragraph 段落

A   Suggest a suitable title for this passage.

B   Which of the following statements are correct:

1   In Alfred's time it was easy for a minstrel to gain access to an enemy camp.

2   Guthrum was the place where the Danish invaders had their camp.

3   Alfred defeated the Danes because he had a large army.

4   During the English attack, the Danes found it difficult to obtain food.

C   The following sentences have been taken from the second paragraph (ll. 5-12). Arrange them in their correct order. Do not refer to the passage until you have finished the exercise:

1   He noticed at once that discipline was slack: the Danes had the self-confidence of conquerors, and their security precautions were casual.

2   These had settled down for the winter at Chippenham: thither Alfred went.

3   There they collected women as well as food and drink, and a life of ease had made them soft.

4   While Alfred's little army slowly began to gather at Athelney, the king himself set out to penetrate the camp of Guthrum, the commander of the Danish invaders.

5   They lived well, on the proceeds of raids on neighbouring regions.

Key structures 关键句型

A   Note how we can use *a lot of* in place of *many (of)* and *much (of)*:

Instead of saying: Alfred had learned *many of* their ballads in his youth. (l.3)

We can say: Alfred had learned *a lot of* their ballads in his youth.

Write these sentences again using *much (of)* or *many (of)* in place of *a lot of*:

1   There were *a lot of* people present at the reception.

2   I haven't got *a lot of* books.

3   I haven't brought *a lot of* luggage with me.

4   *A lot of* the machinery in this factory is out of date.

5   *A lot of* the shops in this area close on Wednesday afternoon.

Unit 2 Lesson 9

B Put the words in parentheses in their correct position in these sentences. Do not refer to the passage until you have finished the exercise:

1 He noticed that discipline was slack. (at once) (l.7)
2 They lived on the proceeds of raids on neighbouring regions. (well) (ll.8-9)
3 But Alfred had deduced that the Danes were fit for prolonged battle. (no longer) (ll.12-13)

C Note how *as well as* can be used to mean *in addition to*:

There they collected women *as well as* food and drink. (l.9)

Write two sentences using *as well as* in the same way.

D Compare these two sentences:

Instead of saying: Their commissariat had *no* organization. (l.13)

We can say: Their commissariat hadn't *any* organization.

Supply suitable compounds with *no* or *any* in the following:

1 _____ called while you were out.
2 Did you go _____ last night?
3 Haven't you got _____ to do?
4 He said he knew _____ about it.
5 I don't know _____ by that name.

E Give the correct form of the verbs in parentheses. Do not refer to the passage until you have finished the exercise:

So, faced with the Danish advance, Alfred not _____ (risk) open battle but _____ (harry) the enemy. He _____ (be) constantly on the move, _____ (draw) the Danes after him. His patrols _____ (halt) the raiding parties: hunger _____ (assail) the Danish army. Now Alfred _____ (begin) a long series of skir-mishes—and within a month the Danes _____ (surrender). (ll.14-17)

Special difficulties 难点

A Study the following pairs of words and then write sentences of your own to bring out the difference:

1 wandering (ll.1-2) — wondering
   I love wandering around second-hand bookshops.
   I'm wondering if we've made a mistake here.
2 learned (l.3) — taught
   I learned to knit when I was eight.
   Who taught you how to knit?
3 noticed (l.7) — remarked
   She noticed that several students seemed restless that morning.
   He remarked, 'You look beautiful today.'
4 conquerors (l.8) — winners
   Military victories were celebrated by parading the defeated chiefs and princes in the streets of Rome, in a display of submission to their conquerors.
   The Oxford team were the winners in last year's Oxford and Cambridge Boat Race.

5   force (l.11) — strength

The captain called together a small force of hand-picked men. (= a group under orders)

The door was opened by force. (= the use of strength)

You need a great deal of strength to be a weight lifter. (= the quality of being strong)

But force and strength are often interchangeable when followed by 'of the':

The force/the strength of the wind was so great that the roof was blown off.

B   Explain the meaning of the verbs and expressions in italics:

1   These had *settled down* for the winter at Chippenham ... (ll.6-7)

2   Have you *settled* your account yet?

3   They *settled* in Australia before the war.

4   It's time we *settled* this question.

5   He *settled* all his property on his wife.

C   Note this compound with *self*:

The Danes had the *self-confidence* of conquerors. (ll.7-8)

Write sentences using the following:

self-assurance; self-denial; self-governing; self-centred.

D   Explain the words and expressions in italics:

1   The Danes were no longer *fit for* prolonged battle. (ll.12-13)

2   Does that coat *fit* you?

3   I can't *fit* all these clothes *into* this suitcase.

4   He may win the race today. He's extremely *fit* and in good form.

5   He wrote that book in a sudden *fit* of energy.

6   It's a good idea, but it doesn't *fit in with* our plans.

Multiple choice questions 选择题

Choose the correct answers to the following questions.

Comprehension 理解

1   Why was it easy for Alfred the Great to visit the Danish camp disguised as a minstrel?

(*a*) Because no one would recognize him.

(*b*) Because he had learned many Danish ballads in his youth.

(*c*) Because minstrels were able to travel freely in those days.

(*d*) Because no one would refuse hospitality to a king.

2   At the Chippenham camp, King Alfred took special note of the fact that _____ .

(*a*) the camp was easy to penetrate

(*b*) the Danish commander, Guthrum, had a lot of confidence

(*c*) winter was setting in

(*d*) the Danes were unprepared for war

3 From what he had seen, Alfred concluded that _____ .

(a) he would have to stay in the Danish camp for a week

(b) his small army was not necessarily a disadvantage

(c) the Danes would be dangerous in a prolonged battle

(d) the Danes could survive indefinitely on irregular raids

4 One of the factors that led to the Danish surrender was that _____ .

(a) the Danes could no longer depend on irregular raids to obtain food

(b) King Alfred engaged in open battle

(c) this was a unique epic of royal espionage

(d) they surrendered within a month

Structure 句型

5 Minstrels were not men _____ in battle. (1.2)

(a) who fight　　　(b) to fight　　　(c) fighting　　　(d) they fight

6 The Danes collected women _____ food and drink. (1.9)

(a) also　　　(b) both　　　(c) in addition to　　　(d) moreover

7 Alfred stayed in the camp a week before _____ to Athelney.

(a) returning　　　(b) to return　　　(c) to returning　　　(d) return

8 So, _____ with the Danish advance, Alfred did not risk open battle. (1.14)

(a) he was faced　　　(b) on being faced　　　(c) he faced　　　(d) in the face

Vocabulary 词汇

9 Alfred was disguised so no one _____ him. (1.1)

(a) recognized　　　(b) understood　　　(c) knew　　　(d) met

10 Alfred _____ at once that discipline was slack. (1.7)

(a) regarded　　　(b) remarked　　　(c) saw　　　(d) attended

11 The force there _____ was trivial compared with the Danish horde. (ll.11-12)

(a) gathered　　　(b) picked up　　　(c) constituted　　　(d) picked

12 His patrols _____ the raiding parties. (1.15)

(a) attacked　　　(b) prevented　　　(c) held back　　　(d) put an end to

Lesson 10　Silicon valley　硅谷

📼 **First listen and then answer the following question.**

听录音, 然后回答以下问题 。

What does the computer industry thrive on apart from anarchy?

Technology trends may push Silicon Valley back to the future. Carver Mead, a pioneer in integrated circuits and a professor of computer science at the California Institute of Technology, notes there are now work-stations that enable engineers to design, test and produce chips right on their desks, much the way an editor creates a newsletter on a Macintosh. As the time and cost of making a chip drop to a few days and a few
5　hundred dollars, engineers may soon be free to let their imaginations soar without being penalized by expensive failures. Mead predicts that inventors will be able to perfect powerful customized chips over a weekend at the office—spawning a new generation of garage start-ups and giving the U.S. a jump on its foreign rivals in getting new products to market fast. 'We've got more garages with smart people,' Mead observes. 'We really thrive on anarchy.'

10　　And on Asians. Already, orientals and Asian Americans constitute the majority of the engineering staffs at many Valley firms. And Chinese, Korean, Filipino and Indian engineers are graduating in droves from California's colleges. As the heads of next-generation start-ups, these Asian innovators can draw on customs and languages to forge tighter links with crucial Pacific Rim markets. For instance, Alex Au, a Stanford Ph.D. from Hong Kong, has set up a Taiwan factory to challenge Japan's near lock on the memory-
15　chip market. India-born N. Damodar Reddy's tiny California company reopened an AT&T chip plant in Kansas City last spring with financing from the state of Missouri. Before it becomes a retirement village, Silicon Valley may prove a classroom for building a global business.

US NEWS AND WORLD REPORT, October 2, 1989

New words and expressions 生词和短语

silicon (title) /'sɪlɪkən/ *n.* 硅
integrated (1.1) /'ɪntɪɡreɪtɪd/ *adj.* 综合的
circuit (1.1) /'sɜːkɪt/ *n.* 线路, 电路
California (l.2) /ˌkælɪ'fɔːnɪə/ *n.* 加利福尼亚（美国州名）
workstation (ll.2-3) /'wɜːkˌsteɪʃən/ *n.* 工作站
chip (1.4) /tʃɪp/ *n.* 芯片, 集成电路片, 集成块
newsletter (1.4) /'njuːzˌletə/ *n.* 时事通讯
Macintosh (1.4) /'mækɪntɒʃ/ *n.* 苹果机（一种个人电脑）
penalize (1.5) /'piːnəlaɪz/ *v.* 处罚, 惩罚
customize (1.6) /'kʌstəmaɪz/ *v.* 定制, 定做
spawn (1.7) /spɔːn/ *v.* 引起, 酿成

thrive (1.9) /θraɪv/ *v.* 兴旺, 繁荣
anarchy (1.9) /'ænəki/ *n.* 无政府状态, 混乱
oriental (1.10) /ˌɔːri'entl/ *n.* 东方人
constitute (1.10) /'kɒnstɪtjuːt/ *v.* 构成
drove (1.11) /drəʊv/ *n.* 群
innovator (1.12) /'ɪnəveɪtə/ *n.* 创新者
forge (1.13) /fɔːdʒ/ *v.* 建立（牢固的关系）
memory-chip (1.14) /'memərɪ-'tʃɪp/ *n.* 内存条
AT&T (1.15) 美国电话电报公司 (American Telephone and Telegraph)
Kansas (1.15) /'kænzəs/ *n.* 堪萨斯（美国州名）
Missouri (1.15) /mɪ'zʊəri/ *n.* 密苏里（美国州名）

Aerial view of Silicon Valley

Notes on the text 课文注释

1   much the way an editor creates a newsletter, 就像一位编辑编出一份时事通讯一样 。
2   be free to, 可以做…… 。
3   in droves, 一批批, 成群地 。
4   draw on, 依靠, 凭借 。

参考译文

　　技术的发展趋势有可能把硅谷重新推向未来 。集成电路的先驱 、加州理工学院的计算机教授卡弗 · 米德——指出, 现在有些计算机工作站使工程技术人员可以在他们的办公桌上设计 、试验和生产芯片, 就像一位编辑在苹果机上编出一份时事通讯一样 。由于制造一块芯片的时间已缩短至几天, 费用也只有几百美元, 因此, 工程技术人员可能很快就可以充分发挥他们的想象力, 而不会因失败而造成经济上的损失 。米德预言发明者可以在办公室用一个周末的时间生产出完美的 、功能很强的 、按客户需求设计的芯片——造就新一代从汽车间起家的技术人员, 在把新产品推向市场方面使美国比它的外国对手们抢先一步 。"我们有更多的汽车间, 而那里有许多聪明人," 米德说 。"我们确实是靠这种无政府状态发展起来的 。"

靠的是亚洲人。硅谷许多公司中工程技术人员的大多数是东方人和亚裔美国人。中国、韩国、菲律宾和印度的工程师一批批地从加州的大学毕业。作为新崛起一代的带头人,亚裔创新者可以凭借他们在习惯和语言上的优势,与关键的太平洋沿岸市场建立起更加牢固的联系。比如说,亚历克斯·奥,一位来自香港的斯坦福大学博士,已经在台湾建厂,对日本在内存条市场上近似垄断的局面提出了挑战。印度出生的N.达莫达·雷迪经营的小小的加州公司去年春天在堪萨斯城重新启用了美国电话电报公司的一家芯片工厂,并从密苏里州获取了财政上的支持。在硅谷变成一个退休村之前,它很可能成为建立全球商业的一个教学场地。

Comprehension 理解

Give short answers to these questions in your own words as far as possible. Use one complete sentence for each answer.

1　Why, in future, will chip engineers be able to 'let their imaginations soar'?

2　What do you think is meant by the phrase 'garage start-ups' (l.7)?

3　What additional non-computer skills can Asian computer engineering staffs provide that are important in Pacific Rim markets?

Vocabulary 词汇

Refer to the text to see how the following words have been used, then write sentences of your own using these words: trends (l.1); soar (l.5); penalized (l.5); a jump (l.7); rivals (l.7); thrive (l.9); links (l.13); crucial (l.13); set up (l.14); near lock (l.14); global (l.17).

The paragraph 段落

A　Which of these statements best expresses the main idea in the first paragraph of the passage? Give reasons for your answer:

1　Computer engineers can design computer chips on their desks.

2　The cost of producing chips has dropped to a few hundred dollars.

3　As the cost of producing chips falls, engineers will be free to make more mistakes.

4　Chip engineers thrive on anarchy.

B　Which of these statements best expresses the main idea in the second paragraph of the passage?
Give reasons for your answer:

1　Most chip engineers are Oriental and Asian Americans.

2　Oriental and Asian American chip engineers can help the US beat the competition.

3　Alex Au has set up a factory in Taiwan.

4　Silicon Valley is a global business.

C　What idea do the two examples quoted in the second paragraph (ll.10-17) illustrate? ('For instance, Alex Au...' ll.12-14)

Unit 2   Lesson 10

Key structure 关键句型

A   Supply *a, an* or *the* only where necessary in the following paragraph. Do not refer to the passage until
you have finished the exercise:

_____ technology trends may push Silicon Valley back to _____ future. Carver Mead, _____ pioneer in _____ integrated circuits and _____ professor of computer science at _____ California Institute of Technology, notes there are now _____ workstations that enable _____ engineers to design, test
and produce _____ chips right on their desks, much _____ way _____ editor creates _____
newsletter on _____ Macintosh. As _____ time and cost of making _____ chip drop to _____
few days and _____ few hundred dollars, _____ engineers may soon be free to let their imaginations
soar without being penalized by _____ expensive failures. Mead predicts that _____ inventors will be
able to perfect _____ powerful customized chips over _____ weekend at _____ office—spawning
_____ new generation of garage start-ups and giving _____ U.S. _____ jump on its foreign rivals
in getting new products to market fast. 'We've got more garages with _____ smart people,' Mead observes. 'We
really thrive on _____ anarchy.' (ll.1-9)

B   Note the use of the *-ing* form after the preposition *without*:
Engineers may soon be free to let their imaginations soar without *being* penalized by expensive failures. (ll.5-6)
Complete the following sentences:
1   A lot of people are afraid of _____ (speak) in public.
2   I always believe in _____ (tell) the truth.
3   Poor eyesight prevents me from _____ (drive) a car.
4   Would you be interested in _____ (buy) a second-hand car?
5   A lot of people object to _____ (smoke) these days.

C   Note the form of the verb after *before*:
Before it becomes a retirement village, Silicon Valley may prove a classroom for building a global business. (ll.16-17)
Complete these sentences with the right form of the verbs:
1   As soon as your sister _____ (arrive) please give me a call.
2   We'd better tidy the house up before my mother _____ (get) back from work.
3   I'm going to wait here until he _____ (arrive).
4   We go through Customs after we _____ (collect) our luggage.

Special difficulties 难点

A   Note the use of the following verb:
Carver Mead *notes* there are now workstations that enable engineers to produce chips right on their
desks. (ll.1-3)
Write sentences using each of these verbs:
notice, observe, remark.

B   There are now workstations that enable engineers to produce chips right on their desks. (ll.2-3)

Write a sentence using the noun chips with an entirely different meaning.

C   Note the use of *set up* in this sentence:

Alex Au has *set up* a Taiwan factory. (ll.13-14)

Suggest meanings for these combinations with *set*:

1   The explorers *set off* at dawn.

2   Winter has *set in* early this year.

3   We'll have to *set by* some money if we want to buy a car.

4   What time do you *set out* tomorrow morning?

5   If we all *set to*, we can finish this job in no time.

Multiple choice questions 选择题

Choose the correct answers to the following questions.

Comprehension 理解

1   Engineers can now _____ .

(*a*) create chips at the California Institute of Technology

(*b*) pioneer integrated circuits in garages

(*c*) create chips on computers without having to manufacture them

(*d*) create newsletters whenever they want to

2   The important thing about this new technology is that _____ .

(*a*) it doesn't matter whether inventors make mistakes

(*b*) there will be more people working in garages

(*c*) the computer industry is in a state of anarchy

(*d*) people will be able to buy chips for a few hundred dollars

3   One great advantage of employing Asian American engineers is they _____ .

(*a*) have an advantage over others in the Pacific Rim markets

(*b*) are graduating in large numbers from California's colleges

(*c*) are now more widely employed than engineers with other backgrounds

(*d*) are more able than other graduates in the computer industry

4   Japan almost has a monopoly of the memory-chip market which _____ .

(*a*) is now being challenged by a Chinese

(*b*) is now facing real competition

(*c*) is about to end

(*d*) an AT&T chip plant in Kansas is going to take over

Structure 句型

5   It is _____ that engineers will soon be free to let their imaginations soar. (1.5)

(*a*) certain   (*b*) true   (*c*) necessary   (*d*) possible

6 Carver Mead predicts that inventors will be capable _____ powerful chips. (l.6)

    (*a*) to perfect   (*b*) to perfecting   (*c*) of perfecting   (*d*) perfecting

7 _____ engineering staffs at Valley firms are orientals and Asian Americans. (ll.10-11)

    (*a*) The most   (*b*) Most   (*c*) Many   (*d*) The greatest

8 N. Damodar Reddy, who _____ in India, has a tiny California company. (l.15)

    (*a*) is born   (*b*) was born   (*c*) born   (*d*) has borne

Vocabulary 词汇

9 There are now work-stations that _____ engineers to design, test and produce chips right on their desks. (ll.2-3)

    (*a*) make possible   (*b*) allowed   (*c*) make it capable for   (*d*) allow

10 If a chip is 'customized', it has been made _____ . (l.6)

    (*a*) in a traditional way   (*b*) according to custom

    (*c*) to suit your needs   (*d*) perfectly

11 Indian engineers are graduating _____ . (l.11)

    (*a*) in large numbers   (*b*) increasingly

    (*c*) like cattle   (*d*) without limits

12 Japan has _____ the memory-chip market. (l.14)

    (*a*) control of   (*b*) locked up   (*c*) the key to   (*d*) the master of

Lesson 11   How to grow old   如何安度晚年

First listen and then answer the following question.

听录音，然后回答以下问题。

What, according to the author, is the best way to overcome the fear of death as you get older?

Some old people are oppressed by the fear of death. In the young there is a justification for this feeling. Young men who have reason to fear that they will be killed in battle may justifiably feel bitter in the thought that they have been cheated of the best things that life has to offer. But in an old man who has known human joys and sorrows, and has achieved whatever work it was in him to do, the fear of death is somewhat abject
5   and ignoble. The best way to overcome it—so at least it seems to me—is to make your interests gradually wider and more impersonal, until bit by bit the walls of the ego recede, and your life becomes increasingly merged in the universal life. An individual human existence should be like a river—small at first, narrowly contained within its banks, and rushing passionately past boulders and over waterfalls. Gradually the river grows wider, the banks recede, the waters flow more quietly, and in the end, without any visible break, they
10   become merged in the sea, and painlessly lose their individual being. The man who, in old age, can see his life in this way, will not suffer from the fear of death, since the things he cares for will continue. And if, with the decay of vitality, weariness increases, the thought of rest will be not unwelcome. I should wish to die while still at work, knowing that others will carry on what I can no longer do, and content in the thought that what was possible has been done.

BERTRAND RUSSELL *How to grow old* from *Portraits from Memory*

Bertrand Russell speaking at a protest meeting in Trafalgar Square

65

Unit 2 Lesson 11

New words and expressions 生词和短语

oppress (l.1) /əˈpres/ v. 忧郁, 压抑

justification (l.1) /ˌdʒʌstɪfɪˈkeɪʃən/ n. 正当理由

justifiably (l.2) /ˈdʒʌstɪfaɪəbli/ adv. 无可非议地

cheat (l.3) /tʃiːt/ v. 欺骗

abject (l.4) /ˈæbdʒekt/ adj. 可怜的

ignoble (l.5) /ɪgˈnəʊbəl/ adj. 不体面的, 可耻的

impersonal (l.6) /ɪmˈpɜːsənəl/ adj. 超脱个人感情影响的

ego (l.6) /ˈiːgəʊ/ n. 自我

recede (l.6) /rɪˈsiːd/ v. 退去

increasingly (l.6) /ɪnˈkriːsɪŋli/ adv. 日益, 不断

passionately (l.8) /ˈpæʃənɪtli/ adv. 激昂地

painlessly (l.10) /ˈpeɪnlɪsli/ adv. 毫无痛苦地

vitality (l.12) /vaɪˈtælɪti/ n. 精力

weariness (l.12) /ˈwɪərinɪs/ n. 疲惫感

Notes on the text 课文注释

1   in the young, 在年轻人身上 。

2   Young men who have reason ... that life has to offer. 这个句子较长, 其中有 3 个 that 。第 1 个 that 引导一个宾语从句 that ... battle, 是 fear 的宾语 。第 2 个 that 引导一个同位语从句 that they ... to offer, 说明 thought 的内容 。第 3 个 that 引导一个定语从句 that life has to offer, 修饰 things 。

3   cheat of ..., 从 …… 那里骗取 …… 。

4   whatever work it was in him to do, 他所能做的任何工作 。

5   so at least it seems to me, 这里一个插入语, 用了倒装语序, 自然的语序是 at least it seems so to me 。

6   bit by bit, 一点一点地 。

7   the thought of rest 是 death 的一种委婉说法 。

参考译文

　　有些老年人因为怕死而感到烦恼 。青年人有这种感觉是情有可原的 。有理由害怕自己会死在战场上的年轻人, 想到自己被剥夺了生活所能给予的最美好的东西时, 感到痛苦, 这是可以理解的 。可是老年人已经饱尝了人间的甘苦, 一切能做的都做了, 如果怕死, 就有点儿可怜又可鄙了 。克服怕死的最好办法——至少在我看来是这样——就是逐渐使自己的兴趣更加广泛, 逐渐摆脱个人狭小的圈子, 直到自我的围墙一点一点地倒塌下来, 自己的生活慢慢地和整个宇宙的生活融合在一起 。个人的存在应该像一条河流, 开始很小, 被紧紧地夹在两岸中间, 接着热情奔放地冲过巨石, 飞下瀑布 。然后河面渐渐地变宽, 两岸后撤, 河水流得平缓起来, 最后连绵不断地汇入大海, 毫无痛苦地失去了自我的存在 。上了年纪的人这样看待生命, 就不会有惧怕死亡的心情了, 因为自己关心的一切事物都会继续下去 。再者, 随着精力的衰退, 老年人的疲惫感会增长, 有长眠的愿望未尝不是一件好事 。我希望工作到死为止, 知道有人会继续我的未竟事业, 想到能做的事都做了, 也就坦然了 。

Comprehension 理解

Give short answers to these questions in your own words as far as possible. Use one complete sentence for each answer.

1   Why, according to the author, is it justifiable for a young man to fear death?

2   How does the author regard the fear of death in old people?

3   What, in the opinion of the author, is the best way for an old person to overcome the fear of death?

Vocabulary 词汇

Refer to the text to see how the following words have been used, then write sentences of your own using these words: oppressed (l.1); justification (l.1); cheated (l.3); recede (l.6); merged (l.7); decay of vitality (l.12); weariness (l.12).

The paragraph 段落

A   Which of these statements best expresses the main idea of the passage? Give reasons for your answer:

1   Old people fear death.

2   While it is justifiable for a young man to fear death, it is not so in an old man who has known human joys and sorrows and has accomplished whatever work it was in him to do.

3   It is justifiable for young people to fear death.

4   An old man will not fear death if he knows that there are others who will carry on what he can no longer do.

B   The following sentences have been taken from lines 7-14. Arrange them in their correct order. Do not refer to the passage until you have finished the exercise:

1   I should wish to die while still at work, knowing that others will carry on what I can no longer do, and content in the thought that what was possible has been done.

2   The man who, in old age, can see his life in this way, will not suffer from the fear of death, since the things he cares for will continue.

3   An individual human existence should be like a river—small at first, narrowly contained within its banks, and rushing passionately past boulders and over waterfalls.

4   Gradually the river grows wider, the banks recede, the waters flow more quietly, and in the end, without any visible break, they become merged in the sea, and painlessly lose their individual being.

5   And if, with the decay of vitality, weariness increases, the thought of rest will be not unwelcome.

Key structures 关键句型

A   Supply the correct form of the verbs in parentheses in the following paragraph. Do not refer to the passage until you have finished the exercise:

Some old people _____ (oppress) by the fear of death. In the young there is a justification for this feeling. Young men who have reason to fear that they _____ (kill) in battle may justifiably feel bitter in the thought that they _____ (cheat) of the best things that life has to offer. But in an old man who _____ (know) human joys and sorrows, and _____ (achieve) whatever work it was in him to do, the fear of death _____ (be) somewhat abject and ignoble. (ll.1-5)

B   Note the form of the verbs used after *until* in this sentence:

Make your interests gradually wider and more impersonal, until bit by bit the walls of the ego *recede*, and your life *becomes* increasingly merged in the universal life. (ll.5-7)

Supply the correct form of the verbs in parentheses in the following sentences:

1   I don't think he will be very pleased when he _____ (find) out the truth.

2   He will send a telegram as soon as he _____ (arrive) in Zurich.

3   We should wait until the weather _____ (change) before we go on holiday.

C   Study these sentences:

Instead of saying: An individual human existence *should* be like a river. (l.7)

We can say: An individual human existence *ought to* be like a river.

Now compare the following sentence with the two given above:

I can't leave now: I *must* finish my work first.

Supply *should* (*ought to*) or *must* in these sentences:

1   I really _____ finish this letter, but I think it can wait until tomorrow.

2   I have no alternative: I _____ do what I am told to do.

3   By rights, you _____ pay a fine on this book as it is long overdue, but it doesn't matter.

4   I _____ be at work on time every morning or I'll lose my job.

D   Supply the missing words in the following sentences. Do not refer to the passage until you have finished the exercise:

Gradually the river grows wider, the banks recede, the waters flow more quietly and _____ the end, without any visible break, they become merged _____ the sea and painlessly lose their individual being. The man who, _____ old age, can see his life _____ this way, will not suffer _____ the fear _____ death, since the things he cares _____ will continue. (ll.8-11)

E   Give the correct form of the verb in parentheses. Do not refer to the passage until you have completed the exercise:

And if, with the decay of vitality, weariness _____ (increase), the thought of rest will be not unwelcome. (ll.11-12)

Special difficulties 难点

A   Study these examples, then write two sentences to bring out the difference between the verbs *flow* (1.9) and *fly*.

The River Thames rises in Gloucestershire and runs eastwards for 210 miles until it *flows* into the North Sea at the Nore, some 40 miles east of London.

The nest in the hedge is empty. The young birds *have flown*.

B   Note that the word *water* is rarely used in the plural: 'the waters flow more quietly' (1.9). Study the example and then write a sentence using *water* in the plural.

The banks of the River Oder had disappeared in the flood, and despairing householders watched from a hill top as the *waters* went on rising.

C   Explain the meaning of *since* in these sentences:

1   Man will not suffer from the fear of death, *since* the things he cares for will continue. (ll.10-11)

2   I have not seen him *since* last year.

D   Note the use of *no longer* and *any longer* in these sentences:

Others will carry on what I can *no longer* do. (ll.12-13)

Others will carry on what I cannot do *any longer*.

Write two sentences using *no longer* and *any longer*.

Multiple choice questions 选择题

Choose the correct answers to the following questions.

Comprehension 理解

1   It is _____ that young people fear they will die.

(*a*) not surprising

(*b*) unnatural

(*c*) oppressive

(*d*) deceitful

2 Fear of death in old people _____ .

(*a*) is not something the writer admires

(*b*) is wider and more impersonal

(*c*) is all right for someone who has known joys and sorrows

(*d*) is truly justified

3　As a person's interests become more impersonal, so _____ .

(*a*) his existence becomes like a river

(*b*) the sense of individuality decreases

(*c*) life flows without a visible break

(*d*) the waters flow more quietly

4　An old person can reach a stage where _____ .

(*a*) the things he cares for will continue

(*b*) he wishes to die while still at work

(*c*) his life will continue

(*d*) he looks forward to death

Structure 句型

5　In the young, this feeling _____ . (l.1)

(*a*) has justified　　　(*b*) was justified　　　(*c*) justified　　　(*d*) is justified

6　In an old man _____ has known human joys and sorrows ... (ll.3-4)

(*a*) what　　　(*b*) which　　　(*c*) -　　　(*d*) that

7　An individual human existence should be like a river. That's how it _____ be. (l.7)

(*a*) ought to　　　(*b*) must　　　(*c*) has to　　　(*d*) is obliged to

8　_____ death will not bring fear to the old man who can see his life in this way. (ll.10-11)

(*a*) A　　　(*b*) The　　　(*c*) Every　　　(*d*) -

Vocabulary 词汇

9　Young men may justifiably feel they have been _____ of the best things in life. (ll.1-2)

(*a*) deceived　　　(*b*) lied　　　(*c*) stolen　　　(*d*) robbed

10　Your life becomes increasingly _____ in the universal life. (ll.6-7)

(*a*) lost　　　(*b*) joined　　　(*c*) sunk　　　(*d*) contained

11　_____ the river grows wider ... (ll.8-9)

(*a*) Less and less　　　(*b*) Step by step　　　(*c*) One by one　　　(*d*) Little by little

12　I should wish to die while still at work, _____ that others will carry on ... (ll.13-14)

(*a*) thinking　　　(*b*) aware　　　(*c*) believing　　　(*d*) accepting

Lesson 12 Banks and their customers 银行和顾客

First listen and then answer the following question.

听录音，然后回答以下问题 。

Why is there no risk to the customer when a bank prints the customer's name on his cheques?

When anyone opens a current account at a bank, he is lending the bank money, repayment of which he may demand at any time, either in cash or by drawing a cheque in favour of another person. Primarily, the banker-customer relationship is that of debtor and creditor—who is which depending on whether the customer's account is in credit or is overdrawn. But, in addition to that basically simple concept, the bank
5 and its customer owe a large number of obligations to one another. Many of these obligations can give rise to problems and complications but a bank customer, unlike, say, a buyer of goods, cannot complain that the law is loaded against him.

The bank must obey its customer's instructions, and not those of anyone else. When, for example, a customer first opens an account, he instructs the bank to debit his account only in respect of cheques drawn
10 by himself. He gives the bank specimens of his signature, and there is a very firm rule that the bank has no right or authority to pay out a customer's money on a cheque on which its customer's signature has been forged. It makes no difference that the forgery may have been a very skilful one: the bank must recognize its customer's signature. For this reason there is no risk to the customer in the practice, adopted by banks, of printing the customer's name on his cheques. If this facilitates forgery, it is the bank which will lose, not the
15 customer.

GORDON BARRIE and AUBREY L. DIAMOND *The Consumer Society and the Law*

National Westminster Bank at Queen St. in Cardiff

New words and expressions 生词和短语

current (l.1) /'kʌrənt/ *adj.* 通用的，流行的

account (l.1) /ə'kaʊnt/ *n.* 账户

cash (l.2) /kæʃ/ *n.* 现金

cheque (l.2) /tʃek/ *n.* 支票

debtor (l.3) /'detə/ *n.* 借方

creditor (l.3) /'kredɪtə/ *n.* 贷方

obligation (l.5) /ˌɒblɪ'geɪʃən/ *n.* 义务

complication (l.6) /ˌkɒmplɪ'keɪʃən/ *n.* 纠纷

debit (l.9) /'debɪt/ *v.* 把 …… 记入借方

specimen (l.10) /'spesɪmɪn/ *n.* 样本

forge (l.12) /fɔːdʒ/ *v.* 伪造

forgery (l.12) /'fɔːdʒəri/ *n.* 伪造（文件，签名等）

adopt (l.13) /ə'dɒpt/ *v.* 采用

facilitate (l.14) /fə'sɪlɪteɪt/ *v.* 使便利

Notes on the text 课文注释

1   open a current account, 开一个活期账号 。

2   draw a cheque in favour of ..., 开一张以 …… 为收款人的支票 。

3   who is which depending on ... is overdrawn, 这是现在分词短语 depending on ... is overdrawn 的独立主格结构 。who is which 是分词短语意思上的主语, which 代表 debtor or creditor 。

4   give rise to, 引起 。

5   be loaded against ..., 于 …… 不利 。

参考译文

　　任何人在银行开一个活期账户, 就等于把钱借给了银行 。这笔钱他可以随时提取, 提取的方式可以是取现金, 也可以是开一张以他人为收款人的支票 。银行与储户的关系主要是债务人和债权人的关系 。究竟谁是债务人谁是债权人, 要看储户的账户是有结余还是透支 。但是, 除了这一基本的简单的概念外, 银行和储户彼此还需承担大量义务 。其中许多义务往往引起问题和纠纷 。但是储户不能像货物的买主那样来抱怨法律对自己不利 。

　　银行必须遵照储户的嘱托办事, 不能听从其他人的指令 。比如, 储户首次在银行开户时, 嘱咐银行他的存款只能凭他本人签字的支票来提取 。他把自己签名的样本交给银行, 对此有一条非常严格的规定: 银行没有任何权利或理由把储户的钱让伪造储户签名的支票取走 。即使伪造得很巧妙, 也不能付款, 因为银行有责任辨认出其储户的签名 。因此, 银行采用了把储户姓名印在支票上的做法 。这种做法对储户毫无风险 。如果因这种做法出现了伪造的话, 受损失的将不是储户, 而是银行 。

Comprehension 理解

Give short answers to these questions in your own words as far as possible. Use one complete sentence for each answer.

1   What is meant by the statement that 'the banker-customer relationship is that of debtor and creditor'? (ll.2-3)

2   Quote a sentence from the second paragraph which illustrates this statement: 'a bank customer ... cannot complain that the law is loaded against him.' (ll.6-7)

3   Why does a customer give the bank specimens of his signature when he first opens an account?

Vocabulary 词汇

Refer to the text to see how the following words have been used, then write sentences of your own using these words: cash (l.2); primarily (l.2); debtor (l.3); creditor (l.3); in credit (l.4); concept (l.4); give rise to (ll.5-6); specimens (l.10); forged (l.12); facilitates (l.14).

The paragraph 段落

A   Write a sentence in your own words expressing what you consider to be the main idea in the first paragraph of the passage.

B   Which of these sentences best expresses the main idea in the second paragraph? Give reasons for your choice:

1   The bank must obey its customer's instructions, and not those of anyone else.
2   The bank must honour a cheque even when the signature on it has been forged.
3   The bank must always recognize its customer's signature.

C   The following sentences have been taken from the second paragraph (lines 8-15). Arrange them in their correct order. Do not refer to the passage until you have finished the exercise:

1   The bank must obey its customer's instructions, and not those of anyone else.
2   For this reason there is no risk to the customer in the practice, adopted by banks, of printing the customer's name on his cheques.
3   It makes no difference that the forgery may have been a very skilful one: the bank must recognize its customer's signature.
4   If this facilitates forgery, it is the bank which will lose, not the customer.
5   He gives the bank specimens of his signature, and there is a very firm rule that the bank has no right or authority to pay out a customer's money on a cheque on which its customer's signature has been forged.
6   When, for example, a customer first opens an account, he instructs the bank to debit his account only in respect of cheques drawn by himself.

Key structures 关键句型

A   Note the way these two sentences have been combined:
When anyone opens a current account at a bank, he is lending the bank money. He may demand repayment of *it* at any time.
When anyone opens a current account at a bank, he is lending the bank money, repayment of *which* he may demand at any time. (ll.1-2)
Combine the following sentences using *which*:

1   The bank has no right or authority to pay out a customer's money on a cheque. Its customer's signature on it has been forged. (ll.10-12)
2   The source is very reliable. I obtained this information from it.
3   We have certain principles. We should act on them.

B   Compare these two sentences:
Instead of saying: The banker-customer relationship is *a relationship of* debtor and creditor.
We can say: The banker-customer relationship is *that of* debtor and creditor. (ll.2-3)
Rewrite these sentences using *that of*:

1   I am not referring to our policy but to the policy of our opponents.
2   The only system I know which will help you to remember what you have heard at a lecture is the system of keeping notes.

C   Compare these two sentences:

Instead of saying: He instructs the bank to debit his account only in respect of cheques *which have been drawn* by himself.

We can say: He instructs the bank to debit his account only in respect of cheques *drawn* by himself. (ll.9-10)

Rewrite these sentences in the same way:

1   The exhibition consists entirely of pictures which have been painted by young children.

2   The report on education which has been prepared by a government committee will soon be published.

3   According to the regulations, income which has been earned overseas will be taxed.

Special difficulties 难点

A   Study the following pairs of words and then write sentences of your own to bring out the difference.

1   current (l.1) — currant
I can't keep up with current fashions.
Corinth produces some of the world's finest currants.

2   lend (l.1) — borrow
Can you lend me £20 please? I'll pay it back tomorrow.
Can I borrow £20 from you please?

3   in favour of (l.2) — for the sake of
Are you in favour of the death penalty?
They both endured a bad marriage for years for the sake of the children.

4   whether (l.3) — weather
I don't know whether you've heard the news.
What's the weather like today?

5   loaded (l.7) — laden
The camera has a sensor that flashes when a film has not been correctly loaded.
The poor woman was so laden with household shopping, she could hardly step up to get on the bus.

6   else (l.8) — other
Take this back and exchange it for something else.
There must be other ways of approaching this problem.

7   specimen (l.10) — example
The research collection at the Royal Botanic Gardens at Kew has six-and-a-half million dried plant specimens.
The fall of Rome in 410 AD is an example of how even the greatest empires decay.

8   customer (l.11) — client
During the sales, the department stores are full of customers.
Small clients demand the same service from their bank as large clients.

9   cheque (l.11) — check
You can pay by cheque if you want to. (British English)
You can pay by check if you want to. (American English)

10   adopted (l.13) — adapted
We have adopted the same sort of assembly methods they use in Japan.
We have adapted the assembly system they use in Japan to suit our circumstances here.

11   print (l.14) — type
I'll print these letters on my laser printer.
I'll ask my secretary to type those letters for you.

B   Explain the meaning of the word *account* in these sentences:
1   When anyone opens a current *account* at a bank, he is lending the bank money. (l.1)
2   I can't settle my *account* until next month.
3   How do you *account* for his change of attitude?
4   He gave an interesting *account* of his travels in China.
5   Please don't go to all this trouble on my *account*.
6   Trains were delayed on *account* of the bad weather.

C   Note how *say* has been used in the sense of *for example* in this sentence:
A bank customer, unlike, *say*, a buyer of goods, cannot complain that the law is loaded against him. (ll.6-7)
Write two sentences using *say* in this way.

D   Note that the verb *obey* is not followed by a preposition:
The bank must *obey* its customer's instructions. (l.8)
Write sentences using the following verbs: enter, discuss, reach and leave.

E   Write sentences using the following words and phrases:
in addition to (l.4); a large number of (l.5); unlike (l.6); in respect of (l.9); for this reason (l.13).

Multiple choice questions 选择题

Choose the correct answers to the following questions.

Comprehension 理解

1   When you have a bank account, you _____ .
    (a) can't draw any money if you're overdrawn
    (b) must always be in credit
    (c) can draw money without notice
    (d) can't pay money to anyone else
2   One of the obligations a bank has to a customer _____ .
    (a) is that it can't take instructions from other people
    (b) is that it can avoid complications and problems
    (c) it must pay money to the customer even if he is seriously overdrawn
    (d) it must print the customer's signature
3   If someone forged your signature and drew money from your account _____ .
    (a) you would lose your money
    (b) you wouldn't lose your money
    (c) the bank wouldn't lose any money
    (d) the bank would always pay money to the forger
4   Which of these statements is true?
    (a) It doesn't matter to a customer if the bank prints his name on cheques.
    (b) Banks never print the names of customers on cheques.
    (c) It's easy to forge a signature on a cheque which prints a customer's name.
    (d) Banks always lose money when they print customers' names on cheques.

Structure 句型

5 He may demand repayment of _____ at any time. (ll.1-2)

　　(*a*) you　　　　　　(*b*) them　　　　　　(*c*) it　　　　　　(*d*) some

6 The bank becomes a creditor if the _____ is overdrawn. (1.4)

　　(*a*) account of a customer's　　　　　　(*b*) account of a customers'

　　(*c*) account of a customer　　　　　　(*d*) customers' account

7 The bank _____ obey its customer's instructions. (1.8)

　　(*a*) is necessary to　　(*b*) may　　　　(*c*) can always　　(*d*) is obliged to

8 Banks print names on cheques _____ risk to their customers.

　　(*a*) without　　　　(*b*) without no　　　(*c*) without some　　(*d*) without none

Vocabulary 词汇

9 When a customer is overdrawn, he has _____ money _____ the bank. (ll.1-4)

　　(*a*) lent ... to　　　(*b*) lent ... from　　(*c*) borrowed ... from　(*d*) borrowed ... to

10 If you are a debtor, someone _____ . (1.3)

　　(*a*) has lent money to you　　　　　　(*b*) has borrowed money from you

　　(*c*) owes money to you　　　　　　(*d*) will receive money from you

11 The bank must _____ its customer's instructions. (1.8)

　　(*a*) follow　　　　(*b*) obey to　　　(*c*) hear　　　　(*d*) listen

12 He gives the bank _____ of his signature. (1.10)

　　(*a*) examples　　　(*b*) samples　　　(*c*) copies　　　(*d*) types

Lesson 13　The search for oil　探寻石油

🎧 **First listen and then answer the following question.**

听录音，然后回答以下问题。

What do oilmen want to achieve as soon as they strike oil?

The deepest holes of all are made for oil, and they go down to as much as 25,000 feet. But we do not need to send men down to get the oil out, as we must with other mineral deposits. The holes are only borings, less than a foot in diameter. My particular experience is largely in oil, and the search for oil has done more to improve deep drilling than any other mining activity. When it has been decided where we are going to drill,
5　we put up at the surface an oil derrick. It has to be tall because it is like a giant block and tackle, and we have to lower into the ground and haul out of the ground great lengths of drill pipe which are rotated by an engine at the top and are fitted with a cutting bit at the bottom.

　　The geologist needs to know what rocks the drill has reached, so every so often a sample is obtained with a coring bit. It cuts a clean cylinder of rock, from which can be seen the strata the drill has been cutting
10　through. Once we get down to the oil, it usually flows to the surface because great pressure, either from gas or water, is pushing it. This pressure must be under control, and we control it by means of the mud which we circulate down the drill pipe. We endeavour to avoid the old, romantic idea of a gusher, which wastes oil and gas. We want it to stay down the hole until we can lead it off in a controlled manner.

T. F. GASKELL *The Search for the Earth's Minerals* from *Discovery*

An oil rig drilling in the Abu Dhabi offshore oilfields
in the Persian Gulf

New words and expressions 生词和短语

mineral (1.2) /'mɪnərəl/ *adj.* 矿物的
boring (1.2) /'bɔːrɪŋ/ *n.* 钻孔
derrick (1.5) /'derɪk/ *n.* 井架
block and tackle (1.5) 滑轮组
haul (1.6) /hɔːl/ *v.* 拖, 拉
rotate (1.6) /rəʊ'teɪt/ *v.* 使转动
cutting bit (1.7) 钻头

geologist (1.8) /dʒi'ɒlədʒɪst/ *n.* 地质学家
coring bit (1.9) /'kɔːrɪŋ-bɪt/ 取芯钻头
cylinder (1.9) /'sɪlɪndə/ *n.* 圆柱体
strata (1.9) /'strɑːtə/ *n.* 岩层 [复]
　　([单] stratum /'strɑːtəm/)
circulate (1.12) /'sɜːkjʊleɪt/ *v.* 注入, 环流
gusher (1.12) /'gʌʃə/ *n.* 喷油井

Notes on the text 课文注释

1　they go down to as much as 25,000 feet,
　　as much as 意为 "多达", "达到 (量)"。
2　as we must with other mineral deposits,
　　must 后面省去了与上句中相同的部分 send men down。
3　a foot in diameter, 直径 1 英尺。
4　every so often, 时常。
5　by means of, 用 ……, 靠 …… 手段。

参考译文

　　在所有洞穴中, 为寻找石油所钻的洞是最深的, 这些洞可深达 25,000 英尺。但是, 我们不必像开采其他矿藏那样, 把人送到地下去把石油取出。这些洞只不过是一些钻孔, 直径不到 1 英尺。我是专门搞石油的, 寻找石油比其他任何采矿活动对改进深孔钻探作的贡献都要大。当确定钻孔地点后, 我们就在那里竖起一个井架。井架必须很高, 因为它像一个巨型滑轮组。我们必须把很长的钻杆一节节地钻入地下, 然后再从地下拉出来。钻杆顶部安装的发动机带动钻杆旋转, 它的底部装有钻头。
　　地质学家需要知道钻头已经到达什么样的岩层, 因此时常要用取芯钻头取样。这种钻头能切割一段光滑的圆柱形岩石, 从中能看出钻头所钻透的地层。一旦到达油层, 石油就会由于地下巨大的压力涌到地面上来, 这种巨大的压力来自地下天然气或水。这种压力必须加以控制, 我们让泥浆顺着钻杆向下循环, 用这种方法来控制压力。我们尽量避免使用过时的不实用的喷井方法, 那样会浪费石油和天然气。我们要让石油留在井下, 直到我们能用一种可控制的方法把它引上来为止。

Comprehension 理解

1　In a single sentence explain the purpose of an oil derrick.
2　Explain in a sentence how oilmen prevent oil from gushing to the surface.

Vocabulary 词汇

Refer to the text to see how the following words have been used, then write sentences of your own using these words: in diameter (1.3); drilling (1.4); haul (1.6); rotated (1.6); every so often (1.8); endeavour (1.12).

Unit 2   Lesson 13

The paragraph 段落

A   Which of these statements do you think the author would agree with? Give reasons for your choice:

1   The search for oil has led to an improvement in drilling techniques.

2   When drilling for oil, it is difficult to obtain samples of the rocks the drill has been cutting through.

3   Once oil has been found, it is impossible to prevent it from gushing to the surface.

B   The following sentences have been taken from the first paragraph (lines 1-7). Arrange them in their correct order. Do not refer to the passage until you have finished the exercise:

1   My particular experience is largely in oil, and the search for oil has done more to improve deep drilling than any other mining activity.

2   When it has been decided where we are going to drill, we put up at the surface an oil derrick.

3   The deepest holes of all are made for oil, and they go down to as much as 25,000 feet.

4   The holes are only borings, less than a foot in diameter.

5   But we do not need to send men down to get the oil out, as we must with other mineral deposits.

6   It has to be tall because it is like a giant block and tackle, and we have to lower into the ground and haul out of the ground great lengths of drill pipe which are rotated by an engine at the top and are fitted with a cutting bit at the bottom.

Key structures 关键句型

A   Supply the correct form of the missing verbs (*must, need* or *have to*) in these sentences. Do not refer to the passage until you have finished the exercise:

1   We do not _____ to send men down to get the oil out, as we _____ with other mineral deposits. (ll.1-2)

2   It _____ be tall because it is like a giant block and tackle and we _____ lower into the ground and haul out of the ground great lengths of drill pipe. (ll.5-6)

3   The geologist _____ to know what rocks the drill has reached. (1.8)

4   This pressure _____ be under control, and we control it by means of the mud which we circulate down the drill pipe. (ll.11-12)

B   Supply *a* or *the* where necessary in the following. Do not refer to the passage until you have finished the exercise:

_____ deepest holes of all are made for _____ oil, and they go down to as much as 25,000 feet. But we do not need to send _____ men down to get _____ oil out, as we must with _____ other mineral deposits. _____ holes are only borings, less than _____ foot in _____ diameter. _____ my particular experience is largely in _____ oil, and _____ search for _____ oil has done more to improve _____ deep drilling than any other mining activity. (ll.1-4)

C   Supply (*be*) *going to* or *will* in these sentences:

1   When it has been decided where we _____ drill, we put up at the surface an oil derrick. (ll.4-5)

2   Ask Mary. I'm sure she _____ be able to help you.

3   He _____ be far more co-operative if you speak to him nicely.

4   If ever you want any information, we _____ always be glad to help you.

5   He's changed his mind again. He _____ make out another will.

D　Note the order of the words in italics:

The geologist needs to know *what rocks the drill has reached*. (1.8)

Complete the following sentences:

1　Tell me where _____ .

2　I don't know why _____ .

3　Ask him how _____ .

4　Did he tell you when _____ ?

E　Note the word order in this sentence:

We want *it* to stay down the hole. (1.13)

Write sentences using the same pattern with the following verbs: allow, ask, teach, cause, warn and advise.

Special difficulties 难点

A　Study the following pairs of words and then write sentences of your own to bring out the difference.

1　hole (1.1) — whole

We'll just dig a hole in the ground and bury the box in it.

You have your whole life ahead of you.

2　engine (1.6) — machine

A car like this needs a powerful engine.

How often should you equip a factory with new machines?

3　fit (1.7) — suit

That jacket really fits you at the shoulders.

Pastel colours suit me.

4　clean (1.9) — clear

Please hand me a clean towel.

You must never do that again. Is that clear?

5　control (1.13) — check

OPEC no longer has control over the price of oil.

It's hard to keep a check on the number of people coming into the country.

B　Supply verbs which could be used in place of the expressions in italics:

1　When it has been decided where we are going to drill, we *put up* at the surface an oil derrick. (ll.4-5)

2　It took them several hours to *put out* the fire.

3　I won't *put up with* this sort of thing any longer.

4　Because of the bad weather, the match has been *put off* until next week.

C　Explain the meaning of the words or phrases in italics:

1　*Once* we get down to the oil, it usually flows to the surface. (1.10)

2　I'm ashamed to say I've only been to the Louvre *once*.

3　*Once upon a time* there was a poor woodcutter who lived in a forest.

4　I see him *once in a while*.

5　I'll come *at once*.

6　*All at once* there was a loud explosion.

D   Write sentences using the following expressions:

under control (1.13); out of control; beyond control.

E   Note the use of *off* in this sentence:

We want it to stay down the hole until we can *lead it off* in a controlled manner. (l.13)

Write sentences using the following verbs:

drive off; cool off; hurry off; switch off; wear off.

Multiple choice questions 选择题

Choose the correct answers to the following questions.

Comprehension 理解

1 Deep drilling techniques have improved greatly because _____ .

(*a*) of the need to locate oil

(*b*) it is necessary to go down as much as 25,000 feet

(*c*) there is no need to send men down deep holes to get oil

(*d*) of the constant search for mineral deposits

2 It's necessary to put up an oil derrick _____ .

(*a*) because it is like a giant block and tackle

(*b*) to rotate the engine at the top

(*c*) to control all the equipment needed to drill a deep hole

(*d*) to decide exactly where to drill for oil

3 The only way of knowing what rocks the drill has reached is to _____ .

(*a*) cut clean cylinders of rock

(*b*) use the coring bit

(*c*) take note of the strata below the surface

(*d*) bring up specimen material from time to time

4 If you don't control the oil pressure _____ .

(*a*) oil will be forced to the surface with great force

(*b*) mud will have to be circulated down the drill pipe

(*c*) you will have to catch the oil at the surface

(*d*) water will gush to the surface

Structure 句型

5 The holes made for oil go down as _____ as 25,000 feet. (l.1)

(*a*) many   (*b*) long   (*c*) far   (*d*) distant

6 Nothing has done as _____ to improve deep drilling as the search for oil. (ll.3-4)

(*a*) many   (*b*) much   (*c*) long   (*d*) far

7 The geologist needs to know _____ rocks the drill has reached. (l.8)

(*a*) that   (*b*) when   (*c*) how   (*d*) which

8 _____ we get down to the oil, it usually flows with great pressure. (l.10)

(*a*) Immediately   (*b*) The first time   (*c*) Until   (*d*) As long as

Vocabulary 词汇

9 The holes are only borings, less than a foot _____ . (ll.2-3)

    (*a*) round   (*b*) across   (*c*) through   (*d*) along

10 The engine at the top makes the drill pipe go _____ . (l.6)

    (*a*) up and down   (*b*) in and out   (*c*) round and round   (*d*) deeper and deeper

11 _____ a sample is obtained with a coring bit. (ll.8-9)

    (*a*) Every now and again   (*b*) In one way or another

    (*c*) Often but not always   (*d*) After a long time

12 We _____ avoid the old, romantic idea of a gusher. (l.12)

    (*a*) make sure we   (*b*) can't   (*c*) attempt   (*d*) try to

Lesson 14　The Butterfly Effect　蝴蝶效应

First listen and then answer the following question.

听录音，然后回答以下问题 。

Why do small errors make it impossible to predict the weather system with a high degree of accuracy?

Beyond two or three days, the world's best weather forecasts are speculative, and beyond six or seven they are worthless.

　　The Butterfly Effect is the reason. For small pieces of weather — and to a global forecaster, small can mean thunderstorms and blizzards — any prediction deteriorates rapidly. Errors and uncertainties multiply,
5　cascading upward through a chain of turbulent features, from dust devils and squalls up to continent-size eddies that only satellites can see.

　　The modern weather models work with a grid of points of the order of sixty miles apart, and even so, some starting data has to be guessed, since ground stations and satellites cannot see everywhere. But suppose the earth could be covered with sensors spaced one foot apart, rising at one-foot intervals all the way to the
10　top of the atmosphere. Suppose every sensor gives perfectly accurate readings of temperature, pressure, humidity, and any other quantity a meteorologist would want. Precisely at noon an infinitely powerful computer takes all the data and calculates what will happen at each point at 12.01, then 12.02, then 12.03 ...

　　The computer will still be unable to predict whether Princeton, New Jersey, will have sun or rain on a day one month away. At noon the spaces between the sensors will hide fluctuations that the computer will
15　not know about, tiny deviations from the average. By 12.01, those fluctuations will already have created small errors one foot away. Soon the errors will have multiplied to the ten-foot scale, and so on up to the size of the globe.

JAMES GLEICK, *Chaos*

New words and expressions 生词和短语

forecast (1.1) /ˈfɔːkɑːst/ *n.* 预报
speculative (1.1) /ˈspekjʊlətɪv/ *adj.* 推测的
blizzard (1.4) /ˈblɪzəd/ *n.* 暴风雪
deteriorate (1.4) /dɪˈtɪərɪəreɪt/ *v.* 变坏, 恶化
multiply (1.4) /ˈmʌltɪplaɪ/ *v.* 增加
cascade (1.5) /kæˈskeɪd/ *v.* 瀑布似地落下
turbulent (1.5) /ˈtɜːbjʊlənt/ *adj.* 狂暴的
dust devil (1.5) /ˈdʌst-ˌdevəl/ 小尘暴, 尘旋风
squall (1.5) /skwɔːl/ *n.* 暴风
eddy (1.6) /ˈedi/ *n.* 旋涡

grid (1.7) /grɪd/ *n.* 坐标方格
sensor (1.9) /ˈsensə/ *n.* 传感器
humidity (1.11) /hjuːˈmɪdɪti/ *n.* 湿度
meteorologist (1.11) /ˌmiːtiəˈrɒlədʒɪst/ *n.* 气象学家
Princeton (1.13) /ˈprɪnstən/ *n.* 普林斯顿 （美国城市名）
New Jersey (1.13) /njuː-ˈdʒɜːzi/ *n.* 新泽西 （美国州名）
fluctuation (1.14) /ˌflʌktʃuˈeɪʃən/ *n.* 起伏, 波动
deviation (1.15) /ˌdiːviˈeɪʃən/ *n.* 偏差

View of the 76 metre diameter Mark 1A radio
telescope at Jodrell Bank near Manchester,
England

Notes on the text 课文注释

1　beyond two or three days, 超过两三天 。
2　of the order of, 大约 。

参考译文

　　世界上最好的两三天以上的天气预报具有很强的猜测性, 如果超过六七天, 天气预报就没有了任何价值 。

　　原因是蝴蝶效应 。对于小片的天气状况——对一个全球性的气象预报员来说, "小" 可以意味着雷暴和暴风雪——任何预测的质量会很快下降 。错误和不可靠性上升, 接踵而来的是一系列湍流的征兆, 从小尘暴和暴风发展到只有卫星上可以看到的席卷整块大陆的旋涡 。

　　现代气象模型以一个坐标图来显示, 图中每个点大约间隔 60 英里 。即使是这样, 有些开始时的资料也不得不依靠推测, 因为地面工作站和卫星不可能看到地球上的每一个地方 。假设地球上可以布满传感器, 每个相隔 1 英尺, 并按 1 英尺的间隔从地面一直排列到大气层的顶端 。再假定每个传感器都极端准确地读出了温度 、气压 、湿度和气象学家需要的任何其他数据 。在正午时分, 一个功能巨大的计算机搜集所有的资料, 并算出在 12:01、12:02、12:03 等每一个点时可能出现的情况 。

　　计算机无法推断出 1 个月以后的某一天, 新泽西州的普林斯顿究竟是晴天还是雨天 。正午时分, 传感器之间的距离会掩盖计算机无法知道的波动——任何偏离平均值的变化 。到 12:01 时, 那些波动就已经会在 1 英尺远的地方造成偏差 。很快这种偏差会增加到 10 英尺的范围, 如此等等, 一直到全球的范围 。

Comprehension 理解

Give short answers to these questions in your own words as far as possible. Use one complete sentence for each answer.

1　What does the author mean by 'small pieces of weather'?
2　How do modern weather models work?
3　What do you think 'the butterfly effect' means in this passage?

Vocabulary 词汇

Refer to the text to see how the following words have been used, then write sentences of your own using these words: speculative (l.1); global (l.3); deteriorates (l.4); rapidly (l.4); multiply (l.4); turbulent (l.5); suppose (l.10); accurate (l.10); precisely (l.11); data (l.12); fluctuations (l.14); average (l.15); errors (l.16).

The paragraph 段落

Which one of these statements do you think the author would agree with?

1   Accurate readings by computers enable us to predict the weather.
2   It will never be possible to predict the weather accurately.
3   The only way to predict the weather accurately is to have sensors one foot apart, rising at one-foot intervals all the way to the top of the atmosphere.

Key structures 关键句型

A   Note how these two sentences have been connected:

Errors and uncertainties multiply. They cascade upward through a chain of turbulent features.

Errors and uncertainties multiply, cascading upward through a chain of turbulent features. (ll.4-5)

Join these sentences in the same way:

1   There's a fault in the earth's crust. It runs along the west coast of the USA.
2   The hurricane hit Florida. It swept away everything in its path.
3   I noticed the lights were on. I assumed they were at home.
4   He emerged from the airport. The president waved to the reporters.

B   We can introduce conditional sentences with conjunctions other than *if*, for example:

Suppose the earth could be covered with sensors spaced one foot apart. (ll.8-9)

Complete these sentences in any way you like:

1   You can go home early, providing (that) _____ .
2   We can offer you a job on condition (that) _____ .
3   You can come in any time you like tomorrow morning so long as _____ .
4   I won't phone you unless _____ .
5   He'll definitely win even if _____ .

C   Study these two sentences:

We will probably have some rain by noon.

By 12.01 those fluctuations will already have created small errors one foot away. (ll.15-16)

Explain the differences in meaning between these pairs of sentences:

1   He won't receive this fax tomorrow morning.
    He will have received this fax by tomorrow morning.
2   He won't leave Beijing until this message arrives.
    By the time this message arrives, he will have left Beijing.
3   They will complete the new motorway by next June.
    They won't have completed the new motorway until next June.

Special difficulties 难点

A Explain the meaning of *since* in these sentences:

1   Some starting data has to be guessed, since ground stations and satellites cannot see everywhere.
2   John feels much happier since he changed his job.
3   Susan left in July and we haven't seen her since.
4   It hasn't stopped raining since eight o'clock this morning.
5   Since you're so clever, see if you can solve the problem!

B The computer will be unable to predict whether Princeton, New Jersey, will have sun or rain on a day one month away. (ll.13-14)

Supply *if* or *whether*; note the sentences where we can use both *if* and *whether*.

1   _____ he has signed the contract (or not) doesn't matter.
2   The question is _____ he has signed the contract.
3   I want to know _____ he has signed the contract.
4   I'm concerned about _____ he has signed the contract.
5   Do you know _____ she's arriving by bus or by car?

Multiple choice questions 选择题

Choose the correct answers to the following questions.

Comprehension 理解

1 The reason it's hard to forecast the weather is that _____ .
   (*a*) conditions rapidly deteriorate
   (*b*) there is always turbulence
   (*c*) only satellites have a panoramic view of conditions
   (*d*) the effect of tiny changes cannot be detected or calculated

2 Even with grid points which are sixty miles apart, forecasters _____ .
   (*a*) have to depend on satellites for information
   (*b*) have to make assumptions about some of the data
   (*c*) work on modern weather models
   (*d*) prevent errors from multiplying

3 Which of these statements is true?
   (*a*) The only way to solve the problem is to have sensors spaced at one-foot intervals.
   (*b*) The only way to solve the problem is to have infinitely powerful computers.
   (*c*) The only way to solve the problem is to have perfectly accurate readings.
   (*d*) At present, there is no way of making absolutely accurate predictions.

4 Tiny variations in temperature, pressure and humidity _____ .
   (*a*) will be picked up by sensors at one-minute intervals
   (*b*) are used to predict the weather one month ahead
   (*c*) can lead to completely unexpected weather conditions
   (*d*) produce expected results

Unit 2　Lesson 14

Structure 句型

5 Generally speaking, any prediction _____ rapidly. (l.2)

   (*a*) is deteriorating   (*b*) has deteriorated   (*c*) will deteriorate   (*d*) had deteriorated

6 Only satellites _____ see continent-size features. (ll.5-6)

   (*a*) are able to   (*b*) could   (*c*) are possible   (*d*) are capable

7 _____ the earth could be covered with sensors. (ll.9-10)

   (*a*) Providing that   (*b*) On condition that   (*c*) Say   (*d*) Allowing that

8 The computer will be incapable _____ whether Princeton will have sun or rain one month away. (ll.13)

   (*a*) predict   (*b*) to predict   (*c*) of predicting   (*d*) predicting

Vocabulary 词汇

9 The world's best weather forecasts are based on _____ . (l.1)

   (*a*) certain knowledge   (*b*) guess work

   (*c*) scientific facts   (*d*) accurate calculation

10 The modern weather models work with a _____ of points. (l.7)

   (*a*) scale   (*b*) balance   (*c*) line   (*d*) network

11 'Humidity' refers to _____ . (l.11)

   (*a*) light   (*b*) water vapour   (*c*) pressure   (*d*) heat

12 An infinitely powerful computer takes in all the data and _____ what will happen. (ll.11-12)

   (*a*) predicts   (*b*) foretells   (*c*) estimates   (*d*) works out

Lesson 15 Secrecy in industry 工业中的秘密

First listen and then answer the following question.

听录音，然后回答以下问题。

Why is secrecy particularly important in the chemical industries?

Two factors weigh heavily against the effectiveness of scientific research in industry. One is the general atmosphere of secrecy in which it is carried out, the other the lack of freedom of the individual research worker. In so far as any inquiry is a secret one, it naturally limits all those engaged in carrying it out from effective contact with their fellow scientists either in other countries or in universities, or even, often enough,
5 in other departments of the same firm. The degree of secrecy naturally varies considerably. Some of the bigger firms are engaged in researches which are of such general and fundamental nature that it is a positive advantage to them not to keep them secret. Yet a great many processes depending on such research are sought for with complete secrecy until the stage at which patents can be taken out. Even more processes are never patented at all but kept as secret processes. This applies particularly to chemical industries, where
10 chance discoveries play a much larger part than they do in physical and mechanical industries. Sometimes the secrecy goes to such an extent that the whole nature of the research cannot be mentioned. Many firms, for instance, have great difficulty in obtaining technical or scientific books from libraries because they are unwilling to have their names entered as having taken out such and such a book, for fear the agents of other firms should be able to trace the kind of research they are likely to be undertaking.

J. D. Bernal *The Social Function of Science*

A scientist working at the 'Arcton' Laboratories in Cheshire

Unit 2　Lesson 15

New words and expressions 生词和短语

secrecy (title) /'si:krəsi/ *n.* 秘密
effectiveness (1.1) /ɪ'fektɪvnɪs/ *n.* 成效, 效力
inquiry (1.3) /ɪn'kwaɪəri/ *n.* 调查研究
positive (1.6) /'pɒzɪtɪv/ *adj.* 确实的

process (1.7) /'prəʊses/ *n.* 过程
patent (1.8) /'peɪtnt/ *n.* 专利; *v.* 得到专利权
agent (1.13) /'eɪdʒənt/ *n.* 情报人员

Notes on the text 课文注释

1　weigh against, 不利于…… 。
2　in so far as ..., 就 …… 而言 。
3　which are of such general and fundamental nature, 其中 to be of 有 "具有" 的意思 。
4　are sought for with complete secrecy, 极端秘密地探索 。
5　such and such a book, 某一本书 。

参考译文

　　有两个因素严重地妨碍着工业中科学研究的效率: 一是科研工作中普遍存在的保密气氛; 二是研究人员缺乏个人自由 。任何一项研究都涉及到保密, 那些从事科研的人员自然受到了限制 。他们不能和其他国家 、其他大学, 甚至往往不能与本公司的其他部门的同行们进行有效的接触 。保密程度自然差别很大 。某些大公司进行的研究属于一般和基础性的研究, 因此不保密对他们才有利 。然而, 依赖这种研究的很多工艺程序是在完全保密的情况下进行的, 直到可以取得专利权的阶段为止 。更多的工艺过程根本就不会取得专利权, 而是作为秘方保存着 。这在化学工业方面尤其突出 。同物理和机械工业相比, 化学工业中偶然发现的机会要多得多 。有时, 保密竟达到了这样的程度, 即连研究工作的整个性质都不准提及 。比如, 很多公司向图书馆借阅科技书籍时感到很困难, 因为它们不愿让人家记下它们公司的名字和借阅的某一本书 。他们生怕别的公司的情报人员发现他们可能要从事的某项科研项目 。

Comprehension 理解

Give short answers to these questions in your own words as far as possible. Use one complete sentence for each answer.

1　Which two factors weigh heavily against the effectiveness of scientific research in industry?
2　Why are some processes in chemical industries never patented at all?
3　Why are some firms reluctant to borrow books from libraries?

Vocabulary 词汇

Refer to the text to see how the following words have been used, then write sentences of your own using these words: weigh heavily against (1.1); lack (1.2); effective contact (1.4); fundamental (1.6); processes (1.7); applies (1.9); trace (1.14); likely (1.14).

The paragraph 段落

A　Which of these statements best expresses the main idea of the passage? Give reasons for your choice:

1　The effectiveness of scientific research in industry is hampered by the general atmosphere of secrecy which surrounds it and by the lack of freedom of the individual research worker.

2 Scientific research in industry is not very effective because big firms wish to keep so many processes secret.

3 Many scientific processes in industry are kept secret until they can be patented.

B The following sentences have been taken from lines 5-10. Arrange them in their correct order. Do not refer to the passage until you have finished the exercise:

1 The degree of secrecy naturally varies considerably.

2 This applies particularly to chemical industries, where chance discoveries play a much larger part than they do in physical and mechanical industries.

3 Some of the bigger firms are engaged in researches which are of such general and fundamental nature that it is a positive advantage to them not to keep them secret.

4 Even more processes are never patented at all but kept as secret processes.

5 Yet a great many processes depending on such research are sought for with complete secrecy until the stage at which patents can be taken out.

Key structures 关键句型

A Change the form of the verbs in each of these sentences. Omit the words in italics. Do not refer to the passage until you have completed the exercise:

1 One is the general atmosphere of secrecy in which *they* carry it out. (ll.1-2)

2 *They* seek for a great many processes with complete secrecy until the stage at which *they* can take out patents. (ll.7-8)

3 Even more processes *they* never patent at all but keep as secret processes. (ll.8-9)

4 Sometimes the secrecy goes to such an extent that *they* cannot mention the whole nature of the research. (l.10-11)

B Give the correct form of the verbs in parentheses in the following sentences. Do not refer to the passage until you have completed the exercise:

1 In so far as any inquiry is a secret one, it naturally limits all those engaged in _____ (carry) it out. (l.3)

2 Many firms, for instance, have great difficulty in _____ (obtain) technical or scientific books from libraries. (ll.11-12)

C Complete the following sentences using a verb after the words in italics:

1 He was engaged in _____ .

2 He was prevented from _____ .

3 He insisted on _____ .

4 If you persist in _____ .

D Note the position of *not* in this sentence:

It is a positive advantage to them *not* to keep them secret. (ll.6-7)

Supply *not* in each of the following sentences:

1 He told me to mention it to you.

2 Please tell him to call in the morning.

3 Didn't I beg you to write to him?

E What is the difference between these two sentences:

They are unwilling *to enter their names* as having taken out such and such a book.

They are unwilling *to have their names entered* as having taken out such and such a book. (ll.12-13)

Write these sentences again using the correct form of *have* with the verbs in italics:

1 We are going to *decorate* this room soon.
2 I *repaired* this watch last year.
3 Will you *install* the television in this room?

F Note that in the following sentence we may use the word *lest* in place of *for fear*:

Many firms are unwilling to have their names entered as having taken out such and such a book *lest* (or *for fear*) the agents of other firms should be able to trace the kind of research they are likely to be undertaking. (ll.11-14)

Write two sentences using *lest* and *for fear*.

Special difficulties 难点

A Note the use of *fellow* in this phrase: 'with their *fellow scientists*' (l.4). Write three sentences using *fellow* with the following words: men; students; workers.

B Write sentences using the following phrases:

in so far as (l.3); often enough (l.4); to such an extent (l.11); the whole nature of (l.11).

C Explain the expressions in italics in the following sentences:

1 In so far as any inquiry is a secret one, it naturally limits all those engaged in *carrying it out*. (l.3)
2 I think we can *carry on* without your help.
3 The audience was completely *carried away by* the wonderful performance of the soloist.
4 The government failed to *carry through* the new bill on housing in the House of Commons last night.

D What do you understand by the phrase in italics:

They are unwilling to have their names entered as having taken out *such and such* a book. (ll.12-13)

Write a sentence using the phrase *such and such*.

Multiple choice questions 选择题

Choose the correct answers to the following questions.

Comprehension 理解

1 Fear of industrial espionage _____ .

(*a*) leads to lack of freedom in scientific research

(*b*) especially applies to scientific research of a general and fundamental nature

(*c*) can lead to secrecy in scientific research

(*d*) creates an atmosphere of distrust in business

2 Which of these statements is true?

(*a*) Some kinds of scientific research are 'more secret' than others.

(*b*) All kinds of scientific research are top secret.

(*c*) Firms never tell anyone anything about their scientific research.

(*d*) Scientific research workers never speak to each other.

3 Firms want to be sure _____ .

  (*a*) they limit all those engaged in carrying out scientific research

  (*b*) that larger companies can't find out about their scientific research

  (*c*) they are working in an atmosphere of complete secrecy

  (*d*) they own the rights to intellectual property before they reveal what they're doing

4 The possibility of making discoveries by accident _____ .

  (*a*) makes it difficult to obtain scientific books from libraries

  (*b*) encourages competition from other agents

  (*c*) increases the need for secrecy

  (*d*) means that every discovery has to be patented

Structure 句型

5 One is the general atmosphere of secrecy _____ . (ll.1-2)

  (*a*) which it is carried out   (*b*) which is carried out

  (*c*) it is carried out   (*d*) it is carried out in

6 _____ any inquiry is a secret one, it naturally limits ... (l.3)

  (*a*) With regard to   (*b*) As well as   (*c*) Supposing that   (*d*) To the extent that

7 Some of the bigger firms are engaged in researches which are _____ general that it is a positive
  advantage to them not to keep them secret. (ll.6-7)

  (*a*) such   (*b*) so   (*c*) so that   (*d*) in order that

8 They _____ even more processes as secret processes. (ll.8-9)

  (*a*) keep   (*b*) kept   (*c*) are kept   (*d*) are keeping

Vocabulary 词汇

9 There is the _____ of freedom of the individual research worker. (l.2)

  (*a*) loss   (*b*) emptiness   (*c*) absence   (*d*) luck

10 It naturally limits all those engaged in _____ . (l.3)

  (*a*) performing it   (*b*) involving it   (*c*) betrothed to it   (*d*) allowing it

11 It is _____ not to keep them secret. (ll.6-7)

  (*a*) with their knowledge   (*b*) on their account

  (*c*) in their best interests   (*d*) for their benefit

12 Sometimes the secrecy goes to such a _____ that ... (l.l.10-11)

  (*a*) degree   (*b*) process   (*c*) limit   (*d*) period

Lesson 16 The modern city 现代城市

What is the author's main argument about the modern city?

In the organization of industrial life the influence of the factory upon the physiological and mental state of the workers has been completely neglected. Modern industry is based on the conception of the maximum production at lowest cost, in order that an individual or a group of individuals may earn as much money as possible. It has expanded without any idea of the true nature of the human beings who run the machines, and
5 without giving any consideration to the effects produced on the individuals and on their descendants by the artificial mode of existence imposed by the factory. The great cities have been built with no regard for us. The shape and dimensions of the skyscrapers depend entirely on the necessity of obtaining the maximum income per square foot of ground, and of offering to the tenants offices and apartments that please them. This caused the construction of gigantic buildings where too large masses of human beings are crowded
10 together. Civilized men like such a way of living. While they enjoy the comfort and banal luxury of their dwelling, they do not realize that they are deprived of the necessities of life. The modern city consists of monstrous edifices and of dark, narrow streets full of petrol fumes and toxic gases, torn by the noise of the taxicabs, lorries and buses, and thronged ceaselessly by great crowds. Obviously, it has not been planned for the good of its inhabitants.

ALEXIS CARREL *Man, the Unknown*

An aerial veiw of Pittsburgh, Pennsylvania

New words and expressions 生词和短语

physiological (l.1) /ˌfɪziə'lɒdʒɪkəl/ *adj.* 生理的

maximum (l.2) /'mæksɪməm/ *adj.* 最大限度的

consideration (l.5) /kənˌsɪdə'reɪʃən/ *n.* 考虑

descendant (l.5) /dɪ'sendənt/ *n.* 子孙, 后代

artificial (l.6) /ˌɑːtɪ'fɪʃəl/ *adj.* 人工的

impose (l.6) /ɪm'pəʊz/ *v.* 强加

dimension (l.7) /daɪ'menʃən/ *n.* 大小, 规模

skyscraper (l.7) /'skaɪˌskreɪpə/ *n.* 摩天大楼

tenant (l.8) /'tenənt/ *n.* 租户

civilized (l.10) /'sɪvəlaɪzd/ *adj.* 文明的

banal (l.10) /bə'nɑːl/ *adj.* 平庸的

luxury (l.10) /'lʌkʃəri/ *n.* 豪华

deprive (l.11) /dɪ'praɪv/ *v.* 剥夺

monstrous (l.12) /'mɒnstrəs/ *adj.* 巨大的

edifice (l.12) /'edɪfɪs/ *n.* 大厦

toxic (l.12) /'tɒksɪk/ *adj.* 有毒的

ceaselessly (l.13) /'siːsləsli/ *adv.* 不停地

throng (l.13) /θrɒŋ/ *v.* 挤满, 拥塞

Notes on the text 课文注释

1 in order that ..., 以使 ……, 为了 ……, 引导目的的状语从句。

2 without any idea of, 完全忽视 ……。

3 without giving any consideration to ..., 完全不考虑 ……。

4 with no regard for, 不考虑 ……。

5 be deprived of, 被剥夺。

参考译文

在工业生活的组织中, 工厂对工人的生理和精神状态的影响完全被忽视了。现代工业的基本概念是: 以最低成本获取最多产品, 为的是让某个人或某一部分人尽可能多地赚钱。现代工业发展起来了, 却根本没想到操作机器的人的本质。工厂把一种人为的生存方式强加给工人, 却不顾及这种生存方式给工人及其后代带来的影响。大城市的建设毫不关心我们。摩天大楼完全是按这样的需要修建的: 每平方英尺地皮取得最大收入和向租房人提供使他满意的办公室和住房。这样就导致了许多摩天大厦拔地而起, 大厦内众多的人挤在一起。文明人喜欢这样一种生活方式。在享受自己住宅的舒适和庸俗的豪华时, 却没有意识到被剥夺了生活所必需的东西。大得吓人的高楼和阴暗狭窄的街道组成了今日现代化的城市。街道上充斥着汽油味和有毒气体, 出租汽车、卡车、公共汽车的噪音刺耳难忍, 络绎不绝的人群挤来挤去。显然, 现代化的城市不是为居民的利益而规划的。

Comprehension 理解

Give short answers to these questions in your own words as far as possible. Use one complete sentence for each answer.

1 In what way is a modern factory similar to a large city?

2 What, according to the author, led to the building of huge skyscrapers?

3 What do those who enjoy living in cities fail to realize?

Vocabulary 词

Refer to the text to see how the following words have been used, then write sentences of your own using these words: physiological (l.1); neglected (l.2); expanded (l.4); artificial mode of existence (l.6); regard (l.6); the maximum income (ll.7-8); construction (l.9); banal (l.10); monstrous edifices (l.12); toxic (l.12); thronged ceaselessly by great crowds (l.13).

The paragraph 段落

A   Which of these statements best expresses the author's main argument? Give reasons for your choice:

1   Modern cities have not been planned for the good of their inhabitants.

2   Man is obsessed by the desire for profit.

3   Great cities, like modern factories, impose on us an artificial way of life.

B   The following sentences are taken from lines 1-6. Arrange them in their correct order. Do not refer to the passage until you have finished the exercise:

Modern industry is based on the conception of the maximum production at lowest cost, in order that an individual or a group of individuals may earn as much money as possible.

In the organization of industrial life the influence of the factory upon the physiological and mental state of the workers has been completely neglected.

It has expanded without any idea of the true nature of the human beings who run the machines, and without giving any consideration to the effects produced on the individuals and on their descendants by the artificial mode of existence imposed by the factory.

Key structures 关键句型

A   Give the correct form of the verbs in parentheses. Do not refer to the passage until you have finished the exercise:

In the organization of industrial life the influence of the factory upon the physiological and mental state of the workers completely _____ (neglect). Modern industry _____ (base) on the conception of the maximum production at lowest cost, in order that an individual or a group of individuals may earn as much money as possible. It _____ (expand) without any idea of the true nature of the human beings who run the machines, and without _____ (give) any consideration to the effect produced on the individuals and on their descendants by the artificial mode of existence imposed by the factory. The great cities _____ (build) with no regard for us. (ll. 1-6)

B   Study the pattern in italics in this sentence:

Modern industry is based on the conception of the maximum production at lowest cost, *in order that an individual or a group of individuals may* (or *might*) earn as much money as possible. (ll.2-4)

Complete the following sentences:

1   He is attending English classes in order that _____ .

2   She works very hard in order that _____ .

3   The Prime Minister has gone abroad in order that _____ .

C   Note the phrase in italics:

In order that an individual or a group of individuals may earn *as much money as possible*. (ll.3-4)

Write sentences using the following phrases:

as many as possible; as far as possible; as few as possible; as little as possible.

D   Write sentences using the following expressions:

influence upon (l.1); based on (l.2); the true nature of (l.4); mode of (l.6); regard for (l.6); depend on (l.7); the necessity of (l.7); deprived of (l.11); consist of (l.11); full of (l.12).

E   Compare these two sentences:

Instead of saying: *Although* they enjoy the comfort and banal luxury of their dwelling, they do not realize that they are deprived of the necessities of life.

We can say: *While* they enjoy the comfort and banal luxury of their dwelling, they do not realize that they are deprived of the necessities of life. (ll.10-11)

Complete the following sentences using your own words:

1   While we are less concerned _____ .

2   While modern cities have grown in size _____ .

3   While factory conditions have improved _____ .

Special difficulties 难点

A   Study the following pairs of words and then write sentences of your own to bring out the difference.

1   physiological (l.1) — psychological

The doctor could not find any physiological cause of his illness.

John says he's got some sort of virus, but I'm sure it's psychological.

2   neglect (l.2) — ignore

Heavy drinking is one reason why some people neglect themselves.

I won't accept any responsibility if you choose to ignore my advice.

3   modern (l.2) — contemporary

The original supermarkets were small by modern standards.

I have no interest at all in contemporary Japanese prints.

4   earn (l.3) — win

He earns nearly 45,000 dollars a year.

Who do you think will win the next election?

5   please (l.8) — beg

It pleases me to say that we got what we wanted as a result of taking your advice.

I beg you to consider carefully before you make up your mind.

B   Note this use of *per* in the sense of *for each*:

The necessity of obtaining the maximum income per square foot of ground ... (ll.7-8)

Write sentences using the following expressions:

per mile; per hour; per person; per yard; per cent.

C   Explain the meaning of the verb *crowd* in these sentences:

1   Large masses of human beings are *crowded* together. (ll.9-10)

2   When it began to rain, everyone *crowded* into the building.

3   He *crowded* a lot of information into the last chapter.

D   What is the plural of the following words:

necessity; mass; bus; gas; lorry; taxicab; city.

Unit 2　Lesson 16

Multiple choice questions 选择题

Choose the correct answers to the following questions.

Comprehension 理解

1 The purpose of modern industry is to _____ .
   (a) produce as much as possible as cheaply as possible
   (b) ignore the mental and physical state of the workers
   (c) enable individuals to earn as much money as possible
   (d) achieve maximum production regardless of cost

2 Factories require people to _____ .
   (a) run machines without thinking
   (b) lead an unnatural way of life
   (c) ignore the effects produced on individuals
   (d) take into account the true nature of human beings

3 According to the writer, some people who live in modern cities _____ .
   (a) try to obtain maximum income from property
   (b) are responsible for the shape and dimensions of skyscrapers
   (c) take pleasure in living in the conditions a city imposes
   (d) offer tenants offices and apartments that please them

4 The writer believes that conditions in modern cities _____ .
   (a) have caused the construction of gigantic buildings
   (b) are deprived of the necessities of life
   (c) are comfortable and luxurious
   (d) are actively harmful to the inhabitants

Structure 句型

5 It is based on maximum production _____ earn as much as possible. (ll.2-3)
   (a) for individuals to　　(b) so as individuals　　(c) for individuals　　(d) in order individuals

6 It has expanded with _____ idea of the true nature of human beings. (l.4)
   (a) little　　　　(b) few　　　　(c) some　　　　(d) no

7 This caused the construction of gigantic buildings _____ too large masses ... (l.9)
   (a) at which　　(b) on which　　(c) to which　　(d) in which

8 _____ they enjoy the comfort and banal luxury of their dwelling ... (ll.10-11)
   (a) During　　(b) Though　　(c) At the time　　(d) When

Vocabulary 词汇

9 The _____ of the factory on workers has been completely neglected. (ll.1-2)
   (a) effect　　(b) affection　　(c) extent　　(d) measurement

10 The city has _____ without any idea of the true nature of human beings. (l.4)
   (a) grown up　　(b) grown　　(c) been grown　　(d) been grown up

11 They are _____ the necessities of life. (l.11)
   (a) denied　　(b) refused　　(c) discarded　　(d) ignored

12 The modern city _____ monstrous edifices and dark narrow streets. (ll.11-12)
   (a) consists　　(b) cohabits　　(c) comprises　　(d) constitutes

96

Unit 3

INSTRUCTIONS TO THE STUDENT

Content

This unit consists of eight passages followed by exercises on Comprehension, Vocabulary, The paragraph, Key structures, Special difficulties and Multiple choice questions.

Aim

To provide more advanced practice in paragraph construction.

How to work

1 Read each passage carefully two or three times.
2 Answer the questions in the order in which they are given.

The paragraph

All the exercises under this heading are based on the passage. The following types of exercise have been given:

1 Writing a list of the points in note form to answer a question on the main ideas contained in part of the passage.
2 Enabling you to reconstruct in your own words a paragraph taken from the passage by providing you with the main ideas in note form.
3 Writing a short paragraph of your own on a subject which is in some way related to the passage.

Lesson 17 A man-made disease 人为的疾病

First listen and then answer the following question.

听录音, 然后回答以下问题。

What factor helped to spread the disease of *myxomatosis?*

In the early days of the settlement of Australia, enterprising settlers unwisely introduced the European rabbit. This rabbit had no natural enemies in the Antipodes, so that it multiplied with that promiscuous abandon characteristic of rabbits. It overran a whole continent. It caused devastation by burrowing and by devouring the herbage which might have maintained millions of sheep and cattle. Scientists discovered that
5 this particular variety of rabbit (and apparently no other animal) was susceptible to a fatal virus disease, *myxomatosis*. By infecting animals and letting them loose in the burrows, local epidemics of this disease could be created. Later it was found that there was a type of mosquito which acted as the carrier of this disease and passed it on to the rabbits. So while the rest of the world was trying to get rid of mosquitoes, Australia was encouraging this one. It effectively spread the disease all over the continent and drastically
10 reduced the rabbit population. It later became apparent that rabbits were developing a degree of resistance to this disease, so that the rabbit population was unlikely to be completely exterminated. There were hopes, however, that the problem of the rabbit would become manageable.

Ironically, Europe, which had bequeathed the rabbit as a pest to Australia, acquired this man-made disease as a pestilence. A French physician decided to get rid of the wild rabbits on his own estate and
15 introduced *myxomatosis*. It did not, however, remain within the confines of his estate. It spread through France, where wild rabbits are not generally regarded as a pest but as a sport and a useful food supply, and it spread to Britain where wild rabbits are regarded as a pest but where domesticated rabbits, equally suscep-tible to the disease, are the basis of a profitable fur industry. The question became one of whether Man could control the disease he had invented.

RITCHIE CALDER *Science Makes Sense*

New words and expressions 生词和短语

settlement (l.1) /'setlmənt/ n. 移民, 开拓
enterprising (l.1) /'entəpraızıŋ/ adj. 有事业心的
settler (l.1) /'setlə/ n. 移居者
Antipodes (l.2) /æn'tıpədiːz/ n. (the ~) 新西兰和
　　澳大利亚 （英）
promiscuous (l.2) /prə'mıskjuəs/ adj. 杂乱的
abandon (l.3) /ə'bændən/ n. 放任, 纵情
overrun (l.3) /'əʊvərʌn/ v. 蔓延, 泛滥
devastation (l.3) /ˌdevə'steıʃən/ n. 破坏, 劫掠
burrow (l.3) /'bʌrəʊ/ v. 挖, 掘
susceptible (l.5) /sə'septıbəl/ adj. 易受感染的
virus (l.5) /'vaıərəs/ n. 病毒

myxomatosis (l.6) /ˌmıksəmə'təʊsıs/ n. 多发性黏液瘤
infect (l.6) /ın'fekt/ v. 传染
epidemic (l.6) /ˌepı'demık/ n. 流行病
mosquito (l.7) /mə'skiːtəʊ/ n. 蚊虫
carrier (l.7) /'kærıə/ n. 带菌者
exterminate (l.11) /ık'stɜːmıneıt/ v. 消灭
ironically (l.13) /aı'rɒnıkli/ adv. 具有讽刺意味地
bequeath (l.13) /bı'kwiːð/ v. 把 …… 传给
pest (l.13) /pest/ n. 害虫,有害动物
pestilence (l.14) /'pestıləns/ n. 瘟疫
confine (l.15) /kən'faın/ n. 范围
domesticate (l.17) /də'mestıkeıt/ v. 驯养

Rabbits drinking at a waterhole in Australia

Notes on the text 课文注释

1   so that it multiplied with that promiscuous abandon characteristic of rabbits, 这里 so that 引导的一个结果状语从句，可译成"因此便以兔子所特有的杂乱交配繁衍后代"。

2   be susceptible to ..., 易受 …… 感染的, 易受 …… 影响的 。

3   let loose, 让乱跑 。

4   pass ... on to, 把 …… 传给 。

参考译文

　　在澳大利亚移民初期，一些有创业精神的移民不明智地把欧洲兔子引进了澳大利亚。这种兔子在澳大利亚及新西兰没有天敌，因此便以兔子所特有的杂乱交配迅猛繁殖起来。整个澳洲兔子成灾。它们在地下打洞，吃掉本可以饲养数百万头牛羊的牧草，给澳洲大陆造成了毁灭性的破坏。科学家们发现，这种特殊品种的兔子（显然不包括别的动物）易患一种叫做"多发性黏液瘤"的致命病毒性疾病。通过让染上此病的动物在洞内乱跑，就可以使这种疾病在一个地区蔓延起来。后来又发现，有一种蚊子是传播这种疾病的媒介，能把此病传染给兔子。因此，世界上其他地方在设法消灭蚊子的时候，澳大利亚却在促使这种蚊子大量繁殖。蚊子把这种疾病扩散到整个澳洲大陆，效果甚佳，结果兔子的数目大为减少。后来，明显看出，兔子对这种疾病已产生了一定程度的免疫力，所以兔子不可能被完全消灭。但是，已有希望解决兔子所带来的问题。

　　具有讽刺意味的是，欧洲把这种兔子作为有害动物传给澳洲，而欧洲自己却染上了这种人为的瘟疫般的疾病。一位法国内科医生决定除掉自己庄园内的野兔子，于是引进了这种多发性黏液瘤疾病。然而，这种疾病并未被局限在他的庄园内，结果在整个法国蔓延开来。野兔在法国一般不被当作有害动物，而被视为打猎取乐的玩物和有用的食物来源。这种疾病又蔓延到了英国。在英国，野兔被当作有害的动物，可是家兔是赚钱的毛皮工业的基础，然而家兔同样易感染这种疾病。现在的问题是，人类能否控制住这种人为的疾病。

Comprehension 理解

Answer these questions:

1　Why is the rabbit regarded as a serious pest in Australia?

2　Why did it prove impossible to exterminate rabbits completely in Australia?

3　How was *myxomatosis* introduced to Europe?

Vocabulary 词汇

Refer to the text to see how the following words have been used, then write sentences of your own using these words: enterprising (l.1); devastation (l.3); burrowing (l.3); devouring the herbage (l.4); susceptible (l.5); fatal (l.5); epidemics (l.6); drastically reduced (ll.9-10); completely exterminated (l.11); bequeathed (l.13); the confines of his estate (l.15); domesticated (l.17).

The paragraph 段落

A　Drawing your information from the first paragraph (lines 1-12), write a list of points in note form to answer the following question:

How did the rabbit overrun the continent of Australia, and what steps were taken to exterminate it?

B　Read the second paragraph again (lines 13-19). Then, using the list of points given below, reconstruct the paragraph in your own words as far as possible. Do not refer to the passage until you have finished the exercise.

1　Australia acquired rabbit from Europe: a pest.

2　Europe acquired from Australia *myxomatosis*: a pestilence.

3　French physician introduced it—estate.

4　It spread.

5　France: rabbit not a pest; sport; food supply.

6　Britain: rabbit: a pest; tame rabbits: fur industry.

7　Could man control his artificial disease?

C　Write a paragraph of about 200 words on one of the following subjects:

1　Pest control.

2　The balance of nature.

Key structures 关键句型

A　Put the words in parentheses in their correct position in these sentences. In many cases, more than one position is possible. Do not refer to the passage until you have finished the exercise:

1　In the early days of the settlement of Australia, enterprising settlers introduced the European rabbit. (unwisely) (ll.1-2)

2　It was found that there was a type of mosquito which acted as the carrier of this disease and passed it on to the rabbits. (later) (ll.7-8)

3　It spread the disease all over the continent and reduced the rabbit population. (effectively, drastically) (ll.9-10)

4　It became apparent that rabbits were developing a degree of resistance to the disease, so that the rabbit population was unlikely to be exterminated. (later, completely) (ll.10-11)

5   Europe, which had bequeathed the rabbit as a pest to Australia, acquired this man-made disease as a pestilence. (ironically) (ll.13-14)

B   Compare these two uses of *so that*:

1   This rabbit had no natural enemies in the Antipodes, *so that* it multiplied with that promiscuous abandon characteristic of rabbits. (ll.2-3)

2   I went to Switzerland last winter so that I could do some skiing.

Write two sentences using *so that* in the ways shown above.

C   Note the form of the verbs in italics in this sentence:

So while the rest of the world *was trying* to get rid of mosquitoes, Australia *was encouraging* this one. (ll.8-9)

Complete the following sentences:

1   While Tom was doing his homework, his sister _____ .

2   While my wife was seeing to the evening meal, I _____ .

D   Supply the missing words in this sentence. Do not refer to the passage until you have finished the exercise:

It spread through France, _____ wild rabbits are not generally regarded as a pest but as a sport and a useful food supply, and it spread to Britain _____ wild rabbits are regarded as a pest but _____ domesticated rabbits, equally susceptible to the disease, are the basis of a profitable fur industry. (ll.15-18)

Special difficulties 难点

A   Study the following pairs of words and then write sentences of your own to bring out the difference.

1   discovered (1.4) — invented

Captain Cook discovered Antarctica when he was exploring the Eastern Pacific Ocean.

Do you have any idea who invented the safety pin?

2   disease (1.5) — decease

Poverty and disease usually go together.

A national crisis was caused by the sudden decease of the President.

3   basis (1.18) — base

What's your basis for making such a decision?

The base of the memorial is engraved with the names of those who died.

4   apparent (1.10) — obvious

It soon became apparent that our opponents were too strong for us.

It was obvious to the parents that Tom was lying.

5   acquired (1.13) — obtained

He has acquired a fearsome reputation.

Further information can be obtained from the information centre.

6   degree (1.10) — rank

To a certain degree, I accept the truth of what you say, even if I disagree with your conclusions. (degree = extent)

The campaign to protect the countryside involves people from all degrees of society, not just the landowning classes. (degree = social class)

What rank was your father when he was in the army? (rank = an official position on a scale)

B   Note the use of *early* in this phrase: in the *early* days (l.1). Write sentences using the following phrases: in the early hours; in the early years; at an early age.

C   Write sentences to illustrate the use of the following verbs: overrun (l.3); overtake; overdo; overlook.

D   Compare the use of *spread* in these two sentences:

1   It (the mosquito) effectively *spread* the disease all over the continent. (l.9)
2   It (the disease) *spread* through France. (ll.15-16)
    Write two sentences to illustrate these uses of spread.

E   Note the spelling of this word: *manageable* (l.12). Add *-able* to the following words, retaining or dropping the *e* where necessary: move; love; peace; knowledge; change; service; believe.

F   Note the use of *own* in this phrase: on his *own* estate (l.14). Write sentences using the following phrases: my own; on my own; of my own.

Multiple choice questions 选择题

Choose the correct answers to the following questions.

Comprehension 理解

1 One of the reasons rabbits multiplied so rapidly in Australia is that they _____ .
   (*a*) were unwisely introduced by enterprising settlers
   (*b*) bred rapidly
   (*c*) overran the continent
   (*d*) overcame their natural enemies in the Antipodes

2 Scientists found _____ of spreading myxomatosis.
   (*a*) one way
   (*b*) two ways
   (*c*) three ways
   (*d*) a large number of ways

3 The disease was spread right across the continent of Australia largely because _____ .
   (*a*) of the mosquito
   (*b*) of the rabbit
   (*c*) scientists let infected animals loose in burrows
   (*d*) Australia encouraged diseased rabbits to migrate to other places

4 Myxomatosis, that was a blessing in Australia, proved to be _____ in Europe.
   (*a*) domesticated
   (*b*) a disease
   (*c*) profitable
   (*d*) a curse

Structure 句型

5 This rabbit had no natural enemies in the Antipodes _____ . (1.2)

　(a) and as a result it multiplied　　　　　(b) in order to multiply

　(c) so that it might multiply　　　　　　(d) because it multiplied

6 It _____ and caused devastation. (1.3)

　(a) burrowing　　　(b) burrowed　　　(c) was burrowing　　　(d) has burrowed

7 _____ were local epidemics created? By infecting animals. (1.6)

　(a) Why　　　(b) How　　　(c) Where　　　(d) When

8 It was _____ to create local epidemics of this disease. (ll.6-7)

　(a) potent　　　(b) able　　　(c) enabled　　　(d) possible

Vocabulary 词汇

9 It caused devastation by _____ the herbage. (ll.3-4)

　(a) burrowing into　　(b) infecting　　(c) consuming　　(d) digging

10 By infecting animals and _____ them loose in burrows ... (1.6)

　(a) allowing　　(b) leaving　　(c) introducing　　(d) turning

11 The rabbits were able to _____ this disease to a certain extent. (1.10)

　(a) react to　　(b) prevent　　(c) withstand　　(d) oppose

12 Australia _____ the rabbit as a pest from Europe. (1.13)

　(a) inherited　　(b) obtained　　(c) assumed　　(d) claimed

Lesson 18 Porpoises 海豚

First listen and then answer the following question.

听录音，然后回答以下问题 。

What would you say is the main characteristic of porpoises?

There has long been a superstition among mariners that porpoises will save drowning men by pushing them to the surface, or protect them from sharks by surrounding them in defensive formation. Marine Studio biologists have pointed out that, however intelligent they may be, it is probably a mistake to credit dolphins with any motive of lifesaving. On the occasions when they have pushed to shore an unconscious human
5 being they have much more likely done it out of curiosity or for sport, as in riding the bow waves of a ship. In 1928 some porpoises were photographed working like beavers to push ashore a waterlogged mattress. If, as has been reported, they have protected humans from sharks, it may have been because curiosity attracted them and because the scent of a possible meal attracted the sharks. Porpoises and sharks are natural enemies. It is possible that upon such an occasion a battle ensued, with the sharks being driven away or killed.

10   Whether it be bird, fish or beast, the porpoise is intrigued with anything that is alive. They are constantly after the turtles, who peacefully submit to all sorts of indignities. One young calf especially enjoyed raising a turtle to the surface with his snout and then shoving him across the tank like an aquaplane. Almost any day a young porpoise may be seen trying to turn a 300-pound sea turtle over by sticking his snout under the edge of his shell and pushing up for dear life. This is not easy, and may require two porpoises working together.
15 In another game, as the turtle swims across the oceanarium, the first porpoise swoops down from above and butts his shell with his belly. This knocks the turtle down several feet. He no sooner recovers his equilibrium than the next porpoise comes along and hits him another crack. Eventually the turtle has been butted all the way down to the floor of the tank. He is now satisfied merely to try to stand up, but as soon as he does so a porpoise knocks him flat. The turtle at last gives up by pulling his feet under his shell and the game is over.

RALPH NADING HILL *Window in the Sea*

New words and expressions 生词和短语

porpoise (title) /'pɔːpəs/ n. 海豚
mariner (1.1) /'mærɪnə/ n. 水手
shark (1.2) /ʃɑːk/ n. 鲨鱼
formation (1.2) /fɔː'meɪʃən/ n. 队形
dolphin (1.3) /'dɒlfɪn/ n. 海豚科动物
unconscious (1.4) /ʌn'kɒnʃəs/ adj. 不省人事的
beaver (1.6) /'biːvə/ n. 海狸
ashore (1.6) /ə'ʃɔː/ adv. 上岸
waterlogged (1.6) /'wɔːtəlɒgd/ adj. 浸满水的
scent (1.8) /sent/ n. 香味
ensue (1.9) /ɪn'sjuː/ v. 接着发生

intrigue (1.10) /ɪn'triːg/ v. 引起兴趣
indignity (1.11) /ɪn'dɪgnɪti/ n. 侮辱
snout (1.12) /snaʊt/ n. 口鼻部
shove (1.12) /ʃʌv/ v. 硬推
aquaplane (1.12) /'ækwəpleɪn/ n. 驾浪滑水板
oceanarium (1.15) /ˌəʊʃə'neərɪəm/ n. 水族馆
swoop (1.15) /swuːp/ v. 猛扑
belly (1.16) /'beli/ n. 腹部
equilibrium (1.16) /ˌiːkwɪ'lɪbriəm/ n. 平衡
butt (1.17) /bʌt/ v. 碰撞
crack (1.17) /kræk/ n. 重击

Dolphins jumping at Marineland in California

Notes on the text 课文注释

1   however intelligent they may be, 不管它们有多聪明, 这是一个让步状语从句。

2   as in riding the bow waves of a ship, 就像它们追逐被船首犁开的浪花一样。

3   If, as has been reported, they have protected humans from sharks ...,
    as 是关系代词, 代替 they have protected humans from sharks。

4   Whether it be bird, fish or beast ...,
    这是一个让步状语从句, 用的是虚拟语气形式。

5   for dear life, 拼命地。

参考译文

　　长期以来, 海员中流传着一种迷信说法, 认为海豚会把快要淹死的人托到水面, 救人性命; 或在人们周围列队保护, 使他们免遭鲨鱼伤害。海洋摄影室的生物学家指出, 无论海豚多么聪明, 认为它们有救人的动机可能是错误的。当它们偶尔把一个失去知觉的人推到岸边时, 更大的可能是出于好奇或游戏, 就像它们追逐被船首犁开的浪花一样。1928年, 有人拍摄到了海豚像海狸一样把浸透水的床垫推上岸的情景。正如报道中所说, 如果海豚保护人不受鲨鱼侵害, 那它们可能是出于好奇; 而鲨鱼可能是闻到了可以美食一顿的香味。海豚和鲨鱼是天然仇敌, 双方可能随之发生搏斗, 搏斗结果是海豚赶走或咬死鲨鱼。

　　凡是活的东西海豚都感兴趣, 不管是鸟、是鱼, 还是野兽。它们经常追逐海龟, 海龟则温顺地忍受着各种侮辱。有一只小海豚特别喜欢用鼻子把海龟推到水面, 然后像滑水板一样把海龟从水池的这一边推到那一边。几乎每天都可以看到一只小海豚把鼻子顶入一只 300 磅重的海龟的硬壳下面, 拼命地把它翻过来。这并非易事, 可能需要两只海豚合伙干才行。在另一场游戏中, 当海龟游过水族馆时, 第一只海豚从上方猛扑下去, 用腹部撞击龟壳。这一下子把海龟撞下去好几英尺。海龟刚恢复平衡, 第二只海豚又冲过来猛击一下。这只海龟最终被撞到池底。此时的海龟, 只要能站起来就满足了, 但它刚站起来, 就被一只海豚击倒。海龟终于屈服了, 将四条腿缩进壳内。游戏到此结束。

Unit 3   Lesson 18

Comprehension 理解

Answer the following question:

Name one outstanding quality which porpoises possess.

Vocabulary 词汇

Refer to the text to see how the following words have been used, then write sentences of your own using these words: superstition (l.1); in defensive formation (l.2); motive (l.4); waterlogged (l.6); ensued (l.9); intrigued (l.10); constantly (l.10); shoving (l.12); sticking his snout (l.13); butts (l.16); recovers his equilibrium (l.16).

The paragraph 段落

A   Drawing your information from the second paragraph (lines 10-19) write a list of points in note form to answer the following question:

How does the author prove that the porpoise is intrigued with anything alive?

B   Read the first paragraph again (lines 1-9). Then, using the list of points given below, reconstruct the paragraph in your own words as far as possible. Do not refer to the passage until you have finished the exercise:

1   Superstition among mariners.
2   Porpoises will save drowning men or protect them—sharks.
3   Marine Studio biologists: probably not true.
4   Done out of curiosity or for sport.
5   E.g. pushing a mattress to the shore.
6   Saving men from sharks: porpoises and sharks: natural enemies.

C   Write a paragraph of about 200 words on one of the following subjects:

1   Dolphins.
2   Intelligence in animals.

Key structures 关键句型

A   Supply the correct form of the verbs in parentheses in the following paragraph. Do not refer to the passage until you have finished the exercise:

There has long been a superstition among mariners that porpoises _____ (save) drowning men by _____ (push) them to the surface, or _____ (protect) them from sharks by _____ (surround) them in defensive formation. Marine Studio biologists _____ (point) out that, however intelligent they may be, it _____ (be) probably a mistake to credit dolphins with any motive of lifesaving. On the occasions when they _____ (push) to shore an unconscious human being they much more likely _____ (do) it out of curiosity or for sport, as in _____ (ride) the bow waves of a ship. In 1928 some porpoises _____ (photograph) _____ (work) like beavers to push ashore a waterlogged mattress. If, as _____ (report), they _____ (protect) humans from sharks, it may have been because curiosity _____ (attract) them and because the scent of a possible meal _____ (attract) the sharks. Porpoises and sharks _____ (be) natural enemies. It _____ (be) possible that upon such an occasion a battle _____ (ensue) with the sharks _____ (drive) away or _____ (kill). (ll.1-9)

106

B   Note the form of the verb used after *enjoyed* in this sentence:

One young calf especially enjoyed *raising* a turtle to the surface. (ll.11-12)

Complete the following sentences using the construction given above:

1   I can't remember _____ .

2   You should avoid _____ .

3   Will you stop _____ ?

4   Fancy _____ !

5   I can't imagine him _____ .

6   Pardon my _____ ?

C   Study the following sentence:

He *no sooner* recovers his equilibrium *than* the next porpoise comes along and hits him another crack. (ll.16-17)

Write a sentence using the phrase *no sooner ... than*.

Special difficulties 难点

A   Study the following pairs of words and then write sentences of your own to bring out the difference.

1   drown (l.1) — choke

She must have swum too far out and drowned.

Something got stuck in my throat and I nearly choked.

2   unconscious (l.4) — insensitive

Someone fainted on the train today and remained unconscious for several minutes.

The two mothers chatted happily, quite unconscious of what their children were planning.

You have to be completely insensitive to other people, to play loud music in the street in the middle of the night.

3   curiosity (l.7) — strangeness

Curiosity killed the cat. (= wanting to know)

It took me a while to get used to the strangeness of my new school. (= the unfamiliar quality)

4   indignity (l.11) — disrespect

Pink and embarassed, she endured the indignity of being rescued from the mud in front of a party of tourists staring in silence.

To avoid any hint of disrespect, most countries sent their most senior officials to represent them at the President's funeral.

5   raise (l.11) — rise

Increased sales tax will raise prices.

We rise at six in the morning.

6   game (l.15) — play

Thousands of people packed the stadium to see the game.

Which is your favourite Shakespeare play?

7   eventually (l.17) — finally

Pneumonia eventually led to his death.

So you've finally decided to get married.

B   Explain the meaning of the words in italics:

1   They have much more *likely* done it out of curiosity or for sport. (l.5)

2   It's rather *unlikely* that he will come now.

Unit 3   Lesson 18

3   That's a *likely* story, I must say.

4   He's a *likely* person, I'm sure he'll help you.

C   Note the verb in italics:

A battle ensued, with the sharks being *driven away* or killed. (l.9)

Write sentences using the following expressions idiomatically: drive off; drive out; drive back; drive up.

D   Explain the verbs in italics:

1   They *are* constantly *after* the turtles. (ll.10-11)

2   The game *is over*. (l.19)

3   You can't see him now. *He's out*.

4   When will he *be back*?

5   Our team will not be playing next week. The match *is off*.

6   The fire *is out*.

7   What's *on* at the Regal today?

E   Explain the meaning of the verb in italics:

The turtle at last *gives up* by pulling his feet under his shell. (l.19)

Write sentences using the following expressions:

give oneself up; give off; give back.

Multiple choice questions 选择题

Choose the correct answers to the following questions.

Comprehension 理解

1   The writer of this piece probably _____ .

(*a*) doubts whether porpoises have a special relationship with humans

(*b*) believes that porpoises have a special interest in humans

(*c*) thinks that porpoises can't tell the difference between a human and a mattress

(*d*) thinks that porpoises are attracted by humans as a possible meal

2   The stories we hear about porpoises suggest that porpoises _____ .

(*a*) take a special interest in us

(*b*) are as intelligent as we are

(*c*) always save humans who are drowning

(*d*) always protect humans from sharks

3   Porpoises often give turtles a bad time because _____ .

(*a*) they are natural enemies

(*b*) they like to play

(*c*) turtles enjoy being badly treated

(*d*) they often share an oceanarium

108

4 One of these statements is true. Which one?

(*a*) Porpoises try to kill turtles by lifting their shells.

(*b*) Porpoises never allow turtles to stand up.

(*c*) Turtles seem to take part in this game played by porpoises.

(*d*) Turtles don't feel any pain when they're ill-treated by porpoises.

Structure 句型

5 The superstition among mariners _____ . (1.1)

(*a*) was very common   (*b*) has been very long   (*c*) existed long ago   (*d*) has lasted a long time

6 _____ intelligent they may be, it is a mistake to ... (1.3)

(*a*) Regardless that   (*b*) Whatever   (*c*) No matter how   (*d*) Whether

7 Whether it _____ bird, fish or beast, the porpoise is intrigued ... (1.10)

(*a*) were   (*b*) has been   (*c*) was   (*d*) is

8 Hardly has the turtle recovered his equilibrium _____ he is knocked down. (ll.16-17)

(*a*) but   (*b*) though   (*c*) when   (*d*) than

Vocabulary 词汇

9 The _____ of a possible meal attracted sharks. (1.8)

(*a*) odour   (*b*) perfume   (*c*) smell   (*d*) aroma

10 The porpoise is _____ with anything that is alive. (1.10)

(*a*) repelled   (*b*) attracted   (*c*) fascinated   (*d*) puzzled

11 One young calf especially enjoyed _____ a turtle to the surface. (ll.11-12)

(*a*) rising   (*b*) lifting   (*c*) arousing   (*d*) elevating

12 The first porpoise _____ down from above. (1.15)

(*a*) dives   (*b*) flies   (*c*) jumps   (*d*) falls

Lesson 19 The stuff of dreams   话说梦的本质

First listen and then answer the following question.

听录音，然后回答以下问题 。

What is going on when a person experiences rapid eye-movements during sleep?

It is fairly clear that the sleeping period must have some function, and because there is so much of it the function would seem to be important. Speculations about its nature have been going on for literally thousands of years, and one odd finding that makes the problem puzzling is that it looks very much as if sleeping is not simply a matter of giving the body a rest. 'Rest', in terms of muscle relaxation and so on, can
5 be achieved by a brief period lying, or even sitting down. The body's tissues are self-repairing and self-restoring to a degree, and function best when more or less continuously active. In fact a basic amount of movement occurs during sleep which is specifically concerned with preventing muscle inactivity.

   If it is not a question of resting the body, then perhaps it is the brain that needs resting? This might be a plausible hypothesis were it not for two factors. First the electroencephalograph (which is simply a device
10 for recording the electrical activity of the brain by attaching electrodes to the scalp) shows that while there is a change in the pattern of activity during sleep, there is no evidence that the total amount of activity is any less. The second factor is more interesting and more fundamental. Some years ago an American psychiatrist named William Dement published experiments dealing with the recording of eye-movements during sleep. He showed that the average individual's sleep cycle is punctuated with peculiar bursts of eye-movements,
15 some drifting and slow, others jerky and rapid. People woken during these periods of eye-movements generally reported that they had been dreaming. When woken at other times they reported no dreams. If one group of people were disturbed from their eye-movement sleep for several nights on end, and another group were disturbed for an equal period of time but when they were not exhibiting eye-movements, the first group began to show some personality disorders while the others seemed more or less unaffected. The
20 implications of all this were that it was not the disturbance of sleep that mattered, but the disturbance of dreaming.

CHRISTOPHER EVANS *The stuff of dreams* from *The Listener*

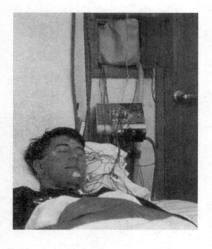

Circadian rhythm experiment. A patient is asleep in a sleep research laboratory. Electrodes are attached to his head to measure brainwaves.

New words and expressions 生词和短语

speculation (l.2) /ˌspekjʊˈleɪʃən/ n. 推测

literally (l.2) /ˈlɪtərəli/ adv. 确实

odd (l.3) /ɒd/ adj. 奇特的

tissue (l.5) /ˈtɪsjuː/ n. 组织

plausible (l.9) /ˈplɔːzəbəl/ adj. 似乎有理的

hypothesis (l.9) /haɪˈpɒθɪsɪs/ n. 假说

electroencephalograph (l.9) /ɪˌlektrəʊɪnˈsefələɡrɑːf/
　n. 脑电图仪

electrode (l.10) /ɪˈlektrəʊd/ n. 电极

scalp (l.10) /skælp/ n. 头皮

psychiatrist (l.12) /saɪˈkaɪətrɪst/ n. 精神病学家

punctuate (l.14) /ˈpʌŋktʃueɪt/ v. 不时介入

jerky (l.15) /ˈdʒɜːki/ adj. 急动的

disorder (l.19) /dɪsˈɔːdə/ n. 失调

implication (l.19) /ˌɪmplɪˈkeɪʃən/ n. 含意, 暗示

Notes on the text 课文注释

1　in terms of muscle relaxation and so on, 从使肌肉得到放松等方面来看。in terms of, 从 …… 方面看。

2　then perhaps it is the brain that needs resting? 这是个陈述句的语序, 但句尾加问号, 表示说话人对这种观点有把握但需进一步证实。

3　were it not for two factors, 这是省略了 if 的条件句, 可译作 "如果不是下面两个因素的话"。

4　several nights on end, 一连几夜。

参考译文

　　很清楚, 睡眠必然具有某种作用。睡眠占去那么多时间, 所以其作用似乎还很重要。人们对睡眠作用的种种猜测, 确实已有数千年之久。一项使人对这个问题感到困惑的奇怪的发现是, 睡眠在很大程度似乎并不仅仅是为了使身体得到休息。"休息", 从使肌肉得到放松等方面来看, 只要稍微躺一躺, 甚至坐一坐就能达到。人体组织在一定程度上有自我修补和自我恢复的能力, 有张有弛地连续活动时, 其功能最佳。事实上, 睡眠状态下仍有着基本的活动量, 以防止肌肉活动停止。

　　如果睡眠的功能不是在于使身体得到休息, 那么也许是让大脑得以休息? 若不是下面两点, 这种假设似乎是有道理的。第一点, 脑电图记录仪 (不过是一种把电极接到头皮上记录脑电活动的仪器) 显示, 人在睡眠时大脑活动的方式有变化, 但没有迹象表明, 其活动总量有任何减少。第二点更有意思, 也更重要。前些年, 美国一位名叫威廉 · 德门特的精神病学者发表了一项实验报告, 报告中记录了眼球在睡眠时的活动情况。他指出, 平常人的睡眠周期中不时伴有一阵阵奇怪的眼球活动, 这些活动有的飘忽而缓慢, 有的急剧而快速。在眼球活动期间被叫醒的人都说自己在做梦; 在其他时间叫醒他们, 则说没做梦。如果有两组人, 一组人连续几夜在眼球活动时被叫醒; 另一组人也是连续几夜被叫醒, 但是在眼球没活动时被叫醒的。结果, 第一组人开始出现性格失常, 而第二组人似乎没受什么影响。这一切暗示我们: 睡眠受到干扰没关系, 而做梦受到干扰是有问题的。

Comprehension 理解

Answer these questions:

1　How does the author disprove the idea that we sleep in order to rest our muscles?

2　What is the relationship between eye-movements during sleep and dreaming?

Vocabulary 词汇

Refer to the text to see how the following words have been used, then write sentences of your own using these words: function (l.1); speculations (l.2); specifically (l.7); plausible hypothesis (l.9); evidence (l.11); fundamental (l.12); punctuated (l.14); jerky and rapid (l.15); implications (l.19).

Unit 3   Lesson 19

The paragraph 段落

1   Drawing your information from the second paragraph (lines 8-21), write a list of points in note form to answer the following question: What appears to be the main function of the sleeping period?

2   Read the first paragraph again (lines 1-7). Then, using the list of points given below, reconstruct the paragraph in your own words as far as possible. Do not refer to the passage until you have finished the exercise:

a   We sleep a great deal: sleep must have a function.

b   Problem has puzzled mankind for thousands of years.

c   Purpose of sleep is not to give the body a rest.

d   We do not have to sleep to relax the muscles: this can be done by lying or sitting down for short periods.

e   Body tissues function best when muscles are active.

f   Movement occurs during sleep to prevent muscle inactivity.

3   Write a paragraph of about 200 words on one of the following subjects:

a   Briefly describe a dream you had and attempt to interpret it.

b   Sleep.

Key structures 关键句型

A   Supply the missing words in the following sentences. Do not refer to the passage until you have finished the exercise:

1   Speculations _____ its nature have been going on _____ literally thousands _____ years. (ll. 2-3)

2   In fact a basic amount _____ movement occurs _____ sleep which is specifically concerned _____ preventing muscle inactivity. (ll.6-7)

3   Some years ago an American psychiatrist named William Dement published experiments dealing _____ the recording _____ eye-movements _____ sleep. (ll.12-13)

4   If one group _____ people were disturbed _____ their eye-movement sleep _____ several nights _____ end, and another group were disturbed _____ an equal period _____ time. (ll.16-18)

B   Note the use of *for* in this sentence:

Speculations about its nature have been going on *for* literally thousands of years. (ll.2-3)

Supply *for* or *since* in the following sentences:

1   He has been going to work regularly _____ he recovered from his illness.

2   They have been working overtime _____ several months.

3   The election results have been coming in steadily _____ midnight.

4   She's been working on her novel _____ the beginning of the year.

C   Study this sentence:

Perhaps it is the brain that needs resting? (l.8)

Write similar sentences using the verbs *want* or *need* with the following words: cleaning; mending; decorating.

112

D　Compare these two sentences:

Instead of saying:　This might be a plausible hypothesis *were it not* for two factors. (ll.8-9)

We can say:　　　This might be a plausible hypothesis *if it* were not for two factors.

Rewrite the following sentences using *if* :

1　Were it possible, I would leave tomorrow.

2　I would take action at once were it not too late.

3　Were this allegation true, he would be arrested.

Special difficulties 难点

A　Study the following pairs of words and then write sentences of your own to bring out the difference.

1　fairly (l.1) — enough

The water is fairly warm.

The water is warm enough to swim in.

2　puzzling (l.3) — confusing

The children showed a puzzling lack of curiosity about where their parents were.

The instructions are so confusing that I can't work out what they're saying.

3　factor (l.12) — fact

The rise in crime is mainly due to social and economic factors.

It is a fact that most deaths from lung cancer are caused by smoking.

B　Explain the meaning of the verbs in italics in these sentences:

1　William Dement published experiments *dealing with* the recording of eye-movements. (l.13)

2　We have been *dealing with* the same firm for a number of years.

3　He's an extremely difficult child. His father is the only person who knows how to *deal with* him.

C　Explain the meaning of the phrases in italics in these sentences:

1　If one group of people were disturbed from their eye-movement sleep for several nights *on end* ... (ll.16-17)

2　It wasn't an accident. That window was broken *on purpose*.

3　*On the whole*, business has been very good this year.

4　The doctor's very tired. He's been *on duty* for fourteen hours.

5　How many soldiers are *on leave*?

6　You mustn't open the door *on any account* when I'm out.

7　It's getting late. I must be *on my way*.

Multiple choice questions 选择题

Choose the correct answers to the following questions.

Comprehension 理解

1 Giving the body a rest _____ .

(*a*) seems to be the main function of sleep

(*b*) doesn't seem to be the main function of sleep

(*c*) means that sleep must have some function

(*d*) prevents muscle inactivity

2 Electrical activity _____ .

    (*a*) is a good indication of the way the body rests during sleep

    (*b*) doesn't seem to diminish during sleep

    (*c*) is a plausible explanation for the function of sleep

    (*d*) must always be recorded during sleep

3 Rapid eye-movements are an indication that _____ .

    (*a*) a person is having a disturbed sleep

    (*b*) sleep is very deep

    (*c*) a sleeper is dreaming

    (*d*) a person is drifting into sleep

4 One of these statements is true. Which one?

    (*a*) The most important function of sleep is dreaming.

    (*b*) Rapid eye-movement is associated with deep sleep.

    (*c*) People who experience rapid eye-movements show personality disorders.

    (*d*) When people are woken, they don't report any dreams.

Structure 句型

5 _____ have speculations gone on? – For thousands of years. (ll.2-3)

    (*a*) How many   (*b*) How often   (*c*) How much   (*d*) How long

6 The body's tissues can repair _____ .

    (*a*) themselves   (*b*) their self   (*c*) itself   (*d*) them

7 Peculiar bursts of eye-movements _____ an individual's sleep. (1.14)

    (*a*) punctuate   (*b*) is punctuating   (*c*) are punctuating   (*d*) have punctuated

8 People woken during these periods of eye-movements generally reported that they had been dreaming _____ . (ll.15-16)

    (*a*) for a while   (*b*) during sleep

    (*c*) before they went to sleep   (*d*) just this moment

Vocabulary 词汇

9 Speculations have been going on for thousands of years _____ . (ll.2-3)

    (*a*) so to speak   (*b*) in history   (*c*) and recorded   (*d*) in fact

10 This might be a plausible _____ . (ll.8-9)

    (*a*) conclusion   (*b*) deduction   (*c*) philosophy   (*d*) theory

11 The second factor is more interesting and more _____ . (1.13)

    (*a*) obvious   (*b*) basic   (*c*) apparent   (*d*) acceptable

12 Some eye-movements were slow, others _____ and rapid. (1.15)

    (*a*) smooth, quick   (*b*) interrupted

    (*c*) sudden, irregular   (*d*) painful, repeated

Lesson 20 Snake poison 蛇毒

🔊 **First listen and then answer the following question.**
听录音,然后回答以下问题 。
What are the two different ways in which snake poison acts?

How it came about that snakes manufactured poison is a mystery. Over the periods their saliva, a mild, digestive juice like our own, was converted into a poison that defies analysis even today. It was not forced upon them by the survival competition; they could have caught and lived on prey without using poison, just as the thousands of non-poisonous snakes still do. Poison to a snake is merely a luxury; it enables it to get its
5 food with very little effort, no more effort than one bite. And why only snakes? Cats, for instance, would be greatly helped; no running fights with large, fierce rats or tussles with grown rabbits—just a bite and no more effort needed. In fact, it would be an assistance to all carnivores though it would be a two-edged weapon when they fought each other. But, of the vertebrates, unpredictable Nature selected only snakes (and one lizard). One wonders also why Nature, with some snakes, concocted poison of such extreme potency.

10   In the conversion of saliva into poison, one might suppose that a fixed process took place. It did not; some snakes manufactured a poison different in every respect from that of others, as different as arsenic is from strychnine, and having different effects. One poison acts on the nerves, the other on the blood.

The makers of the nerve poison include the mambas and the cobras and their venom is called neurotoxic. Vipers (adders) and rattlesnakes manufacture the blood poison, which is known as haemolytic. Both poisons
15 are unpleasant, but by far the more unpleasant is the blood poison. It is said that the nerve poison is the more primitive of the two, that the blood poison is, so to speak, a newer product from an improved formula. Be that as it may, the nerve poison does its business with man far more quickly than the blood poison. This, however, means nothing. Snakes did not acquire their poison for use against man but for use against prey such as rats and mice, and the effects on these of viperine poison is almost immediate.

JOHN CROMPTON *The snake*

New words and expressions 生词和短语

saliva (1.1) /sə'laɪvə/ *n.* 唾液
digestive (1.2) /daɪ'dʒestɪv/ *adj.* 助消化的
defy (1.2) /dɪ'faɪ/ *v.* 使不可能
analysis (1.2) /ə'næləsɪs/ *n.* 分析
prey (1.3) /preɪ/ *n.* 被捕食的动物
fierce (1.6) /fɪəs/ *adj.* 凶猛的
tussle (1.6) /'tʌsəl/ *n.* 扭打
carnivore (1.7) /'kɑːnɪvɔː/ *n.* 食肉动物
vertebrate (1.8) /'vɜːtɪbrɪt/ *n.* 脊椎动物
lizard (1.9) /'lɪzəd/ *n.* 蜥蜴
concoct (1.9) /kən'kɒkt/ *v.* 调制
potency (1.10) /'pəʊtənsi/ *n.* 效力

conversion (1.10) /kən'vɜːʃən/ *n.* 转变
arsenic (1.11) /'ɑːsnɪk/ *n.* 砒霜
strychnine (1.12) /'strɪkniːn/ *n.* 马钱子碱
mamba (1.13) /'mæmbə/ *n.* 树眼镜蛇
cobra (1.13) /'kəʊbrə/ *n.* 眼镜蛇
venom (1.13) /'venəm/ *n.* 毒液
neurotoxic (1.13) /ˌnjʊərəʊ'tɒksɪk/ *adj.* 毒害神经的
viper (1.14) /'vaɪpə/ *n.* 蝰蛇
adder (1.14) /'ædə/ *n.* 蝮蛇
rattlesnake (1.14) /'rætlsneɪk/ *n.* 响尾蛇
haemolytic (1.14) /ˌhiːməʊ'lɪtɪk/ *adj.* 溶血性的
viperine (1.19) /'vaɪpəraɪn/ *adj.* 毒蛇的

An Indian grass snake swallowing a frog

Notes on the text 课文注释

1 How it came about that snakes ... a mystery.

这句话的主语是一个句子: How it came about that snakes manufactured poison, 谓语部分是 is a mystery 。主语从句中的 it 是形式主语, 真正主语是 that snakes manufactured poison, 因为主语太长, 所以使用 it 作先行主语的结构 。

2 over the periods, 经过很长时间 。

3 live on, 靠 …… 生活 。

4 a two-edged weapon, 一把双刃刀, 这里的意思是: 如果食肉动物都有毒液, 就会造成食肉动物之间的互相残杀 。

5 act on, 对 …… 起作用 。

6 by far the more unpleasant, 更难受得多, by far 是 " …… 得多" 的意思 。

7 so to speak, 插入语, 有 "可以这样说", "打个比方说" 的意思 。

8 Be that as it may, 这是一个倒装的让步状语从句, 相当于 however that may be, 可译成 "尽管如此" 。

9 does its business with man, 在人的身上发挥作用, 要人的命 。

10 the effects on these of viperine poison, these 是指 rats and mice, 介词宾语结构 of viperine poison 是作 effects 的定语 。

参考译文

　　蛇是怎样产生毒液的, 这是一个谜 。蛇的唾液本来和我们人的消化液一样柔和, 但经过漫长的时间, 演变成了今天仍无法分析清楚的毒液 。毒液不是生存竞争强加给它们的, 它们也可以不用毒液捕捉动物而生存, 就像今天成千上万的无毒蛇那样 。毒液对毒蛇来说只不过是一种舒适生存的优越手段, 它能使蛇不用费多大力气就能捕获到食物, 轻咬一口即可 。为什么只有蛇才有毒液呢? 譬如说, 如果猫有毒液, 那对猫会大有帮助, 它就不必再和又大又凶的老鼠边跑边搏斗了, 也不必再和大兔子扭斗了, 只要咬一口, 就不必再费力气了 。事实上, 任何食肉动物有了毒液, 都能从中获益 。不过, 当它们相互撕打时, 毒液就成了利弊参半的武器, 可以杀死对方, 也可以被对方的毒液杀死 。然而, 在脊椎动物中, 大自然神秘莫测地只选择了蛇 (还有一种蜥蜴), 人们还弄不清大自然为什么在某些蛇身上调制出如此高效的毒液来 。

人们可能认为，唾液转变成毒液，其中有固定的程序。其实没有。有些蛇产生的毒液在各方面与另外一些毒蛇产生的毒液不相同，就像砒霜不同于马钱子碱一样。不同毒蛇的毒液产生的效果也不同，一种毒液作用于神经，另一种毒液作用于血液。

产生神经毒液的蛇有一种非洲树眼镜蛇和眼镜蛇，它们的毒液称为神经毒素。蝰蛇（蝮蛇）和响尾蛇产生血液毒素，称为溶血性毒液。这两种毒液都很可怕，但溶血性毒液尤其厉害。据说，神经毒液在两种毒液中是较为原始的一种，而溶血性毒液，打个比方说，是根据改良配方生产出的一种较新的产品。不过，神经毒液比溶血性毒液在人身上起作用快得多。但是，这没什么关系，因为蛇有毒液不是用来对付人的，而是对付它的猎物，诸如鼠类，毒液对这些猎物会立刻起作用。

Comprehension 理解

Answer these questions:

1 Why does the author find it odd that snakes should be capable of manufacturing poison?
2 What is the difference between neurotoxic and haemolytic poison?

Vocabulary 词汇

Refer to the text to see how the following words have been used, then write sentences of your own using these words: mild (l.1); converted (l.2); defies analysis (l.2); the survival competition (l.3); carnivore (l.7); a two-edged weapon (ll.7-8); concocted (l.9); extreme potency (l.9); viperine (l.19).

The paragraph 段落

A Drawing your information from the first paragraph (lines 1-9), write a list of points in note form to answer the following question: Why is the author justified in stating that Nature behaved in an unpredictable way in allowing snakes to manufacture poison?

B Read the last paragraph again (lines 13-19). Then, using the list of points given below, reconstruct the paragraph in your own words as far as possible. Do not refer to the passage until you have finished the exercise.

1 Nerve poison (e.g. mambas): neurotoxic.
2 Blood poison (e.g. vipers): haemolytic.
3 Blood poison the more unpleasant.
4 Nerve poison possibly the more primitive.
5 Blood poison a later development.
6 But nerve poison acts more quickly on man.
7 Purpose of poison: not against man, but snake's prey: e.g. rats.

C Write a paragraph of about 200 words on one of the following subjects:
1 Our fear of snakes.
2 The survival competition.

Key structures 关键句型

A   Compare these two sentences:

Instead of saying: *They had the ability to catch and live* on prey without using poison if they wanted to (but they didn't).

We can say: *They could have caught and lived* on prey without using poison. (1.3)

Write sentences using the following expressions:

could have succeeded; could have stayed; could have bought.

B   Write sentences using the following expressions:

force upon (ll.2-3); live on (l.3); conversion into (l.10); different from (l.11); act on (l.12); effect on (l.19).

C   Compare these two sentences:

Instead of saying: They could have caught and lived on prey without using poison, just as the thousands of non-poisonous snakes still *catch and live on prey without using poison*.

We can say: They could have caught and lived on prey without using poison, just as the thousands of non-poisonous snakes still *do*. (ll.3-4)

Complete the following sentences by adding the correct form of *do*:

1   Even though he has retired, he still gets up early just as he always _____ .

2   He certainly enjoys music as much as you _____ .

3   If you act as he _____ you won't be very popular.

D   Study the following sentence:

Both poisons are unpleasant, but by far *the more unpleasant* is the blood poison. (ll.14-15)

Why is *the more* used here and not *the most*?

Write two sentences using *the more* and *the most*.

E   Note how the word *far* has been added for emphasis in this sentence: Nerve poison does its business ... *far more quickly* than ... (l.17)

The word *much* may be used in the same way. We can say *much more quickly*, using *much* in an emphatic way.

Write sentences using the following phrases: much more expensive; far more difficult; far less exciting; much less interesting.

Special difficulties 难点

A   Study the following pairs of words and then write sentences of your own to bring out the difference.

1   merely (1.4) — only

I'm not blaming you. I'm merely trying to find out how this happened.

Only the head of the department can authorize a withdrawal from a course.

2   fierce (1.6) — furious

You can see armed guards along the border accompanied by fierce dogs.

He was terribly annoyed. Indeed, he was furious!

3   take place (1.10) — take part

All these events took place before you were born.

How many of you are taking part in the play?

4   prey (1.3) — pray

The tiger seized its prey and tore it into pieces.

You've done your best. All you can do now is pray for success.

B   Explain the verbs in italics in the following:

1   How it *came about* that snakes manufacture poison is a mystery. (1.1)

2   I'm sorry I said that. I don't know what *came over* me.

3   He *came up with* some very interesting ideas.

4   I *came across* an old friend of yours while I was abroad.

C   Write sentences using the following words and phrases: enable (1.4); running fights (1.6); in fact (1.7); in every respect (1.11); so to speak (1.16); be that as it may (ll.16-17).

D   Supply full stops and commas where necessary in the following paragraph. Do not refer to the passage until you have finished the exercise:

The makers of the nerve poison include the mambas and the cobras and their venom is called neurotoxic vipers (adders) and rattlesnakes manufacture the blood poison which is known as haemolytic both poisons are unpleasant but by far the more unpleasant is the blood poison it is said that the nerve poison is the more primitive of the two that the blood poison is so to speak a newer product from an improved formula be that as it may the nerve poison does its business with man far more quickly than the blood poison this however means nothing snakes did not acquire their poison for use against man but for use against prey such as rats and mice and the effects on these of viperine poison is almost immediate. (ll.13-19)

Multiple choice questions 选择题

Choose the correct answers to the following questions.

Comprehension 理解

1   One of these statements is true. Which one?

(*a*) Snakes need poison to digest their food.

(*b*) Snakes can feed on other animals without the use of poison.

(*c*) Non-poisonous snakes find survival more difficult than poisonous ones.

(*d*) All snakes are capable of manufacturing poison.

2   The possession of poison in the saliva makes hunting _____ .

(*a*) easy for all carnivores

(*b*) a two-edged weapon when carnivores fight each other

(*c*) almost effortless for snakes

(*d*) unpredictable, as Nature intended

3 The poison that acts on the blood _____ .

   (*a*) acts less rapidly than nerve poison

   (*b*) doesn't affect the victim as badly as nerve poison

   (*c*) is made by snakes like mambas and cobras

   (*d*) was probably the first of the two kinds of poison to be developed

4 Human beings _____ .

   (*a*) can't compare with prey such as rats and mice

   (*b*) respond to all snake poisons in the same way

   (*c*) are likely to survive nerve poison but not blood poison

   (*d*) are not the intended victims of snake poison

Structure 句型

5 They _____ have been able to catch and live on prey without using poison. (1.3)

   (*a*) might   (*b*) should   (*c*) would   (*d*) must

6 They could have caught and lived on prey without _____ poison. (1.3)

   (*a*) to use   (*b*) use   (*c*) the use of   (*d*) have used

7 For _____ snakes, poison is merely a luxury. (1.4)

   (*a*) these   (*b*) a   (*c*) -   (*d*) an

8 Blood poison is the more unpleasant _____ . (1.15)

   (*a*) of them all   (*b*) of the two   (*c*) in the world   (*d*) among them both

Vocabulary 词汇

9 Saliva is a natural _____ . (ll.1-2)

   (*a*) oil in the body   (*b*) snake-poison   (*c*) digestive process   (*d*) body fluid

10 Poison would be _____ to all carnivores. (1.7)

   (*a*) an asset   (*b*) a help   (*c*) a necessity   (*d*) a disadvantage

11 Arsenic and strychnine _____ us in different ways. (1.ll.11-12)

   (*a*) effect   (*b*) result   (*c*) affect   (*d*) cause

12 The nerve poison is thought to be _____ (ll.15-16)

   (*a*) less highly developed   (*b*) more potent

   (*c*) more recent   (*d*) less complicated

Lesson 21　William S. Hart and the early 'Western' film
威廉·S.哈特和早期"西部"影片

📼 **First listen and then answer the following question.**

听录音，然后回答以下问题。

How did William Hart's childhood prepare him for his acting role in Western films?

William S. Hart was, perhaps, the greatest of all Western stars, for unlike Gary Cooper and John Wayne he appeared in nothing but Westerns. From 1914 to 1924 he was supreme and unchallenged. It was Hart who created the basic formula of the Western film, and devised the protagonist he played in every film he made, the good-bad man, the accidental-noble outlaw, or the honest-but-framed cowboy, or the sheriff made
5　suspect by vicious gossip; in short, the individual in conflict with himself and his frontier environment.

Unlike most of his contemporaries in Hollywood, Hart actually knew something of the old West. He had lived in it as a child when it was already disappearing, and his hero was firmly rooted in his memories and experiences, and in both the history and the mythology of the vanished frontier. And although no period or place in American history has been more absurdly romanticized, myth and reality did join hands in at least
10　one arena, the conflict between the individual and encroaching civilization.

Men accustomed to struggling for survival against the elements and Indians were bewildered by politicians, bankers and businessmen, and unhorsed by fences, laws and alien taboos. Hart's good-bad man was always an outsider, always one of the disinherited, and if he found it necessary to shoot a sheriff or rob a bank along the way, his early audiences found it easy to understand and forgive, especially when it was
15　Hart who, in the end, overcame the attacking Indians.

Audiences in the second decade of the twentieth century found it pleasant to escape to a time when life, though hard, was relatively simple. We still do; living in a world in which undeclared aggression, war, hypocrisy, chicanery, anarchy and impending immolation are part of our daily lives, we all want a code to live by.

CARL FOREMAN *Virtue and a Fast Gun* from *The Observer*

New words and expressions 生词和短语

supreme (1.2) /suːˈpriːm/ *adj.* 首屈一指的
protagonist (1.3) /prəʊˈtægənɪst/ *n.* 主角
outlaw (1.4) /ˈaʊtlɔː/ *n.* 逃犯，亡命之徒
framed (1.4) /freɪmd/ *adj.* 遭到陷害的
vicious (1.5) /ˈvɪʃəs/ *adj.* 恶毒的
mythology (1.8) /mɪˈθɒlədʒi/ *n.* 神话
vanished (1.8) /ˈvænɪʃd/ *adj.* 消失了的
absurdly (1.9) /əbˈsɜːdli/ *adv.* 荒诞地
arena (1.10) /əˈriːnə/ *n.* 竞技场地
encroaching (1.10) /ɪnˈkrəʊtʃɪŋ/ *adj.* 渐渐渗入的
Indian (1.11) /ˈɪndiən/ *n.* 印第安人

bewilder (1.11) /bɪˈwɪldə/ *v.* 使手足无措
alien (1.12) /ˈeɪliən/ *adj.* 外来的
taboo (1.12) /təˈbuː/ *n.* 戒律
disinherit (1.13) /ˌdɪsɪnˈherɪt/ *v.* 剥夺……继承权
undeclared (1.17) /ˌʌndɪˈkleəd/ *adj.* 未经宣布的
hypocrisy (1.18) /hɪˈpɒkrɪsi/ *n.* 伪善
chicanery (1.18) /ʃɪˈkeɪnəri/ *n.* 诈骗
impending (1.18) /ɪmˈpendɪŋ/ *adj.* 迫近的，迫在眉睫的
immolation (1.18) /ˌɪməˈleɪʃən/ *n.* 杀戮
code (1.18) /kəʊd/ *n.* 准则

William S. Hart in an early Western

Notes on the text 课文注释

1　nothing but, 仅仅, 只是 。
2　in short, 总而言之, 一句话 。
3　the old West, 指密西西比河以西地区 。
4　be rooted in, 生根于 。
5　join hands, 携手联合 。
6　live by, 靠 …… 过活 。

参考译文

　　威廉·S.哈特大概是美国西部电影明星中的佼佼者 。他和加里·古柏 、约翰·韦恩不同, 他只在西部电影中扮演角色 。在 1914 年至 1924 年期间, 他首屈一指, 独霸影坛 。正是他创造了西部电影的基调, 即在他自己拍摄的影片中他所塑造的主人公的形象: 被认为是坏人的好人, 出人意料的高尚的逃犯, 诚实却遭陷害的牛仔, 或因流言蜚语蒙受嫌疑的司法官 。总之, 主人公是一个自相矛盾, 又与他的拓荒环境相矛盾的人物 。

　　哈特与大部分同时代在好莱坞的演员不同, 他确实了解西部早期拓荒生活的一些情况 。作为一个孩子他曾在西部生活过, 当时西部拓荒生活正在消失 。他塑造的英雄人物深深地扎根于他本人的记忆和经历之中, 也扎根于有关已经消失的拓荒生活的历史和神话之中 。虽然在美国历史上没有任何时期或地区像西部拓荒时期那样被荒谬地浪漫主义化了, 但神话和事实至少在某一个舞台上共存, 也就是存在于个人与渐渐闯入的文明这两者的冲突之中 。

　　习惯与大自然和印第安人作斗争以求生存的拓荒者被政客 、银行家和商人搞得晕头转向, 最后被圈地 、法律和外来的清规戒律所击败 。哈特扮演的被误认为坏人的好人总是一个局外人, 总是一个被剥夺继承权的人 。如果他认为在进行过程中有必要枪击一个司法官或抢劫一个银行, 他的早期观众很容易接受, 觉得应原谅他, 特别是当哈特最后战胜了前来进攻的印第安人时, 观众更能原谅他 。

　　生活在 20 世纪 20 年代的观众认为, 逃到一个即使艰苦但比较简朴的时代中去是件愉快的事, 我们今天仍有这种感觉 。如今, 不宣而战的侵略 、战争 、虚伪 、诈骗 、无政府状态以及即将临头的毁灭成了我们日常生活的一部分, 我们都希望有一个赖以生存的行为准则 。

Comprehension 理解

Answer these questions:

1　What, according to the writer, is the basic formula of the Western film?
2　How did the spread of civilization affect the old West?
3　Why have Western films appealed so much to twentieth-century audiences?

Vocabulary 词汇

Refer to the text to see how the following words have been used, then write sentences of your own using these words: supreme (1.2); devised the protagonist (1.3); framed (1.4); in conflict (1.5); environment (1.5); contemporaries (1.6); firmly rooted (1.7); encroaching (1.10); bewildered (1.11); impending immolation (1.18).

The paragraph 段落

A　Drawing your information from the first three paragraphs (lines 1-15), write a list of points in note form to answer the following question: With what justification can the claim be made that William S. Hart was, perhaps, the greatest of all Western stars?

B　Read the fourth paragraph again (lines 16-19). Then, using the list of points given below, reconstruct the paragraph in your own words as far as possible. Do not refer to the passage until you have finished the exercise:

1　Audiences—2nd decade 20th century—escape: appeal of hard and simple life.
2　We still do: world of aggression, hypocrisy—want a code to live by.

C　Write a paragraph of about 200 words on one of the following subjects:

1　A short appreciation of any actor or actress who took part in a Western film you have seen.
2　Westerns.

Key structures 关键句型

A　Which words could be omitted from the following sentences without affecting the sense of the original? Do not refer to the passage until you have finished the exercise:

1　It was Hart who created the basic formula of the Western film, and devised the protagonist whom he played in every film which he made, the good-bad man, the accidental-noble outlaw, or the honest-but-framed cowboy, or the sheriff who has been made suspect by vicious gossip; in short, the individual who is in conflict with himself and with his frontier environment. (ll.2-5)
2　Men who had been accustomed to struggling for survival against the elements and Indians were bewildered by politicians, bankers and businessmen. (ll.11-12)

B　Compare these sentences:

Instead of saying:　He appeared *only* in Westerns.
We can say:　　　　He appeared in *nothing but* Westerns. (ll.1-2)
Or:　　　　　　　　He *did not appear* in *anything but* Westerns.

Write three sentences using the phrase *nothing but*.

C   Supply *a* or *the* where necessary in the following paragraph. Do not refer to the passage until you have finished the exercise:

Unlike _____ most of _____ his contemporaries in _____ Hollywood, _____ Hart actually knew something of _____ old West. He had lived in it as _____ child when it was already disappearing, and _____ his hero was firmly rooted in _____ his memories and _____ experiences, and in both _____ history and _____ mythology of _____ vanished frontier. And although no period or place in _____ American history has been more absurdly romanticized, _____ myth and _____ reality did join hands in at least one arena, _____ conflict between _____ individual and _____ encroaching civilization. (ll.6-10)

D   Note the form of the verb in this sentence:

Myth and reality *did join* hands in at least one arena. (ll.9-10)

We use this form when we wish to place particular emphasis on the verb.

Write these sentences again using this emphatic verb form:

1   I *mentioned* it to him but he wasn't impressed.
2   You *posted* my letter, didn't you?
3   We *enjoyed* ourselves at the party.

E   Compare these two uses of *though:*

Life, *though* (even if it was) hard, was relatively simple. (ll.16-17)

I wish you had told me *though*. (however)

Write two sentences using *though* in the ways shown above.

F   Compare these two sentences:

Instead of saying: We all want a code *by which to live*.

We can say: We all want a code *to live by*. (ll.18-19)

Write sentences which end with the following expressions:

to fight for; to talk about; to act on; to work with.

Special difficulties 难点

A   Study the following pairs of words and then write sentences of your own to bring out the difference.

1   appear (l.2) — seem

Wayne Sleep is appearing in 'Song and Dance.' (= can be seen)

He appeared from nowhere. (= came into view)

It appears/seems odd that he hasn't written to any of us. (= is or may be)

2   devise (l.3) — device

Can you devise a solution to this problem?

An encephalograph is a device for measuring brain activity.

3   suspect (l.5) — suspicious

Police blew up the suspect package.

If travellers look nervous, customs officers get suspicious.

4   memory (l.7) — remembrance

My memory is not as good as it used to be.

This ring is the only remembrance I have of my grandmother.

5   history (1.8) — story

We often know little about the history of our own times.

Climb into bed and I'll read you a bedtime story.

6   rob (1.13) — steal

I lost my address book when the man robbed me of my bag.

The man who stole my handbag took my address book as well.

B   Note this use of *unlike:*

Unlike Gary Cooper and John Wayne he appeared in nothing but Westerns. (ll.1-2)

Complete the following sentences in any way you wish:

1   Unlike most of his contemporaries long dashes (1.6)

2   Unlike some people long dashes

3   Unlike yourself long dashes

C   Write sentences using the following phrases:

in short (1.5); in conflict with (1.5); at least (1.9); in the end (1.15).

Multiple choice questions 选择题

Choose the correct answers to the following questions.

Comprehension 理解

1   The basis of Western films, as defined by William S. Hart, is _____ .

(*a*) contrast

(*b*) conflict

(*c*) evil

(*d*) outlaws

2   William S. Hart's understanding of the West was _____ .

(*a*) absurdly romanticized

(*b*) influenced by his contemporaries in Hollywood

(*c*) part of history and mythology

(*d*) based on direct personal experience

3   The basic theme of early Western films _____ .

(*a*) concerned survival against Indians

(*b*) was about the clash between civilization and Nature

(*c*) was not appreciated by early audiences

(*d*) was about inheritance

4   The passage suggests that audiences, past and present, like _____ .

(*a*) stories about civilization

(*b*) simple living and simple rules

(*c*) impending catastrophe

(*d*) war and bad behaviour

Unit 3   Lesson 21

Structure 句型

5 William S. Hart appeared in nothing _____ Westerns. (ll.1-2)

   (*a*) except   (*b*) although   (*c*) only   (*d*) apart

6 Hart devised the protagonist _____ he played in every film. (1.3)

   (*a*) whom   (*b*) which   (*c*) what   (*d*) where

7 Hart actually knew something about the old West _____ he had lived as a child. (ll.6-7)

   (*a*) to whom   (*b*) which   (*c*) in it   (*d*) in which

8 _____ no period has been more absurdly romanticized, myth and reality did join hands in at least one arena. (ll.8-10)

   (*a*) As   (*b*) Because   (*c*) When   (*d*) While

Vocabulary 词汇

9 Hart devised the _____ he played in every film. (ll.2-3)

   (*a*) leading part   (*b*) fighter   (*c*) cowboy   (*d*) first person

10 His hero was rooted in the mythology of a frontier that had _____ . (ll.7-8)

   (*a*) expanded   (*b*) disappeared   (*c*) become established (*d*) changed

11 This period has been romanticized in _____ fashion. (ll.8-9)

   (*a*) an exaggerated (*b*) a realistic   (*c*) a ridiculous   (*d*) an amusing

12 Men accustomed to struggling for survival were _____ by politicians. (1.11)

   (*a*) confused   (*b*) surrounded   (*c*) pursued   (*d*) welcomed

Lesson 22　Knowledge and progress　知识和进步

First listen and then answer the following question.

听录音，然后回答以下问题 。

In what two areas have people made no 'progress' at all?

Why does the idea of progress loom so large in the modern world? Surely because progress of a particular kind is actually taking place around us and is becoming more and more manifest. Although mankind has undergone no general improvement in intelligence or morality, it has made extraordinary progress in the accumulation of knowledge. Knowledge began to increase as soon as the thoughts of one individual could
5　be communicated to another by means of speech. With the invention of writing, a great advance was made, for knowledge could then be not only communicated but also stored. Libraries made education possible, and education in its turn added to libraries: the growth of knowledge followed a kind of compound interest law, which was greatly enhanced by the invention of printing. All this was comparatively slow until, with the coming of science, the *tempo* was suddenly raised. Then knowledge began to be accumulated according to a
10　systematic plan. The trickle became a stream; the stream has now become a torrent. Moreover, as soon as new knowledge is acquired, it is now turned to practical account. What is called 'modern civilization' is not the result of a balanced development of all man's nature, but of accumulated knowledge applied to practical life. The problem now facing humanity is: What is going to be done with all this knowledge? As is so often pointed out, knowledge is a two-edged weapon which can be used equally for good or evil. It is now being
15　used indifferently for both. Could any spectacle, for instance, be more grimly whimsical than that of gunners using science to shatter men's bodies while, close at hand, surgeons use it to restore them? We have to ask ourselves very seriously what will happen if this twofold use of knowledge, with its ever-increasing power, continues.

G. N. M. Tyrrell *The Personality of Man*

A military field-hospital

127

New words and expressions 生词和短语

loom (l.1) /luːm/ v. 赫然耸起
manifest (l.2) /'mænɪfest/ adj. 明显的
morality (l.3) /mə'rælɪti/ n. 道德
communicate (l.5) /kə'mjuːnɪkeɪt/ v. 交流, 交际
compound (l.7) /'kɒmpaʊnd/ adj. 复合的
enhance (l.8) /ɪn'hɑːns/ v. 增进
tempo (l.9) /'tempəʊ/ n. 速度
trickle (l.10) /'trɪkəl/ n. 涓涓细流

torrent (l.10) /'tɒrənt/ n. 滔滔洪流
humanity (l.13) /hjuː'mænɪti/ n. 人类
indifferently (l.15) /ɪn'dɪfərəntli/ adv. 不在乎地
grimly (l.15) /'grɪmli/ adv. 可怖地
whimsical (l.15) /'wɪmzɪkəl/ adj. 怪诞的
shatter (l.16) /'ʃætə/ v. 毁坏
twofold (l.17) /'tuːfəʊld/ adj. 双重的

Notes on the text 课文注释

1　with the invention of writing, 短语中的 with 是 "由于" 的意思 。
2　education in its turn added to libraries, 教育反过来也丰富了藏书 。
3　a kind of compound interest law, 一种复利法则 。compound interest law 有时也被称作 "雪球法则", 即利上滚利, 增长很快 。
4　turn ... to account, 利用 …… 。
5　Could any spectacle, ... to restore them? 这句话从形式上是个疑问句, 但实质上起一个加强语气的陈述句的作用, 这种疑问句常被称为修辞疑问句 。

参考译文

　　为什么进步这个概念在现代世界显得如此突出? 无疑是因为有一种特殊的进步实际上正在我们周围发生, 而且变得越来越明显 。虽然人类在智力和道德上没有得到普遍提高, 但在知识积累方面却取得了巨大的进步 。人一旦能用语言同别人交流思想, 知识的积累便开始了 。随着书写的发明, 又迈进了一大步, 因为这样一来, 知识不仅能交流, 而且能储存了 。藏书使教育成为可能, 而教育反过来又丰富了藏书, 因为知识的增长遵循着一种 "雪球法则" 。印刷术的发明又大大提高了知识增长的速度 。所有这些发展都比较缓慢, 而随着科学的到来, 增长的速度才突然加快 。于是, 知识便开始有系统有计划地积累起来 。涓涓细流汇成了小溪, 小溪现已变成了奔腾的江河 。而且, 新知识一旦获得, 便得到实际应用 。所谓 "现代文明" 并不是人的天性平衡发展的结果, 而是积累起来的知识应用到实际生活中的结果 。现在人类面临的问题是: 用这些知识去做什么? 正像人们常常指出的, 知识是一把双刃刀, 可以用于造福, 也可用来为害 。人们现在正漫不经心地把知识用于这两个方面, 例如: 炮兵利用科学毁坏人的身体, 而外科医生就在附近用科学抢救被炮兵毁坏的人体, 还有什么情景比这更可怕更怪诞的吗? 我们不得不严肃地问我们自己: 随着日益增长的知识的力量, 如果我们继续利用知识的这种双重性, 将会发生什么样的情况呢?

Comprehension 理解

Answer these questions:

1　How does the author define the word 'progress'?
2　How was the spread of knowledge affected by the coming of science?
3　What problem has the spread of knowledge given rise to?

Vocabulary 词汇

Refer to the text to see how the following words have been used, then write sentences of your own using these words: loom so large (l.1); manifest (l.2); accumulation (l.4); enhanced (l.8); indifferently (l.15); spectacle (l.15); grimly whimsical (l.15); twofold (l.17).

The paragraph 段落

A　Drawing your information from lines 4-13 ('Knowledge began ... practical life.') write a list of points in note form to answer the following question: How did the growth of knowledge follow 'a kind of compound interest law'?

B　Read lines 13-18 again. ('The problem ... continues.') Then, using the list of points given below, reconstruct the author's argument in your own words as far as possible. Do not refer to the passage until you have finished the exercise.

1　Problem facing humanity: what to do with knowledge.
2　Two-edged weapon: good and evil.
3　Used for both.
4　Ironical use of science. E.g. gunner—wounded men—surgeons.
5　Where will this twofold use lead?

C　Write a paragraph of about 200 words on one of the following subjects:
1　Support the author's view that mankind has undergone no general improvement in intelligence or morality.
2　Support the author's view that knowledge is a two-edged weapon.

Key structures 关键句型

A　Supply the correct form of the verbs in parentheses in these sentences. Do not refer to the passage until you have finished the exercise:

1　Knowledge began to increase as soon as the thoughts of one individual _____ (can communicate) to another by means of speech. With the invention of writing, a great advance _____ (make), for knowledge then not only _____ (can communicate) but also _____ (store). (ll.4-6)
2　The growth of knowledge followed a kind of compound interest law, which greatly _____ (enhance) by the invention of printing. All this was comparatively slow until, with the coming of science, the *tempo* suddenly _____ (raise). Then knowledge began to _____ (accumulate) according to a systematic plan. (ll.7-10)
3　Moreover, as soon as new knowledge _____ (acquire), it now _____ (turn) to practical account. (ll.10-11)
4　As so often _____ (point) out, knowledge is a two-edged weapon which _____ (can use) equally for good or evil. It now _____ (use) indifferently for good or evil. (ll.13-14)

B　Study this sentence pattern:
Libraries *made education possible*. (l.6)
Write sentences using *make* in the same pattern with the following words:
unnecessary; desirable; unrecognizable.

C　Compare these two sentences:
Instead of saying:　The problem *which now faces* humanity ...
We can say:　　　　The problem *now facing* humanity ... (l.13)
Complete the following sentences:
1　People emigrating _____
2　All aeroplanes arriving _____
3　Ships sailing _____

D Compare the expressions in italics in these two sentences:

Instead of saying: What is called 'modern civilization' is not the result of a balanced development of all man's nature, but of accumulated *knowledge which has been applied* to practical life.

We can say: What is called 'modern civilization' is not the result of a balanced development of all man's nature, but of accumulated *knowledge applied* to practical life. (ll.11-13)

Complete the following sentences:

1 Photographs taken _____
2 Passports issued _____
3 Passengers delayed _____

Special difficulties 难点

A Study the following pairs of words and then write sentences of your own to bring out the difference.

1 surely (l.1) — certainly
   Surely you can ride a bike!
   I don't know how far it is to Edinburgh, but it's certainly a long way.

2 extraordinary (l.3) — outstanding
   Fancy meeting you here! What an extraordinary coincidence! (= unusual, surprising)
   Sarah is a woman of extraordinary ability.
   Sarah's ability is quite outstanding. (= exceptional, possibly unique)

3 spectacle (l.15) — view
   The National Day parade was a magnificent spectacle.
   We had a really good view of the beach from where we stayed.

B Write sentences using the following words and phrases:
   more and more (l.2); by means of (l.5); in its turn (l.7); a kind of (l.7); comparatively (l.8); according to (l.9); at hand (l.16).

C What do you understand by the following metaphor:
   The trickle became a stream; the stream has now become a torrent. (l.10)

D Note the use of *ever-* in this phrase: its *ever-increasing* power. (l.17)
   Write sentences using the following expressions:
   ever-expanding; ever-changing; ever-diminishing.

Multiple choice questions 选择题

Choose the correct answers to the following questions.

Comprehension 理解

1 One of these statements is true. Which one?
   (*a*) Humans today have greatly improved in moral behaviour.
   (*b*) Advances in human intelligence have made progress possible.
   (*c*) The body of knowledge available to humans becomes greater and greater.
   (*d*) Knowledge increases, morality declines.

2 One of the greatest advances humans have made is in their ability _____ .

  (*a*) to learn about things

  (*b*) to tell other people what they have learned

  (*c*) to think about what they have learned

  (*d*) to keep records of things they have learned

3 One of these statements is true. Which one?

  (*a*) The rate of growth of knowledge becomes faster and faster.

  (*b*) Libraries increase with amazing speed.

  (*c*) The invention of printing had a minor effect on the growth of knowledge.

  (*d*) The compound interest law is the basis of everything.

4 As soon as human beings learn something new, they _____ .

  (*a*) find out more about 'modern civilization'

  (*b*) use it for the benefit of mankind

  (*c*) make it work for them

  (*d*) create a systematic plan

Structure 句型

5 Knowledge began to increase as soon as humans could _____ with each other. (ll.4-5)

  (*a*) communicating   (*b*) communicate   (*c*) to communicate   (*d*) be communicate

6 Knowledge could not only be communicated but stored _____ . (1.6)

  (*a*) as well   (*b*) together   (*c*) both   (*d*) either

7 Knowledge began _____ accumulated according to a systematic plan. (ll.9-10)

  (*a*) to   (*b*) was   (*c*) to being   (*d*) being

8 What are they going _____ with all this knowledge? (1.13)

  (*a*) to be done   (*b*) to do   (*c*) do   (*d*) doing

Vocabulary 词汇

9 Progress of a particular kind is actually _____ around us. (ll.1-2)

  (*a*) doing   (*b*) making   (*c*) occurring   (*d*) taking part

10 The growth of knowledge was greatly _____ by the invention of printing. (ll.7-8)

  (*a*) reduced   (*b*) applied   (*c*) renewed   (*d*) improved

11 As soon as new knowledge is _____ , it is turned to practical account. (ll.10-11)

  (*a*) obtained   (*b*) acknowledged   (*c*) accepted   (*d*) recorded

12 Could any _____ be more grimly whimsical ... (1.15)

  (*a*) landscape   (*b*) sight   (*c*) scene   (*d*) view

Lesson 23　Bird flight　鸟的飞行方法

📼 **First listen and then answer the following question.**
听录音，然后回答以下问题 。
What are the two main types of bird flight described by the author?

No two sorts of birds practise quite the same sort of flight; the varieties are infinite; but two classes may be roughly seen. Any ship that crosses the Pacific is accompanied for many days by the smaller albatross, which may keep company with the vessel for an hour without visible or more than occasional movement of wing. The currents of air that the walls of the ship direct upwards, as well as in the line of its course, are
5　enough to give the great bird with its immense wings sufficient sustenance and progress. The albatross is the king of the gliders, the class of fliers which harness the air to their purpose, but must yield to its opposition. In the contrary school, the duck is supreme. It comes nearer to the engines with which man has 'conquered' the air, as he boasts. Duck, and like them the pigeons, are endowed with steel-like muscles, that are a good part of the weight of the bird, and these will ply the short wings with such irresistible power that they can
10　bore for long distances through an opposing gale before exhaustion follows. Their humbler followers, such as partridges, have a like power of strong propulsion, but soon tire. You may pick them up in utter exhaustion, if wind over the sea has driven them to a long journey. The swallow shares the virtues of both schools in highest measure. It tires not, nor does it boast of its power; but belongs to the air, travelling it may be six thousand miles to and from its northern nesting home, feeding its flown young as it flies, and slipping
15　through a medium that seems to help its passage even when the wind is adverse. Such birds do us good, though we no longer take omens from their flight on this side and that; and even the most superstitious villagers no longer take off their hats to the magpie and wish it good-morning.

WILLIAM BEACH THOMAS *A Countryman's Creed*

A flock of wild geese in flight

132

New words and expressions 生词和短语

albatross (1.2) /'ælbətrɒs/ *n.* 信天翁

sustenance (1.5) /'sʌstənəns/ *n.* 支撑力

glider (1.6) /'glaɪdə/ *n.* 滑翔者

harness (1.6) /'hɑːnɪs/ *v.* 利用

endow (1.8) /ɪn'daʊ/ *v.* 赋有

ply (1.9) /plaɪ/ *v.* 不断地供给

gale (1.10) /geɪl/ *n.* 大风

partridge (1.11) /'pɑːtrɪdʒ/ *n.* 鹧鸪

like (1.11) /'laɪk/*adj.* 类似的

propulsion (1.11) /prə'pʌlʃən/ *n.* 推进力

utter (1.11) /'ʌtə/ *adj.* 完全的

slip (1.14) /slɪp/ *v.* 滑行

adverse (1.15) /'ædvɜːs/ *adj.* 逆的, 相反的

omen (1.16) /'əʊmən/ *n.* 预兆

Notes on the text 课文注释

1   keep company with, 陪伴着…… 。

2   The currents of air that the walls of the ship direct upwards, 沿着船体上升的气流 。

3   steel-like muscles, that are a good part of the weight of the bird, 句中以 that 引导的从句是一个非限定性定语从句, 修饰 muscles, 但用 that 引导非限定性定语从句是很罕见的 。

4   in highest measure, 最大程度地 。

5   It tires not nor does it boast of its power, but belongs to the air, travelling it may be ... adverse.
句中的 tires not 是古英语或诗歌中使用的句式 。boast of 中的 of = about; belong to the air 的意思是: 与天空融为一体 。travelling it may be 是倒装语序, 这是为了强调 travelling 的生动逼真, 自然语序是 it may be travelling ...; nesting home 意为 home for nesting; flown young 中的 flown 意为已会飞的 。a medium （媒介）指 air 。

参考译文

　　没有任何两种鸟的飞行方式是相同的 。鸟的飞行方式千差万别, 但大体上可分为两类 。任何一艘横渡太平洋的轮船都会有一种小信天翁伴随飞行许多天 。它们随船飞行一小时也难得见其扇动一下翅膀 。沿船体上升的气流和沿航线向前的气流给这种巨翼大鸟以足够的浮力和推力 。信天翁是滑翔飞行的鸟类之王, 它能自如地驾驭空气, 但必须顺气流飞行 。与滑翔鸟相对的另一类鸟中, 数野鸭本领最高 。它更近乎于人类自夸 "征服" 了空气的发动机 。野鸭及与它们相似的鸽子有天赐的钢铁般的肌肉, 占了体重的很大一部分 。这些肌肉以巨大的力量扇动短小的翅膀, 使这类鸟能顶着大风飞行很远的路程才会疲劳 。次于野鸭和鸽子的鸟, 如鹧鸪, 有相似的巨大推动力, 但很快会疲劳 。如果海风驱使它们飞行很长距离, 你可捡到一些因筋疲力尽而摔下来的鹧鸪 。燕子充分兼有这两类鸟的长处, 它既不疲劳, 也不炫耀自己的飞翔力; 在空中十分自如, 可以飞行 6000 英里, 可以飞往北方做窝的老家, 再从老家飞回; 一边飞一边喂养会飞的雏燕, 甚至在顶风时也能在气流中滑翔, 似乎气流在帮它前进 。这些鸟对我们是有益的, 虽然我们不再从它们的飞翔姿态来占卜吉凶, 连最迷信的村民也不再对喜鹊脱帽行礼, 祝它早安了 。

Comprehension 理解

Answer these questions:

1   Why is the albatross described as 'the king of the gliders'?

2   Why does the author single out the swallow for special praise?

Vocabulary 词汇

Refer to the text to see how the following words have been used, then write sentences of your own using these words: infinite (l.1); sufficient sustenance (l.5); harness (l.6); yield (l.6); endowed (l.8); irresistible power (l.9); bore (l.9); like (l.11); utter (l.11); adverse (l.15); omens (l.16).

The paragraph 段落

A Drawing your information from lines 1-10 ('No two sorts ... exhaustion follows.') write a list of points in note form to answer the following question: How does the flight of an albatross differ from that of a duck?

B Read lines 12-17 again. ('The swallow shares ... wish it good-morning.') Then, using the list of points given below, reconstruct the author's description in your own words as far as possible. Do not refer to the passage until you have finished the exercise.

1 Swallow: the good qualities of both schools.
2 Does not tire; has great power.
3 Flies as much as 6,000 miles to and from nesting home.
4 Feeds young in flight.
5 Good progress in adverse conditions.
6 Such birds do us good.
7 No omens—even among superstitious villagers.

C Write a paragraph of about 200 words on one of the following subjects:
1 The power of flight.
2 Birds.

Key structures 关键句型

A Supply *a, an* or *the* where necessary in the following. Do not refer to the passage until you have finished the exercise:

No two sorts of _____ birds practise quite _____ same sort of _____ flight; _____ varieties are infinite; but _____ two classes may be roughly seen. Any ship that crosses _____ Pacific is accompanied for many days by _____ smaller albatross, which may keep company with _____ vessel for _____ hour without _____ visible or _____ more than occasional movement of _____ wing. _____ currents of _____ air that _____ walls of _____ ship direct upwards, as well as in _____ line of its course are enough to give _____ great bird with _____ its immense wings sufficient sustenance and _____ progress. _____ albatross is _____ king of _____ gliders, _____ class of _____ fliers which harness _____ air to their purpose, but must yield to its opposition. (ll.1-6)

B Note the form of the verbs in italics:
You *may pick* them up in utter exhaustion, if wind over the sea *has driven* them to a long journey. (ll.11-12)
Complete the following sentences:
1 If you have ever driven at a hundred miles an hour _____

2   If you have never been to New Zealand _____

3   If you have finished your work _____

C   Supply the correct form of the verbs in parentheses. Do not refer to the passage until you have finished the exercise:

The swallow _____ (share) the virtues of both schools in highest measure. It _____ (tire) not, nor _____ (boast) of its power; but _____ (belong) to the air, _____ (travel) it may be six thousand miles to and from its northern nesting home, _____ (feed) its flown young as it _____ (fly), and _____ (slip) through a medium that _____ (seem) to help its passage even when the wind _____ (be) adverse. (ll.12-15)

Special difficulties 难点

A   Study the following pairs of words and then write sentences of your own to bring out the difference:

1   quite (l.1) — quiet

I'm quite happy at my new school.

Please be quiet. I can't think with all that noise you're making.

2   wing (l.4) — feather

He has a good collection of butterflies with beautiful markings on their wings.

Old-fashioned quill pens were made from strong goose feathers.

3   course (l.4) — coarse

The ship had been blown off course in the storm.

He wore an old jacket made of coarse cloth.

B   Note how the words *sort* and *kind* can be used in the singular and in the plural:

No two *sorts* (or *kinds*) of *birds* practise quite the same *sort* (or *kind*) of *flight*. (l.1)

Write two sentences using the words *sort* and *sorts*.

C   Explain the meaning of *rough* and *roughly* in these sentences:

1   Two classes may be *roughly* seen. (ll.1-2)

2   The surface of this road is very *rough*.

3   *Roughly* six hundred people attended the meeting.

4   Last night the sea was very *rough*.

D   Write sentences using the following expressions:

keep company with (l.3); as well as (l.4); take off their hats to (l.17).

E   Note the use of *good* in this phrase: '*a good* part of the weight of the bird' (ll.8-9).

Write sentences using the following phrases:

a good fifteen minutes; a good twenty miles; a good five hundred people; a good many; a good few.

F   Note how *such as* may be used to introduce an example:

Their humbler followers, *such as* partridges, ... (ll.10-11)

Write two sentences using *such as* in this way.

G Note the phrase *do us good* (1.15). Which of the following words are used with *do* and which with *make*: your duty; an excuse; a fortune; wrong; harm; an attempt; a bed; a proposal; sense; a speech; the shopping; a problem; a lesson; a difference; a copy; an announcement; an agreement; some work; a job; money; a mistake; a living; fun of; your best; business; an experiment; friends with; a favour; some homework; trouble; sure; a will; a noise.

With which of the above words would it be possible to use either *do* or *make*?

H Note the phrase: *wish it good-morning* (1.17).

Write sentences using the following phrases:

wish me luck; wish me well; wish me good-night.

Multiple choice questions 选择题

Choose the correct answers to the following questions.

Comprehension 理解

1 The two classes of flight depend on _____ .

(*a*) occasional movement and progress

(*b*) wing span and gliding

(*c*) gliding and muscle-power

(*d*) wind currents and machinery

2 The albatross can keep flying for very long periods because it _____ .

(*a*) actively uses air movement to stay in the sky

(*b*) it is a very great bird

(*c*) recognizes ships at sea

(*d*) it can glide in any direction, regardless of air currents

3 Ducks can fly in any direction _____ .

(*a*) and stay in the air indefinitely

(*b*) but are too heavy to fly for long

(*c*) and uses engine power

(*d*) but can run out of energy

4 The swallow _____ .

(*a*) is often greeted by superstitious villagers

(*b*) is good for people

(*c*) combines both forms of flight

(*d*) is an omen of good luck

Structure 句型

5 The albatross _____ to yield to the opposition of the wind. (1.6)

(*a*) must   (*b*) could   (*c*) has   (*d*) should

6 The duck comes nearer to the engines _____ man has 'conquered' the air with. (ll.7-8)

(*a*) where   (*b*) who   (*c*) whom   (*d*) -

7 Partridges _____ a like power of strong propulsion. (l.11)

   (*a*) contain   (*b*) provide   (*c*) possess   (*d*) display

8 It _____ , nor does it boast of its power. (l.13)

   (*a*) does not tire   (*b*) not tire   (*c*) not tires   (*d*) do not tire

Vocabulary 词汇

9 There is no _____ to the variety of flight practised by birds. (l.1)

   (*a*) opportunity   (*b*) end   (*c*) point   (*d*) goal

10 The great bird has _____ wings. (l.5)

   (*a*) broad   (*b*) long   (*c*) huge   (*d*) wide

11 Duck, like pigeons, are _____ with steel-like muscles. (l.8)

   (*a*) provided   (*b*) gifted   (*c*) talented   (*d*) inherited

12 We no longer look for _____ in the way they fly. (ll.15-16)

   (*a*) guides   (*b*) notices   (*c*) signs   (*d*) signals

Lesson 24 Beauty 美

What do glimpses of beauty, either in nature or art, often suggest to the human mind?

A young man sees a sunset and, unable to understand or to express the emotion that it rouses in him, concludes that it must be the gateway to a world that lies beyond. It is difficult for any of us in moments of intense aesthetic experience to resist the suggestion that we are catching a glimpse of a light that shines down to us from a different realm of existence, different and, because the experience is intensely moving, in
5 some way higher. And, though the gleams blind and dazzle, yet do they convey a hint of beauty and serenity greater than we have known or imagined. Greater too than we can describe; for language, which was invented to convey the meanings of this world, cannot readily be fitted to the uses of another.

That all great art has this power of suggesting a world beyond is undeniable. In some moods, Nature shares it. There is no sky in June so blue that it does not point forward to a bluer, no sunset so beautiful that
10 it does not waken the vision of a greater beauty, a vision which passes before it is fully glimpsed, and in passing leaves an indefinable longing and regret. But, if this world is not merely a bad joke, life a vulgar flare amid the cool radiance of the stars, and existence an empty laugh braying across the mysteries; if these intimations of a something behind and beyond are not evil humour born of indigestion, or whimsies sent by the devil to mock and madden us, if, in a word, beauty means something, yet we must not seek to interpret
15 the meaning. If we glimpse the unutterable, it is unwise to try to utter it, nor should we seek to invest with significance that which we cannot grasp. Beauty in terms of our human meanings *is* meaningless.

C. E. M. JOAD *Pieces of Mind*

New words and expressions 生词和短语

intense (1.3) /ɪn'tens/ *adj.* 强烈的
aesthetic (1.3) /iːs'θetɪk/ *adj.* 审美的
realm (1.4) /relm/ *n.* 世界
serenity (1.5) /sɪ'renɪti/ *n.* 静谧
undeniable (1.8) /ˌʌndɪ'naɪəbəl/ *adj.* 不可否认的
indefinable (1.11) /ˌɪndɪ'faɪnəbəl/ *adj.* 模糊不清的

vulgar (1.11) /'vʌlgə/ *adj.* 平庸的
radiance (1.12) /'reɪdiəns/ *n.* 发光
intimation (1.13) /ɪntɪ'meɪʃən/ *n.* 暗示
unutterable (1.15) /ʌn'ʌtərəbəl/ *adj.* 不可言传的
invest (1.15) /ɪn'vest/ *v.* 赋予

Notes on the text 课文注释

1 in moments of intense aesthetic experience, 在强烈地感受到美的时刻 。

2 in some way higher, in some way 是 "在某种程度上" 的意思, higher 与前面的 different and 是并列的, 作 realm of existence 的定语 。

3 yet do they convey a hint of beauty, 其中的 do 起强调作用, 放在主语之前更具有强调的意义 。

4 In some moods Nature shares it. 在某种状态下, 大自然也具有这种力量 。it 是指前面一句中 this power of suggesting a world beyond 。

138

Detail of Madonna and Child—Filippo Lippi (C. 1406-1469)

参考译文

　　一个年轻人看到日落，由于无法理解或表达日落在他心中唤起的激情，便得出结论：日落处想必是通往遥远世界的大门。无论是谁，在强烈地感受到美的时刻，心中都不禁油然而生一种遐想：我们似乎瞥见从另一个世界射向我们的一线光芒，那个世界不仅不同于我们这个世界，而且由于美感的强烈感染，在某些方面比我们这个世界更美好。虽然这光芒令人眼花缭乱，但它确实给予我们一种不曾经历和无法想象的美感和静谧的启示。这种美感和静谧是我们无法描述的，因为我们发明的语言是用来描述我们这个世界的含义，不能随便拿来去描述另一个世界。

　　不可否认，一切伟大的艺术都具有使人遐想到进入天外世界的魅力。在某种状态下，大自然也有这种魅力。六月蔚蓝的天空总使人遥想一个更加蔚蓝的苍穹；美丽的落日总会引起一个更加绚丽的景象，这景象未及饱览便一闪即逝，并在消逝中给人留下了不可名状的渴望和惆怅。如果这个世界不只是一个拙劣的恶作剧，如果人生不只是群星寒光中平凡的一闪，如果存在不只是对神秘事物的一阵空虚的笑声，如果某种玄妙事物的暗示不是消化不良引起的邪恶情绪，也不是魔鬼为了捉弄我们，使我们发狂而送给我们的邪念，一句话，如果美有某种意义的话，我们千万不要去阐明它的意义。如果我们瞥见了只可意会不可言传的事物，企图把它说出来，那是不明智的；对于我们不理解的事物，我们也不应该去赋予它某种意义。用对我们人类有意义的词句来解释美是没有意义的。

Comprehension 理解

Answer these questions:

1　What, according to the author, have great art and certain moods of Nature in common?
2　Why does the author feel that it is unwise to attempt to interpret beauty?

Vocabulary 词汇

Refer to the text to see how the following words have been used, then write sentences of your own using these words: rouses (l.1); aesthetic (l.3); realm (l.4); moving (l.4); convey (l.5); indefinable longing (l.11); radiance (l.12); braying (l.12); whimsies (l.13); glimpse the unutterable (l.15); invest with significance (ll.15-16).

The paragraph 段落

A Drawing your information from the second paragraph (lines 8-16) write a list of points in note form to answer the following question: How does the author arrive at the conclusion that beauty in terms of our human meanings is meaningless?

B Read the first paragraph again (lines 1-7). Then, using the list of points given below, reconstruct the author's argument in your own words as far as possible. Do not refer to the passage until you have finished the exercise:

1 Effect of sunset on a young man: vision of another world.
2 Aesthetic experiences: suggestion of the existence of a world in some way higher than our own.
3 Hint of beauty and serenity we have never known.
4 Impossible to describe: language ill-equipped.

C Write a paragraph of about 200 words on one of the following subjects:
1 What is beautiful to one individual is ugly to another.
2 Beauty does have a meaning: it reflects the grandeur of God.
3 Beauty has no meaning: it should be accepted for what it is.
4 There is no such thing as 'beauty'. There are merely various phenomena, objects, etc. which we attempt to classify as 'beautiful', but this is a purely subjective evaluation on our part.

Key structures 关键句型

A Compare the uses of *must* in these two sentences:
   A young man sees a sunset and concludes that it *must be* the gateway to a world that lies beyond. (ll.1-2)
   If beauty means something we *must not seek* to interpret the meaning. (ll.14-15)
   In which of the following sentences would it be possible to replace *must* by *has to*?
1 I haven't seen Tom for some time; he *must* be ill.
2 He *must* advertise for a new secretary, now that Miss Perkins has left.
3 He *must* stay in bed for at least a week.
4 I'm afraid he *must* be mistaken.

B Compare the use of *it is* and *there is* in these sentences:
   It is difficult for any of us to resist the suggestion. (ll.2-3)
   There is no sky in June so blue ... (l.9)
   Supply *it* or *there* in the following sentences:
1 _____ must have been after one o'clock when I arrived home.
2 _____ must have been a large number of accidents over the Christmas holidays.
3 You might be asked to make a speech, but I think _____ is highly unlikely.

4 _____ will be difficult to dissuade him now that he has made up his mind.

5 _____ will be difficult times ahead.

C   Compare these two sentences:

Instead of saying: It is undeniable that all great art has this power of suggesting a world beyond.

We can say: That all great art has this power of suggesting a world beyond is undeniable. (l.8)

Write these sentences again so that each one begins with *That*.

1   It is unbelievable that he wrote this story himself.

2   It is astonishing to me that you should believe this to be true.

3   It is quite true that we all feel depressed sometimes.

D   Complete the following sentence in any way you wish. Then compare what you have written with the sentence in the passage:

If we glimpse the unutterable, _____ (l.15)

Special difficulties 难点

A   Study the following pairs of words and then write sentences of your own to bring out the difference.

1   unable (l.1) — enable

I'll be unable to see you on Friday.

Money from his grandfather enabled him to further his education in the United States.

2   rouse (l.1) — raise

If we're going to set out so early, you'll have to rouse us at 6 in the morning.

Will those who agree with me please raise their hands?

3   lie (l.2) — lay

Are you going to lie in bed all morning?

Please lay the book open on the desk.

4   indefinable (l.11) — undefined

She felt a sudden indefinable sadness.

The relationship between them was undefined, but she might have been his wife, I'd guess.

5   vulgar (l.11) — common

I wish you wouldn't use such vulgar expressions in your speech.

In this block we have a common responsibility for maintaining the staircase.

B   Note the words in italics in the following sentences. Use these words again in sentences of your own, giving each word a different meaning from the one it has in the example:

1   A young man sees a sunset and *concludes* that it must be the gateway to a world that lies beyond. (ll.1-2)

2   It is difficult for any of us in moments of intense aesthetic *experience* to resist the suggestion that we are catching a glimpse of a light that shines down to us from a different realm of existence. (ll.2-4)

3   And *though* the gleams blind and dazzle, yet do they convey a hint of beauty. (l.5)

4   Nor should we seek to *invest* with significance that which we cannot *grasp*. (ll.15-16)

5   Beauty in *terms* of our human meanings is meaningless. (l.16)

C Note the use of *fully* in this phrase:

'before it is *fully* glimpsed' (l.10)

Write sentences using the following expressions:

fully realize; fully capable; explain fully.

D Write sentences using the following phrases:

catch a glimpse (l.3); in some way (ll.4-5); seek to (l.15).

Multiple choice questions 选择题

Choose the correct answers to the following questions.

Comprehension 理解

1 When we have an intense experience of beauty we _____ .

  (*a*) are tempted to believe it has some kind of meaning

  (*b*) want to express the emotion it arouses in us

  (*c*) know that it comes from a different realm of existence

  (*d*) are open to suggestions

2 According to the writer, language _____ .

  (*a*) is not powerful enough to describe other-worldly experiences

  (*b*) always conveys meaning

  (*c*) can convey beauty and serenity

  (*d*) has only got one use

3 _____ can suggest a world beyond.

  (*a*) All forms of art and Nature

  (*b*) Only Nature

  (*c*) Not only Nature

  (*d*) Only great art

4 The writer implies that we would all like to _____ .

  (*a*) explain the meaning of life

  (*b*) explain the meaning of beauty

  (*c*) have an explanation of the meaning of life

  (*d*) express the inexpressible

Structure 句型

5 A young man sees a sunset and because he _____ understand ... (l.1)

  (*a*) is enabled to   (*b*) can't   (*c*) is incapable to   (*d*) hasn't potential to

6 We are catching a glimpse of a light _____ down to us ... (ll.2-3)

  (*a*) which shining   (*b*) that it shines   (*c*) shining   (*d*) to shine

7 And, though the gleams blind and dazzle, they _____ convey a hint of beauty. (l.5)

  (*a*) still   (*b*) even   (*c*) up to this time   (*d*) always

8 If life _____ a vulgar flare ... (l.12)

  (*a*) hasn't   (*b*) doesn't   (*c*) will not be   (*d*) isn't

Vocabulary 词汇

9 A young man is unable to express the emotion it _____ in him. (1.1)

   (*a*) is risen   (*b*) raises   (*c*) arises   (*d*) awakens

10 It's difficult to resist the suggestion that we are _____ a light ... (ll.2-3)

   (*a*) briefly seeing   (*b*) viewing   (*c*) examining   (*d*) experiencing

11 In passing it leaves an indefinable _____ and regret. (ll.10-11)

   (*a*) grief   (*b*) sadness   (*c*) desire   (*d*) sorrow

12 Nor should we invest with _____ that which we cannot grasp. (ll.15-16)

   (*a*) explanation   (*b*) force   (*c*) power   (*d*) meaning

IF YOU CAN DO THIS TEST GO ON TO PART 2

Read the following passage carefully, then do the exercises below:

Television is a method of communication. It is about as revolutionary as the invention of printing. Neither printing nor television is in itself an idea, or power, or good or bad. They are simply methods by which ideas and experiences can be communicated faster to more people. It is perhaps because the characteristics of television, which determine what it can best communicate, are so different from those of printing, that
5 professional educationists were reluctant for so long to interest themselves in the newer method.

Printing and television are certainly alike in that both are costly to the producers of the communication and relatively cheap to the receiver. They are both, therefore, mass media which depend upon reaching great numbers. But whereas the printed word, being relatively permanent, can communicate to numbers of like minds over centuries, television is relatively ephemeral and communicates, using both pictures and words,
10 to millions of unlike minds at the same moment in time. Moreover television appeals not only to those who can read but to those who can't.

Professional educationists, accustomed to communication through words, and highly valuing reading and the quality of the like minds reachable through books, saw television, in its early years, not only as a rival for attention but as an enemy of the good. Some ten years ago a friend said to me: 'We in Oxford may
15 be old fashioned and fuddy-duddy,* but most of us think that television is actively detrimental.' Even that great pioneer of teaching by radio, the late Mary Somerville, had no faith in television. 'It won't last,' she said to me. 'It's a flash in the pan.' And many in the world of education no doubt hoped that this was true.

The situation has now altered. It is clear that television is no flash in the pan. So educationists all over the world are trying to get access to its 'power', often by attempting to use traditional methods of academic
20 teaching to inculcate, through television, the ideas and attitudes in which they devotedly believe. But one of the characteristics of television is that it has no power other than that created by the wish of people to watch it. If nobody watches it, then television has no power.

GRACE WYNDHAM GOLDIE *Television and Education* from *The Listener*

* old-fashioned

Comprehension

Answer these questions:

1 Name two qualities which printing and television have in common.
2 Name two ways in which television differs from printing.
3 State two of the objections made by educationists against television.
4 'The situation has altered.' (l.18) Which situation is the author referring to, and how has it altered?

Vocabulary

Explain the meaning of the following words and phrases as they are used in the passage: a method of communication (l.1); characteristics (l.3); reluctant (l.5); relatively (l.7); mass media (l.7); ephemeral (l.9); rival (l.14); detrimental (l.15).

Sentence structure

A Combine the following sentences so as to make one complex statement out of each group. Make any changes you think necessary, but do not alter the sense of the original. Do not refer to the passage until you have finished the exercise:

1 They are simply methods. By these methods ideas and experiences can be communicated faster to more people. (ll.2-3)

2 The characteristics of television are different from those of printing. The characteristics of television determine what it can best communicate. Because of this, professional educationists were reluctant for so long to interest themselves in the newer method. (ll.3-5)

3 Printing and television are certainly alike in one respect. They are costly to the producers of the communication. They are relatively cheap to the receiver. (ll.6-7)

4 They are both, therefore, mass media. They depend on reaching great numbers. (ll.7-8)

5 The printed word is relatively permanent. It can communicate to numbers of like minds over centuries. Television is relatively ephemeral. It communicates to millions of unlike minds at the same moment in time. It uses both pictures and words. (ll.8-10).

B Supply the missing words in the following. Do not refer to the passage until you have finished the exercise:

1 Professional educationists, accustomed to communication through words, _____ highly valuing reading _____ the quality of the like minds reachable through books, saw television, in its early years, _____ as a rival for attention _____ as an enemy of the good. (ll.12-14)

2 So educationists all over the world are trying to get access to its 'power', often _____ attempting to use traditional methods of academic teaching _____ inculcate, through television, the ideas and attitudes in _____ they devotedly believe. (ll.18-20)

The paragraph

A Which of the following words or phrases would best serve as a title for this passage.
Give reasons for your choice:
Television; Television and Printing; Television and Education; Television as a Mass Medium; Mass Media; The Appeal of Television.

B The following sentences have been taken from the first paragraph (lines 1-5). Arrange them in their correct order. Do not refer to the passage until you have finished the exercise:

1 Television is a method of communication.

2 It is perhaps because the characteristics of television, which determine what it can best communicate, are so different from those of printing, that professional educationists were reluctant for so long to interest themselves in the newer method.

3 It is about as revolutionary as the invention of printing.

4 They are simply methods by which ideas and experiences can be communicated faster to more people.

5 Neither printing nor television is in itself an idea, or power, or good or bad.

C Drawing your information from the second paragraph (lines 6-11), write a list of points in note form to answer the following question: In what ways are television and printing similar to each other, and in what ways do they differ from each other?

D Read the last paragraph again (lines 18-22). Using the list of points given below, reconstruct the author's arguments in your own words as far as possible. Do not refer to the passage until you have finished the exercise:

1 Situation altered.
2 Television has come to stay.
3 Educationists: access to its power.
4 Traditional methods of teaching through television.
5 But television can only have power if people watch it.

E Write a paragraph of about 200 words on one of the following subjects:

1 The use of television in education.
2 How can television enrich our lives?
3 What are the arguments against watching television?

Part 2

Unit 4

INSTRUCTIONS TO THE STUDENT

Content

This unit consists of eight passages followed by exercises on Comprehension, Vocabulary, Summary, Composition, Key structures, Special difficulties and Multiple choice questions.

Aim

To employ the skills you have required in constructing sentences and paragraphs in order to write Summary and Composition.

How to work

1   Read each passage carefully two or three times.
2   Answer the questions in the order in which they are given.

Summary

In Part 1 you learnt how to write points in note form to answer a specific question on a passage. When writing Summary, you will be required to do precisely the same thing. This time, however, you will join your points to reconstruct the main ideas of each passage in a limited number of words. Follow the instructions very carefully.

Composition

In Part 1 you learnt how to write a paragraph from notes which were provided. When writing a composition, you will be required to do precisely the same thing. This time, however, the notes given have not been derived from the passage. They are of a general nature and meant to be suggestions only. You may ignore them altogether if you wish. Follow the instructions very carefully.

Lesson 25　Non-auditory effects of noise　噪音的非听觉效应

🔊 **First listen and then answer the following question.**

听录音，然后回答以下问题。

What conclusion does the author draw about noise and health in this piece?

Many people in industry and the Services, who have practical experience of noise, regard any investigation of this question as a waste of time; they are not prepared even to admit the possibility that noise affects people. On the other hand, those who dislike noise will sometimes use most inadequate evidence to support their pleas for a quieter society. This is a pity, because noise abatement really is a good cause, and it is likely
5　to be discredited if it gets to be associated with bad science.

　　One allegation often made is that noise produces mental illness. A recent article in a weekly newspaper, for instance, was headed with a striking illustration of a lady in a state of considerable distress, with the caption 'She was yet another victim, reduced to a screaming wreck'. On turning eagerly to the text, one learns that the lady was a typist who found the sound of office typewriters worried her more and more until
10　eventually she had to go into a mental hospital. Now the snag in this sort of anecdote is of course that one cannot distinguish cause and effect. Was the noise a cause of the illness, or were the complaints about noise merely a symptom? Another patient might equally well complain that her neighbours were combining to slander her and persecute her, and yet one might be cautious about believing this statement.

　　What is needed in the case of noise is a study of large numbers of people living under noisy conditions,
15　to discover whether they are mentally ill more often than other people are. Some time ago the United States Navy, for instance, examined a very large number of men working on aircraft carriers: the study was known as Project Anehin. It can be unpleasant to live even several miles from an aerodrome; if you think what it must be like to share the deck of a ship with several squadrons of jet aircraft, you will realize that a modern navy is a good place to study noise. But neither psychiatric interviews nor objective tests were able to show
20　any effects upon these American sailors. This result merely confirms earlier American and British studies: if there is any effect of noise upon mental health, it must be so small that present methods of psychiatric diagnosis cannot find it. That does not prove that it does not exist; but it does mean that noise is less dangerous than, say, being brought up in an orphanage — which really is a mental health hazard.

D. E. BROADBENT *Non-auditory effects of noise* from *Science Survey*

New words and expressions 生词和短语

auditory (title) /ˈɔːdɪtəri/ *adj.* 听觉的
inadequate (1.3) /ɪnˈædɪkwɪt/ *adj.* 不适当的
plea (1.4) /pliː/ *n.* 要求
abatement (1.4) /əˈbeɪtmənt/ *n.* 减少
discredit (1.5) /dɪsˈkredɪt/ *v.* 怀疑
allegation (1.6) /ˌælɪˈgeɪʃən/ *n.* 断言
caption (1.8) /ˈkæpʃən/ *n.* 插图说明
wreck (1.8) /rek/ *n.* 受到严重损害的人

snag (1.10) /snæg/ *n.* 疑难之处，障碍
anecdote (1.10) /ˈænɪkdəʊt/ *n.* 轶闻
slander (1.13) /ˈslɑːndə/ *v.* 诽谤
persecute (1.13) /ˈpɜːsɪkjuːt/ *v.* 迫害
squadron (1.18) /ˈskwɒdrən/ *n.* 中队
psychiatric (1.19) /ˌsaɪkiˈætrɪk/ *adj.* 精神病学的
diagnosis (1.22) /ˌdaɪəgˈnəʊsɪs/ *n.* 诊断
orphanage (1.23) /ˈɔːfənɪdʒ/ *n.* 孤儿院

An American aircraft carrier

Notes on the text 课文注释

1   the Services, 军队 。

2   On turning eagerly to the text, one learns that ...,
句中 on 的意思是 on the occasion of, directly after（当时, 随后）。

3   aircraft carrier, 航空母舰 。

4   That does not prove that it does not exist; but it does mean that ... 句中出现的 3 个 does 的语法功能并不相同, 前两个 does 是一般现在时的否定式使用的助动词, 第 3 个 does 则是强调用法, 有强化句意的作用 。

参考译文

在工业部门工作和在军队中服役的许多人对噪音有切身的体会, 他们认为对这个问题进行调查是浪费时间, 甚至不愿承认噪音可能对人有影响 。另一方面, 那些讨厌噪音的人有时会用不充分的证据来支持他们希望有一个较为安静的社会环境的要求 。要求减少噪音确实是件好事, 但是如果与拙劣的科学掺杂在一起的话, 就不会被人们所信任, 这是很遗憾的 。

常见的一种指责是, 噪音能引起精神病 。例如, 最近一家周报刊登了一篇文章, 文章上方有一幅引人注目的插图, 是一位表情沮丧的女子 。图的文字说明是:“她是又一个受害者, 成了只会尖叫的可怜虫 。”当人们急切地看完正文后, 便知道这位女子是个打字员, 办公室打字机的声音使她越来越烦恼, 最终住进了精神病医院 。这类奇闻的疑难之处是无法区别因果关系 。是噪音引起了（精神）病呢, 还是（精神）病的症状之一是对噪音的抱怨? 另有一位病人可能同样有理由抱怨说, 她的邻居们正在联合起来对她进行诽谤和迫害, 不过, 人们不会轻信她的抱怨 。

对于噪音问题, 需要对大量生活在噪音中的人进行研究, 看一看他们是否比其他人更易患精神病 。例如, 美国海军前些时候调查了许多在航空母舰上工作的人, 这次调查被称之为:“安内英工程” 。即使住在离机场几英里以外的地方, 机场的噪音也会使人难受 。因此, 如果你能想象出和几个中队的喷气机同在一个甲板上是什么滋味儿的话, 你就会认识到现代海军是研究噪音的好地方 。但是, 不管是进行精神病学的调查访问, 还是进行客观的测试, 都不能显示噪音对这些美国水兵有任何影响 。这个结果只不过证实了美国和英国早些时候的研究结论: 如果噪音对精神健康有影响的话, 那也一定是微乎其微, 以至现有的精神病诊断方法还发现不了 。这并不能证实噪音对健康的影响不存在 。但它确实说明, 噪音的危险性——比如说——比在孤儿院长大所受的危害要小一些, 孤儿院才是真正危害精神健康的地方 。

Comprehension 理解

Answer these questions:

1　What does the author mean by the statement 'Noise abatement really is a good cause, and it is likely to be discredited if it gets to be associated with bad science.'? (ll.4-5)
2　Why is a modern navy a good place to study noise?

Vocabulary 词汇

Refer to the text to see how the following words have been used, then write sentences of your own using these words: investigation (l.1); inadequate evidence (l.3); abatement (l.4); allegation (l.6); snag (l.10); cautious (l.13); hazard (l.23).

Summary 摘要

A　Drawing your information from the first two paragraphs (lines 1-13), write a list of points in note form outlining the author's argument about noise abatement.

B　Using this list of points, reconstruct the author's argument in not more than 90 words. Your answer should be in one paragraph.

Composition 作文

Write a composition of about 300 words on the following subject: *Noise in modern life*.
You may use some or all of the ideas given below if you wish:

1　We have grown accustomed to living and working against a background of noise: traffic in the streets; machines in the factory; office equipment; labour-saving devices in the home; aeroplanes overhead.
2　In a modern industrial society, hardly any place is free from noise; in cities, the problem is acute.
3　Many people learn to live against this background and do not seem to be affected.
4　Some people even seem to require noise as a necessary condition in which to work: e.g. music as a constant background.
5　We seem to be helpless to do anything about noise and have come to accept it as one of the more unpleasant features of modern civilization.

Key structures 关键句型

A　Study this sentence:
Many people in industry and the Services, *who have practical experience of noise*, regard any investigation of this question as a waste of time. (ll.1-2)
Expand the following sentences by inserting suitable clauses beginning with *who* or *which* after the words in italics:

1　*Many roads* _____ were not built for such heavy traffic.
2　*The heavy snow* _____ has now begun to melt.

3   *The party of tourists* _____ left this morning.

4   *The clerk* _____ apologized for the mistake.

B   Compare these two sentences:

Instead of saying: One allegation *that is often made* is that noise produces mental illness.

We can say: One allegation *often made* is that noise produces mental illness. (1.6)

Write sentences using the following phrases:

frequently seen; sometimes heard; generally considered.

C   Note the use of *yet* in these sentences:

1   Has he come *yet*?

2   I haven't seen him *yet*.

3   She was *yet* another victim. (1.8)

Write three sentences using *yet* in the ways shown above.

D   Compare these two sentences:

Instead of saying: *When one turns* eagerly to the text, one learns that the lady was a typist.

We can say: *On turning* eagerly to the text, one learns that the lady was a typist. (ll.8-9)

Write these sentences again so that each one begins with *On*:

1   When I opened the door, I got a surprise.

2   When he saw me approaching, he ran towards me.

3   When he was asked to leave the meeting, he got very angry.

4   When she arrived at the station, she bought a ticket.

E   Write sentences using the following expressions:

reduced to (1.8); cause of (1.11); complaints about (1.11); cautious about (1.13); share with (1.18); effects upon (1.21); methods of (1.21).

Special difficulties 难点

A   Study the following pairs of words and then write sentences of your own to bring out the difference.

1   regard (1.1) — look at

I don't regard a degree as a meal ticket for life.

Just look at those children picking apples.

2   affect (1.2) — effect (1.27)

This hay fever is seriously affecting my work.

This hay fever is having a serious effect on my work.

3   plea (1.4) — please

The accused man entered a plea of Not Guilty.

I only got married to please my parents.

4   objective (1.19) — objection

I need an objective opinion from someone who is not involved. (adjective)

The objective of this meeting is to decide who will represent us on the Planning Committee. (noun)

If no one has any objection, I'll declare the meeting closed.

5　confirm (l.20) — assure

I can confirm that the door was locked. (= say it is true)

I went back to assure myself that I really had locked the door. (= make myself confident)

B　The opposites of these words are to be found in the passage. What are they?

Like; adequate; credit; pleasant.

C　Explain the meaning of the verbs and expressions in italics:

1　It does mean that noise is less dangerous than, say, being *brought up* in an orphanage—which really is a mental health hazard. (ll.22-23)

2　The question was recently *brought up* in Parliament.

3　The boxer was knocked out in the first round. It took a long time to *bring him round*.

4　The whole scene *brought back* the days of my childhood.

5　Their wonderful performance *brought down the house*.

6　Can you *bring to mind* what happened on the fourth of July?

7　Difficult conditions will sometimes *bring out* a man's best qualities.

Multiple choice questions 选择题

Choose the correct answers to the following questions.

Comprehension 理解

1　The reduction of noise is a good cause and it's important to _____ .

(*a*) understand that noise affects people

(*b*) understand the people who dislike noise

(*c*) make sure we have a quieter society

(*d*) prevent it from getting a bad name

2　Stories like the one about the typist _____ .

(*a*) help us to understand the effects of noise

(*b*) do not help us to understand the effects of noise

(*c*) show how noise can produce mental illness

(*d*) cause considerable distress

3　Project Anehin provided an opportunity to _____ .

(*a*) study the effects of noise on a large number of people

(*b*) consider what life is like on aircraft carriers

(*c*) conclude that noise has bad effects on people

(*d*) explore the workings of the United States Navy

4　Project Anehin proved that noise _____ .

(*a*) has no ill effects at all

(*b*) is less dangerous than being brought up in an orphanage

(*c*) is really bad for the health

(*d*) doesn't appear to have any bad effects

Unit 4   Lesson 25

Structure 句型

5 _____ you turned eagerly to the text ... (1.8)

   (a) As   (b) On   (c) While   (d) When

6 Eventually, she _____ go into a mental hospital. (1.10)

   (a) will go   (b) should go   (c) was obliged to   (d) made to

7 What is needed is a study of large numbers to discover _____ they are ill. (ll.14-15)

   (a) if   (b) unless   (c) in case   (d) lest

8 Noise is _____ dangerous _____ being brought up in an orphanage. (ll.22-23)

   (a) not ... as   (b) not so ... than   (c) not so ... as   (d) no as ... as

Vocabulary 词汇

9 It is _____ that noise abatement could be discredited. (ll.4-5)

   (a) perhaps   (b) acceptable   (c) certain   (d) probable

10 _____ she had to go into a mental hospital. (1.10)

   (a) At least   (b) In the end   (c) At the finish   (d) In fact

11 Now the _____ in this sort of anecdote is ... (1.10)

   (a) case   (b) knot   (c) difficulty   (d) weakness

12 This result merely _____ earlier American and British studies. (1.20)

   (a) verifies   (b) certifies   (c) exemplifies   (d) certificates

Lesson 26 The past life of the earth 地球上的昔日生命

听录音,然后回答以下问题。

What is the main condition for the preservation of the remains of any living creature?

It is animals and plants which lived in or near water whose remains are most likely to be preserved, for one of the necessary conditions of preservation is quick burial, and it is only in the seas and rivers, and sometimes lakes, where mud and silt have been continuously deposited, that bodies and the like can be rapidly covered over and preserved.

5   But even in the most favourable circumstances only a small fraction of the creatures that die are preserved in this way before decay sets in or, even more likely, before scavengers eat them. After all, all living creatures live by feeding on something else, whether it be plant or animal, dead or alive, and it is only by chance that such a fate is avoided. The remains of plants and animals that lived on land are much more rarely preserved, for there is seldom anything to cover them over. When you think of the innumerable birds
10 that one sees flying about, not to mention the equally numerous small animals like field mice and voles which you do not see, it is very rarely that one comes across a dead body, except, of course, on the roads. They decompose and are quickly destroyed by the weather or eaten by some other creature.

It is almost always due to some very special circumstances that traces of land animals survive, as by falling into inaccessible caves, or into an ice crevasse, like the Siberian mammoths, when the whole animal
15 is sometimes preserved, as in a refrigerator. This is what happened to the famous Beresovka mammoth which was found preserved and in good condition. In his mouth were the remains of fir trees—the last meal that he had before he fell into the crevasse and broke his back. The mammoth has now been restored in the Palaeontological Museum in St. Petersburg. Other animals were trapped in tar pits, like the elephants, sabre-toothed cats, and numerous other creatures that are found at Rancho la Brea, which is now just a suburb of
20 Los Angeles. Apparently what happened was that water collected on these tar pits, and the bigger animals like the elephants ventured out on to the apparently firm surface to drink, and were promptly bogged in the tar. And then, when they were dead, the carnivores, like the sabre-toothed cats and the giant wolves, came out to feed and suffered exactly the same fate. There are also endless numbers of birds in the tar as well.

ERROL WHITE *The past life of the earth* from *Discovery*

New words and expressions 生词和短语

preservation (1.2) /ˌprezə'veɪʃən/ n. 保存
silt (1.3) /sɪlt/ n. 淤泥
scavenger (1.6) /'skævɪndʒə/ n. 食腐动物
vole (1.10) /vəʊl/ n. 田鼠
decompose (1.12) /ˌdiːkəm'pəʊz/ v. 腐烂
inaccessible (1.14) /ˌɪnək'sesəbəl/ adj. 不能到达的
crevasse (1.14) /krɪ'væs/ n. 缝隙

Siberian (1.14) /saɪ'bɪərɪən/ adj. 西伯利亚的
palaeontological (1.18) /'pælɪˌɒntə'lɒdʒɪkəl/ adj. 古
生物学的
St. Petersburg (1.18) /seɪnt-'piːtəzbɜːg/ n. 圣彼得堡
sabre-toothed (ll.18-19) /'seɪbətuːθt/ adj. 剑齿的
venture (1.21) /'ventʃə/ v. 冒险
bogged (1.21) /bɒgd/ adj. 陷入泥沼的, 陷于困境的

155

The mammoth in the Palaeontological Museum in St. Petersburg. Photographed in 1860

Notes on the text 课文注释

1　第 1 段中有两个由 it is … 引导的强调句。一个是 It is animals and plants which lived in or near water whose remains are most likely to be preserved, 被强调部分是 animals and plants which lived in or near water。另一个强调句是 it is only in the seas and rivers, and sometimes lakes, … that bodies and the like can be …, 这一句中强调的是地点状语。

2　set in, 到来, 开始。

3　whether it be plant or animal, dead or alive,
　　这是让步状语从句, 用的是虚拟语气形式。

参考译文

　　只有生活在水中或水边的动植物尸体最有可能被保存下来, 因为保存的必要条件之一是迅速掩埋, 所以只有在泥沙不停淤积的海洋和江河里, 有时在湖泊里, 尸体之类的东西才能被迅速地覆盖而保存下来。

　　即使是在最有利的环境中, 死去的生物中也只有一小部分能在开始腐烂前, 或更可能在被食腐动物吃掉之前, 被这样保存下来。因为一切生物都是靠吃别的东西来活命的, 不管这种东西是植物还是动物, 死的还是活的, 因此, 生物偶尔才能避免被吃掉的命运。曾在陆地上生活过的动植物的遗体被保存下来的更为罕见, 因为陆地上几乎没有什么东西覆盖它们。你可以想象出天上有看得见的飞来飞去、数不清的鸟, 地上有不显眼的无数的野鼠和田鼠之类的小动物, 但是, 除非在路上, 很少有人遇到这些动物的尸体, 因为它们腐败之后很快就被风化掉, 或被别的动物吃掉了。

　　几乎总是由于某些特殊的条件, 陆地动物的遗体才被保存下来, 如掉进难以到达的洞穴, 或掉进冰河裂缝里, 或者像西伯利亚长毛象那样掉进冰窟中, 有时整个动物像被放在冰箱里一样被保存下来。著名的别林索夫卡长毛象就是这样被保存下来的, 而且保存得很好。它嘴里还留着冷杉——它掉进冰河裂隙折断脊柱之前的最后一顿饭。这头长毛象已被修复, 现存于圣彼得堡古生物学博物馆。有的动物掉进天然沥青坑里被保存了下来, 如在兰桥·拉·布里——现在是洛杉矶的郊区——发现的大象、剑齿虎和许多其他动物。显然, 事情的经过是这样: 沥青坑里积存了水, 像大象那样的大动物冒险到似乎坚固的水面上去饮水, 结果立即掉进了沥青坑。大象死后, 一些食肉动物, 如剑齿虎和大灰狼就来吃大象, 结果遭到了同样的命运。沥青坑里还有无数只鸟的尸体。

Comprehension 理解

Answer these questions:

1 Why are animals or plants which lived in or near water most likely to be preserved?
2 What usually happens to the dead bodies of animals?
3 How were the remains of the Beresovka mammoth accidentally preserved?

Vocabulary 词汇

Refer to the text to see how the following words have been used, then write sentences of your own using these words: preservation (1.2); the like (1.3); a small fraction (1.5); scavengers (1.6); innumerable (1.9); decompose (1.12); inaccessible (1.14); restored (1.17); promptly bogged (1.21).

Summary 摘要

A Drawing your information from the first two paragraphs (lines 1-12), write a list of points in note form outlining the author's main ideas on the preservation of animals.

B Using this list of points, reconstruct the author's account in not more than 80 words. Your answer should be in one paragraph.

Composition 作文

Write a composition of about 300 words on the following subject: Extinct forms of animal life.
You may use some or all of the ideas given below if you wish:

1 Fascination of a natural history museum where the skeletons and fossils of extinct forms of life are on display.
2 The sort of thing one can see: remains of animals that existed in pre-historic times. E.g. Reptiles: dinosaurs, tyrannosaurs. Birds: pterodactyls. Fish: early sharks; fossilized crustaceans. Mammals: perhaps the most fascinating: Neanderthal man.
3 The remains of animals which became extinct recently: e.g. the dodo. Many forms of animal life are in danger of becoming extinct today.
4 A reference to 'living fossils'—primitive forms of life which have surprisingly survived: e.g. the coelacanth; the platypus.

Key structures 关键句型

A Note the form of the verbs in italics:
   Only a small fraction of the creatures that die are preserved in this way *before* decay *sets in* or, even more likely, *before* scavengers *eat* them. (ll.5-6)
   Write sentences using the same construction with these words: until; after; as soon as; when.

B Compare the use of *for* in these two sentences:
1 The remains of plants and animals that lived on land are much more rarely preserved, *for* there is seldom anything to cover them over. (ll.8-9)
2 I think this letter is *for* you.
   Write two sentences using *for* in the ways illustrated above.

C   Supply the correct form of the verbs in the following. Do not refer to the passage until you have finished the exercise:

It is almost always due to some very special circumstances that traces of land animals survive, as by _____ (fall) into inaccessible caves, or into an ice crevasse, like the Siberian mammoths, when the whole animal sometimes _____ (preserve) as in a refrigerator. This is what _____ (happen) to the famous Beresovka mammoth which _____ (find) _____ (preserve) and in good condition. In his mouth _____ (be) the remains of fir trees—the last meal that he _____ (have) before he _____ (fall) into the crevasse and _____ (break) his back. The mammoth now _____ (restore) in the Palaeontological Museum in St. Petersburg. Other animals _____ (trap) in tar pits, like the elephants, sabre-toothed cats, and numerous other creatures that _____ (find) at Rancho la Brea. (ll.13-19)

Special difficulties 难点

A   Study the following pairs of words and then write sentences of your own to bring out the difference.

1   favourable (1.5) — favourite
The new film received favourable reviews.
What is your favourite dish?

2   alive (1.7) — living
Be careful! That lobster is alive.
All living creatures need air and water.

3   avoid (1.8) — prevent
Avoid travelling during the rush hour.
I can't prevent your going if you want to.

B   Note the phrase in italics: Only a small fraction of the creatures that die are preserved *in this way*. (ll.5-6)
Write sentences using the following phrases:
in the way; on the way; in a way; by the way.

C   Explain the meaning of *due to* and *due* in these sentences:

1   It is almost always *due to* some very special circumstances that traces of land animals survive. (1.13)

2   The train is *due to* arrive in three minutes.

3   Give the man his *due*, even if you dislike him.

4   Halifax lies *due* North from here.

D   Study the use of *as* and *like* in this sentence:
It is due to some very special circumstances ... *as* by falling into inaccessible caves, *like* the Siberian mammoths ... (ll.13-14)
Supply *like* or *as* in the following sentences:

1   Please do _____ I say.

2   He was white _____ a sheet.

3   He left _____ suddenly _____ he came.

4   Don't act _____ a baby.

5   The carnivores, _____ the sabre-toothed cats, came out to feed and suffered exactly the same fate. (ll.22-23)

Multiple choice questions 选择题

Choose the correct answers to the following questions.

Comprehension 理解

1 The remains of life forms can only survive intact if they are _____ .

    (*a*) in seas and rivers

    (*b*) under the ground

    (*c*) covered up quickly in the right conditions

    (*d*) preserved near water

2 Inland conditions ensure that the preservation of life forms _____ .

    (*a*) is quite common

    (*b*) is relatively rare

    (*c*) occurs where there are great numbers of species

    (*d*) is always possible in favourable circumstances

3 Unusual circumstances for the preservation of life forms can be provided by _____ .

    (*a*) mammoths

    (*b*) crevasses

    (*c*) freezing conditions

    (*d*) fir trees

4 Animals were trapped in tar because they _____ .

    (*a*) wanted to drink the tar

    (*b*) were deceived by the appearance of the pits

    (*c*) were extremely heavy

    (*d*) were chasing birds

Structure 句型

5 The remains of plants are _____ more rarely preserved. (ll.8-9)

    (*a*) far   (*b*) very   (*c*) quite   (*d*) many

6 There is _____ anything to cover them over. (1.9)

    (*a*) ever   (*b*) never   (*c*) rarely   (*d*) hardly

7 It is almost always _____ special circumstances that traces of land animals survive. (1.13)

    (*a*) as a result   (*b*) owing   (*c*) on account   (*d*) because of

8 In his mouth were the remains of fir trees—the last meal he _____ before he fell. (1.17)

    (*a*) was eaten   (*b*) is eating   (*c*) has eaten   (*d*) ate

Vocabulary 词汇

9 When you think of the _____ birds that one sees ... (ll.9-10)

    (*a*) countless   (*b*) uncountable   (*c*) uncounted   (*d*) unnumbered

10 They _____ and are quickly destroyed by the weather. (ll.11-12)

    (*a*) die   (*b*) decay   (*c*) fall away   (*d*) are buried

11 _____ what happened was that ... (1.20)

    (*a*) It seems that   (*b*) It looks   (*c*) He appears   (*d*) It shows

12 They were _____ bogged in the tar. (1.21)

    (*a*) apparently   (*b*) finally   (*c*) quickly   (*d*) eventually

Lesson 27 The 'Vasa' "瓦萨"号

First listen and then answer the following question.

听录音，然后回答以下问题 。

What happened to the 'Vasa' almost immediately after she was launched?

From the seventeenth-century empire of Sweden, the story of a galleon that sank at the start of her maiden voyage in 1628 must be one of the strangest tales of the sea. For nearly three and a half centuries she lay at the bottom of Stockholm harbour until her discovery in 1956. This was the *Vasa*, royal flagship of the great imperial fleet.

5　　King Gustavus Adolphus, 'The Northern Hurricane', then at the height of his military success in the Thirty Years' War, had dictated her measurements and armament. Triple gun-decks mounted sixty-four bronze cannon. She was intended to play a leading role in the growing might of Sweden.

　　As she was prepared for her maiden voyage on August 10, 1628, Stockholm was in a ferment. From the Skeppsbron and surrounding islands the people watched this thing of beauty begin to spread her sails and 10 catch the wind. They had laboured for three years to produce this floating work of art; she was more richly carved and ornamented than any previous ship. The high stern castle was a riot of carved gods, demons, knights, kings, warriors, mermaids, cherubs; and zoomorphic animal shapes ablaze with red and gold and blue, symbols of courage, power, and cruelty, were portrayed to stir the imaginations of the superstitious sailors of the day.

15　　Then the cannons of the anchored warships thundered a salute to which the *Vasa* fired in reply. As she emerged from her drifting cloud of gun smoke with the water churned to foam beneath her bow, her flags flying, pennants waving, sails filling in the breeze, and the red and gold of her superstructure ablaze with colour, she presented a more majestic spectacle than Stockholmers had ever seen before. All gun-ports were open and the muzzles peeped wickedly from them.

20　　As the wind freshened there came a sudden squall and the ship made a strange movement, listing to port. The Ordnance Officer ordered all the port cannon to be heaved to starboard to counteract the list, but the steepening angle of the decks increased. Then the sound of rumbling thunder reached the watchers on the shore, as cargo, ballast, ammunition and 400 people went sliding and crashing down to the port side of the steeply listing ship. The lower gun-ports were now below water and the inrush sealed the ship's fate. In that 25 first glorious hour, the mighty *Vasa*, which was intended to rule the Baltic, sank with all flags flying—in the harbour of her birth.

ROY SAUNDERS *The Raising of the 'Vasa'* from *The Listener*

New words and expressions 生词和短语

galleon (l.1) /'gæliən/ *n.* 大型帆船
Stockholm (l.3) /'stɒkhəʊm/ *n.* 斯德哥尔摩
flagship (l.3) /'flægʃɪp/ *n.* 旗舰
imperial (l.4) /ɪm'pɪəriəl/ *adj.* 帝国的
hurricane (l.5) /'hʌrɪkən/ *n.* 飓风

armament (l.6) /'ɑːməmənt/ *n.* 军械
triple (l.6) /'trɪpəl/ *adj.* 三层的
mount (l.6) /maʊnt/ *v.* 架有
bronze (l.7) /brɒnz/ *n.* 青铜
cannon (l.7) /'kænən/ *n.* 加农炮

The 'Vasa', now in a museum in Stockholm

might (l.7) /maɪt/ n. 力量
ferment (l.8) /'fɜ:ment/ n. 激动不安
ornament (l.11) /'ɔ:nəmənt/ v. 装饰
riot (l.11) /'raɪət/ n. 丰富
demon (l.11) /'di:mən/ n. 恶魔
mermaid (l.12) /'mɜ:meɪd/ n. 美人鱼
cherub (l.12) /'tʃerəb/ n. 小天使
zoomorphic (l.12) /ˌzəʊəʊ'mɔ:fɪk/ adj. 兽形的
ablaze (l.12) /ə'bleɪz/ adj. 光彩的
portray (l.13) /pɔ:'treɪ/ v. 绘制
drifting (l.16) /'drɪftɪŋ/ adj. 弥漫的
churn (l.16) /tʃɜ:n/ v. 翻滚
pennant (l.17) /'penənt/ n. 三角旗
superstructure (l.17) /'su:pəˌstrʌktʃə/ n. 上部结构

majestic (l.18) /mə'dʒestɪk/ adj. 威严的
muzzle (l.19) /'mʌzəl/ n. 炮口
freshen (l.20) /'freʃən/ v. 变强
squall (l.20) /skwɔ:l/ n. 狂风
list (l.20) /lɪst/ v. 倾斜
port (l.20) /pɔ:t/ n. （船、飞机的）左舷
ordnance (l.21) /'ɔ:dnəns/ n. 军械
heave (l.21) /hi:v/ v. 拖
starboard (l.21) /'stɑ:bəd/ n. （船、飞机的）右舷
counteract (l.21) /ˌkaʊntər'ækt/ v. 抵消
steepen (l.22) /'sti:pən/ v. 变得更陡峭
ballast (l.23) /'bæləst/ n. 压舱物
inrush (l.24) /'ɪnrʌʃ/ n. 水的涌入
Baltic (l.25) /'bɔ:ltɪk/ n. 波罗的海

Notes on the text 课文注释

1   the 'Vasa', "瓦萨号" 战船。这艘船是以瑞典瓦萨王朝（1523-1654）创始人 Gustavus Vasa 的姓氏命名的。Gustavus Vasa（1496-1560）曾领导了反对丹麦统治的暴动，1523 年出任国王，使瑞典成为一个独立、统一、富强的国家。

2   the Thirty Years War, "三十年战争"。这是欧洲历史上的一场多国混战，具有政治和宗教色彩，是新教诸侯和天主教诸侯之间的连年战争（1618-1648），最后在 1648 年签定了《威斯特伐利亚条约》，以天主教诸侯失败而告终。

3   a riot of, 许多……，主要指色彩丰富。

4   with the water churned ..., her flags flying, pennants waving, sails filling ..., and the red and gold ... ablaze ... with 后有 5 个独立主格结构，均作方式状语，修饰动词 emerged。

参考译文

　　1628 年，一艘大帆船在处女航开始时就沉没了，这个从 17 世纪瑞典帝国流传至今的故事无疑是航海史上最离奇的事件之一。这艘大船在斯德哥尔摩港口的海底躺了将近 3 个半世纪，直到 1956 年才被发现。这就是"瓦萨"号，帝国大舰队的皇家旗舰。

　　当时号称"北方飓风"的国王古斯塔夫斯·阿道尔弗斯正处在"三十年战争"的军事鼎盛阶段，他亲自规定了这艘船的规模和武器配备。3 层的火炮甲板上装着 64 门青铜加农炮，目的就是要在不断增长的瑞典势力中起主导作用。

　　1628 年 8 月 10 日，"瓦萨"号准备首航时，斯德哥尔摩一片欢腾。人们从斯开斯布朗和周围的岛屿前来观看这艘美丽的战船扬帆起航，乘风前进。瑞典人辛辛苦苦干了 3 年才建成这件水上艺术品，它比以往任何船只雕刻得都更加精美，装饰得都更加华丽。高耸的船楼上雕刻着令人眼花缭乱的神仙、妖魔、骑士、国王、武士、美人鱼和小天使，还有用红色、金黄色、蓝色绘制的光彩夺目的兽形图案，象征着勇敢、力量和残暴，以激起当时崇尚迷信的水手们的想象。

　　这时，停泊在港口的其他战船向"瓦萨"号鸣炮致礼，"瓦萨"号也鸣炮回礼。当"瓦萨"号从弥漫的礼炮烟云中出现时，船头下浪花四溅，舰旗迎风招展，三角旗随风飘动，微风鼓起风帆，金碧辉煌的船楼闪耀着灿烂的色彩。"瓦萨"号展现的壮观景象是斯德哥尔摩人从未见过的。船上的炮眼都开着，炮口虎视眈眈地向外窥视着。

　　当风力增强时，突然刮来一阵大风，"瓦萨"号奇怪地摇晃了一下，便向左舷倾斜。炮长命令把左舷上所有大炮搬到右舷上来以抵消船的倾斜，但甲板的倾斜度仍在增加。当物品、压舱物、弹药和 400 个人轰地一声滑向陡斜的左舷时，岸上的观众听到船上发出了雷鸣般的轰响。下层炮眼已淹没在水里，涌进船舱的水给"瓦萨"号带来了难以逃脱的厄运。就这样，想要统治波罗的海的大型战舰"瓦萨"号，在它壮丽的起航时刻，带着全身飘扬的彩旗，沉没在了它诞生的港口。

Comprehension 理解

Answer these questions:

1　Why was the *Vasa* regarded as an important ship when she was built?
2　How long did it take to build the *Vasa*?
3　Why is the *Vasa* described as a 'floating work of art'?

Vocabulary 词汇

Refer to the text to see how the following words have been used, then write sentences of your own using these words: galleon (l.1); dictated (l.6); might (l.7); maiden voyage (l.8); in a ferment (l.8); zoomorphic (l.12); ablaze (l.12); portrayed (l.13); churned (l.16); freshened (l.20); sudden squall (l.20); ballast (l.23); inrush (l.24); sealed the ship's fate (l.24).

Summary 摘要

A　Drawing your information from lines 8-26 ('As she was prepared ... her birth.') write a list of points in note form describing what the people in Stockholm harbour saw on August 10, 1628.

B　Using this list of points, reconstruct the author's description of the scene in not more than 100 words. Your answer should be in one paragraph.

Composition 作文

Write a composition of about 300 words on the following subject:

Recovering lost treasure from the sea.

You may use some or all of the ideas given below if you wish:

1   The difficulty of salvaging wrecks in the past.
2   Modern techniques have made salvaging less difficult: skin diving.
3   Hunting for treasure is carried out not only by experts but also by amateurs.
4   Examples of treasure recovered: the Mediterranean: Roman ships; Greek works of art. Off the coast of Florida: gold from Spanish galleons.

Key structures 关键句型

A   Supply the correct form of the verbs in parentheses in the following. Do not refer to the passage until you have finished the exercise:

King Gustavus Adolphus, 'The Northern Hurricane', then at the height of his military success in the Thirty Years' War, _____ (dictate) her measurements and armament. Triple gun-decks _____ (mount) sixty-four bronze cannon. She _____ (intend) to play a leading role in the growing might of Sweden.

   As she _____ (prepare) for her maiden voyage on August 10, 1628, Stockholm _____ (be) in a ferment. From the Skeppsbron and surrounding islands the people _____ (watch) this thing of beauty begin to spread her sails and catch the wind. They _____ (labour) for three years to produce this floating work of art; she more richly _____ (carve) and _____ (ornament) than any previous ship. (ll.5-11)

B   Study this sentence pattern:

The people *watched* this thing of beauty *begin* to spread her sails and *catch* the wind. (ll.9-10)

Complete these sentences using the same pattern:

1   I heard him _____
2   I noticed someone _____
3   Did you see anyone _____

C   Supply *for* or *since* in the following sentences:

1   They had laboured _____ three years to produce this floating work of art. (l.10)
2   _____ 1628 few attempts had been made to salvage the *Vasa*.
3   _____ nearly three and a half centuries she lay at the bottom of Stockholm harbour. (ll.2-3)

D   Note this construction:

As the wind freshened *there came* a sudden squall. (l.20)

Write sentences using the following: there lived; there seemed.

E   Study the construction in italics:

400 people *went sliding and crashing* ... (l.23)

Write sentences using the following expressions:

go shopping; go swimming; go sailing.

Unit 4   Lesson 27

Special difficulties 难点

A Explain the meaning of *spread* in these sentences:

1 The people watched this thing of beauty begin to *spread* her sails. (l.9)

2 You should know better than to *spread* such rumours.

3 *Spread* some jam on your bread.

4 Help me to *spread* the tablecloth.

B Explain the meaning of *produce* in these sentences:

1 They had laboured for three years to *produce* this floating work of art. (l.10)

2 The inspector asked me to *produce* my ticket.

3 Who *produced* this play?

4 This country does not *produce* enough wheat for its needs.

C Explain the meaning of the words in italics:

1 All gun-ports were open and the muzzles *peeped* wickedly from them. (ll.18-19)

2 I opened the door and *peered* into the darkness.

3 I've been so busy, I haven't even *glanced* at today's newspapers.

4 I just *caught a glimpse* of a face at the window.

Multiple choice questions 选择题

Choose the correct answers to the following questions.

Comprehension 理解

1 The loss of the Vasa _____ .

(*a*) was discovered in 1956

(*b*) had been known for centuries

(*c*) played a leading role in the growing might of Sweden

(*d*) increased the King's reputation as 'The Northern Hurricane'

2 At the launch of the Vasa _____ .

(*a*) it must have been immediately obvious she was going to sink

(*b*) everyone in Stockholm was depressed by the event

(*c*) the people of Stockholm must have been very impressed by the spectacle

(*d*) the sailors knew they had been right to be superstitious

3 The Vasa listed to one side because _____ .

(*a*) no one could see anything as a result of the gun smoke

(*b*) all the cannons of the anchored warships thundered a salute

(*c*) all gun ports were open

(*d*) the cannon made one side of the ship too heavy

4 Once _____ , it was impossible to prevent the Vasa from sinking.

(*a*) the wind freshened

(*b*) the sound of rumbling thunder was heard

(*c*) the port-holes were no longer above the surface

(*d*) the Ordnance Officer ordered all the port cannon to be moved to starboard

164

Structure 句型

5 How long has the Vasa _____ at the bottom of Stockholm harbour? (1.2)

(a) lied   (b) laid   (c) lain   (d) lying

6 First they _____ . Then they produced this floating work of art. (1.10)

(a) laboured   (b) had laboured   (c) were labouring   (d) are labouring

7 The cannons thundered a salute which the Vasa replied _____ . (1.15)

(a) at   (b) from   (c) to   (d) in

8 The mighty Vasa sank in the harbour where she _____ .

(a) was borne   (b) born   (c) was born   (d) has borne

Vocabulary 词汇

9 This must be one of the strangest _____ of the sea.

(a) mysteries   (b) tails   (c) storeys   (d) stories

10 She was intended to play a leading role in the growing _____ of Sweden. (1.7)

(a) ability   (b) forces   (c) expectations   (d) power

11 As she prepared for her maiden voyage, Stockholm was _____ . (1.8)

(a) churning   (b) boiling

(c) fermenting   (d) in a state of high excitement

12 The Ordnance Officer ordered all the port cannon to be _____ to starboard. (1.21)

(a) pulled   (b) dropped   (c) lifted   (d) thrown

Lesson 28 Patients and doctors 病人与医生

First listen and then answer the following question.

听录音,然后回答以下问题。

What are patients looking for when they visit the doctor?

This is a sceptical age, but although our faith in many of the things in which our forefathers fervently believed has weakened, our confidence in the curative properties of the bottle of medicine remains the same as theirs. This modern faith in medicines is proved by the fact that the annual drug bill of the Health Services is mounting to astronomical figures and shows no signs at present of ceasing to rise. The majority of the
5 patients attending the medical out-patients departments of our hospitals feel that they have not received adequate treatment unless they are able to carry home with them some tangible remedy in the shape of a bottle of medicine, a box of pills, or a small jar of ointment, and the doctor in charge of the department is only too ready to provide them with these requirements. There is no quicker method of disposing of patients than by giving them what they are asking for, and since most medical men in the Health Services are
10 overworked and have little time for offering time-consuming and little-appreciated advice on such subjects as diet, right living, and the need for abandoning bad habits etc., the bottle, the box, and the jar are almost always granted them.

   Nor is it only the ignorant and ill-educated person who has such faith in the bottle of medicine. It is recounted of Thomas Carlyle that when he heard of the illness of his friend, Henry Taylor, he went off
15 immediately to visit him, carrying with him in his pocket what remained of a bottle of medicine formerly prescribed for an indisposition of Mrs. Carlyle's. Carlyle was entirely ignorant of what the bottle in his pocket contained, of the nature of the illness from which his friend was suffering, and of what had previously been wrong with his wife, but a medicine that had worked so well in one form of illness would surely be of equal benefit in another, and comforted by the thought of the help he was bringing to his friend,
20 he hastened to Henry Taylor's house. History does not relate whether his friend accepted his medical help, but in all probability he did. The great advantage of taking medicine is that it makes no demands on the taker beyond that of putting up for a moment with a disgusting taste, and that is what all patients demand of their doctors—to be cured at no inconvenience to themselves.

KENNETH WALKER *Patients and doctors*

New words and expressions 生词和短语

sceptical (1.1) /'skeptɪkəl/ *adj.* 怀疑的
forefathers (1.1) /'fɔːˌfɑːðəz/ *n.* 祖先
fervently (1.1) /'fɜːvəntli/ *adv.* 热情地
curative (1.2) /'kjʊərətɪv/ *adj.* 治病的
astronomical (1.4) /ˌæstrə'nɒmɪkəl/ *adj.* 天文学的
tangible (1.6) /'tændʒəbəl/ *adj.* 实实在在的

remedy (1.6) /'remɪdi/ *n.* 药物
ointment (1.7) /'ɔɪntmənt/ *n.* 药膏
prescribe (1.16) /prɪ'skraɪb/ *v.* 开药方
indisposition (1.16) /ɪnˌdɪspə'zɪʃən/ *n.* 小病
disgusting (1.22) /dɪs'ɡʌstɪŋ/ *adj.* 令人讨厌的
inconvenience (1.23) /ˌɪnkən'viːniəns/ *n.* 不便

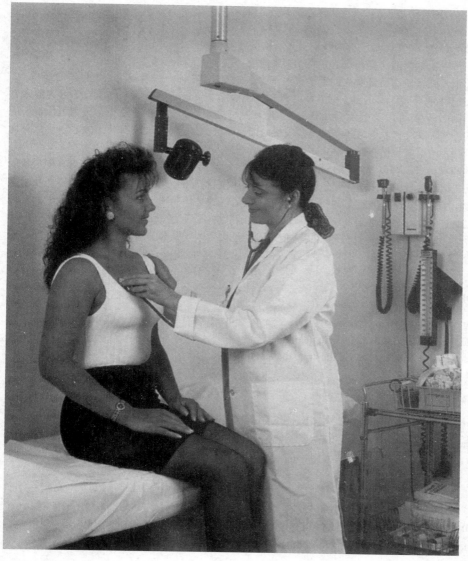

A doctor with her patient

Notes on the text 课文注释

1 the same as theirs, 这里的 theirs 是指 our forefathers'。

2 only too ready to provide, 非常乐意提供。在英语中 too ... to do ... 的结构通常表示否定, 但如果在前面加上 only, 就有 "非常 …… 能做" 的意思。

3 dispose of, 处理。

4 It is recounted of Thomas Carlyle ..., 据说, 托马斯·卡莱尔 …… (有下面这件事)。托马斯·卡莱尔是 19 世纪英国著名的散文作家和历史学家。

5 in all probability, 很可能。

6 put up with, 忍受。

参考译文

　　这是一个怀疑一切的时代，可是虽然我们对我们祖先笃信的许多事物已不太相信，我们对瓶装药品疗效的信心仍与祖辈一样坚定。卫生部门的年度药费上升到了天文数字，并且目前尚无停止上升的迹象，这个事实证实了现代人对药物的信赖。在医院门诊部看病的大多数人觉得，如果不能带回一些看得见、摸得着的药物，如一瓶药水、一盒药丸、一小瓶药膏回家的话，就不算得到充分的治疗。负责门诊的医生也非常乐意为前来看病的人提供他们想要得到的药物，病人要什么就给什么，没有比这样处理病人更快的方法了。因为卫生部门的大多数医生都超负荷工作，所以没有多少时间提出一些既费时而又不受人欢迎的忠告，如注意饮食、生活有规律、需要克服坏习惯等等，结果就是把瓶药、盒药、罐药开给看病的人而完事大吉。

　　并不只是那些无知和没受过良好教育的人才迷信药瓶子。据说托马斯·卡莱尔有过这么一件事：他听说朋友亨利·泰勒病了，就立刻跑去看他，衣袋里装上了他妻子不舒服时吃剩下的一瓶药。卡莱尔不知道药瓶子里装的是什么药，不知道他的朋友得的是什么病，也不知道他妻子以前得的是什么病，只知道一种药对一种病有好处，肯定对另一种病也会有好处。想到能对朋友有所帮助，他感到欣慰，于是急急忙忙来到了亨利·泰勒的家里。他的朋友是否接受了他的药物治疗，历史没有记载，但很可能是接受了。服药的最大优点是：除了暂时忍受一下令人作呕的味道外，对服药人别无其他要求。这也正是病人对医生的要求——病要治好，但不要太麻烦。

Comprehension 理解

Answer these questions:

1　Why do doctors readily provide their patients with medicines?
2　How does the anecdote about Thomas Carlyle illustrate the author's argument?

Vocabulary 词汇

Refer to the text to see how the following words have been used, then write sentences of your own using these words: sceptical (l.1); fervently (l.1); curative properties (l.2); astronomical figures (l.4); tangible (l.6); disposing (l.8); granted (l.12); indisposition (l.16); putting up with (l.22); inconvenience (l.23).

Summary 摘要

A　Drawing your information from the first paragraph (lines 1-12), write a list of points in note form outlining the author's argument that we have great faith in the power of medicine.

B　Using this list of points, reconstruct the author's argument in not more than 80 words. Your answer should be in one paragraph.

Composition 作文

Write a composition of about 300 words on the following subject: 'A public health service is an essential part of social welfare.'

Argue for or against this idea. You may use some or all of the ideas given below if you wish:

1　No one should have the right to buy good health.
2　A public health service is expensive to run and is often abused.
3　No one objects to a public health service more than the doctors.
4　Example of a country where a public health service seems to be an impossibility: America.
5　Examples of countries with successful services: Sweden, Britain, Israel.

Key structures 关键句型

A Note the phrase in italics in this sentence:

Our confidence in the curative properties of the bottle of medicine remains *the same as* theirs. (ll.2-3)

Write two sentences using *the same as* and *different from*.

B Read this sentence:

The fact that the annual drug bill of the Health Services is mounting to astronomical figures proves *this modern faith in medicines*.

Write this sentence again so that it begins with the words in italics. Then compare what you have written with lines 3-4.

C Supply the correct form of the verbs in parentheses in the following sentences. Do not refer to the passage until you have finished the exercise:

1 The annual drugs bill shows no signs at present of _____ (cease) to rise. (ll.3-4)

2 The majority of the patients _____ (attend) the medical out-patients departments feel that they have not received adequate treatment ... (ll.4-6)

3 There is no quicker method of _____ (dispose) of patients than by _____ (give) them what they are asking for, and since most medical men in the Health Services are overworked and have little time for _____ (offer) time-consuming and little-appreciated advice on such subjects as diet, right living, and the need for _____ (abandon) bad habits, etc., the bottle, the box, and the jar are almost always granted them. (ll.8-12)

D Note the form of the verb in italics in this sentence:

Nor *is it* only the ignorant and ill-educated person who has such faith in the bottle of medicine. (l.13)

Write sentences which begin with the following words:

Not only; Never; Only now.

E Write sentences using the following expressions:

believe in (l.2); confidence in (l.2); in charge of (l.7); dispose of (l.8); advice on (l.10); the need for (l.11); prescribed for (l.16); ignorant of (l.16); suffer from (l.17); wrong with (l.18); benefit in (l.19); demand of (l.22); inconvenience to (l.23).

Special difficulties 难点

A Study the following pairs of words and then write sentences of your own to bring out the difference.

1 cease (l.4) — seize

It rained all day without ceasing.

He seized her hand and dragged her into another room.

2 receive (l.5) — take

When did you receive that letter?

He told me to take the keys from his pocket.

3 ask for (l.9) — ask

The school is asking for contributions towards a new swimming pool.

'What time did the train arrive?' he asked.

4 advice (l.10) — advise

She gave me some good advice about jobs.

She advised me about applying for jobs.

5 prescribed (l.16) — proscribed

If these don't work, I may have to prescribe you something stronger.

Gambling was proscribed by the new government.

B Explain the meaning of the words and phrases in italics:

1 The doctor *in charge of* the department is only too ready to provide them with these requirements. (ll.7-8)

2 The soldiers *charged* at the enemy.

3 He was arrested and *charged* with murder.

4 How much did they *charge* you for installing this boiler?

C Note the use of *ill-* in this phrase: ill-educated (l.13).

Write sentences using the following phrases:

ill-advised; ill-informed; ill-prepared.

Multiple choice questions 选择题

Choose the correct answers to the following questions.

Comprehension 理解

1 Patients only feel that they have been adequately treated if they _____ .

(*a*) have some remedy they can take home with them

(*b*) are confident in the curative properties of a bottle of medicine

(*c*) can attend the medical out-patients departments of hospitals

(*d*) see that the state spends more and more money on drugs

2 Because doctors are always working under pressure, they _____ .

(*a*) are not happy about handing out remedies

(*b*) feel morally bound to advise patients about diet and right living

(*c*) are sceptical about the curative powers of medicine

(*d*) are inclined to give patients what they are asking for

3 Even educated people can be misled into believing _____ .

(*a*) that doctors know best

(*b*) you can't be cured by a bottle of medicine

(*c*) that a remedy that will cure one illness is also good for another

(*d*) they are experts in medical matters

4 What patients are looking for is _____ .

(*a*) finding out what is really wrong with them

(*b*) getting out of a doctor's surgery as quickly as possible

(*c*) imposing their will on doctors

(*d*) having remedies which don't inconvenience them in any way

Structure 句型

5 _____ patients attending the medical out-patients departments ... (l.5)

(a) Most　　　　　(b) The most　　　　(c) Majority　　　(d) Majority of

6 They only feel they have received adequate treatment _____ they are able to carry home a tangible remedy. (ll.5-6)

(a) in case　　　　(b) when　　　　　(c) until　　　　(d) unless

7 _____ most medical men are overworked, ... (ll.9-10)

(a) Therefore　　　(b) As a result　　　(c) Because　　　(d) On account

8 It is _____ the ignorant person who has such faith in medicine. (l.13)

(a) not only　　　　(b) both　　　　　(c) neither　　　(d) nor

Vocabulary 词汇

9 Our confidence in the curative _____ of the bottle of medicine remains. (l.2)

(a) substance　　　(b) possessions　　(c) contents　　(d) qualities

10 The annual drugs bill shows no _____ of ceasing to rise. (ll.3-4)

(a) indication　　　(b) signals　　　　(c) signposts　　(d) directions

11 Patients want a remedy they can _____ . (l.6)

(a) drink　　　　　(b) hold in their hands　(c) carry　　(d) eat

12 There is no quicker method of getting _____ patients. (l.8)

(a) on with　　　　(b) away from　　　(c) through　　(d) rid of

Lesson 29 The hovercraft 气垫船

📼 **First listen and then answer the following question.**
听录音, 然后回答以下问题。

What is a hovercraft riding on when it is in motion?

Many strange new means of transport have been developed in our century, the strangest of them being perhaps the hovercraft. In 1953, a former electronics engineer in his fifties, Christopher Cockerell, who had turned to boat-building on the Norfolk Broads, suggested an idea on which he had been working for many years to the British Government and industrial circles. It was the idea of supporting a craft on a 'pad', or
5 cushion, of low-pressure air, ringed with a curtain of higher pressure air. Ever since, people have had difficulty in deciding whether the craft should be ranged among ships, planes, or land vehicles—for it is something in between a boat and an aircraft. As a shipbuilder, Cockerell was trying to find a solution to the problem of the wave resistance which wastes a good deal of a surface ship's power and limits its speed. His answer was to lift the vessel out of the water by making it ride on a cushion of air, no more than one or two
10 feet thick. This is done by a great number of ring-shaped air jets on the bottom of the craft. It 'flies', therefore, but it cannot fly higher—its action depends on the surface, water or ground, over which it rides.

The first tests on the Solent in 1959 caused a sensation. The hovercraft travelled first over the water, then mounted the beach, climbed up the dunes, and sat down on a road. Later it crossed the Channel, riding smoothly over the waves, which presented no problem.

15 Since that time, various types of hovercraft have appeared and taken up regular service. The hovercraft is particularly useful in large areas with poor communications such as Africa or Australia; it can become a 'flying fruit-bowl', carrying bananas from the plantations to the ports; giant hovercraft liners could span the Atlantic; and the railway of the future may well be the 'hovertrain', riding on its air cushion over a single rail, which it never touches, at speeds up to 300 m.p.h.—the possibilities appear unlimited.

EGON LARSEN *The Pegasus Book of Inventors*

New words and expressions 生词和短语

hovercraft (title) /'hɒvəkrɑːft/ *n.* 气垫船
Norfolk Broads (1.3) /ˌnɔːfək'brɔːdz/ *n.* 诺福克郡布罗兹区
cushion (1.5) /'kʊʃən/ *n.* 座垫
ring (1.5) /rɪŋ/ *v.* 围

Solent (1.12) /'səʊlənt/ *n.* （英国的）苏伦特海峡
sensation (1.12) /sen'seɪʃən/ *n.* 轰动
dune (1.13) /djuːn/ *n.* 沙丘
plantation (1.17) /plæn'teɪʃən/ *n.* 种植园
hovertrain (1.18) /'hɒvətreɪn/ *n.* 气垫火车

Notes on the text 课文注释

1 the strangest of them being perhaps the hovercraft, 这是现在分词 being 的独立主格结构。
2 in between, 介乎 …… 之间, 这是一种组合介词。

A hovercraft

3   a surface ship, 水面船只 。
4   may well be, 很可能是 。

参考译文

　　本世纪已研制出许多新奇的交通工具, 其中最新奇的要数气垫船了 。1953 年, 有一位 50 多岁名叫克里斯托弗·科克雷尔的原电子工程师, 改行在诺福克郡布罗兹区从事造船业, 他向英国政府和工业界提出了他研究多年的一项计划 。他的设想是: 用一个低压空气垫或软垫来支撑船体, 软垫周围用高压空气环绕 。自那以后, 人们很难决定是否应该将这种运载工具列为轮船 、飞机, 或是陆上交通工具, 因为它是介于船和飞机之间 。作为一个船舶技师, 科克雷尔在寻找解决波浪阻力的方法, 因为波浪阻力浪费掉了船在水面行驶的大量动力, 从而限制了船的速度 。他的解决办法是把船体提离水面, 让船在一个气垫上行驶, 气垫只有一两英尺厚 。船底装上大量环状喷气嘴以实现这一目的 。这样, 船就能飞了, 但飞不高 。它的飞行取决于它所悬浮的水面或地面 。

　　1959 年, 在苏伦特海峡进行的首次试航引起了轰动 。气垫船先是在水面上行驶, 后又登上海岸, 爬上沙丘, 最后停在路上 。后来气垫船跨越英吉利海峡, 平稳地在波浪上行驶, 波浪不再产生阻力 。

　　从那以后, 各种各样的气垫船出现了, 并开始了定期航行服务 。气垫船在非洲 、澳大利亚等幅员辽阔 、交通不发达的地区特别有用 。它能成为 "飞行水果盘子", 把香蕉从种植园运到港口 。大型的气垫班轮或许能跨越大西洋 。未来的火车或许能成为 "气垫火车", 靠气垫在单轨上行驶而不接触轨道, 时速可达每小时 300 英里 。气垫船的前途是不可限量的 。

Comprehension 理解

1   State briefly how a hovercraft works.
2   Name two ways in which the hovercraft may transform sea and land transport.

Vocabulary 词汇

Refer to the text to see how the following words have been used, then write sentences of your own using these words: a former (l.2); ringed with (l.5); ranged (l.6); a solution to the problem (ll.7-8); caused a sensation (l.12); riding smoothly (ll.13-14); span (l.17).

Summary 摘要

A Drawing your information from the first two paragraphs (lines 1-14), write a list of points in note form describing how the hovercraft was developed.

B Using this list of points, reconstruct the author's account in not more than 90 words. Your answer should be in one paragraph.

Composition 作文

Write a composition of about 300 words on the following subject: Modern means of transport.

You may use some or all of the ideas given below if you wish:

1　The main emphasis in all forms of transport is speed and comfort. The world has become a smaller place.
2　Air travel: the jet aeroplane; the helicopter; future possibilities in the rocket.
3　Sea: ocean liners; the hydrofoil; the hovercraft.
4　Land: electric trains; automatic control (e.g. Japan); the car; the building of motorway networks.
5　Of all modern means of transport, the car is creating most problems as it is causing serious congestion in cities. No satisfactory solution to this problem has yet been found.

Key structures 关键句型

A Note the use of *being* in this sentence:

Many strange new means of transport have been developed in our century, the strangest of them *being* perhaps the hovercraft. (ll. 1-2)

Complete these sentences using the same construction:

1　Many international exhibitions have been held, the most recent one _____
2　New York is full of skyscrapers, the tallest one _____

B Supply the correct form of the verbs in parentheses in the following. Do not refer to the passage until you have finished the exercise:

In 1953, a former electronics engineer in his fifties, Christopher Cockerell, who _____ (turn) to boat-building on the Norfolk Broads, _____ (suggest) an idea on which he _____ (work) for many years to the British Government and industrial circles. It _____ (be) the idea of _____ (support) a craft on a 'pad', or cushion, of low-pressure air, _____ (ring) with a curtain of higher pressure air. Ever since, people _____ (have) difficulty in _____ (decide) whether the craft _____ (should range) among ships, planes, or land vehicles. (ll.2-6)

C   Supply *among* or *between* in the following sentences:

1   People have had difficulty in deciding whether the craft should be ranged _____ ships, planes, or land vehicles. (ll.5-6)

2   It is something in _____ a boat and an aircraft. (ll.6-7)

3   Diplomatic relations _____ the two countries have been broken.

4   Strictly _____ you and me, this whole business is beginning to get me down.

D   Note the phrase *a good deal of* in this sentence:

'Wave resistance ... wastes *a good deal of* a surface ship's power.' (l.8)

Write sentences using the following phrases: a great deal of; a great many; a good many; a good few.

E   Note the form of the verbs in italics:

His answer was to lift the vessel out of the water by *making* it *ride* on a cushion of air. (ll.8-9)

Complete the following sentences:

1   I made him _____

2   The teacher made the class _____

3   He trained the team by making them _____

F   Compare these two sentences:

Instead of saying: *It is quite likely that* the railway of the future will be the 'hovertrain'.

We can say: The railway of the future *may* (or *might*) *well* be the 'hovertrain'. (l.18)

Write two sentences using *may* (or *might*) *well* in this way.

Special difficulties 难点

A   Study the following pairs of words and then write sentences of your own to bring out the difference.

1   engineer (l.2) — mechanic

It is every engineer's dream to design a machine that will use water as fuel.

Can I have a word with the mechanic who serviced my car?

2   solution (l.7) — solvent

The ozone layer is depleting and there's no easy solution to this problem.

Water is the commonest solvent.

B   Explain the meaning of the verbs in italics:

1   He had *turned to* boat-building on the Norfolk Broads. (ll.2-3)

2   Please *turn off* the tap.

3   Aunt Matilda *turned up* unexpectedly last night.

4   The soldiers marched to the other side of the park, *turned about*, and marched back.

C   Note the use of the verb *ride* in this sentence:

It crossed the Channel, *riding* smoothly over the waves. (ll.13-14)

Write sentences using the following expressions:

ride a horse; go for a ride (in a car, on a bicycle); give someone a ride.

Multiple choice questions 选择题

Choose the correct answers to the following questions.

Comprehension 理解

1 The hovercraft depends on _____ to keep off the ground.

   (*a*) electronics

   (*b*) rings

   (*c*) air pressure

   (*d*) a curtain

2 Christopher Cockerell had been working on this idea _____ .

   (*a*) for the British Government

   (*b*) in industrial circles

   (*c*) on his own

   (*d*) in the boat-building industry

3 The extraodinary thing about the hovercraft is that it can travel at speed _____ .

   (*a*) over land and water

   (*b*) exactly like a helicopter

   (*c*) because it resists waves

   (*d*) on air pressure

4 The exciting thing about the hovercraft principle is that it _____ .

   (*a*) can be used as a 'flying fruit-bowl'

   (*b*) is good for communications

   (*c*) has been applied to cross the Atlantic

   (*d*) has implications for other modes of transport

Structure 句型

5 _____ , people have had difficulty ... (1.5)

   (*a*) As a result   (*b*) Because of this   (*c*) Up till then   (*d*) From that time

6 Ever since, people have _____ difficulty in deciding ... (ll.5-6)

   (*a*) obtained   (*b*) possessed   (*c*) experienced   (*d*) enjoyed

7 That's the _____ he made it ride on a cushion of air. (1.9)

   (*a*) direction   (*b*) how   (*c*) way   (*d*) idea

8 Its action depends on the surface _____ . (1.11)

   (*a*) it rides over   (*b*) riding over it   (*c*) it rides   (*d*) which it rides

Vocabulary 词汇

9 Cockerell was trying to find the _____ the problem. (1.7)

   (*a*) solvent for   (*b*) explanation of   (*c*) result of   (*d*) answer to

10 This is done by a great number of air jets _____ the craft. (1.10)

   (*a*) under   (*b*) at the depth of   (*c*) deeper than   (*d*) at the basis of

11 The hovercraft travelled first over the water, then _____ the beach. (1.12-13)

   (*a*) hit   (*b*) climbed up   (*c*) crashed into   (*d*) met

12 Since that time _____ types of hovercraft have appeared. (1.15)

   (*a*) many   (*b*) unusual   (*c*) different   (*d*) developed

Lesson 30 Exploring the sea-floor 海底勘探

First listen and then answer the following question.

听录音，然后回答以下问题 。

How did people probably imagine the sea-floor before it was investigated?

Our knowledge of the oceans a hundred years ago was confined to the two-dimensional shape of the sea surface and the hazards of navigation presented by the irregularities in depth of the shallow water close to the land. The open sea was deep and mysterious, and anyone who gave more than a passing thought to the bottom confines of the oceans probably assumed that the sea bed was flat. Sir James Clark Ross had obtained
5 a sounding of over 2,400 fathoms in 1839, but it was not until 1869, when H. M. S. *Porcupine* was put at the disposal of the Royal Society for several cruises, that a series of deep soundings was obtained in the Atlantic and the first samples were collected by dredging the bottom. Shortly after this the famous H. M. S. *Challenger* expedition established the study of the sea-floor as a subject worthy of the most qualified physicists and geologists. A burst of activity associated with the laying of submarine cables soon confirmed the *Challenger's*
10 observation that many parts of the ocean were two to three miles deep, and the existence of underwater features of considerable magnitude.

Today, enough soundings are available to enable a relief map of the Atlantic to be drawn and we know something of the great variety of the sea bed's topography. Since the sea covers the greater part of the earth's surface, it is quite reasonable to regard the sea floor as the basic form of the crust of the earth, with,
15 superimposed upon it, the continents, together with the islands and other features of the oceans. The continents form rugged tablelands which stand nearly three miles above the floor of the open ocean. From the shore line, out to a distance which may be anywhere from a few miles to a few hundred miles, runs the gentle slope of the continental shelf, geologically part of the continents. The real dividing line between continents and oceans occurs at the foot of a steeper slope.

20 This continental slope usually starts at a place somewhere near the 100-fathom mark and in the course of a few hundred miles reaches the true ocean floor at 2,500-3,500 fathoms. The slope averages about 1 in 30, but contains steep, probably vertical, cliffs, and gentle sediment-covered terraces, and near its lower reaches there is a long tailing-off which is almost certainly the result of material transported out to deep water after being eroded from the continental masses.

T. F. GASKELL *Exploring the Sea-floor* from *Science Survey*

New words and expressions 生词和短语

navigation (1.2) /ˌnævɪ'geɪʃən/ n. 航海
sounding (1.5) /'saʊndɪŋ/ n. 水深度
fathom (1.5) /'fæðəm/ n. 英寻（1 英寻约等于1.8米）
porcupine (1.5) /'pɔːkjʊpaɪn/ n. 箭猪
dredge (1.7) /dredʒ/ v. 挖掘
expedition (1.8) /ˌekspɪ'dɪʃən/ n. 远征
physicist (1.8) /'fɪzɪsɪst/ n. 物理学家
magnitude (1.11) /'mægnɪtjuːd/ n. 很多

topography (1.13) /tə'pɒgrəfi/ n. 地形
crust (1.14) /krʌst/ n. 地壳
rugged (1.16) /'rʌgɪd/ adj. 崎岖不平的
tableland (1.16) /'teɪbəl-lænd/ n. 高地
sediment (1.22) /'sedɪmənt/ n. 沉淀物
terrace (1.22) /'terəs/ n. 阶地
erode (1.24) /ɪ'rəʊd/ v. 侵蚀

H. M. S. *Challenger* at St. Paul's Rocks near the Equator

Notes on the text 课文注释

1 be confined to, 仅限于 …… 。

2 shallow water, 浅水区 。

3 open sea, 无边际的大海 。

4 gave more than a passing thought to, 稍微想过 。

5 H. M. S. 是 Her/His Majesty's Ship（英国皇家海军舰艇）的缩写 。

6 at the disposal of, 交由 …… 支配 。

7 a relief map, 地形图 。

8 with, superimposed upon it, the continents, together with the islands and other features of the oceans, 这是 with 引导的一个过去分词独立主格结构 。因逻辑主语太长, 所以使用了倒装语序 。superimposed upon it 是逻辑谓语部分 。

9 continental shelf ,大陆架 。

10 1 in 30, 1/30 。

参考译文

　　100 年前, 我们只知道海洋是二维平面形的, 以及靠近陆地浅水区的深浅不一能给航行带来危险 。无边无际的海洋深邃而又神秘, 凡是稍稍想过大海海底的人大概都会认为海底是平坦的 。1839年, 詹姆斯·克拉克·罗斯爵士曾测得海水深度超过 2400 英寻; 但直到 1869 年, 皇家学会用英国 "豪猪" 号舰艇进行了几次巡航后, 才在大西洋测得一个个海水深度, 同时通过挖掘海底, 取得了研究海底的首批样品 。此后不久, 英国著名的 "挑战者" 号舰艇对海底的那次考察, 把对海床的研究确立为一个值得一流物理学家和地质学家从事的研究课题 。铺设海底电缆的热潮很快证实了 "挑战者" 号的观察结果: 海洋中很多地方可深达两三英里, 水下特征差异极大 。

　　现在已有足够的水深测量数据来绘制一张大西洋洋底地形图, 而且我们对海底地形的千变万化也有了一定的了解 。既然海洋覆盖着地球的大部分表面, 因此完全有理由把海床看作地壳的基本模壳, 上面附加着大陆以及岛屿和海洋的其他形态 。大陆是崎岖不平的高地, 高出辽阔海洋海底近三英里 。从海岸线向大海延伸几英里到几百英里的区域是大陆架慢坡，从地质学上来说，它是大陆的一部分。大陆和海洋的真正分界线是在陡坡脚下。

　　大陆架慢坡一般是从差不多 100 英寻深的地方开始的，一直延伸到几百英里远深达 2500 至 3500 英寻深的地方，那里才是真正的海底。坡度平均约为 1/30，但其中包括陡峭的，乃至垂直的峭壁和沉积物覆盖的缓和的阶梯地带，在这个地带的低处是很长的一段尾沙地段，基本上可以断定这个地段是大陆块体上侵蚀下来的物质被水冲到深水处形成的。

Comprehension 理解

Answer these questions:

1　What does the author mean by the phrase 'the two-dimensional shape of the sea surface'? (ll.1-2)

2　Which sentence in the first paragraph suggests that before the expedition of H. M. S. *Challenger* the sea bed was not considered as an object for serious study?

3　What lies immediately between the continental slope and the true ocean floor?

Vocabulary 词汇

Refer to the text to see how the following words have been used, then write sentences of your own using these words: hazards of navigation (l.2); dredging (l.7); submarine (l.9); considerable magnitude (l.11); relief (l.12); crust (l.14); superimposed (l.14); vertical (l.22); tailing-off (l.23); eroded (l.24).

Summary 摘要

A　Drawing your information from the first two paragraphs (lines 1-19), write a list of points in note form, outlining the author's account of the study of the sea bed.

B　Using this list of points, reconstruct the author's account in not more than 120 words. Your answer should be in one paragraph.

Composition 作文

Write a composition of about 300 words on the following subject:

Man has done relatively little to exploit the wealth of the sea.

You may use some or all of the ideas given below if you wish:

1　The intensive study of the sea is comparatively recent.

2　The sea as a source of power: harnessing the tides to provide electricity.

3　The sea as a source of food: distilling water from the sea; fish; plankton as a source of protein to feed growing world population; 'cultivating' the sea bed.

4　The sea as a source of wealth: obtaining minerals; oil or gas under the sea (e.g. the North Sea).

5　The setting up of permanent villages under the sea; the pioneer work of Jacques Cousteau.

Key structures 关键句型

A　Supply the correct form of the verbs in parentheses. Do not refer to the passage until you have finished the exercise:

1　Our knowledge of the oceans a hundred years ago _____ (confine) to the two-dimensional shape of the sea surface. (ll.1-2)

2   It was not until 1869, when H. M. S. *Porcupine* _____ (put) at the disposal of the Royal Society for several
    cruises, that a series of deep soundings _____ (obtain) in the Atlantic and the first samples _____ (collect)
    by dredging the bottom. (ll.5-7)

3   Today enough soundings are available to enable a relief map of the Atlantic _____ (draw) and we know
    something of the great variety of the sea bed's topography. (ll.12-13)

B   Compare these two sentences:
    Instead of saying: It was *only in 1869* ... that a series of deep soundings was obtained in the Atlantic.
    We can say: It was not until 1869 ... that a series of deep soundings was obtained in the Atlantic. (ll.5-7)
    Change the following sentences in the same way:

1   I only understood what had happened when I read the report in the newspaper.
2   The plane will only take off again when the engine has been checked.
3   Tom only got home at four o'clock this morning.
4   I shall return this book to the library only after I have read it.
5   He agreed to deliver the goods only after I had paid for them.

C   Compare the uses of *since* in these two sentences:

1   *Since* the sea covers the greater part of the earth's surface, form of the crust of the earth. (ll.13-14)
2   I have not seen him *since* last week.
    Write two sentences illustrating these two uses of *since*.

Special difficulties 难点

A   Study the following pairs of words and then write sentences of your own to bring out the difference.
1   flat (l.4) — level
    In front of the hotel is a perfectly flat sandy beach. (= smooth without hollows and bumps)
    You have to adjust it so that the front is level with the back. (= horizontal and in the same place)
2   disposal (l.6) — disposition
    Waste paper is one of the biggest problems in rubbish disposal.
    This old house may be charming, but the disposition of the rooms is hardly ideal. (= the way they are placed)
    Verity has a sweet disposition. (= nature, temperament)
3   worthy (l.8) — valuable
    Nothing particularly worthy of notice occurred during the two following days.
    I won't waste any more of your valuable time.
4   confirm (l.9) — assure
    Overnight reports of an explosion were officially confirmed the next day.
    The police assured us that everything that could be done had been done.
5   rugged (l.16) — ragged
    North Cornwall has a rugged coastline, with high cliffs.
    The begger slept on a pile of ragged blankets.

B   Write two sentences using the phrases 'the open sea' (l.3) and 'the open air'.

C   Note that the word *series* (l.6) is singular. Write sentences using the following words:
    mathematics, news, physics, billiards.

D   Write sentences using the following words and phrases:

shortly after (1.7); shortly before; shortly.

E   Explain the meaning of the word *feature* in these sentences:

1   A burst of activity soon confirmed the existence of underwater *features* of considerable magnitude. (ll.9-11)

2   I never enjoy *feature* films.

3   The present world tour of the President of the United States *is featured* prominently in all today's newspapers.

4   I hardly recognized him when I saw him again: his *features* have changed with the years.

F   What do you understand by the phrase: 'the slope averages about *1 in 30*.' (1.21) ?

Write sentences using the following expressions:

1 in 10; 1 in 1,000. '... the slope averages about *1 in 30* ... ' (1.21)

Multiple choice questions 选择题

Choose the correct answers to the following questions.

Comprehension 理解

1   A hundred years ago, probably no one thought the deep ocean floor was _____ .

(*a*) two dimensional

(*b*) a hazard for navigation

(*c*) irregular

(*d*) flat

2   The H.M.S. Challenger expedition _____ .

(*a*) gave the study of the ocean floor scientific respectability

(*b*) took a sounding of over 2,400 fathoms

(*c*) was devoted to dredging the ocean

(*d*) was devoted to laying submarine cables

3   Continents and islands are standing on _____ .

(*a*) the topography of the sea bed

(*b*) the earth's crust

(*c*) the greater part of the earth's surface

(*d*) superimposed features of the continents

4   The continental slope _____.

(*a*) starts immediately at the seashore

(*b*) consists entirely of steep, probably vertical cliffs

(*c*) ends at the 100-fathom mark

(*d*) gradually stretches out to the sea bed

Structure 句型

5   It was only _____ 1869 that H.M.S. Porcupine obtained soundings. (ll.5-6)

(*a*) on   (*b*) at   (*c*) until   (*d*) in

6   The sea floor became a subject _____ studying.

(*a*) worthy   (*b*) worth   (*c*) is worth   (*d*) worths

Unit 4 Lesson 30

7 Submarine cables were _____ across the Atlantic. (1.9)

    (*a*) lying   (*b*) lain   (*c*) laid   (*d*) lied

8 It is _____ to regard the sea-floor as the earth's crust. (1.14)

    (*a*) less reasonable   (*b*) enough reasonable   (*c*) reasonable enough   (*d*) so reasonable

Vocabulary 词汇

9 The Royal Society was allowed the _____ of the H.M.S. Porcupine. (ll.5-6)

    (*a*) use   (*b*) loan   (*c*) rental   (*d*) exploration

10 A burst of activity _____ with the laying of submarine cables ... (1.9)

    (*a*) coupled   (*b*) communicated   (*c*) connected   (*d*) reckoned

11 ... together with the islands and other _____ of the oceans. (1.15)

    (*a*) studies   (*b*) observations   (*c*) characters   (*d*) characteristics

12 ... after being _____ from the continental masses. (ll.23-24)

    (*a*) worn down   (*b*) worn through   (*c*) worn away   (*d*) worn out

Lesson 31 The sculptor speaks 雕塑家的语言

First listen and then answer the following question.

听录音, 然后回答以下问题 。

What do you have to be able to do to appreciate sculpture?

Appreciation of sculpture depends upon the ability to respond to form in three dimensions. That is perhaps why sculpture has been described as the most difficult of all arts; certainly it is more difficult than the arts which involve appreciation of flat forms, shape in only two dimensions. Many more people are 'form-blind' than colour-blind. The child learning to see, first distinguishes only two-dimensional shape; it cannot judge
5 distances, depths. Later, for its personal safety and practical needs, it has to develop (partly by means of touch) the ability to judge roughly three-dimensional distances. But having satisfied the requirements of practical necessity, most people go no further. Though they may attain considerable accuracy in the perception of flat form, they do not make the further intellectual and emotional effort needed to comprehend form in its full spatial existence.

10 This is what the sculptor must do. He must strive continually to think of, and use, form in its full spatial completeness. He gets the solid shape, as it were, inside his head—he thinks of it, whatever its size, as if he were holding it completely enclosed in the hollow of his hand. He mentally visualizes a complex form *from all round* itself; he knows while he looks at one side what the other side is like; he identifies himself with its centre of gravity, its mass, its weight; he realizes its volume, as the space that the shape displaces in the air.

15 And the sensitive observer of sculpture must also learn to feel shape simply as shape, not as description or reminiscence. He must, for example, perceive an egg as a simple single solid shape, quite apart from its significance as food, or from the literary idea that it will become a bird. And so with solids such as a shell, a nut, a plum, a pear, a tadpole, a mushroom, a mountain peak, a kidney, a carrot, a tree-trunk, a bird, a bud, a lark, a ladybird, a bulrush, a bone. From these he can go on to appreciate more complex forms or
20 combinations of several forms.

HENRY MOORE *The Sculptor Speaks* from *The Listener*

New words and expressions 生词和短语

colour-blind (1.4) /ˈkʌlə-blaɪnd/ *adj.* 色盲的
perception (1.8) /pəˈsepʃən/ *n.* 知觉
comprehend (1.8) /ˌkɒmprɪˈhend/ *v.* 理解
spatial (1.9) /ˈspeɪʃəl/ *adj.* 空间的
visualize (1.12) /ˈvɪʒuəlaɪz/ *v.* 使具形象, 设想
reminiscence (1.16) /ˌremɪˈnɪsəns/ *n.* 回忆, 联想
tadpole (1.18) /ˈtædpəʊl/ *n.* 蝌蚪

mushroom (1.18) /ˈmʌʃruːm/ *n.* 蘑菇
carrot (1.18) /ˈkærət/ *n.* 胡萝卜
bud (1.18) /bʌd/ *n.* 花蕾
lark (1.19) /lɑːk/ *n.* 云雀
ladybird (1.19) /ˈleɪdɪbɜːd/ *n.* 瓢虫
bulrush (1.19) /ˈbʊlrʌʃ/ *n.* 芦苇

Notes on the text 课文注释

1   form-blind, 这是作者仿照 colour-blind （色盲）生造的一个词, 意指 "形盲"。
2   in its full spatial completeness, 存在于空间的整个（形体）。

183

Henry Moore and his sculpture, *Reclining Figure*

3   as it were, 可以说是 。

4   whatever its size, 这是一个省略了 may be 的让步状语从句 。

5   from all round itself, 从它的各个角度构想 。

6   centre of gravity, 重心 。

7   apart from, 除了……外 。

参考译文

对雕塑的鉴赏力取决于对立体的反应能力 。雕塑被说成是所有艺术中最难的艺术, 可能就是这个道理 。欣赏雕塑品当然比欣赏平面的艺术品要难 。 "形盲" 的人数比 "色盲" 的人数要多得多 。正在学看东西的儿童起初只会分辨二维形态, 不会判断距离和深度 。慢慢地, 由于自身安全和实际需要, 儿童必须发展 (部分通过触觉) 粗略判断三维空间距离的能力 。但是, 大部分人在满足了实际需要后, 就不再继续发展这种能力了 。虽然他们对平面形式的感觉能达到相当准确的程度, 但他们没有在智力和情感上进一步努力去理解存在于空间的整个形态 。

而雕塑家就必须做到这一点 。他必须勤于想象并且利用形体在空间中的完整性 。可以这样说, 当他想象一个物体时, 不管其大小如何, 他脑子里得到的是一个立体的概念, 就好像完全握在自己手心里一样 。他的大脑能从物体的各个角度勾画出其复杂的形象, 他看物体的一边时, 便知道另一边是个什么样子 。他把自身和物体的重心 、质量 、重量融为一体 。他能意识到物体的体积, 那就是它的形状在空气中所占的空间 。

因此, 敏锐的雕塑观赏者也必须学会把形体作为形体来感觉, 不要靠描述和联想去感觉 。以鸟蛋为例, 观赏者必须感觉到它是一个单一的实体形态, 而完全不靠它的食用意义或它会变成鸟这样的文学概念来感觉 。对于其他实体, 如贝壳 、核桃 、李子 、梨子 、蝌蚪 、蘑菇 、山峰 、肾脏 、胡萝卜 、树干 、鸟儿 、花蕾 、云雀 、瓢虫 、芦苇以及骨头也应这样来感觉 。从这些形体出发, 观赏者可进一步观察更为复杂的形体或若干形体的组合 。

Comprehension 理解

Answer these questions:

1   What does the author mean when he says that many people are 'form-blind'? (l.3)

2   What do you understand by the following statement: 'The sensitive observer of sculpture must also learn to feel shape simply as shape, not as a description or reminiscence.'? (ll.15-16)

Vocabulary 词汇

Refer to the text to see how the following words have been used, then write sentences of your own using these words: in three dimensions (l.1); involve (l.3); distinguishes (l.4); roughly (l.6); they may attain considerable accuracy in the perception (ll.7-8); strive (l.10); visualizes (l.12); combinations (ll.19-20).

Summary 摘要

A   Drawing your information from the first two paragraphs (lines 1-14), write a list of points in note form to answer the following question: How does a sculptor's appreciation of form differ from that of an ordinary person?

B   Using this list of points, reconstruct the author's argument in not more than 90 words. Your answer should be in one paragraph.

Composition 作文

Write a composition of about 300 words on the following subject:

'The arts (music, literature, painting and sculpture) cannot be enjoyed unless one has a specialized knowledge of them.'

Argue against this statement. You may use some or all of the ideas given below if you wish:

1   Many people enjoy listening to music, reading novels or poetry, looking at pictures or sculpture without knowing anything about the technical difficulties involved in creating works of art.

2   There is a difference between appreciation and enjoyment: in order to appreciate a work of art, one should have a great deal of specialized knowledge; in order to enjoy a work of art, no such knowledge is necessary.

3   Specialized knowledge can increase one's enjoyment: a trained mind knows what to look for.

4   Specialized knowledge can diminish one's enjoyment: it may make you hypercritical and interfere with your response.

5   Artists do not create works of art for those who have specialized knowledge only: often they attempt to communicate to large numbers of people.

6   If specialized knowledge were necessary to enjoy the arts, then only those engaged in the arts would be in a position to enjoy them—something which is demonstrably untrue.

Key structures 关键句型

A   Supply the missing words in the following sentences. Do not refer to the passage until you have finished the exercise:

1   That is perhaps why sculpture has been described as _____ _____ difficult _____ all arts; certainly it is _____ difficult _____ the arts which involve appreciation of flat forms. (ll.1-3)

2   _____ _____ people are 'form-blind' _____ colour-blind. (ll.3-4)

3   But having satisfied the requirements of practical necessity, _____ people go no _____ . (ll.6-7)

B   Compare these two sentences:

Instead of saying: *When they have satisfied* the requirements of practical necessity, most people go no further.

We can say: *Having satisfied* the requirements of practical necessity, most people go no further. (ll.6-7)

Write three sentences beginning with *Having*.

C   Rewrite each of these sentences replacing *has to* by *must*:

1   This is what the sculptor has to do. (l.10)

2   He has to strive continually to think of, and use, form in its full spatial completeness. (ll.10-11)

3   And the sensitive observer of sculpture also has to learn to feel shape simply as shape, not as description or reminiscence. (ll.15-16)

4   He has, for example, to perceive an egg as a simple single solid shape. (l.16)

D   Note the construction in italics:

He thinks of it *as if he were holding* it completely enclosed in the hollow of his hand. (ll.11-12)

Complete the following sentences using the same construction:

1   He acted as if _____

2   He talked as if _____

3   It looked as if _____

Special difficulties 难点

A   Study the following pairs of words and then write sentences of your own to bring out the difference.

1   appreciation (l.1) — estimation

I wish to express my appreciation of the numerous courtesies extended to me by the company.

Your estimation of the time needed seems about right. (= approximate calculation, judgment)

2   distinguish (l.4) — perceive

We have to distinguish carefully between fact and legend.

I don't perceive any improvement in the economy.

3   depth (l.5) — deeps

What depth is this well?

Up till now, we have known more about Space than about the deeps/depths of the oceans on this planet.

4   displace (l.14) — replace

Coal is being displaced by natural gas as a major source of energy.

They are replacing the old windows with double glazing.

5   single (l.16) — unique

There is not a single public phone in the village.

Each person's fingerprints are unique.

B   Explain the meaning of the word *form* in these sentences:

1   It is more difficult than the arts which involve appreciation of flat *forms*. (ll.2-3)

2   A new golf club has just been *formed* in our district.

3   How many children are there in your *form*?

4   I don't feel like playing tennis. I haven't been in very good *form* lately.

5   There were not enough chairs to go round so we had to sit on *forms*.

6   Would you please fill up this *form*?

C   Explain the meaning of the phrases in italics:

1   ... he knows while he looks at one side what the other side *is like*. (l.13)

2   What *is* your new school *like*?

3   What *was* the weather *like* yesterday?

Multiple choice questions 选择题

Choose the correct answers to the following questions.

Comprehension 理解

1 Sculpture has been described as the most difficult of the arts because _____ .

   (a) it is not two-dimensional

   (b) most people are 'form-blind'

   (c) of the difficulty of working in stone

   (d) it depends on special abilities

2 We all learn about three dimensions _____ .

   (a) as a matter of practical necessity and no more

   (b) to appreciate sculptural forms

   (c) through intellectual and emotional effort

   (d) with considerable accuracy

3 A sculptor must be able to _____ .

   (a) hold his sculpture in the hollow of his hand

   (b) think of his sculpture viewed from every angle

   (c) identify himself with his sculpture

   (d) carry his sculpture inside his head

4 The important thing for a sculptor is the appreciation of the _____ of objects.

   (a) form   (b) ideas behind   (c) meaning   (d) description

Structure 句型

5 _____ more people are 'form-blind'. (1.3)

   (a) Lots of   (b) Lot of   (c) A lot of   (d) A lot

6 But _____ the requirements of practical necessity ... (1.7)

   (a) to satisfy   (b) when it has satisfied

   (c) it has satisfied   (d) having to satisfy

7 He knows _____ he looks at one side what the other side is like. (1.13)

   (a) as   (b) that   (c) since   (d) during

8 And so with solids _____ . (1.17)

   (a) like to shells   (b) as shells   (c) such as shell   (d) like shells

Vocabulary 词汇

9 It depends on the ability to _____ form in three dimentions. (1.1)

   (a) surrender to   (b) reply to   (c) answer   (d) react to

10 The child learning to see, first makes _____ only two-dimensional shape. (1.4)

   (a) away   (b) off   (c) out   (d) off

11 They do not make the _____ intellectual effort. (1.8)

   (a) exceptional   (b) additional   (c) more   (d) farther

12 He must learn to feel shape not as description or _____ . (ll.15-16)

   (a) souvenir   (b) remembrance   (c) memorial   (d) something remembered

Lesson 32   Galileo reborn   伽利略的复生

▭ **First listen and then answer the following question.**

听录音, 然后回答以下问题 。

What has modified our traditional view of Galileo in recent times?

In his own lifetime Galileo was the centre of violent controversy; but the scientific dust has long since settled, and today we can see even his famous clash with the Inquisition in something like its proper perspective. But, in contrast, it is only in modern times that Galileo has become a problem child for historians of science.

5　　The old view of Galileo was delightfully uncomplicated. He was, above all, a man who experimented: who despised the prejudices and book learning of the Aristotelians, who put his questions to nature instead of to the ancients, and who drew his conclusions fearlessly. He had been the first to turn a telescope to the sky, and he had seen there evidence enough to overthrow Aristotle and Ptolemy together. He was the man who climbed the Leaning Tower of Pisa and dropped various weights from the top, who rolled balls down
10　inclined planes, and then generalized the results of his many experiments into the famous law of free fall.

　　But a closer study of the evidence, supported by a deeper sense of the period, and particularly by a new consciousness of the philosophical undercurrents in the scientific revolution, has profoundly modified this view of Galileo. Today, although the old Galileo lives on in many popular writings, among historians of science a new and more sophisticated picture has emerged. At the same time our sympathy for Galileo's
15　opponents has grown somewhat. His telescopic observations are justly immortal; they aroused great interest at the time, they had important theoretical consequences, and they provided a striking demonstration of the potentialities hidden in instruments and apparatus. But can we blame those who looked and failed to see what Galileo saw, if we remember that to use a telescope at the limit of its powers calls for long experience and intimate familiarity with one's instrument? Was the philosopher who refused to look through Galileo's
20　telescope more culpable than those who alleged that the spiral nebulae observed with Lord Rosse's great telescope in the eighteen-forties were scratches left by the grinder? We can perhaps forgive those who said the moons of Jupiter were produced by Galileo's spyglass if we recall that in his day, as for centuries before, curved glass was the popular contrivance for producing not truth but illusion, untruth; and if a single curved glass would distort nature, how much more would a pair of them?

MICHAEL HOSKIN *Galileo Reborn* from *The Listener*

New words and expressions 生词和短语

controversy (1.1) /ˈkɒntrəvɜːsi/ n. 争议, 争论

dust (1.1) /dʌst/ n. 纠纷, 骚动

clash (1.2) /klæʃ/ n. 冲突

Inquisition (1.2) /ˌɪŋkwɪˈzɪʃən/ n. （罗马天主教的）宗教法庭

perspective (1.3) /pəˈspektɪv/ n. 观点, 看法

despise (1.6) /dɪsˈpaɪz/ v. 蔑视

Aristotelian (1.6) /ˌærɪstəˈtiːljən/ n. 亚里士多德学派的人

Aristotle (1.8) /ˈærɪstɒtl/ n. 亚里士多德 （公元前 384-322, 古希腊哲学家）

Ptolemy (1.8) /ˈtɒlɪmi/ n. 托勒密 （公元 90-168, 古希腊天文学家）

Leaning Tower of Pisa (1.9) 比萨斜塔

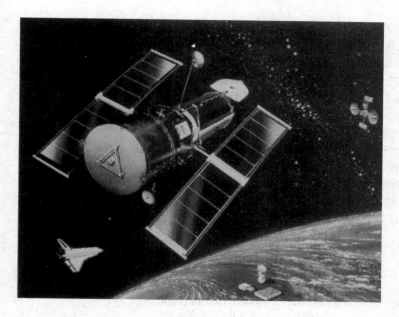

Artist concept of the space telescope showing the shuttle, TDRSS,
and a ground station

generalize (l.10) /ˈʤenərəlaɪz/ v. 归纳

undercurrent (l.12) /ˈʌndəˌkʌrənt/ n. 潜流

theoretical (l.16) /θɪəˈretɪkəl/ adj. 理论上的

potentiality (l.17) /pəˌtenʃiˈælɪti/ n. 潜能

intimate (l.19) /ˈɪntɪmɪt/ adj. 详尽的

familiarity (l.19) /fəˌmɪliˈærɪti/ n. 熟悉

culpable (l.20) /ˈkʌlpəbəl/ adj. 应受谴责的

spiral (l.20) /ˈspaɪərəl/ adj. 螺旋状的

nebula (l.20) /ˈnebjʊlə/ （[复] nebulae /ˈnebjʊliː/)
　　　n. 星云

scratch (l.21) /ˈskrætʃ/ n. 擦痕

contrivance (l.23) /kənˈtraɪvəns/ n. 器械

distort (l.24) /dɪsˈtɔːt/ v. 歪曲

Notes on the text 课文注释

1　something like, 多少, 大约。

2　a problem child, problem 作定语, 修饰 child。这是一种比喻修辞法, 意思是 "新出现的问题"。

3　a man who ... who ... who ... who ..., 这里一连用了 4 个定语从句, 均用 who 引导, 构成了排比结构, 起加强
　语气的作用。

4　at the time, 当时。

5　use a telescope at the limit of its powers, 用望远镜的极限放大率。

参考译文

　　伽利略在世时是激烈论战的中心。但是, 自他逝世以来, 那场科学上的纷争早已平息了下来, 甚至他和宗教
法庭的著名冲突, 我们今天也能正确如实地看待。但是相比之下, 对于科学史家来说, 伽利略只是在现代才变成
一个新的难题。

　　令人高兴的是, 过去对伽利略的看法并不复杂。他首先是个实验工作者, 他蔑视亚里士多德学派的偏见和
空洞的书本知识。他向自然界而不是向古人提出问题, 并大胆地得出自己的结论。他是第一个把望远镜对准天
空的人, 观察到的论据足以把亚里士多德和托勒密一起推翻。他就是那个曾经爬上比萨斜塔, 从塔顶向下抛掷

各种重物的人; 他就是那个使球体沿斜面向下滚动, 然后将多次实验结果概括成著名的自由落体定律的人 。

　　但是, 对那个时代的深化了解, 尤其是以科学革命中哲学潜流的新意识为依据, 进一步仔细研究, 就会极大地改变对伽利略的看法 。今天, 虽然已故的伽利略继续活在许多通俗读物中, 但在科学史家中间, 一个新的更加复杂的伽利略的形象出现了 。与此同时, 我们对伽利略的反对派的同情也有所增加 。伽利略用望远镜所作的观察确实是不朽的, 这些观察在当时引起了人们极大的兴趣, 具有重要的理论意义, 并充分显示出了仪表和仪器的潜在力量 。但是, 如果我们想到, 使用一架倍数有限的望远镜需要长期的经验和对自己仪器的熟悉程度, 那么我们怎么能去责备观察了天空但没有看到伽利略所看到的东西的那些人呢? 某位哲学家曾拒绝使用伽利略的望远镜去观察天空; 到了 19 世纪 40 年代, 有人硬把用罗斯勋爵高倍望远镜观测到的螺旋状星云说成是磨镜工留下的磨痕 。难道反对伽利略的哲学家比诋毁罗斯勋爵造谣者应受到更严厉的谴责吗? 如果我们回想一下伽利略之前的几个世纪期间, 曲面镜一直是一种用于产生幻影而不是产生真相的把戏装置, 那么我们就会原谅那些当初把伽利略观察到的木星卫星说成是伽利略用他的小望远镜变出来的人们, 如果一片曲面镜就可歪曲自然, 那么伽利略的两片曲面镜对自然的歪曲又该多大呢?

Comprehension 理解

Answer these questions:

1   State in a sentence the main difference between the old and the modern view of Galileo.

2   How does the author justify Galileo's contemporaries' failure to see what he saw?

Vocabulary 词汇

Refer to the text to see how the following words have been used, then write sentences of your own using these words: violent controversy (l.1); clash (l.2); proper perspective (ll.2-3); despised the prejudices (l.6); consciousness (l.12); profoundly modified (l.12); consequences (l.16); potentialities (l.17); culpable (l.20); contrivance (l.23); distort (l.24).

Summary 摘要

A   Drawing your information from the last paragraph (lines 11-24), write a list of points in note form to answer the following question: How has a closer study of the evidence profoundly modified the old view of Galileo?

B   Using this list of points, reconstruct the author's argument in not more than 90 words. Your answer should be in one paragraph.

Composition 作文

Write a composition of about 300 words on the following subject:

'New ideas can never be readily accepted by those who cling to old beliefs.'

Argue in favour of this statement. You may use some or all of the ideas given below if you wish:

1   Why new ideas are resisted: prejudice, fear, narrow sensibilities. Examples: the length of time the views of Aristotle and Ptolemy persisted. Copernicus' reluctance to publish his work.

2   New ideas which are resisted when they first make their appearance are gradually assimilated until they finally become commonplace. Examples: The observation of Copernicus that the earth goes round the sun; the views of Galileo: the scientific method; Kepler's ideas on planetary motions; Darwin's idea of evolution; Freud's ideas on psychology.

3   There are, however, exceptions. Some great ideas have been accepted almost without question from the time they made their appearance: Newton's ideas on gravitation were acclaimed in the eighteenth century just as Einstein's ideas on relativity were acclaimed in the twentieth.

Key structures 关键句型

A   Supply the missing words in the following paragraph. Do not refer to the passage until you have finished the exercise:

He had been the first to turn a telescope _____ the sky, and he had seen there evidence enough to overthrow Aristotle and Ptolemy together. He was the man who climbed the Leaning Tower _____ Pisa and dropped various weights _____ the top, who rolled balls _____ inclined planes, and then generalized the results _____ his many experiments _____ the famous law _____ free fall. (ll.7-10)

B   Supply *a* or *the* where necessary in the following paragraph. Do not refer to the passage until you have finished the exercise:

But _____ closer study of _____ evidence, supported by _____ deeper sense of _____ period, and particularly by _____ new consciousness of _____ philosophical undercurrents in _____ scientific revolution, has profoundly modified this view of _____ Galileo. Today, although _____ old Galileo lives on in _____ many popular writings, among _____ historians of _____ science _____ new and more sophisticated picture has emerged. (ll.11-14)

C   Compare these two sentences:

Instead of saying: *Using* a telescope at the limit of its powers calls for long experience and intimate familiarity with one's instrument.

We can say: *To use* a telescope at the limit of its powers calls for long experience and intimate familiarity with one's instrument. (ll.18-19)

Write sentences which begin with the following words: To build; Reading; To eat; Smoking.

Special difficulties 难点

A   Study the following pairs of words and then write sentences of your own to bring out the difference.

1   plane (l.10) — plain

The problem of drawing this on paper is the problem of representing a three-dimensional object in a single plane.

The mountain rises sharply from the plain.

2   popular (l.13) — folk

You can always hear a lot of popular songs on radio request programs.

Some composers like Bartok made use of folk music.

3   sympathy (l.14) — affection

Those children need a lot more than sympathy now that they've lost their mother.

His affection for his family is obvious.

4   blame (l.17) — accuse

Don't blame me for our missing the train. You didn't allow enough time.

He was falsely accused of stealing.

5   refuse (l.19) — deny

I offered to pay him for his help but he refused.

The secretary denies all knowledge of the missing letter.

6   scratch (1.21) — scrape

You're bound to get one or two scratches in the paintwork as soon as you begin using the car. (= lines that make the surface imperfect)

We listened to the scrape of heavy furniture being dragged across the floor upstairs. (= the process of one thing being pushed across another roughly)

B   Explain the meaning of the verb *settle* in these sentences:

1   Have you *settled down* in your new house yet?

2   I *settled down* in an armchair to read a book.

3   I shall *settle* my account next week.

4   We must *settle* this problem once for all.

5   His ancestors *settled* in Boston in the eighteen fifties.

C   Note the use of *on* in this sentence to indicate continuity:

The old Galileo lives *on* in many popular writings. (1.13)

Write sentences using the following verbs: keep on; carry on; go on; drive on; walk on; read on.

D   Explain the verbs in italics:

1   To use a telescope *calls for* long experience. (1.18)

2   I'll *call on* you on my way home from work.

3   I'll *call you up* at the office tomorrow morning.

4   It's impossible to have a party tomorrow. Why don't we *call* the whole thing *off*?

5   May I leave this suitcase here? I'll *call for* it later.

6   I think you'd better *call in* a doctor.

Multiple choice questions 选择题

Choose the correct answers to the following questions.

Comprehension 理解

1 Before Galileo, people _____ .

(a) did exactly as they were told because of their fear of the Inquisition

(b) believed what they read in Aristotle and Ptolemy

(c) made observations about the universe by using telescopes

(d) depended on the evidence of their eyes to understand the universe

2 The old view of Galileo was delightfully uncomplicated probably because _____ .

(a) he was the first to turn a telescope to the sky

(b) he put his questions to nature instead of to the ancients

(c) he performed various experiments with weights and balls

(d) we considered his achievements from only one point of view

3 Before we had a better understanding of the period, we probably _____ .

(a) overrated Galileo's achievements

(b) underrated Galileo's achievements

(c) were over-critical of his opponents

(d) agreed with his opponents

4 We have to conclude that in Galileo's time, optical instruments were _____ .

(*a*) sufficiently developed to enhance our view of the sky

(*b*) rather primitive

(*c*) full of scratches left by glass grinders

(*d*) created to produce not truth but illusion

Structure 句型

5 The scientific dust settled _____ . (ll.1-2)

(*a*) a long time ago   (*b*) since a long time   (*c*) for a long time still   (*d*) a long time yet

6 Before modern times, Galileo _____ a problem child for historians. (1.3)

(*a*) did not   (*b*) had not been   (*c*) has not been   (*d*) was not

7 Before Galileo, no one _____ a telescope to the sky. (ll.7-8)

(*a*) was turning   (*b*) had turned   (*c*) has turned   (*d*) will turn

8 Can we blame those who looked and failed to see _____ Galileo saw? (ll.17-18)

(*a*) that   (*b*) the which   (*c*) which   (*d*) the things that

Vocabulary 词汇

9 Today we can see even his famous _____ with the Inquisition ... (1.2)

(*a*) crash   (*b*) contrast   (*c*) conflict   (*d*) opposition

10 He was, above all, a man who _____ the prejudices of the Aristotelians. (ll.4-5)

(*a*) had a low opinion of   (*b*) condemned

(*c*) accepted   (*d*) denied

11 A closer study of the evidence has profoundly _____ this view of Galileo. (1.11-13)

(*a*) confirmed   (*b*) altered   (*c*) increased   (*d*) sharpened

12 The old Galileo lives on in many _____ .

(*a*) writings by different people   (*b*) writings of the people

(*c*) widely read and admired writings   (*d*) folk tales

Unit 5

Content

This unit consists of eight passages followed by exercises on Comprehension, Vocabulary, Summary, Composition, Key structures, Special difficulties and Multiple choice questions.

Aim

To carry the skills acquired in the previous unit a stage further.

How to work

1 Read each passage carefully two or three times.
2 Answer the questions in the order in which they are given.

Summary

You will be required to write a summary of a part of each passage in a limited number of words. Your work should fall into three distinct parts:

1 Write a list of points in note form deriving the specific information required by the question.
2 Join these points to write a draft summary in your own words as far as possible. When you have completed the draft, correct and amend it making sure you have not exceeded the word limit.
3 Write a fair copy of your summary. At the end, state the number of words you have used.

Composition

You will be required to write a composition of about 400 words on a subject connected in some way with the passage. Your work should fall into two distinct parts:

1 Write a list of ideas in note form which might be used to discuss the subject.
2 Write a composition based on these ideas.

194

Lesson 33 Education 教育

First listen and then answer the following question.

听录音，然后回答以下问题 。

Why is education democratic in bookless, tribal societies?

Education is one of the key words of our time. A man without an education, many of us believe, is an unfortunate victim of adverse circumstances, deprived of one of the greatest twentieth-century opportunities. Convinced of the importance of education, modern states 'invest' in institutions of learning to get back 'interest' in the form of a large group of enlightened young men and women who are potential leaders.
5 Education, with its cycles of instruction so carefully worked out, punctuated by textbooks—those purchasable wells of wisdom—what would civilization be like without its benefits?

So much is certain: that we would have doctors and preachers, lawyers and defendants, marriages and births—but our spiritual outlook would be different. We would lay less stress on 'facts and figures' and more on a good memory, on applied psychology, and on the capacity of a man to get along with his fellow-
10 citizens. If our educational system were fashioned after its bookless past we would have the most democratic form of 'college' imaginable. Among tribal people all knowledge inherited by tradition is shared by all; it is taught to every member of the tribe so that in this respect everybody is equally equipped for life.

It is the ideal condition of the 'equal start' which only our most progressive forms of modern education try to regain. In primitive cultures the obligation to seek and to receive the traditional instruction is binding
15 to all. There are no 'illiterates'—if the term can be applied to peoples without a script—while our own compulsory school attendance became law in Germany in 1642, in France in 1806, and in England in 1876, and is still non-existent in a number of 'civilized' nations. This shows how long it was before we deemed it necessary to make sure that all our children could share in the knowledge accumulated by the 'happy few' during the past centuries.

20 Education in the wilderness is not a matter of monetary means. All are entitled to an equal start. There is none of the hurry which, in our society, often hampers the full development of a growing personality. There, a child grows up under the ever-present attention of his parents; therefore the jungles and the savannahs know of no 'juvenile delinquency'. No necessity of making a living away from home results in neglect of children, and no father is confronted with his inability to 'buy' an education for his child.

JULIUS E. LIPS *The Origin of Things*

New words and expressions 生词和短语

adverse (1.2) /'ædvɜːs/ *adj.* 不利的
purchasable (1.6) /'pɜːtʃəsəbəl/ *adj.* 可买到的
preacher (1.7) /'priːtʃə/ *n.* 传教士
defendant (1.7) /di'fendənt/ *n.* 被告
outlook (1.8) /'aʊtlʊk/ *n.* 视野
capacity (1.9) /kə'pæsɪti/ *n.* 能力

democratic (1.11) /ˌdemə'krætɪk/ *adj.* 民主的
tribal (1.11) /'traɪbəl/ *adj.* 部落的
tribe (1.12) /traɪb/ *n.* 部落
illiterate (1.15) /ɪ'lɪtərət/ *n.* 文盲
compulsory (1.16) /kəm'pʌlsərɪ/ *adj.* 义务的
deem (1.17) /diːm/ *v.* 认为

The library at the University of Sussex

means (1.20) /miːnz/ *n.* 方法, 手段, 财产, 资力
hamper (1.21) /'hæmpə/ *v.* 妨碍
savannah (1.22) /sə'vænə/ *n.* 大草原

juvenile (1.23) /'ʤuːvənaɪl/ *adj.* 青少年的
delinquency (1.23) /dɪ'lɪŋkwənsɪ/ *n.* 犯罪

Notes on the text 课文注释

1　Education, with its cycles ..., punctuated by textbooks ..., 这句话中的主语 Education 与 punctuated 并不是一种主谓关系, 因此, 这句话在语法上被称作单元句 。

2　So much is certain, 有承上启下的作用: 一方面回答了前一段最后一句的提问, 另一方面开始列举没有教育将会给社会文明带来的影响 。

3　be fashioned after, 按 …… 做成 。

4　without a script, 没有文字的 。

参考译文

　　教育是我们这个时代的关键词之一 。我们许多人都相信, 一个没有受过教育的人, 是逆境的牺牲品, 被剥夺了 20 世纪最优越的机会之一 。现代国家深深懂得教育的重要性, 对教育机构投资, 收回的 "利息" 便是培养出大批有知识的男女青年, 这些人可能会成为未来的栋梁 。教育, 以其教学周期如此精心地安排, 并以教科书——那些可以买到的智慧源泉——予以强化, 如果不受其惠, 文明将会是个什么样子呢?

　　至少, 这些是可以肯定的: 虽然我们还会有医生和牧师 、律师和被告 、婚姻和生育, 但人们的精神面貌将是另一个样子 。人们不会再重视 "资料和数据", 而靠好记性 、实用心理学和与同伴相处的能力 。如果我们的教育制度仿效没有书籍的古代教育, 我们的学院将具有可以想象得出的最民主的形式了 。在部落中, 通过传统继承的知识为所有人共享, 并传授给部落中的每一个成员 。从这个意义上讲, 每个人受到的有关生活本领的教育是相等的 。

　　这就是我们最进步的现代教育试图恢复的 "平等起步" 的理想状况 。在原始文化中, 寻求和接受传统教育的义务对全民都有约束力, 因而没有 "文盲" (如果这个字眼儿可以用于没有文字的民族的话) 。而我们的义务教育成为法律在德国是在 1642 年, 在法国是在 1806 年, 在英国是在 1876 年 。今天, 在许多 "文明" 国家里,义务教育迄今尚未实行。这说明，经过了多么漫长的时间之后，我们才认识到，有必要确保我们的孩子享有多少个世纪以来由"少数幸运者"所积累起来的知识。

　　荒凉地区的教育不是钱的问题，所有的人都享有平等起步的权利。那里没有我们今天社会中的匆忙生活，而匆忙的生活常常妨碍个性的全面发展。荒凉地区的孩子无时无刻不在父母关怀下成长。因此，丛林和荒凉地区不知道什么叫"青少年犯罪"。人们没有必要离家谋生，所以不会产生孩子无人管的问题，也不存在父亲无力为孩子支付教育费用而犯难的问题。

Comprehension 理解

Answer these questions:

1　In what way can education be said to be 'an investment'?
2　Give one reason why the author appears to be opposed to formal education.
3　Give one reason why, according to the author, a primitive society is superior to a civilized society.

Vocabulary 词汇

Refer to the text to see how the following words have been used, then write sentences of your own using these words: key (l.1); adverse circumstances (l.2); enlightened (l.4); potential (l.4); lay less stress (l.8); binding (l.14); illiterates (l.15); compulsory (l.16); monetary means (l.20); entitled (l.20); juvenile delinquency (l.23).

Summary 摘要

Drawing your information from lines 7-24 ('So much ... for his child.') write a summary of the author's argument that real equality of opportunity is only to be found in a primitive society. Do not write more than 100 words. Your answer should be in one paragraph.

Composition 作文

A　Write a list of ideas in note form which could be used to discuss this subject: 'A man without an education, many of us believe, is an unfortunate victim of adverse circumstances deprived of one of the greatest twentieth-century opportunities.' (ll.1-2)

B　Drawing on your list of ideas, write a composition of about 400 words.

Key structures 关键句型

A　Supply the missing words in the following paragraph. Do not refer to the passage until you have finished the exercise:

Education is one _____ the key words _____ our time. A man _____ an education, many _____ us believe, is an unfortunate victim _____ adverse circumstances deprived _____ one _____ the greatest twentieth-century opportunities. Convinced _____ the importance _____ education, modern states 'invest' _____ institutions _____ learning to get back 'interest' _____ the form _____ a large group _____ enlightened young men and women who are potential leaders. Education, _____ its cycles _____ instruction so carefully worked _____ , punctuated _____ textbooks—those purchasable wells _____ wisdom—what would civilization be like _____ its benefits? (ll.1-6)

B   A great many words and phrases are enclosed in inverted commas in this passage. What purpose do the inverted commas serve? Justify your answer with reference to three phrases.

C   Supply *less* or *fewer* in the following sentences:

1   We would lay _____ stress on 'facts and figures'. (1.8)

2   There were _____ opportunities to get a good education in the past.

3   _____ people die of tuberculosis these days.

4   I have _____ time now than I used to have.

5   If there were _____ buses on the roads it would be easier to drive to work.

D   Supply *who, whom* or *which* in the following sentences. Do not refer to the passage until you have finished the exercise:

1   Modern states get back 'interest' in the form of a large group of enlightened young men and women _____ are potential leaders. (ll.3-4)

2   Among the people _____ we like to call savages all knowledge inherited by tradition is shared by all. (ll.11-12)

3   It is the ideal condition of the 'equal start' _____ only our most progressive forms of modern education try to regain. (ll.13-14)

E   Study the pattern in italics:

This shows how long it was before we *deemed it necessary* to make sure that all our children could share in the knowledge accumulated by the 'happy few' during the past centuries. (ll.17-19)

Write sentences using the same pattern with the following verbs: consider, find, think, feel, believe.

Special difficulties 难点

A   Study the following pairs of words and then write sentences of your own to bring out the difference.

1   opportunity (l.2) — chance

Our holiday gave us a chance/an opportunity of getting fit.

Book now, or you won't have a chance of getting a seat.

We met by chance at London Airport.

2   potential (l.4) — potent

Think of him as a potential friend rather than an alarming stranger.

The film is full of potent images of war.

3   imaginable (l.11) — imaginative

Posters were plastered on every imaginable surface.

Congratulations on finding such an imaginative solution to the problem.

4   tribe (l.12) — race

The Seringa tribe will be wiped out by the construction of the new dam.

Global warming poses a threat to the survival of the human race.

5   compulsory (l.16) — necessary

In China, education is compulsory between the ages of 6 and 15.

Is it necessary to wear a tie?

B Explain the meaning of the words in italics:

1 Our spiritual *outlook* would be different. (l.8)

2 He's usually such a quiet person. I can't account for this *outburst*, can you?

3 There was an *outbreak* of dysentery among the troops.

4 One unexpected *outcome* of the new policy has been a fall in prices.

C Comment on the use of *all* in these sentences:

All knowledge ... *is* shared by *all*. (ll.11-12)

All are entitled to an equal start. (l.20)

Multiple choice questions 选择题

Choose the correct answers to the following questions.

Comprehension 理解

1 A modern state hopes to _____ for what an individual's education has cost.

(*a*) repay

(*b*) reap a reward

(*c*) charge interest

(*d*) make an investment

2 According to the writer, among tribal peoples, the most important thing is _____ .

(*a*) their spiritual outlook

(*b*) democracy

(*c*) to live without books

(*d*) to learn how to live together

3 Formal school education in modern societies _____ .

(*a*) makes sure there are no illiterates

(*b*) is relatively recent

(*c*) is enjoyed by a 'happy few'

(*d*) gives everyone an equal start

4 According to the writer, in primitive cultures, _____ .

(*a*) children have time to develop at their own pace

(*b*) fathers can't afford to buy an education for their children

(*c*) the jungles and savannahs are the source of knowledge

(*d*) parents don't pay much attention to their children

Structure 句型

5 _____ of the importance of education, modern societies ... (l.3)

(*a*) Being convincing (*b*) Convincing

(*c*) Having convinced (*d*) Being convinced

6 _____ would civilization be without its benefits? (l.6)

(*a*) How (*b*) Where (*c*) Why (*d*) Which

7 It is taught to every member of the tribe. _____ , everybody is equipped ... (l.12)

    (*a*) Because   (*b*) In fact   (*c*) Consequently   (*d*) However

8 No 'illiterates' _____ in primitive cultures. (ll.14-15)

    (*a*) grow   (*b*) believe   (*c*) exist   (*d*) are

Vocabulary 词汇

9 A man without an education is an unfortunate victim of adverse _____ . (ll.1-2)

    (*a*) cases   (*b*) states   (*c*) situations   (*d*) conditions

10 We would lay more stress on _____ . (ll.8-9)

    (*a*) souvenirs   (*b*) memorisation   (*c*) recall   (*d*) remembrance

11 We would have the most democratic form of 'college' that can be _____ (ll.10-11)

    (*a*) imaginative   (*b*) imagined   (*c*) imaginary   (*d*) fantasized

12 Our own _____ school attendance became law relatively recently. (ll.15-16)

    (*a*) obligatory   (*b*) compelling   (*c*) compulsive   (*d*) commanding

Lesson 34   Adolescence   青春期

First listen and then answer the following question.

听录音，然后回答以下问题。

What do adolescents respect in parents?

Parents are often upset when their children praise the homes of their friends and regard it as a slur on their own cooking, or cleaning, or furniture, and often are foolish enough to let the adolescents see that they are annoyed. They may even accuse them of disloyalty, or make some spiteful remark about the friends' parents. Such a loss of dignity and descent into childish behaviour on the part of the adults deeply shocks the
5 adolescents, and makes them resolve that in future they will not talk to their parents about the places or people they visit. Before very long the parents will be complaining that the child is so secretive and never tells them anything, but they seldom realize that they have brought this on themselves.

Disillusionment with the parents, however good and adequate they may be both as parents and as individuals, is to some degree inevitable. Most children have such a high ideal of their parents, unless the
10 parents themselves have been unsatisfactory, that it can hardly hope to stand up to a realistic evaluation. Parents would be greatly surprised and deeply touched if they realized how much belief their children usually have in their character and infallibility, and how much this faith means to a child. If parents were prepared for this adolescent reaction, and realized that it was a sign that the child was growing up and developing valuable powers of observation and independent judgment, they would not be so hurt, and
15 therefore would not drive the child into opposition by resenting and resisting it.

The adolescent, with his passion for sincerity, always respects a parent who admits that he is wrong, or ignorant, or even that he has been unfair or unjust. What the child cannot forgive is the parents' refusal to admit these charges if the child knows them to be true.

Victorian parents believed that they kept their dignity by retreating behind an unreasoning authoritarian
20 attitude; in fact they did nothing of the kind, but children were then too cowed to let them know how they really felt. Today we tend to go to the other extreme, but on the whole this is a healthier attitude both for the child and the parent. It is always wiser and safer to face up to reality, however painful it may be at the moment.

DORIS ODLUM *Journey Through Adolescence*

New words and expressions 生词和短语

adolescence (title) /ˌædəˈlesəns/ *n*. 青春期
slur (1.1) /slɜː/ *n*. 诋毁
adolescent (1.2) /ˌædəˈlesənt/ *n*. 青少年（12-18岁）
disloyalty (1.3) /dɪsˈlɔɪəlti/ *n*. 不忠实
spiteful (1.3) /ˈspaɪtfəl/ *adj*. 恶意的，怀恨的
disillusionment (1.8) /ˌdɪsɪˈluːʒənmənt/ *n*. 幻灭感
evaluation (1.10) /ɪˌvæljuˈeɪʃən/ *n*. 评价
infallibility (1.12) /ɪnˌfæləˈbɪlɪti/ *n*. 一贯正确

resent (1.15) /rɪˈzent/ *v*. 怨恨
sincerity (1.16) /sɪnˈserɪti/ *n*. 诚挚
victorian (1.19) /vɪkˈtɔːriən/ *adj*. 维多利亚式的
retreat (1.19) /rɪˈtriːt/ *v*. 后退
unreasoning (1.19) /ʌnˈriːzənɪŋ/ *adj*. 不凭理智的
authoritarian (1.19) /ɔːˌθɒrɪˈteəriən/ *adj*. 专制的
cow (1.20) /kaʊ/ *v*. 吓唬

An English family at home

Notes on the text 课文注释

1　on the part of, 在 …… 一边 。
2　they have brought this on themselves, 他们是咎由自取 。
3　stand up to, 经得起 。
4　face up to, 正视 。

参考译文

　　家长听到孩子赞扬自己朋友的家时, 总感到不安, 认为这是孩子在嫌弃自家的饭菜 、卫生或家具, 而且愚蠢地让孩子看出自己的烦恼 。他们甚至责备孩子不忠, 或者讲些小朋友家长的坏话 。家长这种有失身份和孩子气的做法使青春期的孩子大为震惊, 决心以后不再向父母讲述去过的地方和见过的人 。不要很久, 家长就会抱怨孩子守口如瓶, 什么事也不告诉他们, 殊不知这是他们咎由自取 。

　　不管家长的人品有多么好, 作为父母有多么合格, 孩子们对家长幻想的破灭在某种程度上是不可避免的 。除非父母自身不能令人满意, 大多数孩子对父母估价过高, 以致这种估价很难指望经受住现实的考验 。如果家长意识到孩子们通常是多么相信家长的品行和绝对正确, 意识到孩子们的这种信念会对孩子产生多么大的影响, 那么家长会大为吃惊和深受感动的 。如果家长对青少年的这种反应有思想准备, 并且意识到这象征着孩子们正在成熟和正在形成宝贵的观察力 、独立判断力, 那么他们就不会那样伤心, 也就不会由于怨恨和抵触这种反应, 而把孩子推到自己的对立面去 。

　　青少年酷爱真诚, 对于能够承认错误或无知, 甚至承认自己做得不公平或不公正的父母, 他们总是尊敬的 。孩子们所不能原谅的是: 父母错了, 孩子们也看出来了, 可是做父母的还不肯承认 。

　　维多利亚时代的父母认为, 他们可以靠无理的独断专行来维护自己的尊严, 实际上那是根本不行的 。孩子们只不过被吓得不敢让父母知道自己的想法罢了 。虽然现在我们倾向于走向另一个极端, 但总的来看, 孩子和家长的态度都比较端正 。遇事采取面对现实的态度总是比较明智和稳妥的, 尽管会有暂时的痛苦 。

Comprehension 理解

Answer these questions:

1   What sort of behaviour among parents does the author characterize as 'childish'?
2   Why, according to the author, is it inevitable that adolescents should become disillusioned with their parents?
3   How does our attitude towards adolescents differ from that of the Victorians?

Vocabulary 词汇

Refer to the text to see how the following words have been used, then write sentences of your own using these words: slur (l.1); spiteful remark (l.3); resolve (l.5); disillusionment (l.8); to some degree inevitable (l.9); evaluation (l.10); touched (l.11); infallibility (l.12); resenting (l.15); charges (l.18); retreating behind an unreasoning authoritarian attitude (ll.19-20).

Summary 摘要

Drawing your information from lines 1-15 ('Parents ... resisting it.') write a summary of the author's argument that it is inevitable that adolescents should react against their parents. Do not write more than 100 words. Your answer should be in one paragraph.

Composition 作文

A   Write a list of ideas in note form which could be used to discuss this subject:

   Account for the fact that children seem to grow up more quickly today than they did in the past.

B   Drawing on your list of ideas, write a composition of about 400 words.

Key structures 关键句型

A   Put the words in parentheses in their correct position in these sentences. In many cases, more than one position is possible. Do not refer to the passage until you have finished the exercise:

1   Parents are upset when their children praise the homes of their friends. (often) (l.1)
2   Such a loss of dignity and descent into childish behaviour on the part of the adults shocks the adolescents. (deeply) (ll.4-5)
3   They realize that they have brought this on themselves. (seldom) (l.7)
4   Parents would be surprised and touched if they realized how much belief their children have in their character and infallibility. (greatly, deeply, usually) (ll.11-12)

B   Compare the uses of *enough* in these two sentences:

1   Parents are ... often *foolish enough* to let the adolescents see that they are annoyed. (ll.1-3)
2   Have you had *enough tea*, or would you like some more?
   Write two sentences using *enough* in the ways shown above.

C   Note the form of the verbs used after *let* and *make* in these two sentences:

1   Parents are often foolish enough to *let* the adolescents *see* that they are annoyed. (ll.2-3)

2   Such a loss of dignity *makes* them *resolve* that in future they will not talk to their parents. (ll.4-5)

Complete the following sentences:

1   They let us _____

2   We made them _____

3   Will you let him _____

4   Why make me _____

D   Supply the correct form of the verbs in parentheses in these sentences. Do not refer to the passage until you have finished the exercise:

1   Parents greatly (surprise) _____ if they realized how much this faith means to a child. (ll.11-12)

2   If parents were prepared for this adolescent reaction, and _____ (realize) that it _____ (be) a sign that the child _____ (grow) up and _____ (develop) valuable powers of observation and independent judgment, they not _____ (be) so hurt, and therefore not _____ (drive) the child into opposition by resenting and resisting it. (ll.12-15)

E   Compare these two sentences:

Instead of saying: *The thing* the child cannot forgive is the parents' refusal to admit these charges.

We can say: *What* the child cannot forgive is the parents' refusal to admit these charges. (ll.17-18)

Write three statements similar in form to the one above beginning with *What*.

Special difficulties 难点

A   Study the following pairs of words and then write sentences of your own to bring out the difference.

1   enough (l.2) — fairly

The water is warm enough to swim in.

The water is fairly warm.

2   loss (l.4) — lose

Our company made a big loss last year.

Try not to lose your ticket.

3   descent (l.4) — decent

The pilot managed an emergency descent and landed in a field.

Decent citizens have nothing to fear from this legislation.

4   belief (l.11) — loyalty

Try to have more belief in your own ability.

Family loyalty makes it impossible for him to say anything negative about his relations.

5   grow up (l.13) — grow

What do you want to do when you grow up?

Livia grows all her own vegetables.

6   hurt (l.14) — pain

I'm sorry if I hurt your feelings.

I banged against the table and hurt my knee. My knee hurts.

I had such a pain in the stomach after eating oysters.

7   refusal (1.17) — denial

A journalist's refusal to identify his source of information has landed him in prison before now.

He gave the statement an unqualified denial.

The journalist's denial that he had handled stolen documents was not believed at the inquiry.

B   Write sentences using the following phrases:

on the part of (1.4); before very long (1.6); to stand up to (1.10); nothing of the kind (1.20); on the whole (1.21); to face up to (1.22); at the moment (ll.22-23).

Multiple choice questions 选择题

Choose the correct answers to the following questions.

Comprehension 理解

1 Adolescents often fail to communicate _____ .

  (*a*) when parents feel their children are criticising their cooking

  (*b*) because they don't want to talk about the places or people they visit

  (*c*) because they don't want to annoy their parents

  (*d*) in response to negative behaviour from their parents

2 When adolescents feel disillusion with their parents _____ .

  (*a*) they don't really mean it

  (*b*) they want to hurt them

  (*c*) it's often a sign they're developing into maturity

  (*d*) they are expressing their dissatisfaction with them

3 Adolescents are likely to _____ .

  (*a*) show more respect for parents who don't think they're always right

  (*b*) resent and resist parents whatever the parents do

  (*c*) respect their parents' infallibility

  (*d*) treat their parents unfairly and unjustly

4 In Victorian times, adolescents _____ .

  (*a*) had more respect for their parents than today

  (*b*) always faced up to reality, however painful it might be

  (*c*) were too afraid to show their true feelings

  (*d*) admired the authoritarian attitude of their parents

Structure 句型

5 Parents are often _____ foolish _____ show they are annoyed. (ll.1-2)

  (*a*) so ... that   (*b*) so ... as to   (*c*) so ... to   (*d*) such ... to

6 They may even make spiteful remarks about the parents of their _____ . (1.3)

  (*a*) friend   (*b*) friends'   (*c*) friend's   (*d*) friends

7 Soon parents will complain that the child never _____ anything to them. (ll.6-7)

  (*a*) says   (*b*) tells   (*c*) talks   (*d*) speaks

8 _____ parents are unsatisfactory, children won't have high ideals of them. (ll.9-10)

    (*a*) Until   (*b*) As long   (*c*) If   (*d*) Though

Vocabulary 词汇

9 Such a loss of dignity makes them _____ that they won't talk to their parents. (ll.4-5)

    (*a*) deny   (*b*) refuse   (*c*) explain   (*d*) decide

10 Disillusionment with parents, however _____ they may be, is inevitable. (ll.8-9)

    (*a*) outstanding   (*b*) satisfactory   (*c*) promising   (*d*) enough

11 Most children have such a high ideal, it can hardly stand up to realistic _____ . (ll.9-10)

    (*a*) valuation   (*b*) estimate   (*c*) assessment   (*d*) estimation

12 The adolescent always respects a parent who _____ that he is wrong. (l.16)

    (*a*) confesses   (*b*) confides   (*c*) explains   (*d*) excepts

Lesson 35 Space odyssey 太空探索

🔊 **First listen and then answer the following question.**
听录音, 然后回答以下问题 。

When will it be possible for us to think seriously about colonising Mars?

The Moon is likely to become the industrial hub of the Solar System, supplying the rocket fuels for its ships, easily obtainable from the lunar rocks in the form of liquid oxygen. The reason lies in its gravity. Because the Moon has only an eightieth of the Earth's mass, it requires 97 per cent less energy to travel the quarter of a million miles from the Moon to Earth-orbit than the 200 mile-journey from Earth's surface into orbit!

5   This may sound fantastic, but it is easily calculated. To escape from the Earth in a rocket, one must travel at seven miles per second. The comparable speed from the Moon is only 1.5 miles per second. Because the gravity on the Moon's surface is only a sixth of Earth's (remember how easily the Apollo astronauts bounded along), it takes much less energy to accelerate to that 1.5 miles per second than it does on Earth. Moon-dwellers will be able to fly in space at only three per cent of the cost of similar journeys by their terrestrial
10   cousins.

Arthur C. Clark once suggested a revolutionary idea passes through three phases:

1 'It's impossible — don't waste my time.'

2 'It's possible, but not worth doing.'

3 'I said it was a good idea all along.'

15   The idea of colonising Mars — a world 160 times more distant than the Moon — will move decisively from the second phase to the third, when a significant number of people are living permanently in space. Mars has an extraordinary fascination for would-be voyagers. America, Russia and Europe are filled with enthusiasts — many of them serious and senior scientists — who dream of sending people to it. Their aim is understandable. It is the one world in the Solar System that is most like the Earth. It is a world of red sandy
20   deserts (hence its name — the Red Planet), cloudless skies, savage sandstorms, chasms wider than the Grand Canyon and at least one mountain more than twice as tall as Qomolangma. It seems ideal for settlement.

7 DAYS, February 19, 1989

New words and expressions 生词和短语

hub (1.1) /hʌb/ n. （活动的）中心
lunar (1.2) /ˈluːnə/ adj. 月球的
oxygen (1.2) /ˈɒksɪdʒən/ n. 氧气
Apollo (1.7) /əˈpɒləʊ/ n. 阿波罗
accelerate (1.8) /əkˈseləreɪt/ v. 加速
terrestrial (1.9) /tɪˈrestrɪəl/ adj. 地球的

permanently (1.16) /ˈpɜːmənəntli/ adv. 永远地
fascination (1.17) /ˌfæsɪˈneɪʃən/ n. 魅力
senior (1.18) /ˈsiːnɪə/ adj. 资历深的, 年长的
chasm (1.20) /ˈkæzəm/ n. 断层, 裂口
canyon (1.21) /ˈkænjən/ n. 峡谷

Sojourner, the roving little robot sent aboard the Mars probe Pathfinder
arrived Sunday July 6, 1997 on the planet Mars.

Notes on the text 课文注释

1　the comparable speed from the Moon, 从月球出发的相应的速度, 这里是指摆脱月球引力所需达到的速度 。

2　the Apollo astronauts, 指 1969 年 7 月 20 日美国 "阿波罗 11 号" 宇宙飞船第一次载人登月球 。

3　the Grand Canyon, 指位于美国亚利桑那州西北部的科罗拉多大峡谷 。

参考译文

　　月球很可能成为太阳系的工业中心 。从月球上的岩石中很容易提炼出液态氧, 作为航天飞船的燃料 。其原因在于月球的重力 。因为月球的质量只有地球的 1/80, 因此, 从月球到地球的25万英里所消耗的能量要比从地球表面进入地球轨道的200英里所耗能量少 97% 。

　　这点听起来令人难以置信, 但却很容易计算出来 。要乘坐一枚火箭飞离地球, 火箭的速度要达到每秒 7 英里, 而从月球出发的相应速度只是每秒 1.5 英里 。由于月球表面的重力仅是地球表面的 1/6——还记得阿波罗飞船中的宇航员轻松地跳跃——在月球上加速到每秒 1.5 英里比在地球上所用能源要少得多 。月球居民在太空遨游的费用仅是地球上朋友飞越同样路程所需费用的 3% 。

　　亚瑟 · C.克拉克曾指出, 一种创新的想法要经过以下 3 个阶段:

1　"根本不可能, 不要浪费我的时间 。"

2　"可能, 但不值得做 。"

3　"我一直说这是个好想法 。"

　　如果有相当数量的人永久性地住在太空, 征服火星的计划——一个比月球远 160 倍的星球——就可以明确地从第 2 阶段进入第 3 阶段 。火星对未来的星际旅客来说有着特殊的魅力 。美国 、俄罗斯和欧洲都有许多热心此项事业的人——其中的不少人是认真和资深的科学家, 他们一直梦想着把人送上火星 。他们的目标是可以理解的 。火星是太阳系里与地球最相似的一颗行星 。这是一个红色沙漠的世界 (因而得名: 红色行星), 无云的天空, 凶猛的沙暴, 比科罗拉多大峡谷还宽的裂缝, 起码有一座山有珠穆朗玛峰的近两倍高 。看起来, 它很适合居住 。

Comprehension 理解

Answer these questions:

1 Why would a rocket leave the surface of the moon more rapidly than it leaves the surface of the earth?
2 Give two reasons why space travel from the moon would be cheaper than space travel from the earth.
3 When will people begin to consider seriously the possibility of colonising Mars?

Vocabulary 词汇

Refer to the text to see how the following words have been used, then write sentences of your own using these words: hub (l.1); supplying (l.1); lunar (l.2); requires (l.3); one (l.5); comparable (l.6); terrestrial (l.9); significant (l.16); like (l.19); ideal for settlement (l.21).

Summary 摘要

Write a summary of the first two paragraphs ('The Moon ... cousins') explaining why the moon is likely to become the industrial centre of the Solar System. Do not write more than 90 words. Your answer should be in one paragraph.

Composition 作文

A Write a list of ideas in note form about the future of space travel. Follow up the ideas introduced in the passage to predict what space travel might be like in fifty years' time.

B Drawing on your list of ideas, write a composition of about 400 words.

Key structures 关键句型

A Supply the missing words in the following. Do not refer to the passage until you have finished the exercise:

1 The Moon is likely to become the industrial hub _____ the Solar System, supplying the rocket fuels _____ its ships, easily obtainable _____ the lunar rocks _____ the form _____ liquid oxygen. The reason lies _____ its gravity. Because the Moon has only an eightieth _____ the Earth's mass, it requires 97 per cent less energy to travel the quarter _____ a million miles _____ the Moon _____ Earth-orbit than the 200 mile-journey _____ Earth's surface _____ orbit! (ll.1-4)
2 To escape _____ the Earth _____ a rocket, one must travel _____ seven miles per second. The comparable speed _____ the Moon is only 1.5 miles per second. Because the gravity _____ the Moon's surface is only a sixth _____ Earth's (remember how easily the Apollo astronauts bounded _____), it takes much less energy to accelerate _____ that 1.5 miles _____ second than it does _____ Earth. Moon-dwellers will be able to fly _____ space _____ only three per cent _____ the cost _____ similar journeys _____ their terrestrial cousins. (ll.5-10)
3 The idea _____ colonising Mars—a world 160 times more distant _____ the Moon—will move decisively _____ the second phase _____ the third, when a significant number _____ people are living permanently _____ space. (ll.15-16)

4   Mars has an extraordinary fascination _____ would-be voyagers. America, Russia and Europe are filled with enthusiasts—many _____ them serious and senior scientists—who dream _____ sending people _____ it. Their aim is understandable. It is the one world _____ the Solar System that is most like the Earth. (ll.17-19)

B   Note the use of the verb *sound* in this sentence:

This may *sound* fantastic, but it is easily calculated. (l.5)

Supply suitable forms of the verbs *sound, seem, taste, feel* and *look* in place of be in these sentences.

Sometimes more than one replacement is possible.

1   It is very hot today.
2   This chocolate is very bitter.
3   You can see from her face that she isn't well.
4   The price is about right, but I hope they can offer us a bigger discount.
5   How much did you say? That is expensive!

Special difficulties 难点

A   Study the following pairs of words and then write sentences of your own to bring out the difference.

1   industrial (l.1) — industrious
    Japan is an industrial nation.
    The Japanese people are very industrious.
2   supplying (l.1) — providing
    Who supplies you with fresh vegetables?
    Our parents provided us with everything we needed while we were growing up.
3   less (l.3) — lesser
    His new novel had less success than expected.
    This is a lesser problem compared with pollution.
4   bound (l.7) — bounds
    A great black dog came bounding out towards us.
    There are no bounds to his ambition. (= limits)
5   bind — bound for
    Don't bind that so tight. A bandage bound as tight as that will restrict the patient's circulation.
    Where are you bound for? — I'm off to Scotland for a week.
6   fly (l.9) — flow
    It's hard to imagine that anyone could fly some of the old planes you see in museums.
    Originally, the river flowed several miles north of this point.
7   idea (l.11) — ideal
    Whose idea was it that we should invite him?
    You'll find an ideal place for a picnic on the other side of the lake.
8   at least (l.21) — at last
    There isn't much news about the missing climbers, but at least we know they're safe.
    After days of anxiety, at last we learnt the climbers were safe.

B   Supply alternative words in place of the words in italics:

1   The Moon *is likely to* become the industrial hub of the Solar System.

2   This *may* sound fantastic ... (1.5)

3   It takes *much* less energy ... (1.8)

C   Note the use of *who* in the sentence:

There are would-be voyagers *who* dream of sending people to Mars. (compare ll.17-18)

Supply *who* or *which*:

1   In my opinion, this laptop computer is the only one _____ is light enough to carry when you're travelling.

2   Some of the buildings _____ were put up in the 1960s are in very bad shape.

3   The giant panda is one of those animals _____ is most at risk of extinction.

4   There are a lot of people _____ are prepared to take business risks.

5   I think it was your mother _____ answered the phone.

Multiple choice questions 选择题

Choose the correct answers to the following questions.

Comprehension 理解

1   The moon is likely to become the centre of the Solar System because _____ .

(*a*) it has only an eightieth of the Earth's mass

(*b*) it will be an industrial centre

(*c*) it will be cheaper and easier to launch rockets from there

(*d*) there is plenty of fuel available on its surface

2   Compared with the earth, you need to travel _____ to take off from the moon.

(*a*) much faster

(*b*) at far less speed

(*c*) seven miles per second

(*d*) one sixth of the speed

3   We will only be ready to think of colonising Mars when _____ .

(*a*) there are enough enthusiasts to volunteer

(*b*) we have passed three phrases

(*c*) quite a few people have permanently left the earth

(*d*) we are prepared to travel 160 times further than the Moon

4   According to the writer, Mars seems ideal for settlement because _____ .

(*a*) it is the planet that most closely resembles the earth

(*b*) many senior scientists are in favour of it

(*c*) it is a world frull of red sandy deserts

(*d*) it is a fascinating place

Structure 句型

5   _____ escape from the Earth in a rocket, you must travel ... (1.5)

(*a*) For to   (*b*) In order   (*c*) If you want to   (*d*) For

6 How much energy _____ to accelerate 1.5 miles per second? (1.7)

(*a*) does it take   (*b*) it takes   (*c*) takes   (*d*) takes it

7 _____ a significant number of people are living in space can we move from the second phase to the third. (ll.15-16)

    (*a*) Until   (*b*) Not until   (*c*) Unless   (*d*) Although

8 Many serious and senior scientists are _____ enthusiasm. (ll.17-18)

    (*a*) filled of   (*b*) full of   (*c*) full   (*d*) full with

Vocabulary 词汇

9 This may sound _____ , but it is easily calculated. (l.5)

    (*a*) unlikely   (*b*) imaginative   (*c*) imaginary   (*d*) amazing

10 They will be able to fly at only three per cent of the cost of _____ journeys by their terrestrial cousins. (ll.9-10)

    (*a*) proximate   (*b*) the same   (*c*) like   (*d*) identical

11 I said it was a good idea _____ ..(l.3)

    (*a*) a long time   (*b*) always   (*c*) all the time   (*d*) forever

12 Mars has an extraordinary fascination for would-be _____ . (l.17)

    (*a*) flyers   (*b*) journeymen   (*c*) trippers   (*d*) travellers

Lesson 36 The cost of government 政府的开支

📠 **First listen and then answer the following question.**

听录音, 然后回答以下问题 。

What is the most important factor, both in government or business, for keeping running costs low?

If a nation is essentially disunited, it is left to the government to hold it together. This increases the expense of government, and reduces correspondingly the amount of economic resources that could be used for developing the country. And it should not be forgotten how small those resources are in a poor and backward country. Where the cost of government is high, resources for development are correspondingly low.

5　　This may be illustrated by comparing the position of a nation with that of a private business enterprise. An enterprise has to incur certain costs and expenses in order to stay in business. For our purposes, we are concerned only with one kind of cost—the cost of managing and administering the business. Such administrative overheads in a business are analogous to the cost of government in a nation. The administrative overheads of a business are low to the extent that everyone working in the business can be trusted to behave

10 in a way that best promotes the interests of the firm. If they can each be trusted to take such responsibilities, and to exercise such initiative as falls within their sphere, then administrative overheads will be low. It will be low because it will be necessary to have only one man looking after each job, without having another man to check upon what he is doing, keep him in line, and report on him to someone else. But if no one can be trusted to act in a loyal and responsible manner towards his job, then the business will require armies of

15 administrators, checkers, and foremen, and administrative overheads will rise correspondingly. As administrative overheads rise, so the earnings of the business after meeting the expense of administration, will fall; and the business will have less money to distribute as dividends or invest directly in its future progress and development.

　　It is precisely the same with a nation. To the extent that the people can be relied upon to behave in a loyal
20 and responsible manner, the government does not require armies of police and civil servants to keep them in order. But if a nation is disunited, the government cannot be sure that the actions of the people will be in the interests of the nation; and it will have to watch, check, and control the people accordingly. A disunited nation therefore has to incur unduly high costs of government.

RAYMOND FROST *The Backward Society*

New words and expressions 生词和短语

disunited (l.1) /ˌdɪsjuˈnaɪtɪd/ *adj.* 分裂的
correspondingly (l.2) /ˌkɒrɪˈspɒndɪŋli/ *adv.* 相应地
backward (l.3) /ˈbækwəd/ *adj.* 落后的
incur (l.6) /ɪnˈkɜː/ *v.* 承担
administer (l.7) /ədˈmɪnɪstə/ *v.* 管理
administrative (l.8) /ədˈmɪnɪstrətɪv/ *adj.* 行政
　管理的

analogous (l.8) /əˈnæləgəs/ *adj.* 类似的
overheads (l.8) /ˈəʊvəhedz/ *n.* 一般费用
initiative (l.11) /ɪˈnɪʃɪətɪv/ *n.* 主动, 积极性
checker (l.15) /ˈtʃekə/ *n.* 检查人员
foreman (l.15) /ˈfɔːmən/ *n.* 监工
dividend (l.17) /ˈdɪvɪdənd/ *n.* 红利
unduly (l.23) /ʌnˈdjuːli/ *adv.* 过度地

213

The Ministry of Natural Resources and
Local Government, Zomba, Malawi

The Home Office, Whitehall, London

Notes on the text 课文注释

1　economic resources, 经济资源 。
2　stay in business, 维持营业 。
3　be analogous to ..., 与 …… 类似 。
4　as falls within their sphere, 属于他们分内的 。
5　keep someone in line, 控制住某人 。
6　keep them in order, 管理他们 。
7　be in the interests of ..., 符合 …… 的利益 。

参考译文

　　如果一个国家实际上处于分裂状态, 使之联合起来就是政府的事了 。这样一来就增加了政府的开支, 从而相应地减少了可以用来发展国家的那部分经济资源 。不应忘记, 在一个贫穷落后的国家里, 那部分财力是很有限的 。凡是政府管理费用高的地方, 用于发展国家经济的资金就会相应地减少 。

　　把国家的状况同私人企业的状况加以比较, 就可以看清这个问题 。一个企业为了继续经营, 不得不支出一定的费用和开销 。就我们的目的而言, 我们只关心一种费用——企业行政管理费 。一家企业的这种行政管理开支类似于一个国家的政府管理所用的开支 。如果企业中的每个人都在真诚地为提高企业利润而工作, 那么企业的管理费用就会降低到相应的程度 。如果企业的每个人都信得过, 人人都认真负责, 在各自的工作范围内发挥主动性, 行政管理费用就会降低 。行政管理费用降低的原因是: 每项工作只需一个人去完成, 用不着另外再有一个人检查他的工作, 督促他遵守章程, 或向有关人士汇报他的工作 。但是, 如果企业中谁也不可信赖会对工作尽忠守职, 那么企业就会需要大批的管理人员 、检查人员和带班人员, 管理费用就会相应地增加 。管理费用增加了, 那么在扣除管理费用后, 企业的收入就降低了 。因而用于分红的金额或直接用于将来开拓和发展的投资就相应地减少了 。

　　一个国家的情况也完全相同 。如果人民忠于职守, 举止规矩, 能受到政府的信赖, 那么政府就不需要大批的警察和文职人员去促使人民遵纪守法 。但是, 如果一个国家处于分裂状态, 政府不能相信人民的行动有利于国家, 那么政府就不得不对人民进行监督 、检查和控制 。因此, 一个处于分裂状态的国家必然要支付过高的行政管理费用 。

Comprehension 理解

Answer these questions:

1   Why is the expense of government increased if a nation is disunited?
2   What do you understand by the phrase 'administrative overheads'? (ll.8-9)

Vocabulary 词汇

Refer to the text to see how the following words have been used, then write sentences of your own using these words: reduces correspondingly the amount of economic resources (l.2); incur (l.6); analogous (l.8); promotes (l.10); distribute as dividends (l.17); precisely (l.19); unduly (l.23).

Summary 摘要

Drawing your information from lines 5-23 ('This may be ... costs of government'), show how the running of a business enterprise can be compared with the running of a country. Do not write more than 120 words. Your answer should be in one paragraph.

Composition 作文

A   Write a list of ideas in note form which could be used to discuss this subject:
Ideally, a civil service should consist of a permanently appointed body of men who are not necessarily affiliated to the political party that is in power at any particular time.

B   Drawing on your list of ideas, write a composition of about 400 words.

Key structures 关键句型

A   Supply the correct form of the verbs in parentheses in the following sentences. Do not refer to the passage until you have completed the exercise:

1   This reduces the amount of economic resources that could be used for _____ (develop) the country. (ll.1-3)
2   This may be illustrated by _____ (compare) the position of a nation with that of a private business enterprise. (l.5)
3   We are concerned only with the cost of _____ (manage) and _____ (administer) the business. (ll.6-7)
4   It will be low because it will be necessary to have only one man _____ (look) after each job, without _____ (have) another man to check upon what he is doing. (ll.11-13)
5   The earnings of the business, after _____ (meet) the expense of administration, will fall. (l.16)

B   Write these sentences again so that they begin with the words given in parentheses. Make any other necessary changes. Do not refer to the passage until you have completed the exercise:

1   We should not forget how small these resources are. (It) (l.3)
2   We may illustrate this by comparing the position of a nation with that of a private business enterprise. (This) (l.5)
3   Only one kind of cost concerns us. (We) (ll.6-7)
4   We can trust each of them to take such responsibilities. (They) (l.10)
5   We cannot trust anyone to act in a loyal and responsible manner. (No one) (ll.13-14)
6   We can rely upon the people to behave in a loyal and responsible manner. (The people) (ll.19-20)

C   In which of the following sentences would it be possible to use *in order to* in place of *to*? Do not refer to the passage until you have completed the exercise:

1   An enterprise has to incur certain costs and expenses *to* stay in business. (1.6)

2   They can be trusted *to* take such responsibilities. (1.10)

3   No one can be trusted *to* act in a loyal and responsible manner. (ll.13-14)

4   The government does not require armies of police and civil servants *to* keep them in order. (ll.20-21)

D   Note the use of *best* in this sentence:

Everyone working in the business can be trusted to behave in a way that *best* promotes the interest of the firm. (ll.9-10)

Write sentences using the following expressions:

best illustrates; best describes; best explains.

Special difficulties 难点

A   Study the following pairs of words and then write sentences of your own to bring out the difference.

1   earnings (1.16) — profits

The foreign earnings of the company this year are down because of the high exchange value of the dollor. (= money from work or trade)

Our profits figure for the current year will be sharply reduced by provision for bad debts arising from war in Africa. (= money earned from trade after all costs have been deducted)

2   watch (1.22) — follow

I'm watching the game on TV.

The dog followed me all the way home.

Sorry! The phone rang, and I haven't quite followed what you were saying. (i.e. with the mind: understood)

3   check (1.22) — control (1.22)

Check the tyres before you leave.

The state no longer controls the price of grain.

B   Explain the meaning of the words in italics:

1   And it should not be forgotten how small those resources are in a poor and *backward* country. (ll.3-4)

2   The train had to go *backwards* for half a mile.

3   She is concerned with the care of *backward* children.

C   How does the position of *only* affect the meaning of the following sentences:

1   We are concerned *only* with one kind of cost. (ll.6-7)

2   We *only* are concerned.

3   We are concerned with *only* one kind of cost.

4   We are concerned with one kind of cost *only*.

Multiple choice questions 选择题

Choose the correct answers to the following questions.

Comprehension 理解

1 If a country has to spend a lot of money on government, it _____ .

 (a) won't have much over for other expenditure

 (b) will remain essentially disunited

 (c) will become a poor and backward nation

 (d) will be able to develop rapidly

2 A private business enterprise can only stay in business _____ .

 (a) by relating to the cost of government in a nation

 (b) if it distributes dividends on a regular basis

 (c) by spending money

 (d) by assessing the cost of each job

3 The costs of running a business can be kept low, if _____ .

 (a) business earnings remain high

 (b) there is an atmosphere of trust in a company

 (c) people enjoy their jobs

 (d) there is a good system for checking all employees

4 The cost of government _____ .

 (a) includes the employment of armies of administrators

 (b) cannot be compared in any way with running a business

 (c) is in direct proportion to the responsible behaviour of its citizens

 (d) always rises regardless of circumstances

Structure 句型

5 You can illustrate this _____ compare the position of a nation ... (l.5)

 (a) though you   (b) would you   (c) if you   (d) to

6 For our purposes, what _____ us is only one kind of cost. (ll.6-7)

 (a) concerns   (b) is concerned   (c) is concerning   (d) concerning

7 The administrative overheads in a business are low _____ everyone ... (ll.8-9)

 (a) even if   (b) however much   (c) in so far as   (d) supposing

8 _____ the people can be relied upon to behave ... (l.19)

 (a) Even if   (b) However much   (c) As long as   (d) Supposing

Vocabulary 词汇

9 This increase reduces _____ the amount that could be used for ... (ll.1-2)

 (a) together   (b) in response   (c) in writing   (d) proportionately

10 We are concerned only with the cost of managing and _____ the business. (ll.6-7)

 (a) organizing   (b) conducting   (c) establishing   (d) developing

11 The business will have less money to _____ or invest ... (ll.17-18)

 (a) share out   (b) acquire   (c) dispose   (d) amass

12 A disunited nation has to incur _____ high costs of government. (ll.22-23)

 (a) unacceptably   (b) unexpectedly   (c) excessively   (d) extremely

Lesson 37 The process of ageing 衰老过程

First listen and then answer the following question.

听录音，然后回答以下问题。

What is one of the most unpleasant discoveries we make about ourselves as we get older?

At the age of twelve years, the human body is at its most vigorous. It has yet to reach its full size and strength, and its owner his or her full intelligence; but at this age the likelihood of death is least. Earlier, we were infants and young children, and consequently more vulnerable; later, we shall undergo a progressive loss of our vigour and resistance which, though imperceptible at first, will finally become so steep that we
5 can live no longer, however well we look after ourselves, and however well society, and our doctors, look after us. This decline in vigour with the passing of time is called ageing. It is one of the most unpleasant discoveries which we all make that we *must* decline in this way, that if we escape wars, accidents and diseases we shall eventually 'die of old age', and that this happens at a rate which differs little from person to person, so that there are heavy odds in favour of our dying between the ages of sixty-five and eighty.
10 Some of us will die sooner, a few will live longer—on into a ninth or tenth decade. But the chances are against it, and there is a virtual limit on how long we can hope to remain alive, however lucky and robust we are.

   Normal people tend to forget this process unless and until they are reminded of it. We are so familiar with the fact that man ages, that people have for years assumed that the process of losing vigour with time,
15 of becoming more likely to die the older we get, was something self-evident, like the cooling of a hot kettle or the wearing-out of a pair of shoes. They have also assumed that all animals, and probably other organisms such as trees, or even the universe itself, must in the nature of things 'wear out'. Most animals we commonly observe do in fact age as we do, if given the chance to live long enough; and mechanical systems like a wound watch, or the sun, do in fact run out of energy in accordance with the second law of thermodynamics
20 (whether the whole universe does so is a moot point at present). But these are not analogous to what happens when man ages. A run-down watch is still a watch and can be rewound. An *old* watch, by contrast, becomes so worn and unreliable that it eventually is not worth mending. But a watch could never repair itself—it does not consist of living parts, only of metal, which wears away by friction. We could, at one time, repair ourselves—well enough, at least, to overcome all but the most instantly fatal illnesses and accidents.
25 Between twelve and eighty years we gradually lose this power; an illness which at twelve would knock us over, at eighty can knock us out, and into our grave. If we could stay as vigorous as we are at twelve, it would take about 700 years for half of us to die, and another 700 for the survivors to be reduced by half again.

ALEX COMFORT *The process of ageing*

New words and expressions 生词和短语

likelihood (l.2) /'laɪklihʊd/ *n.* 可能性
infant (l.3) /'ɪnfənt/ *n.* 婴儿
vulnerable (l.3) /'vʌlnərəbəl/ *adj.* 脆弱的
imperceptible (l.4) /ˌɪmpə'septəbəl/ *adj.* 感觉不到的

steep (l.4) /stiːp/ *adj.* 急转直下的
ageing (l.6) /'eɪdʒɪŋ/ *n.* 老化
odds (l.9) /ɒdz/ *n.* 可能性
virtual (l.11) /'vɜːtʃuəl/ *adj.* 实际上的

Two tortoises, both from the Seychelles; the small one is a year old, the large one is over a hundred

robust (l.11) /'rəʊbʌst/ *adj.* 强健的
organism (l.16) /'ɔːgənɪzəm/ *n.* 有机体
thermodynamics (l.19) /ˌθɜːməʊdaɪ'næmɪks/
　n. 热力学

moot (l.20) /muːt/ *adj.* 争论未决的
run-down (l.21) /ˌrʌn-'daʊn/ *adj.* 破旧的
friction (l.23) /'frɪkʃən/ *n.* 摩擦

Notes on the text 课文注释

1　at its most vigorous, 生命力最旺盛的时候 。
2　with the passing of time, 随着时间的流失 。
3　It is one of the most unpleasant discoveries ... that ..., that ..., and that ... ，3 个以 that 引导的从句是 discoveries 的同位语 。
4　a wound watch, 上紧了发条的表 。

参考译文

　　人体在 12 岁时是生命力最旺盛的时期 。虽然在这个时期人的身材 、体力和智力还有待发展和完善, 但在这个年龄死亡的可能性最小 。再早一些, 我们是幼儿和小孩子, 身体较脆弱; 再迟一些, 我们就要经历生命力和抵抗力逐步衰退的过程 。虽然这个过程起初难以觉察, 但最终会急转直下, 不管我们怎样精心照料我们自己, 不管社会和医生怎样对我们进行精心照顾, 我们也无法再活下去了 。生命力随时间的流失而衰退叫做衰老 。人类发现的最不愉快的一个事实是: 人必然会衰老 。即使我们能避开战争 、意外的事故和各种疾病, 我们最终也会"老死"; 衰老的速度在人与人之间相差甚微, 我们最可能死亡的年龄在 65 至 80 岁之间, 有些人会死得早一些, 少数人寿命会长一些——活到八十几岁或九十几岁, 但这种可能性很小 。不管我们多么幸运, 多么健壮, 我们所希望的长寿实际上是有限度的 。

　　衰老的过程, 不经提起, 正常人容易忘记; 一经提醒, 才会记起 。我们对人总是要衰老的现象并不陌生, 多年来就已认识到 。生命力随着时间流失而丧失活力, 人随着年龄的增长而接近死亡, 这是不言而喻的, 就像一壶热水迟早会凉下来, 一双鞋渐渐会磨破一样 。人们不但认识到所有的动物, 大概也认识到所有的有机物, 如树木, 甚至宇宙本身, 从事物的本质上来说都会"磨损掉" 。我们通常看到的大多数动物, 即使能让它们活得足够长久的话, 也会像我们一样衰老的 。像上紧发条的手表那样的机械装置, 或太阳, 也都会依照热学第二定律消耗完其能量 (整个宇宙是否如此, 目前尚有争论) 。不过, 这些衰老的情况同人并不相似 。手表停了依然是只手表, 还可以重上好发条 。然而一只老掉牙的手表, 磨损太厉害, 老得一点儿也不准了, 最终会不值得修理了 。但是, 手表决不会自行修理, 它不是由有生命的部件组成, 而是由金属组成, 而金属可以随着磨擦而磨损殆尽 。而

Unit 5 Lesson 37

我们人, 在一定时间内是可以自行修复的, 除了暴病而死或意外事故外, 至少足以克服一切一般疾病和事故 。在 12 岁至 80 岁之间, 我们逐渐丧失这种能力 。能使我们在 12 岁时病倒的疾病, 到了 80 岁可能会使我们一蹶不振而进入坟墓 。假如我们能保持 12 岁时的旺盛生命力, 那么我们当中的一半人过 700 年才会死去, 剩下的一半人再过 700 年, 才会又减少一半 。

Comprehension 理解

Answer these questions:

1 Why is the likelihood of death least when we are twelve years old?

2 Why are there heavy odds in favour of our dying between the ages of sixty-five and eighty?

3 Which power do we gradually lose between the ages of twelve and eighty?

Vocabulary 词汇

Refer to the text to see how the following words have been used, then write sentences of your own using these words: likelihood (1.2); vulnerable (1.3); imperceptible (1.4); decline in vigour (1.6); rate (1.8); robust (1.11); self-evident (1.15); moot (1.20); fatal (1.24).

Summary 摘要

Drawing your information from the second paragraph (lines 13-27), write a summary of the author's description of the process of ageing. Do not write more than 100 words. Your answer should be in one paragraph.

Composition 作文

A Write a list of ideas in note form which could be used to discuss the following subject: Suggest reasons why we in the twentieth century can expect to live longer than people who lived in bygone times.

B Drawing on your list of ideas, write a composition of about 400 words.

Key structures 关键句型

A Supply *the* where necessary in the following sentences:

1 It is one of _____ most unpleasant discoveries which we all make. (ll.6-7)

2 _____ most animals we commonly observe do in fact age as we do. (ll.17-18)

3 Death is something which _____ most people fear.

4 Make _____ most of what you've got.

5 _____ most of the things I've got were bought overseas.

B Compare the use of *however* in these sentences.

1 There is a virtual limit on how long we can hope to remain alive, *however* lucky and robust we are. (ll.11-12)

2 No one will deny that many of the programmes shown on television are very poor. There are, *however*, a fair number which are very fine indeed.

Write two sentences using *however* in the ways shown above.

C   Complete these sentences in any way you wish. Then compare what you have written with the sentences in the passage:

1   We shall undergo a progressive loss of our vigour and resistance which, _____ , will finally become so steep that _____ (ll.3-4)

2   We are so familiar with the fact that man ages, that _____ (ll.13-14)

3   An *old* watch, by contrast, becomes so worn and unreliable that _____ (ll.21-22)

Special difficulties 难点

A   Study the following pairs of words and then write sentences of your own to bring out the difference.

1   infant (l.3) — baby

The State provides a programme of health checks for all infants up to a year old. (Infant is only used in official contexts.)

We were innoculated against diphtheria when we were babies.

2   imperceptible (l.4) — unperceived

The changes, at first so small as to be imperceptible, become more obvious as time passes.

So much money was involved that it was impossible for the forgery to remain unperceived.

3   alive — living

It was a surprise to learn that he had just died, since I hadn't realized he was still alive!

Until August 1997, the oldest living person was a French woman from Arles aged a hundred and twenty-two.

B   Explain the meaning of the verbs in italics:

1   ... we shall undergo a progressive loss of our vigour ... however well we *look after* ourselves ... (ll.3-5)

2   *Look out*! There's a bus coming!

3   I am *looking forward to* the summer holidays.

4   Everybody *looks on* him as a leader.

5   If there are any words in the passage you don't understand, *look* them *up* in the dictionary.

6   Business was very slack before Christmas, but things are *looking up* now.

7   I shall certainly *look up* all my old friends when I go back home.

8   Why don't you *look in* next week. I'm sure he'll be back by then.

C   Explain the meaning of the verbs in italics:

1   ... mechanical systems ... *run out* of energy ... (ll.18-19)

2   My new car hasn't been *run in* yet.

3   That little boy was nearly *run over* by a bus.

4   He *ran through* all the money he had inherited in less than a year.

5   While on holiday in Spain, we *ran into* our next-door neighbours.

6   Look at that lamp-post. It looks as if a car *ran into* it.

D   Explain the meaning of the verbs in italics:

1   ... an illness which at twelve would *knock us over*, at eighty can *knock us out* ... (ll.25-26)

2   There's so much work to do in the office these days, I never *knock off* before six o'clock.

Unit 5   Lesson 37

Multiple choice questions 选择题

Choose the correct answers to the following questions.

Comprehension 理解

1 Our first twelve years _____ .

    (*a*) are followed by a rapid decline

    (*b*) represent the peak of our development as human beings

    (*c*) are succeeded by a gradual ageing process

    (*d*) are the time when the human body is at its most vigorous

2 No matter how lucky and robust we are, we _____ .

    (*a*) cannot avoid the ageing process

    (*b*) make unpleasant discoveries

    (*c*) will died between the ages of sixty-five and eighty

    (*d*) will all die at the same time

3 The process in humans and animals of losing vigour with time _____ .

    (*a*) is something we would all like to forget   (*b*) is not something we question very much

    (*c*) is like a watch that wears out   (*d*) follows the second law of thermodynamics

4 Humans could live for very long periods indeed if they _____ .

    (*a*) retained the capacity for self-repair they enjoyed at twelve

    (*b*) didn't become run down

    (*c*) survived the first 700 years

    (*d*) weren't worn down by friction

Structure 句型

5 _____ reached its full size and strength. (ll.1-2)

    (*a*) It hasn't before   (*b*) It hasn't even   (*c*) It still hasn't   (*d*) Yet it hasn't

6 At this age, the possibilities of death are _____ .

    (*a*) few   (*b*) fewer   (*c*) the fewest   (*d*) fewest

7 We can live no longer, _____ we look after ourselves. (ll.4-5)

    (*a*) whatever   (*b*) no matter how much

    (*c*) how much   (*d*) whichever way

8 So familiar _____ with the fact that man ages, that ... (ll.13-14)

    (*a*) have we   (*b*) we have   (*c*) are we   (*d*) we are

Vocabulary 词汇

9 The body has yet to arrive _____ its full size. (l.1)

    (*a*) -   (*b*) to   (*c*) in   (*d*) at

10 They run out of energy _____ the second law of thermodynamics. (l.19)

    (*a*) similar   (*b*) in contrast to   (*c*) in line with   (*d*) in harmony with

11 Whether the whole universe runs out of energy is _____ point. (l.20)

    (*a*) a mute   (*b*) an undecided   (*c*) a lost   (*d*) a big

12 A watch could never repair itself — it is not made _____ living parts. (ll.22-23)

    (*a*) out   (*b*) away with   (*c*) over to   (*d*) up of

Lesson 38 Water and the traveller 水和旅行者

First listen and then answer the following question.

听录音, 然后回答以下问题 。

What does this text describe?

Contamination of water supplies is usually due to poor sanitation close to water sources, sewage disposal into the sources themselves, leakage of sewage into distribution systems or contamination with industrial or farm waste. Even if a piped water supply is safe at its source, it is not always safe by the time it reaches the tap. Intermittent tap-water supplies should be regarded as particularly suspect.

5   Travellers on short trips to areas with water supplies of uncertain quality should avoid drinking tap-water, or untreated water from any other source. It is best to keep to hot drinks, bottled or canned drinks of well-known brand names—international standards of water treatment are usually followed at bottling plants. Carbonated drinks are acidic, and slightly safer. Make sure that all bottles are opened in your presence, and that their rims are clean and dry.

10   Boiling is always a good way of treating water. Some hotels supply boiled water on request and this can be used for drinking, or for brushing teeth. Portable boiling elements that can boil small quantities of water are useful when the right voltage of electricity is available. Refuse politely any cold drink from an unknown source.

Ice is only as safe as the water from which it is made, and should not be put in drinks unless it is known
15 to be safe. Drinks can be cooled by placing them on ice rather than adding ice to them.

Alcohol may be a medical disinfectant, but should not be relied upon to sterilize water. Ethanol is more effective at a concentration of 50-70 per cent; below 20 per cent, its bactericidal action is negligible. Spirits labelled 95 proof contain only about 47 per cent alcohol. Beware of methylated alcohol, which is very poisonous, and should never be added to drinking water.

20   If no other safe water supply can be obtained, tap water that is too hot to touch can be left to cool and is generally safe to drink. Those planning a trip to remote areas, or intending to live in countries where drinking water is not readily available, should know about the various possible methods for making water safe.

RICHARD DAWOOD *Travellers' Health*

New words and expressions 生词和短语

contamination (l.1) /kənˌtæmɪ'neɪʃən/ *n.* 污染
sanitation (l.1) /ˌsænɪ'teɪʃən/ *n.* 卫生, 卫生设备
sewage (l.1) /'sjuːɪʤ/ *n.* 污水
leakage (l.2) /'liːkɪʤ/ *n.* 泄漏
intermittent (l.4) /ˌɪntə'mɪtənt/ *adj.* 间歇的, 断断续续的
carbonated (l.8) /'kɑːbəneɪtɪd/ *adj.* 碳化的, 碳酸的
acidic (l.8) /ə'sɪdɪk/ *adj.* 酸的, 酸性的

alcohol (l.16) /'ælkəhɒl/ *n.* 酒精
disinfectant (l.16) /ˌdɪsɪn'fektənt/ *n.* 消毒剂
sterilize (l.16) /'sterɪlaɪz/ *v.* 消毒
ethanol (l.16) /'eθənɒl/ *n.* 乙醇
bactericidal (l.17) /bækˌtɪərɪ'saɪdəl/ *adj.* 杀菌的
negligible (l.17) /'neglɪʤɪbəl/ *adj.* 可以忽略的, 微不足道的
methylated (l.18) /'meθɪleɪtɪd/ *adj.* 加入甲醇的

223

A woman is drawing water from a well.

Notes on the text 课文注释

1   keep to, 局限于 。
2   Ice is only as safe as the water from which it is made. 冰块只是当制造冰块的水安全时才是安全的 。
3   know about, 知道 …… 的情况, 了解 。

参考译文

　　水源的污染通常是由于接近水源的地方卫生条件太差而造成的: 污水排入水源, 污水渗入给水系统或工农业污水造成污染 。即使管道供水系统在水源处是安全的, 等水到达龙头时就不一定总是安全的了 。断断续续的水管应该被视为是非常可疑的 。

　　短途旅行到水质不保险的地区时, 旅游者应避免饮用水龙头的水或未经处理的任何其他来源的水 。最好仅饮用开水、名牌瓶装或罐装水——装瓶厂通常遵循国际水处理的标准 。碳酸饮料是酸性的, 就更安全一些 。确保瓶子是当着你的面开启的, 瓶口清洁干燥 。

　　烧开一直是水处理的一种好办法 。有的酒店根据要求可提供开水, 这些开水可用于饮用和刷牙 。如果有相配的电压, 可以煮少量水的便携式热水装置是有用的 。应谢绝任何不明来源的冷饮 。

　　冰块只有当制造冰块的水安全时才是保险的, 只有知道冰块安全时才能加入饮料 。可以把饮料置于冰块之上来冷却, 而不是把冰块加进饮料之中 。

　　酒精可用作医学上的消毒剂, 但决不可用来消毒饮用水 。乙醇的浓度为 50% 至 70% 时比较有效, 浓度低于 20% 时, 杀菌能力基本上就不存在了 。强度标为 95 的酒中含 47% 的酒精 。要提防甲基化酒精, 那是剧毒的, 永远不能掺入饮用水 。

　　如果没有其他安全的饮用水, 水管中流出的烫手的水可以留下来冷却 。这种水一般是安全的 。那些计划去偏远地区旅行 、或在没有现成饮用水的国家居住的人, 应该知道如何使水适于饮用的各种办法 。

Comprehension 理解

Answer these questions:

1　What kind of piped water could be dangerous to the health?

2　Why does the author recommend that travellers on short trips should drink canned drinks of well-known brand names?

3　Why could ice in drinks be dangerous to the health?

4　Why wouldn't you be safe if you added 95 proof alcohol to contaminated water?

5　What kind of tap water is generally safe to drink in the absence of other sources?

Vocabulary 词汇

Refer to the text to see how the following words have been used, then write sentences of your own using these words: poor (l.1); contamination (l.2); regarded (l.4); areas (l.5); plants (l.7); in your presence (l.8); supply (l.10); on request (l.10); refuse (l.12); remote (l.21); various (l.22).

Summary 摘要

Refer to lines 1-5 ('Contamination ... adding ice to them,'). In not more than 80 words write seven sentences giving advice to travellers about drinking water. Begin each sentence with the word 'always'. The first sentence has been done for you:

Always avoid intermittent tap-water supplies.

Composition 作文

A　A foreigner is going to travel to some of the remote regions of your country. Write some notes giving him/her good advice under each of these headings: the people, accommodation, food, water.

B　Refer to your notes and write four paragraphs of advice to a traveller in about 400 words.

Key structures 关键句型

A　Compare these active and passive uses of *should* for giving direct and indirect advice:

You should regard intermittent tap-water supplies as particularly suspect.

Intermittent tap-water supplies should be regarded as particularly suspect. (l.4)

Turn these sentences into the passive in order to give indirect advice:

1　You should avoid drinking tap-water.

2　You should prefer well-known brand names of bottled drinks.

3　They should open all bottles in your presence.

4　You should request boiled water in hotels.

5　You should boil water before drinking it.

B   Compare these active and passive uses of *shouldn't* for giving direct and indirect advice:

You shouldn't regard intermittent tap-water supplies as safe.

Intermittent tap-water supplies shouldn't be regarded as safe.

Turn these sentences into the passive in order to give indirect advice.

1   You shouldn't drink tap-water.

2   You shouldn't accept bottles of water that haven't been opened in your presence.

3   You shouldn't put ice in drinks.

4   You shouldn't rely on alcohol to sterilize water.

5   You shouldn't add methylated alcohol to drinking water.

Special difficulties 难点

A   Compare the *-ing* form in these four sentences:

Boiling is always a good way of treating water. (l.10) (boiling-*noun*)

Portable boiling elements that can boil small quantities of water ... (l.11) (boiling-*compound noun*: i.e. elements used for boiling)

I was scalded with boiling water. (boiling-*adjective*: i.e. water which was boiling)

The water is boiling. (boiling-*participle*: part of the verb form)

Identify the *-ing* forms as nouns, adjectives or participles in these sentences:

1   Travellers should avoid drinking tap water. (ll.5-6)

2   International standards of water treatment are usually followed at bottling plants. (l.7)

3   Methylated alcohol should never be added to drinking water. (ll.18-19)

4   Those planning a trip to remote areas should know about various methods ... (ll.21-22)

5   Making water safe to drink is a matter of life or death.

6   We are planning a trip to the remote areas of the country.

B   Compare the *-ed* form in these two sentences:

Piped water supply is safe at its source. (l.3) (piped-*adjectival past participle*)

The water has been *piped* across thousands of miles. (piped-*past participle*: part of the verb form)

Identify the *-ed* forms as adjectives or past participles in these sentences:

1   Some water supplies should be regarded as particularly suspect.

2   Bottled or canned drinks are usually safe. (ll.6-7)

3   Carbonated drinks are acidic. (l.8)

4   Make sure that all bottles are opened in your presence. (ll.8-9)

5   Drinks can be cooled by placing them on ice. (l.15)

6   Spirits labelled 95 proof contain only about 47 per cent alcohol. (ll.17-18)

Multiple choice questions 选择题

Choose the correct answers to the following questions.

Comprehension 理解

1 Piped water could be contaminated, especially if _____ .

(*a*) it is supplied from the sewage system

(*b*) it isn't safe by the time it reaches the tap

(c) doesn't flow continuously through the pipes

(d) it comes from farmland

2 Make sure that bottled drinks are opened in your presence, presumably _____ .

(a) to be assured that it was filled at a bottling plant

(b) to make sure that it isn't too acidic to drink

(c) to check that the rim of the bottle is clean and dry

(d) because water supplies are uncertain

3 You should avoid ice in drinks because _____ .

(a) you don't know if it has been made with contaminated water

(b) you can be sure it hasn't been boiled first

(c) because it always comes from an unknown source

(d) it hasn't been treated in your presence

4 You can't use alcoholic drinks to sterilize water because _____ .

(a) only ethanol is capable of doing this

(b) the alcoholic content is rarely sufficiently concentrated to do the job

(c) methylated alcohol is very poisonous

(d) it's not a very good disinfectant

Structure 句型

5 Piped water _____ safe at its source, _____ it isn't always safe. (1.3)

(a) must be ... and   (b) may be ... but   (c) should be ... though   (d) will be ... even if

6 It _____ to drink tap water of uncertain quality. (1.5)

(a) isn't advisable   (b) is advisable   (c) isn't required   (d) is required

7 Drinks can be cooled _____ them on ice. (1.15)

(a) so as to place   (b) in placing   (c) if you place   (d) to place

8 _____ rely on alcohol to sterilize water. (1.16)

(a) Not   (b) Don't   (c) Must not   (d) Not to

Vocabulary 词汇

9 Make sure that all bottles are opened _____ . (1.8)

(a) at once   (b) now   (c) at present   (d) in front of you

10 _____ any cold drink from an unknown source. (1.12)

(a) Discard   (b) Prevent   (c) Deny   (d) Don't accept

11 You should not _____ on alcohol to sterilize water. (1.16)

(a) depend   (b) insist   (c) lean   (d) support

12 Those planning a trip to _____ places ... (1.21)

(a) away   (b) far away   (c) contaminated   (d) overseas

Lesson 39　What every writer wants　作家之所需

📼 **First listen and then answer the following question.**

听录音, 然后回答以下问题 。

How do professional writers ignore what they were taught at school about writing?

I have known very few writers, but those I have known, and whom I respect, confess at once that they have little idea where they are going when they first set pen to paper. They have a character, perhaps two; they are in that condition of eager discomfort which passes for inspiration; all admit radical changes of destination once the journey has begun; one, to my certain knowledge, spent nine months on a novel about Kashmir,
5　then reset the whole thing in the Scottish Highlands. I never heard of anyone making a 'skeleton', as we were taught at school. In the breaking and remaking, in the timing, interweaving, beginning afresh, the writer comes to discern things in his material which were not consciously in his mind when he began. This organic process, often leading to moments of extraordinary self-discovery, is of an indescribable fascination. A blurred image appears; he adds a brushstroke and another, and it is gone; but something was
10　there, and he will not rest till he has captured it. Sometimes the yeast within a writer outlives a book he has written. I have heard of writers who read nothing but their own books; like adolescents they stand before the mirror, and still cannot fathom the exact outline of the vision before them. For the same reason, writers talk interminably about their own books, winkling out hidden meanings, super-imposing new ones, begging response from those around them. Of course a writer doing this is misunderstood: he might as well try to
15　explain a crime or a love affair. He is also, incidentally, an unforgivable bore.

　　This temptation to cover the distance between himself and the reader, to study his image in the sight of those who do not know him, can be his undoing: he has begun to write to please.

　　A young English writer made the pertinent observation a year or two back that the talent goes into the first draft, and the art into the drafts that follow. For this reason also the writer, like any other artist, has no
20　resting place, no crowd or movement in which he may take comfort, no judgment from outside which can replace the judgment from within. A writer makes order out of the anarchy of his heart; he submits himself to a more ruthless discipline than any critic dreamed of, and when he flirts with fame, he is taking time off from living with himself, from the search for what *his* world contains at its inmost point.

JOHN LE CARRÉ *What every writer wants* from *Harper's*

New words and expressions 生词和短语

confess (1.1) /kən'fes/ *v.* 承认
inspiration (1.3) /ˌɪnspə'reɪʃən/ *n.* 灵感
Kashmir (1.4) /kæʃ'mɪə/ *n.* 克什米尔
interweave (1.6) /ˌɪntə'wiːv/ *v.* 交织
afresh (1.6) /ə'freʃ/ *adv.* 重新
discern (1.7) /dɪ'sɜːn/ *v.* 辨明, 领悟
indescribable (1.8) /ˌɪndɪs'kraɪbəbəl/ *adj.* 无法描述的
blur (1.9) /blɜː/ *v.* 使 …… 模糊不清

yeast (1.10) /jiːst/ *n.* 激动
fathom (1.12) /'fæðəm/ *v.* 领悟, 彻底了解
interminably (1.13) /ɪn'tɜːmɪnəbəli/ *adv.* 没完没了地
winkle (1.13) /'wɪŋkəl/ *v.* 挖掘
incidentally (1.15) /ˌɪnsɪ'dentli/ *adv.* 顺便说一下
pertinent (1.18) /'pɜːtɪnənt/ *adj.* 中肯的
flirt (1.22) /flɜːt/ *v.* 调情
inmost (1.23) /'ɪnməʊst/ *adj.* 内心深处的

A scene from the film of John le Carré's book, *The Spy Who Came in from the Cold*

Notes on the text 课文注释

1 where they are going, 他们要写什么, 怎么写 。

2 set pen to paper, 开始写作 。

3 pass for, "被当作", 但常指蒙骗 、假冒 。

4 to my certain knowledge, 据我所知 。

5 nothing but, 仅, 只 。

6 like adolescents they stand before the mirror, and still cannot fathom the exact outline of the vision before them. 他们如同少年, 站在镜前, 不能辨认出自身的真面目 。此句出自古希腊的一则神话: 有一漂亮少年, 他热恋上了水中自身的映像, 最后憔悴而死, 化为水仙花 。

7 in the sight of, 从 …… 角度来看 。

参考译文

　　我所认识的作家寥寥无几, 然而凡是我所认识和尊敬的作家, 都坦率地承认在他们动笔时, 不清楚要写什么, 怎么写 。他们心中有一个或两个角色 。他们处于急切不安的状态, 而这被当作是灵感 。他们无不承认, 一旦 "旅程" 开始, "目的地" 常有急剧的变化 。据我所知, 有位作家花了 9 个月的时间写了一部有关克什米尔的小说, 后来却把整个故事背景换成了苏格兰高地 。我从未听说过任何一位作家像我们在学校学的那样, 动笔前先列什么提纲 。作家在剪裁修改 、构思时间 、穿插情节 、甚至从头重写的过程中, 会领悟到素材中有很多东西是他刚动笔时所未意识到的 。这种有机的加工过程往往达到不寻常的自我发现的境界, 具有难以言表的构思魅力 。一个朦胧的形象出现在作家的脑海里, 他左添一笔, 右添一笔, 形象反而消逝了; 可是, 好像还有什么东西存在着, 不把它捕捉到, 作家是不会罢休的 。有时, 一个作家一本书写完了, 但兴奋仍不消散 。我听说一些作家, 除了自己的书外, 别的书一概不读, 犹如希腊神话中那位漂亮少年, 站在镜前, 不能辨认出自身的真面目 。由于这个原因, 作家喋喋不休地谈论自己的书, 挖掘其隐晦的含义, 增添新的含义, 询问周围人的反应 。作家如此行事当然会被人误解 。他还不如给人讲一个犯罪案件或一个恋爱故事 。顺便说一句, 他也是个不可饶恕的令人厌烦的人 。

这种企图消除自己和读者之间距离的做法，企图用不了解自己的人的观点来研究自己塑造的形象的做法，会导致作家的毁灭，因为他已经开始为取悦他人而写作了。

一两年前，一位年轻的英国作家发表了中肯的看法。他说，初稿是才华，以后各稿是艺术。也是由于这个原因，作家同任何艺术家一样，找不到可休息的场所，找不到伙伴和活动使自己得到安逸。任何局外人的判断也比不上他自己内心的正确判断。一旦作家从内心的紊乱中理出头绪，就应按任何评论家想象不到的无情规范约束自己去写作；当他沽名钓誉时，他就脱离了自我生活，脱离了对自己灵魂最深处世界的探索。

Comprehension 理解

Answer these questions:

1   What do you understand by this sentence: 'All admit radical changes of destination once the journey has begun.'? (ll.3-4)
2   What do you understand by the phrase 'organic process'? (l.8)
3   Quote a sentence from the passage from which you could deduce that a writer must be a lonely person.

Vocabulary 词汇

Refer to the text to see how the following words have been used, then write sentences of your own using these words: eager discomfort (l.3); passes for (l.3); skeleton (l.5); beginning afresh (l.6); discern (l.7); a blurred image (l.9); fathom (l.12); interminably (ll.12-13); winkling out (l.13); anarchy (l.21); ruthless (l.22); taking time off (l.22).

Summary 摘要

Drawing your information from the first paragraph (lines 1-15) write a summary of the author's account of how a writer works. Do not write more than 100 words. Your answer should be in one paragraph.

Composition 作文

A   Write a list of ideas in note form which could be used to discuss this subject:

Which do you prefer reading: novels, plays, poetry or non-fiction?

Give reasons for your choice.

B   Drawing on your list of ideas, write a composition of about 400 words.

Key structures 关键句型

A   Supply *who, whom* or *which* where necessary in the following sentences. Do not refer to the passage until you have finished the exercise:

1   I have known very few writers, but those _____ I have known, and _____ I respect confess at once that they have little idea where they are going when they first set pen to paper. (ll.1-2)
2   The writer comes to discern things in his material _____ were not consciously in his mind when he began. (ll.6-7)
3   Sometimes the yeast within a writer outlives a book _____ he has written. (l.10)
4   I have heard of writers _____ read nothing but their own books. (l.11)

B Note the use of *little* in this sentence: They have *little* idea where they are going. (ll.1-2)

Write sentences using the following expressions: little expectation; little appreciation; little improvement.

C Compare these two sentences:

Instead of saying: I never heard of anyone *who made* a 'skeleton', as we were taught at school.

We can say: I have never heard of *anyone making* a 'skeleton', as we were taught at school. (ll.5-6)

Change the following sentences in the same way:

1 This organic process, *which often leads* to moments of extraordinary self-discovery, is of indescribable fascination. (ll.7-9)

2 I have often heard of writers *who read* nothing but their own books. (l.11)

3 A writer *who does* this is misunderstood. (l.14)

D Note the use of *may/might as well* in the following sentences:

1 Of course a writer doing this is misunderstood: he *might* (or *may*) *as well* try to explain a crime or love affair. (ll.14-15)

2 I haven't got anything else to do so I *might* (or *may*) *as well* do some gardening.

Write two sentences using *may/might as well* in the ways shown above.

E Note the use of *back* in place of *ago* in the following:

A young English writer made the pertinent observation a year or two *back* ... (l.18)

Write two sentences using *back* in this way.

Special difficulties 难点

A Study the following pairs of words and then write sentences of your own to bring out the difference.

1 destination (l.3) — destiny

Passengers flying on to other destinations in Europe must first clear their baggage at this airport.

Surely you don't believe someone can tell your destiny by looking at a pack of cards or a crystal ball.

2 indescribable (l.8) — undescribed

When they reached the top of the hill, they saw a scene of indescribable beauty.

Stephen's journey back home is undescribed in the novel.

3 capture (l.10) — arrest

Captured by the enemy, the soldiers were in danger of being shot.

He was arrested by the police for theft.

4 misunderstood (l.14) — not understood

That is not what I meant. He must have misunderstood or misheard me.

Apparently this is not understood by all the students.

5 draft (l.19) — draught

It is said that he completed the first draft of the play within two days.

Can you close that window a bit, please, on account of the draught. (= cold air current)

6 judgment (l.20) — criticism

Find out everything you can, then make a judgment based on the facts.

Young people deeply resent any criticism of their friends by their parents.

Unit 5　Lesson 39

B　The words in italics in the following sentences are used metaphorically. What is their literal meaning?

1　He adds a *brushstroke* and another, and it is gone, ... (1.9)

2　Sometimes the *yeast* within a writer outlives a book he has written. (1.10)

3　Like adolescents they stand before the mirror and still cannot *fathom* the exact outline of the vision before them. (ll.11-12)

4　When he *flirts* with fame, he is taking time off from living with himself ... (ll.22-23)

Multiple choice questions 选择题

Choose the correct answers to the following questions.

Comprehension 理解

1　According to the author, most writers he has known _____ .

　　(*a*) often change the location in which their novel is set

　　(*b*) do not work to a detailed preconceived plan

　　(*c*) follow the method of writing they were taught at school

　　(*d*) rely on inspiration from the moment they start until they finish

2　According to the writer, the process of writing _____ .

　　(*a*) is predictable and methodical

　　(*b*) brings out ideas that the writer was conscious of

　　(*c*) is rather chaotic

　　(*d*) depends on skilful planning

3　If a writer becomes too concerned with the reader, he _____ .

　　(*a*) might fail because he will lose touch with the creative process

　　(*b*) will learn a lot about himself and his work will benefit

　　(*c*) will find conversations with other people very boring

　　(*d*) will understand the vision he is pursuing

4　The key to good writing is not so much the original inspiration, but _____ .

　　(*a*) ruthless discipline

　　(*b*) the anarchy of the writer's heart

　　(*c*) the number of drafts that follow the first one

　　(*d*) the quality of editing that follows the original draft

Structure 句型

5　I have known very few writers _____ . (1.1)

　　(*a*) in my life　　　(*b*) recently　　　(*c*) last year　　　(*d*) since last year

6　_____ at school to make a 'skeleton'. (ll.5-6)

　　(*a*) We taught　　　　　　　　　(*b*) They taught us

　　(*c*) They were taught by us　　　(*d*) They taught to us

7　I have heard of writers _____ nothing but their own books. (1. 11)

　　(*a*) who they read　　(*b*) that they read　　(*c*) which they read　　(*d*) reading

8　Of course a writer _____ this is misunderstood. (1.14)

　　(*a*) who doing　　(*b*) that doing　　(*c*) that he does　　(*d*) that does

Vocabulary 词汇

9 All admit _____ changes of destination. (l.3)

  (*a*) important   (*b*) fundamental   (*c*) unforeseen   (*d*) predictable

10 _____ image appears. (l.9)

  (*a*) A false   (*b*) A visionary   (*c*) A sudden   (*d*) An indistinct

11 They stand before a mirror _____ adolescents. (l.11)

  (*a*) as though   (*b*) as if they were   (*c*) as if to be   (*d*) as

12 A young English writer made the _____ observation ... (l.18)

  (*a*) relative   (*b*) extraordinary   (*c*) relevant   (*d*) cheeky

Lesson 40 Waves 海浪

听录音, 然后回答以下问题 。

What false impression does an ocean wave convey to the observer?

Waves are the children of the struggle between ocean and atmosphere, the ongoing signatures of infinity. Rays from the sun excite and energize the atmosphere of the earth, awakening it to flow, to movement, to rhythm, to life. The wind then speaks the message of the sun to the sea and the sea transmits it on through waves—an ancient, exquisite, powerful message.

5   These ocean waves are among the earth's most complicated natural phenomena. The basic features include a crest (the highest point of the wave), a trough (the lowest point), a height (the vertical distance from the trough to the crest), a wave length (the horizontal distance between two wave crests), and a period (which is the time it takes a wave crest to travel one wave length).

Although an ocean wave gives the impression of a wall of water moving in your direction, in actuality
10 waves move through the water leaving the water about where it was. If the water was moving with the wave, the ocean and everything on it would be racing in to the shore with obviously catastrophic results.

An ocean wave passing through deep water causes a particle on the surface to move in a roughly circular orbit, drawing the particle first towards the advancing wave, then up into the wave, then forward with it and then—as the wave leaves the particles behind—back to its starting point again.

15 From both maturity to death, a wave is subject to the same laws as any other 'living' thing. For a time it assumes a miraculous individuality that, in the end, is reabsorbed into the great ocean of life.

The undulating waves of the open sea are generated by three natural causes: wind, earth movements or tremors, and the gravitational pull of the moon and the sun. Once waves have been generated, gravity is the force that drives them in a continual attempt to restore the ocean surface to a flat plain.

from *World Magazine* (BBC Enterprises)

New words and expressions 生词和短语

signature (1.1) /'sɪgnətʃə/ *n.* 签名, 标记
infinity (1.1) /ɪn'fɪnɪti/ *n.* 无穷
ray (1.2) /reɪ/ *n.* 光线
energize (1.2) /'enədʒaɪz/ *v.* 给予 …… 能量
rhythm (1.3) /'rɪðəm/ *n.* 节奏
transmit (1.3) /trænz'mɪt/ *v.* 传送
exquisite (1.4) /ɪk'skwɪzɪt/ *adj.* 高雅的
phenomena (1.5) /fɪ'nɒmɪnə/ （复数）（phenomenon 单数）*n.* 现象
crest (1.6) /krest/ *n.* 浪峰

trough (1.6) /trɒf/ *n.* 波谷
vertical (1.6) /'vɜːtɪkəl/ *adj.* 垂直的
horizontal (1.7) /ˌhɒrɪ'zɒntl/ *adj.* 水平的
actuality (1.9) /ˌæktʃu'ælɪti/ *n.* 现实
catastrophic (1.11) /ˌkætə'strɒfɪk/ *adj.* 大灾难的
particle (1.12) /'pɑːtɪkəl/ *n.* 微粒
maturity (1.15) /mə'tʃʊərɪti/ *n.* 成熟
undulate (1.17) /'ʌndjʊleɪt/ *v.* 波动, 形成波浪
tremor (1.18) /'tremə/ *n.* 震颤
gravitational (1.18) /ˌgrævɪ'teɪʃənəl/ *adj.* 地心引力的

Waves, a paintng by Utagawa Hirosigi
(1797-1858)

Notes on the text 课文注释

1　back to its starting point again, 又返回出发点 。
2　be subject to, 受 …… 的支配, 服从于 …… 。

参考译文

　　海浪是大海和空气相斗的产物, 一种象征永恒的生动体现 。太阳光刺激了地球的大气层, 并给予它能量; 阳光使空气开始流动, 产生节奏, 获得生命。然后, 风把太阳的信息带给了大海, 海洋用波浪的形式传递这个信息——一个源远流长 、高雅而有力的信息 。

　　这些海浪属于地球上最复杂的自然现象 。它们的基本特征包括浪峰 （波浪的最高点） 、波谷 （最低点） 、浪高 （从波谷到浪峰的垂直距离） 、波长 （两个浪峰间的水平距离） 和周期 （浪峰走过一个波长所需的时间） 。

　　虽然, 海浪给人的印象是一堵由水组成的墙向你压过来, 而实际上, 浪从水中移过, 而水则留在原处 。如果水和浪一起移动的话, 那么大海和海里所有的东西就会向岸边疾涌而来, 带来明显的灾难性后果 。

　　穿过深水的海浪使水面上的一个微粒按照一种近乎圆形的轨道移动, 先把微粒拉向前移的海浪, 然后推上波浪, 随着波浪移动, 然后——当波浪把微粒留在身后时——又回到出发点 。

　　从成熟到消亡, 波浪和其他任何 "活动中" 的东西一样, 都受制于共同的法则 。一度它获得非凡的个性, 但最终又被重新融进生命的大洋 。

　　公海上起伏的波浪是由 3 个自然因素构成的: 风 、地球的运动或震颤和月亮 、太阳的引力 。一旦波浪形成, 地心引力是持续不断企图使海面复原为平面的力量 。

Comprehension 理解

Answer these questions:

1   Why isn't 'a wave a wall of moving water'?
2   What would happen if a wave were actually moving?
3   What is the effect of gravity on the ocean?

Vocabulary 词汇

Refer to the text to see how the following words have been used, then write sentences of your own using these words: struggle (l.1); transmits (l.3); features (l.5); racing in to the shore (l.11); catastrophic results (l.11); roughly (l.12); assumes (l.16); undulating (l.17); generated (l.17); force (l.19).

Summary 摘要

Drawing your information from the last three paragraphs of the passage ('Although an ocean wave ... flat plain.'), write a summary of what a wave is and does. Do not write more than 80 words. Your answer should be in one paragraph.

Composition 作文

A   The passage is a mixture of poetic writing and scientific writing. Choose one of these styles, poetic or scientific and write a list of ideas in note form about the ocean.

B   Drawing on your list of ideas, write a composition of about 400 words.

Key structures 关键句型

A   Supply the correct verb forms. Do not refer to the passage until you have finished the exercise:

1   Waves are the children of the struggle between ocean and atmosphere, the ongoing signatures of infinity. Rays from the sun excite and energize the atmosphere of the earth, awakening it to flow, to movement, to rhythm, to life. The wind then _____ (speak) the message of the sun to the sea and the sea _____ (transmit) it on through waves — an ancient, exquisite, powerful message. (ll.1-4)

2   Although an ocean wave _____ (give) the impression of a wall of water moving in your direction, in actuality waves _____ (move) through the water leaving the water about where it was. (ll.9-10)

3   An ocean wave passing through deep water _____ (cause) a particle on the surface to move in a roughly circular orbit, drawing the particle first towards the advancing wave, then up into the wave, then forward with it and then — as the wave _____ (leave) the particles behind — back to its starting point again. (ll.12-14)

B   Supply the missing prepositions. Do not refer to the passage until you have finished the exercise:

1   Waves are the children of the struggle _____ ocean and atmosphere. Rays _____ the sun excite and energize the atmosphere ... the earth, awakening it to flow, _____ movement, _____ rhythm, _____ life. The wind then speaks the message _____ the sun _____ the sea and the sea transmits it on _____ waves — an ancient, exquisite, powerful message. (ll.1-4)

2   Although an ocean wave gives the impression _____ a wall _____ water moving _____ your direction, _____ actuality waves move _____ the water leaving the water about where it was. If the water was moving _____ the wave, the ocean and everything _____ it would be racing in _____ the shore with obviously catastrophic results. (ll.9-11)

3   An ocean wave passing _____ deep water causes a particle _____ the surface to move _____ a roughly circular orbit, drawing the particle first _____ the advancing wave, then up _____ the wave, then forward _____ it and then — as the wave leaves the particles behind — back _____ its starting point again. (ll.11-14)

Special difficulties 难点

A *Phenomena* (1.5) is the irregular plural of *phenomenon*. Give the plurals of the following nouns (sometimes a noun has two plural forms): index, automaton, appendix, alumnus, stratum, analysis, criterion.

B Note the use of *other* in this sentence:

From both maturity to death, a wave is subject to the same laws as any other 'living' thing. (1.15)

Supply *other, the other, the others* or *others* in these sentences:

1   I think we ought to hurry so that we catch up with _____ .
2   You've seen my best pictures. _____ aren't worth looking at.
3   I'm taking two novels on holiday. One is by Jane Austen. _____ is by Charles Dickens.
4   Some people enjoy watching football; _____ don't.
5   You should be more considerate of _____ people.

C *Death* (1.15) is the noun from the verb *die*. Give the noun forms derived from the following verbs: excite, live, move, assume, generate, restore.

Multiple choice questions 选择题

Choose the correct answers to the following questions.

Comprehension 理解

1 How many essential characteristics can be discerned in waves?
   (*a*) Two.
   (*b*) Three.
   (*c*) Four.
   (*d*) Five.
2 A wave is described as _____ .
   (*a*) a wall of moving water
   (*b*) the energy of the sun
   (*c*) a motion through water
   (*d*) an ancient powerful message
3 As a wave moves forward, it _____ .
   (*a*) carries everything with it
   (*b*) leads to catastrophic results
   (*c*) advances and then retreats
   (*d*) leaves behind the water that it disturbed

4 As far as gravity is concerned, the ideal condition in the sea is _____ .

 (*a*) a totally level surface

 (*b*) rising and falling

 (*c*) constant motion

 (*d*) leaving particles behind

Structure 句型

5 These ocean waves are _____ the earth's most complicated phenomena. (l.5)

 (*a*) considered   (*b*) between   (*c*) one of   (*d*) several of

6 The basic features _____ of a crest ... (ll.5-6)

 (*a*) consist   (*b*) consisting   (*c*) have consisted   (*d*) are consisting

7 An ocean wave _____ give the impression of a wall of water, but in actuality ... (l.9)

 (*a*) must   (*b*) has to   (*c*) should   (*d*) may

8 _____ of undulating waves is caused by wind, earth movement, and gravity. (ll.17-18)

 (*a*) A generation   (*b*) Generations   (*c*) Generation   (*d*) The generation

Vocabulary 词汇

9 Waves are the _____ signatures of infinity. (l.1)

 (*a*) going on   (*b*) carrying on   (*c*) moving forward   (*d*) continuing

10 Although an ocean wave _____ the impression of a wall of water ... (l.9)

 (*a*) creates   (*b*) receives   (*c*) demands   (*d*) contributes

11 It would be racing to the shore with obviously catastrophic _____ . (l.11)

 (*a*) loss   (*b*) damage   (*c*) causes   (*d*) consequences

12 Gravity is the force that drives them in _____ attempt to restore the ocean surface. (ll.18-19)

 (*a*) an unceasing   (*b*) a constant but intermittent

 (*c*) a fluctuating   (*d*) a desperate

Unit 6

INSTRUCTIONS TO THE STUDENT

Content
This unit consists of eight passages followed by exercises on Comprehension, Vocabulary, Summary, Composition, Key structures, Special difficulties and Multiple choice questions.

Aim
To provide more advanced practice in Summary and Composition.

How to work
1　Read each passage carefully two or three times.
2　Answer the questions in the order in which they are given.

Summary and Composition
Carry out the instructions given in the introduction to Unit 5.

Lesson 41　Training elephants　训练大象

First listen and then answer the following question.

听录音，然后回答以下问题。

At what point does the training of a captive wild elephant begin?

Two main techniques have been used for training elephants, which we may call respectively the tough and the gentle. The former method simply consists of setting an elephant to work and beating him until he does what is expected of him. Apart from any moral considerations this is a stupid method of training, for it produces a resentful animal who at a later stage may well turn man-killer. The gentle method requires more
5　patience in the early stages, but produces a cheerful, good-tempered elephant who will give many years of loyal service.

　　The first essential in elephant training is to assign to the animal a single mahout who will be entirely responsible for the job. Elephants like to have one master just as dogs do, and are capable of a considerable degree of personal affection. There are even stories of half-trained elephant calves who have refused to feed
10　and pined to death when by some unavoidable circumstance they have been deprived of their own trainer. Such extreme cases must probably be taken with a grain of salt, but they do underline the general principle that the relationship between elephant and mahout is the key to successful training.

　　The most economical age to capture an elephant for training is between fifteen and twenty years, for it is then almost ready to undertake heavy work and can begin to earn its keep straight away. But animals of this
15　age do not easily become subservient to man, and a very firm hand must be employed in the early stages. The captive elephant, still roped to a tree, plunges and screams every time a man approaches, and for several days will probably refuse all food through anger and fear. Sometimes a tame elephant is tethered nearby to give the wild one confidence, and in most cases the captive gradually quietens down and begins to accept its food. The next stage is to get the elephant to the training establishment, a ticklish business which is achieved
20　with the aid of two tame elephants roped to the captive on either side.

　　When several elephants are being trained at one time, it is customary for the new arrival to be placed between the stalls of two captives whose training is already well advanced. It is then left completely undisturbed with plenty of food and water so that it can absorb the atmosphere of its new home and see that nothing particularly alarming is happening to its companions. When it is eating normally, its own training
25　begins. The trainer stands in front of the elephant holding a long stick with a sharp metal point. Two assistants, mounted on tame elephants, control the captive from either side, while others rub their hands over his skin to the accompaniment of a monotonous and soothing chant. This is supposed to induce pleasurable sensations in the elephant, and its effects are reinforced by the use of endearing epithets, such as 'ho! my son', or 'ho! my father', or 'my mother', according to the age and sex of the captive. The elephant is not
30　immediately susceptible to such blandishments, however, and usually lashes fiercely with its trunk in all directions. These movements are controlled by the trainer with the metal-pointed stick, and the trunk eventually becomes so sore that the elephant curls it up and seldom afterwards uses it for offensive purposes.

RICHARD CARRINGTON *Elephants*

A wild Indian elephant is roped to two trained ones during the first few days of training.

New words and expressions 生词和短语

technique (l.1) /tek'niːk/ *n.* 技术

tough (l.1) /tʌf/ *adj.* 强硬的

resentful (l.4) /rɪ'zentfəl/ *adj.* 忿恨不满的

assign (l.7) /ə'saɪn/ *v.* 分配, 指派

mahout (l.7) /mɑː'huːt/ *n.* 驯象的人

calf (l.9) /kɑːf/ *n.* 幼仔

pine (l.10) /paɪn/ *v.* 消瘦

underline (l.11) /ˌʌndə'laɪn/ *v.* 着重说明, 强调

keep (l.14) /kiːp/ *n.* 生计

subservient (l.15) /səb'sɜːviənt/ *adj.* 屈从的

plunge (l.16) /plʌndʒ/ *v.* 向前冲

tame (l.17) /teɪm/ *adj.* 驯服了的

tether (l.17) /'teðə/ *v.* （用绳）拴

ticklish (l.19) /'tɪklɪʃ/ *adj.* 难对付的, 棘手的

alarming (l.24) /ə'lɑːmɪŋ/ *adj.* 引起惊恐的

accompaniment (l.27) /ə'kʌmpənɪmənt/ *n.* 伴奏

soothe (l.27) /'suːð/ *v.* 镇定

chant (l.27) /tʃɑːnt/ *n.* 单调的歌

reinforce (l.28) /ˌriːɪn'fɔːs/ *v.* 加强

endearing (l.28) /ɪn'dɪərɪŋ/ *adj.* 惹人喜爱的

epithet (l.28) /'epɪθet/ *n.* 称呼

susceptible (l.30) /sə'septəbəl/ *adj.* 易受感动的

blandishment (l.30) /'blændɪʃmənt/ *n.* 奉承

lash (l.30) /læʃ/ *v.* 猛烈地甩

curl (l.32) /kɜːl/ *v.* 使卷曲

Notes on the text 课文注释

1   by some unavoidable circumstance, 由于某些不可避免的情况 。

2   with a grain of salt, 有保留地 。

3   a very firm hand, 一个强有力的人 。

4   with the aid of, 在 …… 的帮助下 。

5   This is supposed, 据说…… 。

参考译文

　　驯象有两种主要的方法，我们分别称之为强硬法和温柔法。强硬法就是驱使象去干活，把它打到顺从为止。且不说道义问题，这本身就是一种愚蠢的训练方法，因为这种方法训练会使动物反感，在以后某个时期可能会变成伤人的动物。温柔法要求在最初阶段保持较大的耐心，但这种方法可以训练出性情愉快、脾气温顺、能忠实为人服务多年的大象。

　　驯象中至关重要的是指派一名专门的驯象员，全面负责这项工作。大象和狗一样，喜欢有一个专一的主人，而且会对主人产生相当深厚的私人感情。甚至有这样的故事：训练了一半的小象，由于不可避免的情况与他们的主人分离后，竟拒绝吃食，消瘦至死。这种极端的事例虽不可全信，但强调了一项基本原则，象和驯象员之间的关系是驯象成功与否的关键。

　　捕捉15至20岁的大象进行训练最为经济。这个年龄的象差不多已能干重活，可以很快挣回饲养它的开支。但这个年龄的象不易驯服，因此开始阶段需要一位强有力的老手。刚捕来拴在树上的大象，每当有人走近它时，就会向前猛冲并发出尖叫，甚至一连几天由于愤怒和恐惧而拒绝进食。有时，把一头已驯服的象拴在旁边能给野象以信心。在大多数情况下，刚捕来的象会慢慢静下来，接着开始吃食。下一步就是把象带到训练场所，这是一件棘手的事，需要在它两侧拴上两头驯服的大象帮忙才能完成。

　　几只象同时训练时，通常是把新到的安置在两头训练得很好的大象的象厩中间，然后给它以充足的食物和水，一定不要惊扰它，以便让它能适应新居的气氛，并且看到自己的同伴身上没有发生让自己担惊受怕的事。当它进食正常了，训练就开始。训练员手持一根有锋利金属尖头的长棒，站在象前。两位助手骑在驯服的象的背上，从两侧控制新捕的象，其他人唱着单调舒缓的歌声用手抚摸象的皮肤。据说这是为了使象产生愉快的感觉，为了加强这种效果，人们还按象的年龄和性别，给以亲切的称呼，如"嗨! 我的孩子""嗨! 我的爸爸""嗨! 我的妈妈"。然而大象不会立刻被这些讨好的话感动，而往往是用鼻子朝各个方向猛烈地甩动。训练员要用有锋利金属尖的长棒控制它的这种举动，象鼻子最后疼得卷了起来，以后它就很少用鼻子去进攻了。

Comprehension 理解

Answer these questions:

1　Why does the author consider the 'tough' method of training elephants to be stupid?
2　In what way can elephants be compared with dogs?
3　What, according to the author, is the key to successful elephant training?
4　What is the main advantage of training an elephant of between fifteen and twenty years old?
5　What is the main disadvantage of training an elephant of between fifteen and twenty years old?
6　How can tame elephants be used to help in the training of wild elephants?

Vocabulary 词汇

Refer to the text to see how the following words have been used, then write sentences of your own using these words: moral considerations (1.3); turn (1.4); assign (1.7); capable of a considerable degree of personal affection (ll.8-9); pined to death (1.10); underline (1.11); subservient (1.15); tethered (1.17); particularly alarming (1.24); monotonous and soothing chant (1.27); blandishments (1.30); lashes fiercely (1.30).

Summary 摘要

Drawing your information from the last paragraph (lines 21-32) write an account of the method used for training several elephants at one time. Use your own words as far as possible. Do not write more than 80 words. Your answer should be in one paragraph.

Composition 作文

Write a composition of about 600 words on one of the following subjects:

1   Pets.
2   Animals in scientific research.
3   'It is cruel to train animals to perform tricks for our amusement.' Discuss.

Key structures 关键句型

A   Note the use of the word *who* in this sentence:

The gentle method produces a cheerful, good-tempered elephant *who* will give many years of loyal service. (ll.4-6)
Write two sentences in which it would be preferable to use *who* instead of *which* when referring to animals.

B   Rewrite the sentences given below using the opening words or phrases provided. Do not refer to the passage until you have finished the exercise:

1   The two main techniques which have been used for training elephants we may call respectively the tough and the gentle.
Two main techniques _____ (l.1)
2   We must probably take such extreme cases with a grain of salt.
Such extreme cases _____ (l.11)
3   When training several elephants at one time we usually place the new arrival between the stalls of two captives whose training is already well advanced.
When training several elephants ... it is customary for _____ (l.21)
4   The trainer controls these movements with the metal-pointed stick.
These movements _____ (l.31)

Special difficulties 难点

A   Study the following pairs of words and then write sentences of your own to bring out the difference.
1   train (l.1) — educate
You need to be very patient when you train dogs.
The best investment any country can make in its future is to educate its children.
2   apart from (l.3) — except
Apart from you/Except for you, everyone has helped in some way.
We're open every day apart from/except Saturday.
3   degree (l.9) — rank
I think that's true to a degree.
What rank was your father when he was in the army?
4   afterwards (l.32) — after
We had dinner first. Afterwards, we went to a show.
Come and see me after work.

B   Use the following expressions in sentences of your own: must be taken with a grain of salt (l.11); a ticklish business (l.19)

Unit 6 Lesson 41

Multiple choice questions 选择题

Choose the correct answers to the following questions.

Comprehension 理解

1 The ill-treatment of an elephant during training _____ .

  (a) can have unpleasant consequences later   (b) is the most effective method available

  (c) increases the time it takes to train the animal   (d) ensures loyal service for years to come

2 An elephant will only be trained successfully if _____ .

  (a) the mahout is a responsible person   (b) elephant calves don't refuse to feed

  (c) the mahout and the elephant get on well together   (d) several trainers are assigned to the job

3 The main attraction of training mature elephants is _____ .

  (a) early financial returns   (b) their willingness to obey their trainers

  (c) the avoidance of anxiety in the elephant   (d) that elephants are difficult to keep

4 A mature elephant is only subjected to training when _____ .

  (a) it is with other elephants

  (b) the mahout has established a good relationship with it

  (c) the animal is feeding normally

  (d) it needs to be controlled with a sharp pointed stick

Structure 句型

5 Moral considerations _____ , this is a stupid method ... (l.3)

  (a) besides   (b) except   (c) instead   (d) aside

6 Elephants enjoy _____ one master just as dogs do. (l.8)

  (a) in having   (b) have   (c) having   (d) to have

7 Extreme cases _____ must be taken with a grain of salt. (l.11)

  (a) like so   (b) of this kind   (c) such that   (d) as this

8 Two assistants control the captive, while _____ others rub the elephant. (ll.25-26)

  (a) eventually   (b) at the same time   (c) during   (d) during which

Vocabulary 词汇

9 Elephants do not easily become _____ to man. (ll.14-15)

  (a) a service   (b) obedient   (c) acceptable   (d) responsive

10 A captive elephant will probably _____ all food. (ll.16-17)

  (a) destroy   (b) repel   (c) deny   (d) reject

11 Sometimes a tame elephant is _____ nearby ... (l.17)

  (a) trained   (b) tied   (c) fed   (d) placed

12 Its effects are _____ by the use of endearing epithets. (l.29)

  (a) imposed   (b) confirmed   (c) intensified   (d) established

Lesson 42　Recording an earthquake　记录地震

First listen and then answer the following question.

听录音，然后回答以下问题。

What does a pen have to do to record on paper the vibrations generated by an earthquake?

An earthquake comes like a thief in the night, without warning. It was necessary, therefore, to invent instruments that neither slumbered nor slept. Some devices were quite simple. One, for instance, consisted of rods of various lengths and thicknesses which would stand up on end like ninepins. When a shock came, it shook the rigid table upon which these stood. If it were gentle, only the more unstable rods fell. If it were
5　severe, they all fell. Thus the rods, by falling, and by the direction in which they fell, recorded for the slumbering scientist the strength of a shock that was too weak to waken him, and the direction from which it came.

　　But instruments far more delicate than that were needed if any really serious advance was to be made. The ideal to be aimed at was to devise an instrument that could record with a pen on paper, the movements
10　of the ground or of the table as the quake passed by. While I write my pen moves, but the paper keeps still. With practice, no doubt, I could in time learn to write by holding the pen still while the paper moved. That sounds a silly suggestion, but that was precisely the idea adopted in some of the early instruments (seismo-meters) for recording earthquake waves. But when table, penholder and paper are all moving, how is it possible to write legibly? The key to a solution of that problem lay in an everyday observation. Why does a
15　person standing in a bus or train tend to fall when a sudden start is made? It is because his feet move on, but his head stays still. A simple experiment will help us a little further. Tie a heavy weight at the end of a long piece of string. With the hand held high in the air, hold the string so that the weight nearly touches the ground. Now move the hand to and fro and around but not up and down. It will be found that the weight moves but slightly or not at all. Imagine a pen attached to the weight in such a way that its point rests upon
20　a piece of paper on the floor. Imagine an earthquake shock shaking the floor, the paper, you and your hand. In the midst of all this movement, the weight and the pen would be still. But as the paper moved from side to side under the pen point, its movement would be recorded in ink upon its surface. It was upon this principle that the first instruments were made, but the paper was wrapped round a drum which rotated slowly. As long as all was still, the pen drew a straight line, but while the drum was being shaken, the line that the pen was
25　drawing wriggled from side to side. The apparatus thus described, however, records only the horizontal component of the wave movement, which is, in fact, much more complicated. If we could actually see the path described by a particle, such as a sand grain in the rock, it would be more like that of a bluebottle buzzing round the room; it would be up and down, to and fro and from side to side. Instruments have been devised and can be so placed that all three elements can be recorded in different graphs.

30　When the instrument is situated at more than 700 miles from the earthquake centre, the graphic record shows three waves arriving one after the other at short intervals. The first records the arrival of longitudinal vibrations. The second marks the arrival of transverse vibrations which travel more slowly and arrive several minutes after the first. These two have travelled through the earth. It was from the study of these that so much was learnt about the interior of the earth. The third, or main wave, is the slowest and has travelled round the earth through the surface rocks.

H. H. Swinnerton　*The Earth beneath Us*

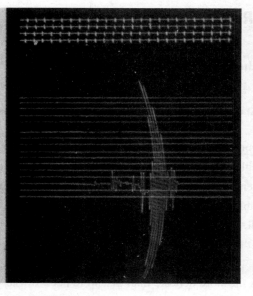

The Shaw seismograph at the
Science Museum, London

An earthquake recorded on a seismograph

New words and expressions 生词和短语

earthquake (title) /ˈɜːθkweɪk/ *n.* 地震
slumber (l.2) /ˈslʌmbə/ *v.* 睡眠
ninepin (l.3) /ˈnaɪnpɪn/ *n.* 九柱戏中的木柱
rigid (l.4) /ˈrɪdʒɪd/ *adj.* 坚硬的
delicate (l.8) /ˈdelɪkɪt/ *adj.* 灵敏的
seismometer (ll.12-13) /saɪzˈmɒmɪtə/ *n.* 地震仪
penholder (l.13) /penˈhəʊldə/ *n.* 笔杆
legibly (l.14) /ˈledʒəbli/ *adv.* 字迹清楚地

drum (l.23) /drʌm/ *n.* 鼓状物
wriggle (l.25) /ˈrɪgəl/ *v.* 扭动
bluebottle (l.27) /ˈbluːbɒtl/ *n.* 绿头苍蝇
graph (l.29) /græf/ *n.* 图表
graphic (l.30) /ˈgræfɪk/ *adj.* 图示的
longitudinal (l.31) /ˌlɒndʒɪˈtjuːdɪnəl/ *adj.* 纵向的
transverse (l.32) /ˈtrænzvɜːs/ *adj.* 横向的

Notes on the text 课文注释

1   stand up on end, 竖立着 。
2   the ideal to be aimed at, 理想的目标 。
3   I could in time ..., 我最终能够 …… 。
4   help us a little further, 帮助我们进一步搞清这个问题 。
5   with the hand ... hold the string ..., 这是一个祈使句, 谓语动词是 hold, with the hand held high in the air 是
    介词短语作方式状语 。
6   to and fro, 来回地 。

参考译文

　　地震就像夜间的小偷, 不打招呼就来了 。因此, 有必要发明一种仪器, 既不打盹儿, 也不睡觉 。有些装置非常简单 。例如, 有一种装置是由一些长短 、粗细不同的木棒组成, 就像九柱戏的木棒一样竖立着, 一旦有地震, 就会震动竖立在坚硬的桌子上的木棒 。如果地震轻微, 只有不稳定的木棒倒下; 如果地震剧烈, 所有的木棒都会倒下 。由于地震太弱而未惊醒科学家时, 木棒倒下的多少和倒下的方向就为科学家记录下了地震的强度和地震方向 。

　　但是, 如果要取得真正重大的进展, 需要有比这种装置精细得多的仪器 。理想的目标是设计出这样一种仪器: 当地震发生时, 它能用笔在纸上记录下大地和桌子的运动情况 。我写字时, 笔是移动的, 纸是静止的 。毫无疑问, 经过练习, 我最终能够学会笔不动而纸动来写字 。这听起来似乎是一种愚蠢的想法, 但是早期记录地震波的仪器 (测震仪) 正是采用了这种思路 。可是, 当桌子 、笔杆 、纸都在移动时, 怎么能书写得清楚呢? 可以从我们的日常生活观察中找到这个问题的答案 。一个人站在公共汽车或火车上, 当车突然开动时, 他为什么会倾倒呢? 这是因为他的脚动了, 而他的头保持着静止 。一个简单的实验可以帮助我们进一步理解这个问题 。把一个重物拴在一根长绳子的一端, 把手高高举在空中握住绳子, 让重物几乎接触地面 。然后把手前后左右以及旋转摆动, 但不要上下摆动 。结果会发现, 重物是动了, 但动得很小, 甚至没动 。假定把一支笔拴在重物上, 笔尖落在地板上的一张纸上, 假定地震发生了, 地板 、纸 、你和你的手都会动, 重物和笔却都不运动 。由于纸在笔尖下来回运动, 纸的表面就会用墨水记录下地板运动的情况 。根据这一原理, 制造出了最初的地震仪器, 但是纸是卷在慢慢旋转的圆筒上的 。只要一切都是静止的, 笔就会画出一条直线; 但是, 圆筒受到震动, 笔所画出的线就会左右摆动 。然而, 这里所说的仪器记录下来的只是地震波运动中的水平部分, 地震波的运动实际比这要复杂得多 。假如我们真能看到诸如岩石中一个沙粒分子的运动轨迹, 那就像一只嗡嗡叫的绿头苍蝇在屋内飞行的轨迹, 呈现出上上下下 、来来回回 、左左右右 3 种运动形式 。已经设计出了一些仪器, 把它们按照一定的方式安放就可测绘出这三种运动的曲线图 。

　　如果把这种仪器安装在距震中 700 多英里远的地方, 曲线记录就能显示出前后相间的这 3 种地震波 。首先记录下的是纵向波的到达; 然后记录下的是横向波的到达, 横向波比纵向波传播得慢, 在纵向波到达几分钟后才能到达 。这两种波都是穿过地球而来的 。正是从这两种波的研究中, 我们可以了解到地球内部的许多情况 。第三种波, 即主波, 是最慢的, 是围绕地球通过表面岩石传来的 。

Comprehension 理解

Answer these questions:

1　Explain how the device consisting of rods of various lengths and thicknesses could be used to indicate the extent of an earthquake.

2　Why was this simple seismometer worked by rods unsatisfactory?

3　Which everyday observation enabled scientists to improve seismometers?

4　'Instruments have been devised and can be so placed that all three elements can be recorded in different graphs.' (ll.28-29) What are these 'elements'?

5　Why, during an earthquake, is the third wave the last to be recorded?

Vocabulary 词汇

Refer to the text to see how the following words have been used, then write sentences of your own using these words: rigid (l.4); slumbering (l.6); delicate (l.8); silly suggestion (l.12); legibly (l.14); everyday (l.14); tend (l.15); to and fro (l.18); slightly (l.19); rotated (l.23); wriggled (l.25); the path described by a particle (ll.26-27); bluebottle (l.27).

Unit 6   Lesson 42

Summary 摘要

Drawing your information from lines 9-28 ('The ideal ... side to side.'), describe how the seismometer used for recording the horizontal component of wave movements works. Do not write more than 120 words. Use your own words as far as possible. Your answer should be in one paragraph.

Composition 作文

Write a composition of about 600 words on one of the following subjects:

1   A description, real or imaginary, of an earthquake.
2   The hidden forces of nature.
3   Man's efforts to understand and control natural calamities. (E.g. earthquakes, floods, hurricanes, tornadoes, tidal waves, volcanic eruptions, avalanches, forest fires.)

Key structures 关键句型

A   Complete the following sentences in any way you wish. Then compare what you have written with the sentences in the passage:

1   When a shock came, it shook the rigid table upon which these stood. If it were gentle, _____ (ll.3-4)
2   _____ if any really serious advance was to be made. (l.8)
3   If we could actually see the path described by a particle, _____ (ll.26-28)

B   Rewrite the sentences given below using the opening phrases provided. Do not refer to the passage until you have finished the exercise:

1   Though that sounds a silly suggestion, that was precisely the idea adopted in some of the early instruments.
     That sounds _____ (ll.11-13)
2   The reason for this is that his feet move on, but his head stays still.
     It is because _____ (ll.15-16)
3   Imagine that an earthquake shock shook the floor.
     Imagine an _____ (l.20)
4   However, only the horizontal component of the wave movement, which is, in fact, far more complicated, is recorded by the apparatus thus described.
     The apparatus thus described, however, _____ (ll.25-26)

Special difficulties 难点

A   Study the following pairs of words and then write sentences of your own to bring out the difference.

1   device (l.2) — devise (l.9)
     The juice extractor is a practical household device.
     He has devised a scheme for earning more money.
2   travel (l.32) — trip
     She travels to London at least three times a month.
     I'm just back from a business trip.
3   adopted (l.12) — adapted
     The company has persuaded the workers to adopt more flexible working practices so as to increase efficiency.
     Our Geology teacher has adapted an old washing-machine so he can use it to polish gem-stones.

B   Note that the word *record* is differently pronounced in each of these sentences:

1   ... the graphic record shows three waves ... (ll.30-31)

2   The first records the arrival of longitudinal vibrations. (ll.31-32)

Write pairs of sentences using the following words as *nouns* and as *verbs*: export; import; produce; conduct.

In each sentence indicate the syllable which should be stressed.

Multiple choice questions 选择题

Choose the correct answers to the following questions.

Comprehension 理解

1 Even a primitive instrument with rods can _____ .

   (*a*) record the movement of an earthquake

   (*b*) indicate roughly how strong an earthquake is and its direction

   (*c*) wake up a sleeping scientist when an earthquake is in progress

   (*d*) rise and fall in line with the movement of an earthquake

2 In a more sophisticated instrument to measure an earthquake _____ .

   (*a*) the pen moves up and down as paper moves steadily beneath it

   (*b*) the pen and the paper beneath it move together in response to the earthquake

   (*c*) the pen remains still while recording the irregular movement of the paper beneath it

   (*d*) the pen rotates with the moving drum beneath it

3 The instrument, consisting of a pen and paper moving round a rotating drum, _____ .

   (*a*) gives a full picture of an earthquake

   (*b*) records deep wave movements only

   (*c*) does not provide a comprehensive record of an earthquake

   (*d*) only reflects vertical movement

4 Instruments have been devised which will _____ .

   (*a*) record all three movements of a nearby earthquake

   (*b*) give a comprehensive record of an earthquake more than 700 miles away

   (*c*) send information about the interior of the earth

   (*d*) reflect the effect of an earthquake on surface rocks

Structure 句型

5 Falling rods recorded a shock that _____ to wake up the scientist. (ll.5-6)

   (*a*) was not enough strong   (*b*) was strong enough

   (*c*) was too strong   (*d*) was not strong enough

6 Instruments of far _____ delicacy were needed. (l.8)

   (*a*) improved   (*b*) greater   (*c*) better   (*d*) finer

7 Where did the key to that problem _____ ? (l.14)

   (*a*) laid   (*b*) lied   (*c*) lay   (*d*) lie

8 _____ all was still, the pen drew a straight line. (ll.23-4)

   (*a*) Provided   (*b*) Suppose   (*c*) Imagine   (*d*) Supposed

Vocabulary 词汇

9 While I write my pen moves, but the paper _____ . (l.10)

   (a) moves yet   (b) changes direction   (c) remains solid   (d) does not

10 It will be found that the weight moves _____ slightly. (ll.18-19)

   (a) even   (b) unless   (c) only   (d) except

11 Instruments have been _____ and can be so placed ... (ll.28-29)

   (a) invented   (b) described   (c) sold   (d) discovered

12 The graphic record shows three waves arriving _____ . (ll.30-31)

   (a) in a synchronised fashion   (b) almost together

   (c) irregularly   (d) with brief breaks in between

Lesson 43 Are there strangers in space? 宇宙中有外星人吗？

First listen and then answer the following question.

听录音，然后回答以下问题 。

What does the 'uniquely rational way' for us to communicate with other intelligent beings in space depend on?

We must conclude from the work of those who have studied the origin of life, that given a planet only approximately like our own, life is almost certain to start. Of all the planets in our own solar system, we are now pretty certain the Earth is the only one on which life can survive. Mars is too dry and poor in oxygen, Venus far too hot, and so is Mercury, and the outer planets have temperatures near absolute zero and
5 hydrogen-dominated atmospheres. But other suns, stars as the astronomers call them, are bound to have planets like our own, and as the number of stars in the universe is so vast, this possibility becomes virtual certainty. There are one hundred thousand million stars in our own Milky Way alone, and then there are three thousand million other Milky Ways, or galaxies, in the universe. So the number of stars that we know exist is now estimated at about 300 million million million.

10 Although perhaps only 1 per cent of the life that has started somewhere will develop into highly complex and intelligent patterns, so vast is the number of planets, that intelligent life is bound to be a natural part of the universe.

If then we are so certain that other intelligent life exists in the universe, why have we had no visitors from outer space yet? First of all, they may have come to this planet of ours thousands or millions of years ago,
15 and found our then prevailing primitive state completely uninteresting to their own advanced knowledge. Professor Ronald Bracewell, a leading American radio astronomer, argued in *Nature* that such a superior civilization, on a visit to our own solar system, may have left an automatic messenger behind to await the possible awakening of an advanced civilization. Such a messenger, receiving our radio and television signals, might well re-transmit them back to its home-planet, although what impression any other
20 civilization would thus get from us is best left unsaid.

But here we come up against the most difficult of all obstacles to contact with people on other planets —the astronomical distances which separate us. As a reasonable guess, they might, on an average, be 100 light years away. (A light year is the distance which light travels at 186,000 miles per second in one year, namely 6 million million miles.) Radio waves also travel at the speed of light, and assuming such an
25 automatic messenger picked up our first broadcasts of the 1920's, the message to its home planet is barely halfway there. Similarly, our own present primitive chemical rockets, though good enough to orbit men, have no chance of transporting us to the nearest other star, four light years away, let alone distances of tens or hundreds of light years.

Fortunately, there is a 'uniquely rational way' for us to communicate with other intelligent beings, as
30 Walter Sullivan has put it in his excellent book, *We Are not Alone*. This depends on the precise radio frequency of the 21-cm wavelength, or 1420 megacycles per second. It is the natural frequency of emission of the hydrogen atoms in space and was discovered by us in 1951; it must be known to any kind of radio astronomer in the universe.

Once the existence of this wave-length had been discovered, it was not long before its use as the uniquely
35 recognizable broadcasting frequency for interstellar communication was suggested. Without something of

this kind, searching for intelligences on other planets would be like trying to meet a friend in London without a pre-arranged rendezvous and absurdly wandering the streets in the hope of a chance encounter.

ANTHONY MICHAELIS *Are There Strangers in Space*? from *The Weekend Telegraph*

Simulation of a hypothetical sighting of a UFO (unidentified flying object) in the small town of Belleville, Wisconsin, USA. For several months in 1986-1989, the town was plagued by UFO sightings.

New words and expressions 生词和短语

Mercury (1.4) /'mɜːkjʊri/ *n.* 水星

hydrogen (1.5) /'haɪdrədʒən/ *n.* 氢气

prevailing (1.15) /prɪ'veɪlɪŋ/ *adj.* 普遍的

radio astronomer (1.16) /'reɪdɪəʊ ə'strɒnəmə/ 射电天文学家

uniquely (1.29) /juː'niːkli/ *adv.* 唯一地

rational (1.29) /'ræʃənəl/ *adj.* 合理的

radio frequency (ll.30-31) /'reɪdɪəʊ 'friːkwənsi/ 无线电频率

cm (1.31) (= centimetre /'sentɪˌmiːtə/) *n.* 厘米

megacycle (1.31) /'megəˌsaɪkəl/ *n.* 兆周

emission (1.31) /ɪ'mɪʃən/ *n.* 散发

interstellar (1.35) /ˌɪntə'stelə/ *adj.* 星际的

rendezvous (1.37) /'rɒndɪvuː/ *n.* 约会地点

encounter (1.37) /ɪn'kaʊntə/ *n.* 相遇

Notes on the text 课文注释

1   that given a planet ... certain to start, 这是一个宾语从句，作动词 conclude 的宾语，其中 given a planet ... our own, 过去分词短语作条件状语，given 与 if 的意思相近，这个过去分词短语可译成"如果一个行星与我们所在的行星大致相同的话"。

2   is best left unsaid, 最好不去说（它）。

3   come up against, 遇到。

参考译文

　　根据研究生命起源的人们所做的工作，我们必然会得出这样的结论：如果设想有一颗行星和我们地球的情况基本相似，那几乎肯定会产生生命。我们目前可以肯定的是，在我们太阳系的所有行星中，地球是生命能存在的唯一行星。火星太干燥又缺氧，金星太热，水星也一样。除此以外，太阳系的其他行星的温度都接近绝对零度，并围绕着以氢气为主的大气层。但是，其他的太阳，即天文学家所说的恒星，肯定会有像我们地球一样的行星。因为宇宙中恒星的数目极其庞大，所以存在着产生有生命星球的这种可能性几乎是确定无疑的。仅我们的银河系就有 1000 亿颗恒星，况且在宇宙中还有 30 亿个天河，即银河系。因此，我们所知道的现有恒星数目估计约有 30 亿 × 1000 亿颗。

　　虽然在已经产生生命的某个地方，可能只有 1% 会发展成高度复杂有智力的生命形态，但是行星的数目是那么庞大，有智力的生命必然是宇宙的自然组成部分。

　　既然我们如此坚信宇宙中存在着其他有智力的生命，那么我们为什么还未见到外层空间来访的客人呢？首先，他们可能在几千年前或几百万年前已来过我们地球，并且发现我们地球当时普遍存在着的原始状态同他们先进的知识相比是索然无味的。美国一位重要的射电天文学家罗纳德·布雷斯韦尔教授在《自然》杂志上提出了这样的观点：假如有如此高级文明生命访问了我们的太阳系，很可能会在离开太阳系时留下自动化信息装置，等待先进文明的觉醒。这种自动化信息装置，在接收到我们的无线电和电视信号后，完全有可能把这些信号发回到原来的行星。至于其他文明行星对我们地球会有什么印象，还是不说为好。

　　然而，在和外星人联系中我们遇到的最大困难是分隔我们的天文距离。据合理推算，外星人离我们平均距离也有 100 光年之遥（1 光年是光以每秒 186,000 英里的速度在一年内走的距离，即 6 万亿英里）。无线电波也是以光速传播的。假定外星人的这种自动化信息装置接收到了我们 20 世纪 20 年代的第一次广播信号，那么这个信号在发回到原来的行星途中刚刚走了一半路程。同样，我们目前使用的原始化学火箭，虽然可以把人送入轨道，但尚不可能把我们送到离我们最近、相距 4 光年的其他恒星上去，更不用说几十光年或几百光年远的地方了。

　　幸运的是，有一种我们可以和其他智力生命通讯联系的"唯一合理的方法"，正如沃尔特·沙利文在其杰作《我们并不孤独》中阐述的。这种通讯联系要靠 21 厘米波段，即每秒 1420 兆周的精确无线电频率。这个频率是空间氢原子释放的自然频率，是在 1951 年被人类发现的。这个频率是宇宙中任何射电天文学家都应该熟悉的。

　　一旦这种波长的实际存在被发现，提出把它作为星际间唯一可辨认的广播频率就为期不远了。没有这种手段，要想寻觅其他星球上的智力生命，就如同去伦敦见一位朋友，事先未约定地点，而荒唐地在街上游逛，以期碰巧遇上一样。

Comprehension 理解

Answer these questions:

1　What do you understand by the word 'galaxy'?
2　Why, according to the author, is it highly probable that life exists in other parts of the universe?
3　Why would it be extremely difficult to visit another planet even if one were travelling at 186,000 miles per second?
4　How might it be possible to accomplish interstellar communication?

Vocabulary 词汇

Refer to the text to see how the following words have been used, then write sentences of your own using these words: approximately (l.2); prevailing primitive state (l.15); automatic messenger (l.17); obstacles (l.21); orbit (l.26); interstellar (l.35); chance encounter (l.37).

Summary 摘要

Drawing your information from lines 21-37 ('But here ... chance encounter.'), write an account of the difficulties of interstellar communication. Do not write more than 100 words. Use your own words as far as possible. Your answer should be in one paragraph.

Composition 作文

Write a composition of about 600 words on one of the following subjects:

1   The universe.
2   Flying saucers.
3   If an outside observer were given the opportunity to spend a year on earth, what impression might he get of its inhabitants?

Key structures 关键句型

A   Note the form of the verb in italics:

But other suns *are bound to* have planets like our own. (ll.5-6)

Write sentences using the following expressions:

sure to; about to; due to.

B   Rewrite the sentences given below using the opening phrases provided. Do not refer to the passage until you have finished the exercise:

1   As the number of planets is so vast, intelligent life is bound to be a natural part of the universe.
    So vast _____ (l.11)
2   First of all, it is possible that they came to this planet of ours thousands or millions of years ago.
    First of all, they may _____ (l.14)
3   It was argued in *Nature* by Professor Ronald Bracewell, a leading American radio astronomer, that such a superior civilization, on a visit to our own solar system, may have left an automatic messenger behind.
    Professor Ronald Bracewell, _____ (ll.16-17)
4   Even if our own present primitive chemical rockets are good enough to orbit men, they have no chance of transporting us to the nearest other star.
    Our own present ... though _____ (ll.26-27)

Special difficulties 难点

A   Study the following pairs of words and then write sentences of your own to bring out the difference.

1   planet (l.2) — star (l.6)
    Live images of the robotic vehicle, Sojourner, have been relayed from the planet Mars to our T.V. screens in seconds.
    There must be other stars, like our own sun, with orbiting planets similar to Earth.
2   estimated (l.9) — esteemed
    The cost of repair has been estimated at $45.
    German mechanical engineering is highly esteemed world-wide.

3   natural (1.11) — physical

It's quite natural for a boy's voice to break when he is about 14.

Boxers take a lot of physical punishment.

4   unsaid (1.20) — untold

Some things are better left unsaid.

The floods have caused untold misery to hundreds of thousands of farmers this year.

5   search for (1.36) — search

The whole village has been searching for the missing boy.

The security guards are searching each passenger.

B   Note the use of *let alone* in this sentence:

Similarly, our own present primitive chemical rockets, though good enough to orbit men, have no chance of transporting us to the nearest other star, four light years away, *let alone* distances of tens or hundreds of light years. (ll.26-28)

Complete the following sentences:

1   He's incapable of adding up a simple list of figures, let alone _____

2   He doesn't earn enough to support himself, let alone _____

Multiple choice questions 选择题

Choose the correct answers to the following questions.

Comprehension 理解

1 The possibility that life exists on other planets is almost certain because _____ .

(*a*) there are plenty of planets like our own

(*b*) the other planets in our solar system are unlikely to support life

(*c*) our own galaxy is so large

(*d*) of the sheer number of planets in the universe

2 According to the writer, _____ .

(*a*) there is a possibility that we constantly have visitors from outer space

(*b*) our planet may have been visited at some time during the distant past

(*c*) an automatic messenger was left on our planet at some time in the past

(*d*) our civilization is just awakening and is of interest to other beings

3 Travel in the universe is difficult because _____ .

(*a*) even at the speed of light, distances are immense

(*b*) light travels at 186,000 miles per hour

(*c*) planets are 100 light years away

(*d*) there are no rockets in the universe powerful enough

4 The discovery of the natural frequency of emission of hydrogen atoms in space is important because _____ .

(*a*) it's a precise radio frequency of 1420 megacycles per second

(*b*) it would be universally recognized by intelligent life anywhere in the universe

(*c*) it makes the discovery of intelligent life elsewhere virtually certain

(*d*) hydrogen is abundant exclusively in our own solar system

Unit 6   Lesson 43

Structure 句型

5 Life _____ present on a planet approximately like our own. (ll.1-2)

    (*a*) was   (*b*) might be   (*c*) must be   (*d*) is

6 Why have we had no visitors from outer space _____ ? (ll.13-14)

    (*a*) before   (*b*) in the past   (*c*) so far   (*d*) till then

7 They were not _____ our primitive state. (l.15)

    (*a*) interesting to   (*b*) interesting in   (*c*) interested to   (*d*) interested in

8 We have no chance _____ by our own primitive chemical rockets. (ll.26-27)

    (*a*) to be transporting   (*b*) to transport

    (*c*) of transporting   (*d*) of being transported

Vocabulary 词汇

9 They are _____ to have planets like our own. (ll.5-6)

    (*a*) almost certain   (*b*) obliged   (*c*) required   (*d*) due

10 What impression they would get of us is best left _____ . (ll.19-20)

    (*a*) unspoken   (*b*) untold   (*c*) unmentioned   (*d*) unrecounted

11 We come up against the most difficult of all obstacles to _____ people. (l.21)

    (*a*) speaking to   (*b*) being in touch with   (*c*) touching   (*d*) reaching out to

12 This depends on the _____ radio frequency of the 21cm wavelength. (ll.30-31)

    (*a*) measurable   (*b*) exact   (*c*) established   (*d*) known

Lesson 44 Patterns of culture 文化的模式

听录音，然后回答以下问题 。

What influences us from the moment of birth?

Custom has not commonly been regarded as a subject of any great moment. The inner workings of our own brains we feel to be uniquely worthy of investigation, but custom, we have a way of thinking, is behaviour at its most commonplace. As a matter of fact, it is the other way around. Traditional custom, taken the world over, is a mass of detailed behaviour more astonishing than what any one person can ever evolve in
5   individual actions, no matter how aberrant. Yet that is a rather trivial aspect of the matter. The fact of first-rate importance is the predominant role that custom plays in experience and in belief, and the very great varieties it may manifest.

No man ever looks at the world with pristine eyes. He sees it edited by a definite set of customs and institutions and ways of thinking. Even in his philosophical probings he cannot go behind these stereotypes;
10 his very concepts of the true and the false will still have reference to his particular traditional customs. John Dewey has said in all seriousness that the part played by custom in shaping the behaviour of the individual, as against any way in which he can affect traditional custom, is as the proportion of the total vocabulary of his mother tongue against those words of his own baby talk that are taken up into the vernacular of his family. When one seriously studies the social orders that have had the opportunity to develop autonomously,
15 the figure becomes no more than an exact and matter-of-fact observation. The life history of the individual is first and foremost an accommodation to the patterns and standards traditionally handed down in his community. From the moment of his birth, the customs into which he is born shape his experience and behaviour. By the time he can talk, he is the little creature of his culture, and by the time he is grown and able to take part in its activities, its habits are his habits, its beliefs his beliefs, its impossibilities his impossibilities.
20 Every child that is born into his group will share them with him, and no child born into one on the opposite side of the globe can ever achieve the thousandth part. There is no social problem it is more incumbent upon us to understand than this of the role of custom. Until we are intelligent as to its laws and varieties, the main complicating facts of human life must remain unintelligible.

The study of custom can be profitable only after certain preliminary propositions have been accepted,
25 and some of these propositions have been violently opposed. In the first place, any scientific study requires that there be no preferential weighting of one or another of the items in the series it selects for its consideration. In all the less controversial fields, like the study of cacti or termites or the nature of nebulae, the necessary method of study is to group the relevant material and to take note of all possible variant forms and conditions. In this way, we have learned all that we know of the laws of astronomy, or of the habits of
30 the social insects, let us say. It is only in the study of man himself that the major social sciences have substituted the study of one local variation, that of Western civilization.

Anthropology was by definition impossible, as long as these distinctions between ourselves and the primitive, ourselves and the barbarian, ourselves and the pagan, held sway over people's minds. It was necessary first to arrive at that degree of sophistication where we no longer set our own belief against our

257

35 neighbour's superstition. It was necessary to recognize that these institutions which are based on the same premises, let us say the supernatural, must be considered together, our own among the rest.

RUTH BENEDICT *Patterns of Culture*

A Padaung girl from Burma in her brass necklace

New words and expressions 生词和短语

commonplace (1.3) /ˈkɒmənpleɪs/ *adj.* 平凡的

aberrant (1.5) /ˈæbərənt/ *adj.* 脱离常规的, 异常的

trivial (1.5) /ˈtrɪvɪəl/ *adj.* 微不足道的, 琐细的

predominant (1.6) /prɪˈdɒmɪnənt/ *adj.* 占优势的, 起支配作用的

manifest (1.7) /ˈmænɪfest/ *v.* 表明

pristine (1.8) /ˈprɪstiːn/ *adj.* 纯洁的, 质朴的

stereotype (1.9) /ˈsterɪətaɪp/ *n.* 陈规

vernacular (1.13) /vəˈnækjʊlə/ *n.* 方言

accommodation (1.16) /əˌkɒməˈdeɪʃən/ *n.* 适应

incumbent (1.21) /ɪnˈkʌmbənt/ *adj.* 义不容辞的, 有责任的

preliminary (1.24) /prɪˈlɪmɪnəri/ *adj.* 初步的

proposition (1.25) /ˌprɒpəˈzɪʃən/ *n.* 主张

preferential (1.26) /ˌprefəˈrenʃəl/ *adj.* 优先的

controversial (1.27) /ˌkɒntrəˈvɜːʃəl/ *adj.* 引起争论的

cactus (1.27) /ˈkæktəs/ (复数 cacti /ˈkæktaɪ/) *n.* 仙人掌

termite (1.27) /ˈtɜːmaɪt/ *n.* 白蚁

variant (1.28) /ˈveərɪənt/ *adj.* 不同的

barbarian (1.33) /bɑːˈbeərɪən/ *n.* 野蛮人

pagan (1.33) /ˈpeɪgən/ *n.* 异教徒

sophistication (1.34) /səˌfɪstɪˈkeɪʃən/ *n.* 老练

premise (1.36) /ˈpremɪs/ *n.* 前提

supernatural (1.36) /ˌsuːpəˈnætʃərəl/ *adj.* 超自然的

Notes on the text 课文注释

1　The inner workings of our own brains, 这一部分是 feel 的宾语, 为了强调而把宾语提前了, to be uniquely worthy of investigation 是宾语补足语。

2　the other way around, 正好相反。

3　taken the world over, 是过去分词短语, 作 Traditional custom 的定语, taken 前省略了 it is, 意为: 被全世界所接受的。

4　go behind these stereotypes, 摆脱这些旧框框。

5　his very concepts, 其中的 very 是形容词, 用于加强语气。

6　have reference to, 参照……, 与 …… 有关。

7　as against ... is as ... against ..., 意为: 与 …… 相比较就如同 …… 与 …… 相比。

8　be taken up into, 被接纳进。

9　first and foremost, 首先。

10　the thousandth part, 等于 the thousandth part of the customs。

11　let us say, 譬如说。

参考译文

风俗一般未被认为是什么重要的课题。我们觉得, 只有我们大脑内部的活动情况才值得研究, 至于风俗呢, 只是些司空见惯的行为而已。事实上, 情况正好相反。从世界范围来看, 传统风俗是由许多细节性的习惯行为组成, 它比任何个人养成的行为都更加引人注目, 不管个人行为多么异常。这只是问题的一个次要的方面。最重要的是, 风俗在实践中和信仰上所起的举足轻重的作用, 以及它所表现出来的极其丰富多彩的形式。

没有一个人是用纯洁而无偏见的眼光看待世界。人们所看到的是一个受特定的风俗习惯、制度和思想方式剪辑过的世界。甚至在哲学领域的探索中, 人们也无法超越这些定型的框框。人们关于真与伪的概念依然和特定的传统风俗有关。约翰·杜威曾经非常严肃地指出: 风俗在形成个人行为方面所起的作用和一个人对风俗的任何影响相比, 就好像他本国语言的总词汇量和自己咿呀学语时他家庭所接纳的他的词汇量之比。当一个人认真地研究自发形成的社会秩序时, 杜威的比喻就是他实事求是观察得来的形象化的说法。个人的生活史首先就是适应他的社会世代相传形成的生活方式和准则。从他呱呱坠地的时刻起, 他所生于其中的风俗就开始塑造他的经历和行为规范。到他会说话时, 他就是传统文化塑造的一个小孩子了; 等他长大了, 能做各种事了, 他的社会的习惯就是他的习惯, 他的社会的信仰就是他的信仰, 他的社会不能做的事就是他不能做的事。每一个和他诞生在同一个社会中的孩子和他一样具有相同的风俗; 而在地球的另一边, 诞生在另一个社会的孩子与他就很少有相同的风俗。没有任何一个社会问题比得上风俗的作用问题更要求我们对它理解。直到我们理解了风俗的规律性和多样性, 我们才能明白人类生活中主要的复杂现象。

只有在某些基本的主张被接受下来、同时有些主张被激烈反对时, 对风俗的研究才是全面的, 才会有收获。首先, 任何科学研究都要求人们对可供考虑的诸多因素不能厚此薄彼, 偏向某一方面。在一切争议较小的领域里, 如对仙人掌、白蚁或星云性质的研究, 应采取的研究方法是, 把有关各方面的材料汇集起来, 同时注意任何可能出现的异常情况和条件。例如, 用这种方法, 我们完全掌握了天文学的规律和昆虫群居的习性。只是在对人类自身的研究中, 各主要的社会学科才用对一个局部地区各种情况的研究 (如对西方文明的研究)来代替对全人类的研究。

只要我们同原始人、我们同野蛮人、我们同异教徒之间存在的区别在人的思想中占主导地位, 那么人类学按其定义来说就无法存在。我们首先需要达到这样一种成熟的程度: 不用自己的信仰去反对我们邻居的迷信。必须认识到, 这些建立在相同前提基础上的风俗, 暂且可以说是超自然的东西, 必须放在一起加以考虑, 我们自己的风俗和其他民族的风俗都在其中。

Comprehension 理解

Answer these questions:

1   What do you understand by this statement: 'No man ever looks at the world with pristine eyes.'? (1.18)

2   How has the study of man differed from the study of less controversial subjects?

3   What criterion must the anthropologist accept before he can undertake the study of man objectively?

Vocabulary 词汇

Refer to the text to see how the following words have been used, then write sentences of your own using these words: moment (1.1); aberrant (1.5); predominant role (1.6); manifest (1.7); probings (1.9); vernacular (1.13); autonomously (1.14); incumbent (1.21); intelligent (1.22); unintelligible (1.23); preferential weighting (1.26); controversial (1.27); held sway (1.33).

Summary 摘要

Drawing your information from lines 1-21 ('Custom has not ... achieve the thousandth part.'), describe how our attitude to life is shaped by custom. Do not write more than 100 words. Use your own words as far as possible. Your answer should be in one paragraph.

Composition 作文

Write a composition of about 600 words on one of the following subjects:

1   Tradition and the individual.

2   How can the study of cultures different from our own lead to a better understanding of man's nature?

3   'There can be no absolute standards of right and wrong since our moral attitudes are conditioned by the society in which we live.' Discuss.

Key structures 关键句型

Rewrite the sentences given below using the opening words and phrases provided. Do not refer to the passage until you have finished the exercise:

1   We have not commonly regarded custom as a subject of any great moment.
Custom _____ (1.1)

2   We feel that the inner working of our own brains are uniquely worthy of investigation.
The inner workings of our own brains we feel to _____ (ll. 1-2)

3   What he sees is edited by a definite set of customs and institutions and ways of thinking.
He sees _____ (1.8)

4   From the moment of his birth his experience and behaviour are shaped by the customs into which he is born.
From the moment of his birth the customs _____ (1.17)

5   We had to arrive first at that degree of sophistication where we no longer set our own belief against our neighbour's superstition.
It was necessary _____ (ll.33-35)

Special difficulties 难点

A   Study the following pairs of words and then write sentences of your own to bring out the difference.

1   custom (l.1) — habit

Sending birthday cards is not a very old custom.

Overeating can easily become a bad habit.

2   aspect (l.5) — view

Why don't we consider the wider aspects of the problem?

There's an excellent view from my window.

3   proportion (l.12) — percentage

The amount of work to be done seems to expand in proportion to the amount of time available to do it.

The percentage of income taken in tax has stayed the same now for four years.

4   unintelligible (l.23) — unintelligent

The nurses found what he said unintelligible, but his wife could understand him well enough.

People with gross physical disabilities are not necessarily unintelligent as well.

5   controversial (l.27) — argumentative

Euthanasia, even voluntary euthanasia, must always be a controversial subject.

It's hard to teach someone who is habitually argumentative, because they are thinking of how to disgrace instead of paying attention.

B   Write sentences using the following words differently from the way in which they have been used in the passage:

accommodation (l.16); creature (l.18); globe (l.21); intelligent (l.22).

Multiple choice questions 选择题

Choose the correct answers to the following questions.

Comprehension 理解

1 Our view of life and the world is largely the product of _____ .

(a) the society we are born into

(b) the inner workings of our own brains

(c) individual development and preference

(d) a mass of detail

2 According to the writer, the thoughts and ideas of an individual _____ .

(a) are minimal compared with the power of tradition

(b) will often dominate the patterns and standards handed down in the community

(c) shape his own beliefs and behaviour

(d) are often completely unintelligible

3 According to the writer, it is unlikely that a child born into one culture _____ .

(a) will acquire the customs and traditions of another

(b) will ever learn anything about a different culture

(c) will be intelligible to a child of another culture

(d) will ever travel to the opposite side of the globe

4 Anthropologists can only study human societies objectively if they _____ .

    (*a*) regard all cultures as having equal value

    (*b*) distinguish between themselves and barbarians

    (*c*) believe in the supernatural

    (*d*) have a good understanding of Western civilization

Structure 句型

5 We feel the inner workings of our brain to be worth _____ . (ll.1-2)

    (*a*) to investigate   (*b*) investigating   (*c*) of investigation   (*d*) for investigating

6 _____ is of first-rate importance is the predominant role of custom. (ll.5-6)

    (*a*) That   (*b*) What   (*c*) Which   (*d*) The thing

7 _____ we are intelligent about its laws, human life will become intelligible. (ll.22-23)

    (*a*) Until   (*b*) When   (*c*) As if   (*d*) Unless

8 _____ we have learned all we know about the laws of astronomy. (l.29)

    (*a*) That's when   (*b*) That's how   (*c*) That's so   (*d*) That's as if

Vocabulary 词汇

9 He sees it _____ by a definite set of customs. (l.8)

    (*a*) examined   (*b*) cut down   (*c*) excluded   (*d*) modified

10 The life-history of an individual is _____ an accommodation ... (ll.15-16)

    (*a*) in the first place   (*b*) only   (*c*) above all   (*d*) exclusively

11 The study of custom can be profitable only after certain _____ propositions have been accepted. (ll.24-25)

    (*a*) required   (*b*) initial   (*c*) advanced   (*d*) exceptional

12 Scientific study requires that there be no _____ towards one side. (ll.25-26)

    (*a*) bias   (*b*) attitude   (*c*) belief   (*d*) indication

Lesson 45 *Of men and galaxies* 人和星系

📼 **First listen and then answer the following question.**

听录音，然后回答以下问题。

What is the most influential factor in any human society?

In man's early days, competition with other creatures must have been critical. But this phase of our development is now finished. Indeed, we lack practice and experience nowadays in dealing with primitive conditions. I am sure that, without modern weapons, I would make a very poor show of disputing the ownership of a cave with a bear, and in this I do not think that I stand alone. The last creature to compete
5 with man was the mosquito. But even the mosquito has been subdued by attention to drainage and by chemical sprays.

Competition between ourselves, person against person, community against community, still persists, however; and it is as fierce as it ever was.

But the competition of man against man is not the simple process envisioned in biology. It is not a simple
10 competition for a fixed amount of food determined by the physical environment, because the environment that determines our evolution is no longer essentially physical. Our environment is chiefly conditioned by the things we believe. Morocco and California are bits of the Earth in very similar latitudes, both on the west coasts of continents with similar climates, and probably with rather similar natural resources. Yet their present development is wholly different, not so much because of different people even, but because of the
15 different thoughts that exist in the minds of their inhabitants. This is the point I wish to emphasize. The most important factor in our environment is the state of our own minds.

It is well known that where the white man has invaded a primitive culture, the most destructive effects have come not from physical weapons but from ideas. Ideas are dangerous. The Holy Office knew this full well when it caused heretics to be burned in days gone by. Indeed, the concept of free speech only exists in
20 our modern society because when you are inside a community, you are conditioned by the conventions of the community to such a degree that it is very difficult to conceive of anything really destructive. It is only someone looking on from outside that can inject the dangerous thoughts. I do not doubt that it would be possible to inject ideas into the modern world that would utterly destroy us. I would like to give you an example, but fortunately I cannot do so. Perhaps it will suffice to mention the nuclear bomb. Imagine the
25 effect on a reasonably advanced technological society, one that still does not possess the bomb, of making it aware of the possibility, of supplying sufficient details to enable the thing to be constructed. Twenty or thirty pages of information handed to any of the major world powers around the year 1925 would have been sufficient to change the course of world history. It is a strange thought, but I believe a correct one, that twenty or thirty pages of ideas and information would be capable of turning the present-day world upside
30 down, or even destroying it. I have often tried to conceive of what those pages might contain, but of course I cannot do so because I am a prisoner of the present-day world, just as all of you are. We cannot think outside the particular patterns that our brains are conditioned to, or, to be more accurate, we can think only a very little way outside, and then only if we are very original.

FRED HOYLE *Of Men and Galaxies*

An aerial view of Sausalito, California

New words and expressions 生词和短语

dispute (1.3) /dɪs'pjuːt/ v. 争夺
mosquito (1.5) /mə'skiːtəʊ/ n. 蚊子
subdue (1.5) /səb'djuː/ v. 征服
drainage (1.5) /'dreɪnɪdʒ/ n. 下水系统
envision (1.9) /ɪn'vɪʒən/ v. 预想
Morocco (1.12) /mə'rɒkəʊ/ n. 摩洛哥

latitude (1.12) /'lætɪtjuːd/ n. 纬度
heretic (1.19) /'herətɪk/ n. 异教徒, 异端邪说
conceive (1.21) /kən'siːv/ v. 想象
suffice (1.24) /sə'faɪs/ v. 足够
nuclear (1.24) /'njuːklɪə/ adj. 原子弹的
original (1.33) /ə'rɪdʒɪnəl/ adj. 有独到见解的

Notes on the text 课文注释

1 make a very poor show, 出丑 。
2 I stand alone, 仅我一人 。
3 the last creature to compete with man, 其中的 last 有 "极不可能的" 的意思 。
4 The Holy Office knew this full well when it caused heretics to be burned in days gone by. the Holy Office 是指罗马天主教的宗教法庭; full well 中的 full 是副词, 有 very 的意思; gone by 作 days 的定语, 整个词组的意思是 "过去的日子" 。

参考译文

　　在人类早期, 人类与其他生物的竞争一定是必不可少的 。但这个发展阶段已经结束 。确实, 我们今天缺乏对付原始环境的实践和经验 。我断定, 如果没有现代化的武器, 要我和一只熊去争洞穴, 我会出洋相的; 我也相信, 出洋相者并非我一人 。能与人竞争的生物最后只有蚊子了 。然而, 即使是蚊子, 也由于我们注意清理污水和喷洒化学药品而被制服了 。

　　然而人类之间的竞争, 人与人, 团体与团体, 依然在进行着, 而且和以前一样激烈 。

　　但是, 人与人的竞争并不像生物学中想象的那样是一个简单的过程 。它已不是为了争得物质环境所决定的有限食物而进行的简单竞争了, 因为决定我们进化环境的主要方面已不再是物质 。我们的环境由我们信仰的东西所决定 。摩洛哥和加利福尼亚是地球上纬度极其相似的两个地方, 都在各自大陆的西海岸, 气候相似, 自然资源也可能相似。但是，这两个地方目前的发展程度完全不一样。这倒不是因为人民不同，而是由于居民头脑中的思想不同。这就是我要强调的论点。我们环境中最重要的因素就是我们的思想状况。

众所周知，凡是白人侵入原始文化的地方，破坏作用最大的不是杀人的武器，而是思想。思想是危险的。宗教法庭对此是非常清楚的，因此从前它总是把异教徒烧死。的确，言论自由的概念只存在于我们现代社会中，因为当你生活在一个社会当中时，社会的风俗习惯会严格地制约你，使你很难有破坏性的想法。只有外部的旁观者才能灌输危险的思想。向现代世界灌输一种思想以便摧毁我们人类是可能的事，对此我并不怀疑。我愿为你举个例子，但幸亏我举不出。也许提一下核弹就足以说明了。对一个尚未拥有核弹但科技相当发达的社会，如果告诉它制造核弹的可能性，而且向它提供制造核弹的细节，那么可以设想，这将对这个社会产生何等的影响。如果把二三十页的情报交给1925年前后的任何一个世界强国，就足以改变世界历史的进程。二三十页材料中的思想和情报会使当今的世界天翻地覆，甚至毁灭这个世界。这是个离奇的想法，不过我认为这个想法是正确的。我常常试图想象这些纸上所写的东西，不过我是做不到的，因为我和你们大家一样，是当今世界上的凡人。我们不能脱离我们大脑所限定的模式去思考问题，我们只能稍微离开一点儿，就这也需要我们有独创的思想。

Comprehension 理解

Answer these questions:

1 Which idea in the first paragraph is illustrated by the following statement: 'I would make a very poor show of disputing the ownership of a cave with a bear.'? (ll.3-4)
2 How does the author account for the fact that the inhabitants of Morocco differ from those of California?
3 What do you understand by this statement: 'When you are inside a community you are conditioned by the conventions of the community.'? (ll.20-21)
4 What, in the author's view, could change the course of world history?
5 What must a person with original ideas be capable of doing?

Vocabulary 词汇

Refer to the text to see how the following words have been used, then write sentences of your own using these words: critical (l.1); phase (l.1); I would make a very poor show (l.3); subdued (l.5); the environment that determines our evolution (ll.10-11); wholly (l.14); factor (l.16); utterly (l.23); course (l.28); accurate (l.32).

Summary 摘要

Drawing your information from the last paragraph (lines 17-33), explain why ideas can be more dangerous than weapons. Do not write more than 110 words. Use your own words as far as possible. Your answer should be in one paragraph.

Composition 作文

Write a composition of about 600 words on one of the following subjects:

1 The evolution of man.
2 Brainwashing.
3 'Our environment is chiefly conditioned by the things we believe.' Support or attack this view.

Key structures 关键句型

A Study this sentence:

In man's early days, competition with other creatures *must have been* critical. (l.1)

Write two sentences illustrating the difference between *must have been* and *had to be*.

B Rewrite the sentences given below using the opening phrases provided. Do not refer to the passage until you have finished the exercise:

1 I am sure that, if I did not have any weapons, I would make a very poor show of disputing the ownership of a cave with a bear.

I am sure that, without _____ (ll.3-4)

2 It is the things we believe that chiefly condition our environment.

Our environment _____ (ll.11-12)

3 It is well known that where a primitive culture has been invaded by the white man, the most destructive effects have come not from physical weapons but from ideas.

It is well known that where the white man _____ (ll.17-18)

4 I do not doubt that we would be utterly destroyed if it were possible to inject ideas into the modern world.

I do not doubt that it would be _____ (ll.22-23)

5 Imagine how a reasonably advanced technological society would be affected.

Imagine the effect _____ (ll.24-26)

Special difficulties 难点

Note the words in italics in the following sentences. Use these words again in sentences of your own, giving each word a different meaning from the one it has in the example:

1 Competition with other creatures must have been *critical*. (l.1)

2 The most important factor in our environment is the *state* of our own minds. (ll.15-16)

3 The concept of *free* speech only exists in our modern society because when you are inside a community you are conditioned by the conventions of the community. (ll.19-21)

Multiple choice questions 选择题

Choose the correct answers to the following questions.

Comprehension 理解

1 Competition in the world _____ .

(*a*) takes place between humans and other animals

(*b*) has not been confined to humans versus mosquitoes

(*c*) exists mainly in a human context

(*d*) is the result of lack of experience in dealing with primitive conditions

2 The writer is arguing that, where humans are concerned, _____ .

(*a*) beliefs are more important than physical environment

(*b*) climate influences what people believe

(*c*) human development is the product of physical environment

(*d*) people compete for the fixed amount of food available in our environment

3 According to the writer, human societies _____ .

   (a) attempt to influence each other with dangerous thoughts

   (b) are always threatened by the invasion of other people

   (c) tend to destroy primitive cultures

   (d) can be threatened by unfamiliar ideas

4 We cannot imagine what ideas would destroy our society because _____ .

   (a) our imaginations are strictly limited by the cultures we live in

   (b) the concept of free speech is not universally acceptable

   (c) we know exactly the kind of information that would turn the world upside-down

   (d) no one on earth ever has any original ideas

Structure 句型

5 There is little doubt that in man's early days competition _____ critical. (1.1)

   (a) had been   (b) would be   (c) was   (d) has been

6 Competition between ourselves _____ persist. (1.6)

   (a) is enabled to   (b) is seen to   (c) continues to   (d) attempts to

7 _____ it would be possible to inject ideas into the modern world. (ll.22-23)

   (a) There is no doubt   (b) It is no doubt

   (c) What is not doubtful   (d) It isn't doubtless that

8 If twenty pages _____ handed down to any of the major world powers around the year 1925, they would have been sufficient to change the course of world history. (ll.26-28)

   (a) could be   (b) would have been   (c) had been   (d) have been

Vocabulary 词汇

9 I would make a poor show of _____ the ownership of a cave with a bear. (ll.3-4)

   (a) engaging in   (b) quarrelling with   (c) discussing   (d) arguing about

10 The competition of man against man is not the simple process _____ in biology. (1.9)

   (a) seen   (b) obvious   (c) imagined   (d) established

11 The Holy Office knew this full well when it caused _____ to be burned. (ll.18-19)

   (a) philosophers   (b) missionaries   (c) enemies   (d) dissidents

12 You are conditioned by the _____ of the community. (ll.19-20)

   (a) laws   (b) regulations   (c) accepted behaviour   (d) boundaries

Lesson 46 Hobbies 业余爱好

First listen and then answer the following question.

听录音, 然后回答以下问题 。

Who, according to the author, are 'Fortune's favoured children'?

A gifted American psychologist has said, 'Worry is a spasm of the emotion; the mind catches hold of something and will not let it go.' It is useless to argue with the mind in this condition. The stronger the will, the more futile the task. One can only gently insinuate something else into its convulsive grasp. And if this something else is rightly chosen, if it is really attended by the illumination of another field of interest, gradually, and often quite swiftly, the old undue grip relaxes and the process of recuperation and repair begins.

The cultivation of a hobby and new forms of interest is therefore a policy of the first importance to a public man. But this is not a business that can be undertaken in a day or swiftly improvised by a mere command of the will. The growth of alternative mental interests is a long process. The seeds must be carefully chosen; they must fall on good ground; they must be sedulously tended, if the vivifying fruits are to be at hand when needed.

To be really happy and really safe, one ought to have at least two or three hobbies, and they must all be real. It is no use starting late in life to say: 'I will take an interest in this or that.' Such an attempt only aggravates the strain of mental effort. A man may acquire great knowledge of topics unconnected with his daily work, and yet get hardly any benefit or relief. It is no use doing what you like; you have got to like what you do. Broadly speaking, human beings may be divided into three classes: those who are toiled to death, those who are worried to death, and those who are bored to death. It is no use offering the manual labourer, tired out with a hard week's sweat and effort, the chance of playing a game of football or baseball on Saturday afternoon. It is no use inviting the politician or the professional or business man, who has been working or worrying about serious things for six days, to work or worry about trifling things at the weekend.

As for the unfortunate people who can command everything they want, who can gratify every caprice and lay their hands on almost every object of desire—for them a new pleasure, a new excitement is only an additional satiation. In vain they rush frantically round from place to place, trying to escape from avenging boredom by mere clatter and motion. For them discipline in one form or another is the most hopeful path.

It may also be said that rational, industrious, useful human beings are divided into two classes: first, those whose work is work and whose pleasure is pleasure; and secondly, those whose work and pleasure are one. Of these the former are the majority. They have their compensations. The long hours in the office or the factory bring with them as their reward, not only the means of sustenance, but a keen appetite for pleasure even in its simplest and most modest forms. But Fortune's favoured children belong to the second class. Their life is a natural harmony. For them the working hours are never long enough. Each day is a holiday, and ordinary holidays, when they come, are grudged as enforced interruptions in an absorbing vocation. Yet to both classes, the need of an alternative outlook, of a change of atmosphere, of a diversion of effort, is

essential. Indeed, it may well be that those whose work is their pleasure are those who most need the means
35 of banishing it at intervals from their minds.

WINSTON CHURCHILL *Painting as a Pastime*

Sir Winston Churchill painting in Switzerland in 1946

New words and expressions 生词和短语

gifted (1.1) /ˈgɪftɪd/ *adj.* 有天才的
psychologist (1.1) /saɪˈkɒlədʒɪst/ *n.* 心理学家
spasm (1.1) /ˈspæzəm/ *n.* 一阵（感情）发作
futile (1.3) /ˈfjuːtaɪl/ *adj.* 无用的
insinuate (1.3) /ɪnˈsɪnjueɪt/ *v.* 使潜入，暗示
convulsive (1.3) /kənˈvʌlsɪv/ *adj.* 起痉挛的
illumination (1.4) /ɪˌluːmɪˈneɪʃən/ *n.* 启发，照明
undue (1.5) /ˌʌnˈdjuː/ *adj.* 不适当的，过度的
grip (1.5) /grɪp/ *n.* 紧张
recuperation (1.5) /rɪˌkuːpəˈreɪʃən/ *n.* 休息
improvise (1.8) /ˈɪmprəvaɪz/ *v.* 临时作成
sedulously (1.10) /ˈsedjʊləsli/ *adv.* 孜孜不倦地
vivify (1.10) /ˈvɪvɪfaɪ/ *v.* 使生气勃勃
aggravate (1.14) /ˈægrəveɪt/ *v.* 加剧

trifling (1.20) /ˈtraɪflɪŋ/ *adj.* 微小的
gratify (1.22) /ˈgrætɪfaɪ/ *v.* 使满意
caprice (1.22) /kəˈpriːs/ *n.* 任性
satiation (1.24) /ˌseɪʃiˈeɪʃən/ *n.* 满足
frantically (1.24) /ˈfræntɪkəli/ *adv.* 狂乱地
avenge (1.24) /əˈvendʒ/ *v.* 替 …… 报复
boredom (1.25) /ˈbɔːdəm/ *n.* 厌烦
clatter (1.25) /ˈklætə/ *n.* 喧闹的谈话
sustenance (1.29) /ˈsʌstənəns/ *n.* 生计
appetite (1.29) /ˈæpɪtaɪt/ *n.* 欲望
grudge (1.32) /grʌdʒ/ *v.* 怨恨
absorbing (1.32) /əbˈsɔːbɪŋ/ *adj.* 引人入胜的
banish (1.35) /ˈbænɪʃ/ *v.* 排除，放弃

Unit 6   Lesson 46

Notes on the text 课文注释

1   catch hold of, 抓住 ……; let ... go, 放掉 …… 。
2   lay one's hands on, 得到 ……，抓到 …… 。
3   Fortune's favoured children 中的 Fortune 是指 "命运女神"。

参考译文

　　一位天才的美国心理学家曾经说过："烦恼是感情的发作，此时脑子纠缠住了某种东西又不肯松手。"在这种情况下，你和头脑争吵让它松手是无济于事的。这种意志越是强烈，这种尝试越是徒劳。你只能缓和而巧妙地让另一种东西进入痉挛僵持的头脑中。如果选得合适，而且的确受到别的领域的情趣的启迪，那么渐渐地，往往也是很顺利地，原先过度的紧张就会松弛下来，恢复和修整的过程就会开始。

　　因此，对一个从事社会活动的人来说，培养一种业余爱好和各种新的兴趣是头等重要的作法。但这并非一日之功，也不是单凭意志一蹴而就的事。精神上多种情趣的培养是一个长期的过程。要想在需要的时候可随手摘取充满生机的果实，那就必然从精选良种做起，然后将其植入肥沃的土地，还需要精心地护理。

　　一个人要想真正感到幸福和平安，至少应有两三种爱好，而且都比较实际。到了晚年才开始说："我会对这个或那个发生兴趣"，已没有用了。这种愿望只能加剧精神紧张。一个人可能会获得与其日常工作无关的某些课题的渊博知识，而没有从中得到什么实益或宽慰。干你所喜欢的事是没有用的，你得喜欢你所干的事。泛泛地说，人可以分为 3 类：劳累至死的人、忧虑至死的人、无聊至死的人。对于流汗出力干了一周苦活的体力劳动者来说，让他们在星期六下午再踢足球或打垒球是不合适的；同样，对于为严肃的公务操劳或烦恼了 6 天的政界人士、专业技术人员、商人来说，在周末再让他们为琐事而动脑子和忧虑也是无益的。

　　至于那些能任意支配一切的"可怜的人"，他们能够恣意妄为，能染指一切追求的目标。对这种人来说，多一种新的乐趣、多一种新的刺激只是增加一分厌腻而已。他们到处狂奔乱跑，企图以闲聊和乱窜来摆脱无聊对他们的报复，但这是徒劳的。对他们来说，用某种形式的纪律约束他们一下才能有希望使他们走上正道。

　　也可以这样说，理智的、勤劳的、有用的人可以分为两类：第一类是分清工作是工作，娱乐是娱乐的人；第二类人的工作和娱乐是一回事。这两类人当中，第一类人是大多数，他们能够得到补偿。在办公室或工厂里长时间的工作给他们带来了酬劳，这不仅是谋生的手段，而且还带来了寻找乐趣的强烈欲望，哪怕是最简单的、最低等的乐趣。但是，命运之神的宠儿是第二类人，他们的生活是一种自然的和谐，对他们来说，工作时间总不会太长，每天都是假日，而通常的假期到来时，他们却惋惜这假期强制打断了他们埋头从事的工作。然而对这两种人来说，都需要换一换脑子，改变一下气氛，转移一下注意力，这是不可缺少的。说实在的，把工作当作享受的那些人可能最需要每隔一段时间把工作从头脑中撤开。

Comprehension 理解

Answer these questions:

1   In what way is the definition of worry quoted in the first paragraph relevant to the author's argument?
2   Why does the author class as unfortunate those people who can command everything they want?
3   How can people who have everything they want find relief from boredom?
4   What is the essential difference between the two classes of human beings defined by the author? (ll.26-28)
5   Why is it particularly important for people whose work is their pleasure to cultivate a hobby?

Vocabulary 词汇

Refer to the text to see how the following words have been used, then write sentences of your own using these words: spasm (l.1); futile (l.3); insinuate (l.3); recuperation (l.5); alternative mental interests (l.9); vivifying (l.10); toiled to death (l.16); trifling (l.20); caprice (l.22); satiation (l.24); enforced interruptions in an absorbing vocation (l.32).

Summary 摘要

Drawing your information from lines 7-21 ('The cultivation ... things at the weekend.'), summarize the author's views on cultivating a hobby. Do not write more than 90 words. Use your own words as far as possible. Your answer should be in one paragraph.

Composition 作文

Write a composition of about 600 words on one of the following subjects:

1   Worry.
2   Your favourite hobby.
3   'Human beings are divided into two classes: first, those whose work is work and whose pleasure is pleasure; and secondly, those whose work and pleasure are one.' (ll.26-28) Which class, in your view, would it be preferable to belong to?

Key structures 关键句型

A   Complete the following sentences in any way you wish, then compare what you have written with the sentences in the passage:

1   It is useless to _____ (l.2)
2   It is no use _____ (l.13)

B   Rewrite the sentences given below using the opening phrases provided. Do not refer to the passage until you have finished the exercise:

1   It is of the first importance to a public man to cultivate a hobby and new forms of interest.
    The cultivation _____ (ll.7-8)
2   If one wishes to be really happy and really safe, one ought to have at least two or three hobbies, and they must all be real.
    To be _____ (ll.12-13)
3   Not only do the long hours in the office or the factory bring with them the means of sustenance as their reward, but a keen appetite for pleasure even in its simplest and most modest forms.
    The long hours _____ (ll.28-30)

Special difficulties 难点

A   Study the following pairs of words and then write sentences of your own to bring out the difference.

1   late (l.13) — lately
    The train arrived late.
    We haven't seen you lately.

2   hardly (l.15) — hard (l.18)

He's so old now, he hardly works at all.

I'll pass the exam if I work hard.

3   alternative (l.33) — alternating

That's what we must do then, unless you have an alternative suggestion.

I visit my parents on alternating weekends.

B   Use each of the following words figuratively in sentences of your own. Do not refer to the passage until you have finished the exercise:

seeds (l.9); fruits (l.10); sweat (l.18).

C   Use the following expressions in sentences of your own. Do not refer to the passage until you have completed the exercise: broadly speaking (l.16); as for (l.22); the former (l.28).

Multiple choice questions 选择题

Choose the correct answers to the following questions.

Comprehension 理解

1 The only way to stop worrying is _____ .

(*a*) through an effort of the will

(*b*) to become absorbed in some other activity

(*c*) to let go whatever it is that's worrying you

(*d*) relax until you recuperate

2 The cultivation of a hobby _____ .

(*a*) prevents you from being bored to death

(*b*) can only occur over a long period of time

(*c*) is particularly suitable for the professional or business man

(*d*) is always a benefit

3 People who can spend as much money as they like _____ .

(*a*) are Fortune's favoured children

(*b*) never feel bored

(*c*) enjoy a life that is full of excitement

(*d*) are truly unlucky

4 The people the writer admires most are those who _____ .

(*a*) can spend their entire lives on holiday

(*b*) don't distinguish between work and pleasure

(*c*) are rational, industrious and useful

(*d*) work hard and can therefore enjoy their leisure

Structure 句型

5 It's no use _____ with the mind in this condition. (l.2)

(*a*) in arguing   (*b*) argue   (*c*) to argue   (*d*) arguing

6 The seeds _____ carefully chosen. (1.9)

  (*a*) have to be   (*b*) should be   (*c*) were probably   (*d*) are probably

7 Human beings may be divided into three classes: _____ who are ... (1.16)

  (*a*) that   (*b*) the ones   (*c*) the which   (*d*) them

8 The long hours in the office bring with them _____ the means of sustenance _____ a keen appetite for pleasure. (11.28-29)

  (*a*) not only ... and   (*b*) either ... or   (*c*) both ... and   (*d*) and ... and

Vocabulary 词汇

9 The stronger the will the more _____ the task. (1.3)

  (*a*) elaborate   (*b*) desirable   (*c*) fertile   (*d*) pointless

10 The seeds must be sedulously _____ . (11.9-10)

  (*a*) cared for   (*b*) grown   (*c*) watered   (*d*) followed

11 A manual labourer works with _____ . (1.17)

  (*a*) his firm   (*b*) his hands   (*c*) machines   (*d*) his mind

12 It may be said that rational, _____ , useful human beings ... (1.26)

  (*a*) professional   (*b*) employed   (*c*) industrial   (*d*) hard-working

Lesson 47 The great escape 大逃亡

First listen and then answer the following question.

听录音，然后回答以下问题 。

What is one of the features of modern camping where nationality is concerned?

Economy is one powerful motive for camping, since after the initial outlay upon equipment, or through hiring it, the total expense can be far less than the cost of hotels. But, contrary to a popular assumption, it is far from being the only one, or even the greatest. The man who manoeuvres carelessly into his twenty pounds' worth of space at one of Europe's myriad permanent sites may find himself bumping a Bentley. More likely,
5 Ford Escort will be hub to hub with Renault or Mercedes, but rarely with bicycles made for two.

That the equipment of modern camping becomes yearly more sophisticated is an entertaining paradox for the cynic, a brighter promise for the hopeful traveller who has sworn to get away from it all. It also provides—and some student sociologist might care to base his thesis upon the phenomenon—an escape of another kind. The modern traveller is often a man who dislikes the Splendide and the Bellavista, not because
10 he cannot afford, or shuns their material comforts, but because he is afraid of them. Affluent he may be, but he is by no means sure what to tip the doorman or the chambermaid. Master in his own house, he has little idea of when to say boo to a *maître d'hôtel* .

From all such fears camping releases him. Granted, a snobbery of camping itself, based upon equipment and techniques, already exists; but it is of a kind that, if he meets it, he can readily understand and deal with.
15 There is no superior 'they' in the shape of managements and hotel hierarchies to darken his holiday days.

To such motives, yet another must be added. The contemporary phenomenon of car worship is to be explained not least by the sense of independence and freedom that ownership entails. To this pleasure camping gives an exquisite refinement.

From one's own front door to home or foreign hills or sands and back again, everything is to hand. Not
20 only are the means of arriving at the holiday paradise entirely within one's own command and keeping, but the means of escape from holiday hell (if the beach proves too crowded, the local weather too inclement) are there, outside—or, as likely, part of—the tent.

Idealists have objected to the practice of camping, as to the package tour, that the traveller abroad thereby denies himself the opportunity of getting to know the people of the country visited. Insularity and
25 self-containment, it is argued, go hand in hand. The opinion does not survive experience of a popular Continental camping place. Holiday hotels tend to cater for one nationality of visitors especially, sometimes exclusively. Camping sites, by contrast, are highly cosmopolitan. Granted, a preponderance of Germans is a characteristic that seems common to most Mediterranean sites; but as yet there is no overwhelmingly specialized patronage. Notices forbidding the open-air drying of clothes, or the use of water points for car
30 washing, or those inviting 'our camping friends' to a dance or a boat trip are printed not only in French or Italian or Spanish, but also in English, German and Dutch. At meal times the odour of sauerkraut vies with that of garlic. The Frenchman's breakfast coffee competes with the Englishman's bacon and eggs.

Whether the remarkable growth of organized camping means the eventual death of the more independent kind is hard to say. Municipalities naturally want to secure the campers' site fees and other custom. Police
35 are wary of itinerants who cannot be traced to a recognized camp boundary or to four walls. But most

probably it will all depend upon campers themselves: how many heath fires they cause; how much litter they leave; in short, whether or not they wholly alienate landowners and those who live in the countryside. Only good scouting is likely to preserve the freedoms so dear to the heart of the eternal Boy Scout.

NIGEL BUXTON *The Great Escape* from *The Weekend Telegraph*

Modern camping

New words and expressions 生词和短语

assumption (1.2) /əˈsʌmpʃən/ n. 假定

manoeuvre (1.3) /məˈnuːvə/ v. （驱车）移动

myriad (1.4) /ˈmɪriəd/ adj. 无数的

paradox (1.6) /ˈpærədɒks/ n. 自相矛盾的事

cynic (1.7) /ˈsɪnɪk/ n. 愤世嫉俗者

sociologist (1.8) /ˌsəʊsiˈɒlədʒɪst/ n. 社会学家

shun (1.10) /ʃʌn/ v. 避开

affluent (1.10) /ˈæfluənt/ adj. 富有的

chambermaid (1.11) /ˈtʃeɪmbəmeɪd/ n. 女招待员

boo (1.12) /buː/ n. 呸的一声

maître d'hôtel (1.12) /ˌmetrə-dəʊˈtel/ n. [法语]总管

snobbery (1.13) /ˈsnɒbəri/ n. 势利

hierarchy (1.15) /ˈhaɪrɑːki/ n. 等级制度

entail (1.17) /ɪnˈteɪl/ v. 使成为必要

inclement (1.21) /ɪnˈklemənt/ adj. 险恶的

package tour (1.23) /ˈpækɪdʒ-tʊə/ 由旅行社安排一切的一揽子旅游

insularity (1.24) /ˌɪnsjʊˈlærɪti/ n. 偏狭

cater (1.26) /ˈkeɪtə/ v. 迎合

exclusively (1.27) /ɪkˈskluːsɪvli/ adv. 排他地

cosmopolitan (1.27) /ˌkɒzməˈpɒlɪtən/ adj. 世界的

preponderance (1.27) /prɪˈpɒndərəns/ n. 优势

overwhelmingly (1.28) /ˌəʊvəˈwelmɪŋli/ adv. 以压倒优势地, 清一色地

patronage (1.29) /ˈpætrənɪdʒ/ n. 恩惠, 惠顾

sauerkraut (1.31) /ˈsaʊəkraʊt/ n. 泡菜

vie (1.31) /vaɪ/ v. 竞争

municipality (1.34) /mjuːˌnɪsɪˈpælɪti/ n. 市政当局

itinerant (1.35) /aɪˈtɪnərənt/ n. 流动人口

heath (1.36) /hiːθ/ n. 荒地

alienate (1.37) /ˈeɪliəneɪt/ v. 使疏远

eternal (1.38) /ɪˈtɜːnəl/ adj. 永久的

Notes on the text 课文注释

1 it is far from ..., 远不是…… 。

2 twenty pounds' worth of space, 价值 20 镑的空地, 其中 worth 是名词 。

3 hub to hub with, 轮毂与…… 轮毂相接 。

4 the Splendide and the Bellavista, 两大酒店的名字 。

5 say boo to a *maître d'hôtel*, 对酒店的经理表示不满 。say boo to a *maître d'hôtel*, 是从 not say boo to a goose（非常胆小, 不敢得罪）演变而来的 。在这个成语中, a goose 常被人们幽默地换成其他字眼 。

6 Granted, ... but ...（虽然…… 但是……）这种句型中的 Granted 总放在句首, 意思是 Yes, 相当于一个连接副词的作用 。

7 in the shape of, 以…… 形式出现的 。

8 be to hand, 垂手可得 。

9 cater for, 迎合…… 。

10 be wary of, 提防…… 。

11 Boy Scout, 童子军 。

参考译文

图省钱是露营的一个主要动机, 因为除了开始时购置或是租借一套露营装备外, 总费用算起来要比住旅馆开支少得多 。但是, 和一般的看法相反, 这绝非是仅有的, 甚至不是最主要的动机 。如果一位游客漫不经心地驾车驶入欧洲无数常年营地之一, 花 20 镑租用一个空位, 那么他可能会碰见一辆宾利汽车, 更可能会望见一辆福特雅仕和一辆雷诺或一辆梅塞德斯并排停放, 不过双人自行车则不容易看到 。

现代露营装备一年比一年讲究, 这对那些愤世嫉俗者来说是一件有趣的自相矛盾的事情 。而对于发誓用露营来摆脱烦恼的人来说, 却带来了更光明的前景 。学社会学的大学生来露营是另一种形式的摆脱现实, 其目的很可能是根据观察到的露营现象去写论文 。现代露营旅游的人往往讨厌住"斯普兰迪德"和"贝拉维斯塔"这样的大酒店, 这并不是因为他们付不起钱, 也不是为了躲避物质享受, 而是因为他们害怕酒店 。他们可能很富有, 但给看门人和房间女服务员多少小费, 心中却根本没有数; 他们在家可能是主人, 但不知道什么时候才能对酒店的经理表示不满 。

露营使人们免除了这些忧虑 。诚然, 露营地本身也存在以露营装备和方式取人的势利现象, 但如果有这种情况, 露营者也容易理解, 知道如何对付 。在露营地里根本不会有管人的"人上人"和酒店里的等级制度来使露营者的假日过得阴郁低沉 。

除了以上动机外, 还应再加上一个 。当前崇拜汽车现象可以用与所有权相伴的独立和自由意识来解释 。因此开车去露营会给这种快乐意识增加一种优雅意境 。

从自己的家门出发到国内国外的山区或沙滩上露营后返回, 一切都很便利 。完全在自己掌握之中的私人汽车不仅是到达假日天堂的工具, 而且也是逃离假日地狱（如海滩太挤、当地天气恶劣）的方便工具, 因为汽车就停在帐篷外面, 或者汽车本身可能就是露营帐篷的一个组成部分 。

理想主义者像反对旅行社安排一切的一揽子旅游一样反对露营的做法, 说这种封闭的做法使到国外旅游者失去了了解所去国家人民的机会 。他们争论说, 心胸狭窄和自我封闭是并存的 。但这种说法在受人欢迎的欧洲露营场地是站不住脚的 。假日旅馆有只接待来自一个国家的旅游者的倾向, 有时会达到排他的程度 。而露营驻地则相反, 是高度世界性的 。在大多数地中海露营地里, 德国人占优势似乎是个普遍现象, 确实如此, 但并没有特别的优待 。禁止露天晒衣服、禁止用水龙头冲洗汽车的布告和邀请露营朋友参加舞会、乘船观光的招贴不仅印成法语、意大利语、西班牙语, 而且也印成英语、德语、荷兰语 。用饭的时候, 德国泡菜味和大蒜味争相散发, 法国人的早点咖啡和英国人的咸肉煎蛋竞相比美 。

有组织的露营活动显著增长是否意味着较独立的自我封闭式露营的最终消失, 还很难说 。市政当局当然希望获得露营者的场地费和其他光临的好处, 警察则对那些查不出有固定营地或住处的游荡者保持警惕 。但最重要的或许是露营者自己，即他们引起了多少场野火，留下了多少垃圾 。总之，他们是否弄得土地的主人和乡间的居民同他们反目 。只有优良的童子军活动才能保持不朽的童子军所衷心热爱的各项自由 。

Comprehension 理解

Answer these questions:

1   Name three factors which induce people to go camping.
2   What do you understand by this statement: 'To this pleasure camping gives an exquisite refinement.'? (ll.17-18)
3   Why have idealists objected to the practice of camping and how have they been proved wrong?
4   What factors may lead to the death of the more independent kind of camping?

Vocabulary 词汇

Refer to the text to see how the following words have been used, then write sentences of your own using these words: motive (l.1); initial outlay upon equipment (l.1); hub to hub (l.5); to say boo to (l.12); granted (l.13); inclement (l.21); package tour (l.23); insularity (l.24); exclusively (l.27); cosmopolitan (l.27); preponderance (l.27); wary of itinerants (l.35); litter (l.36).

Summary 摘要

Drawing your information from lines 6-32 ('That the equipment ... bacon and eggs.'), write an account of modern camping. Do not write more than 160 words. Use your own words as far as possible. Your answer should be in one paragraph.

Composition 作文

Write a composition of about 600 words on one of the following subjects:

1   Holiday camps.
2   Package tours.
3   What, in your opinion, are the requirements of an ideal holiday?

Key structures 关键句型

Rewrite the sentences given below using the opening phrases provided. Do not refer to the passage until you have finished the exercise:

1   Though the modern traveller is often a man who can afford and does not shun the material comforts of the Splendide and the Bellavista, he dislikes them because he is afraid of them.
    The modern traveller _____ not because _____ (ll.9-10)
2   The means of arriving at the holiday paradise are not only entirely within one's own command and keeping, but the means of escape from holiday hell are there, outside—or, as likely, part of—the tent.
    Not only _____ (ll.20-22)
3   They argue that insularity and self-containment go hand in hand.
    Insularity and self-containment, it _____ (ll.24-25)
4   The freedoms so dear to the heart of the eternal Boy Scout are only likely to be preserved by good scouting.
    Only good _____ (ll.37-38)

Special difficulties 难点

A   Study the following pairs of words and then write sentences of your own to bring out the difference.

1   initial (l.1) — primary
The lawyer charged 50 dollars for the initial consultation.
The safety of our passengers is our primary concern.

2   hire (l.2) — rent
I want to hire a car for my trip to London.
We've rented a villa in the south of France for the summer.

3   total (l.2) — whole
The total bill came to $894.
You can't give an opinion unless you've read the whole book.

4   shun (l.10) — avoid
He was shunned by his former friends.
You should avoid being late for work again.

5   worship (l.16) — warship
Religious leaders have always denounced the worship of money as the root of all evil.
The Spanish warships sent to conquer Britain in the 16th century were wrecked by an exceptionally violent storm.

6   by contrast (l.27) — opposite to
This new manager is really competent, especially by contrast with his predecessor.
This new manager is the complete opposite to what you would expect.

B   Note the words in italics in the following sentences. Use these words again in sentences of your own, giving each word a different meaning from the one it has in the example:

1   The man who manoeuvres carelessly into his twenty pounds' worth of space may find himself *bumping* a Bentley. (ll.3-4)

2   *Granted*, a snobbery of camping itself already exists. (ll.13-14)

3   Municipalities naturally want to secure the campers' site fees and other *custom*. (l.34)

Multiple choice questions 选择题

Choose the correct answers to the following questions.

Comprehension 理解

1   The main reason people enjoy camping is _____ .

(*a*) they can spend less on their holidays

(*b*) their enjoyment of owning camping equipment

(*c*) not necessarily so that they are saving money

(*d*) because they can show off their cars

2   Many modern campers are certainly rich enough to _____ .

(*a*) stay at hotels, but prefer not to

(*b*) have holidays, but choose not to

(*c*) buy expensive cars, but prefer cheap models

(*d*) visit camping sites, but generally avoid them

3 One of these statements is true. Which one?

(*a*) Modern campers enjoy considerable mobility.

(*b*) Modern campers look down on people who stay at expensive hotels.

(*c*) Modern campers are always moving from one place to another.

(*d*) Modern campers enjoy camping even in bad weather.

4 People of different nationalities at camping sites _____ .

(*a*) like to keep to themselves

(*b*) often have arguments about the use of facilities

(*c*) frequently disobey the camping site rules

(*d*) like to mix freely and get to know each other

Structure 句型

5 _____ an entertaining paradox that equipment becomes more sophisticated. (l.6)

(*a*) There is　　　　　(*b*) It is　　　　　(*c*) There has　　　　　(*d*) It has

6 _____ he may be affluent, he isn't sure what to tip the doorman. (ll.10-11)

(*a*) Since　　　　　(*b*) Because　　　　　(*c*) Though　　　　　(*d*) As

7 _____ master in his own house, _____ he has little idea ... (ll.11-12)

(*a*) He is ... but　　　(*b*) He has ... and　　　(*c*) He does ... but　　　(*d*) He was ... though

8 _____ the contemporary phenomenon of car worship ... (l.16)

(*a*) It is explained　　(*b*) To explain　　(*c*) You can explain　　(*d*) To be explained

Vocabulary 词汇

9 The equipment of modern camping becomes yearly more _____ . (l.6)

(*a*) superseded　　(*b*) demanding　　(*c*) complicated　　(*d*) refined

10 – not because he _____ or shuns their material comforts ... (ll.9-10)

(*a*) ridicules　　(*b*) can't pay for　　(*c*) has contempt for　　(*d*) dislikes

11 The _____ phenomenon of car worship ... (l.16)

(*a*) latest　　(*b*) modern　　(*c*) up-to-date　　(*d*) recent

12 Holiday hotels tend to _____ one nationality of visitors. (l.26)

(*a*) acknowledge　　(*b*) appeal to　　(*c*) provide for　　(*d*) include

Lesson 48　Planning a share portfolio　规划股份投资

听录音，然后回答以下问题。

How does the older investor differ in his approach to investment from the younger investor?

There is no shortage of tipsters around offering 'get-rich-quick' opportunities. But if you are a serious private investor, leave the Las Vegas mentality to those with money to fritter. The serious investor needs a proper 'portfolio'—a well-planned selection of investments, with a definite structure and a clear aim. But exactly how does a newcomer to the stock market go about achieving that?

5　Well, if you go to five reputable stock brokers and ask them what you should do with your money, you're likely to get five different answers—even if you give all the relevant information about your age, family, finances and what you want from your investments. Moral? There is no one 'right' way to structure a portfolio. However, there are undoubtedly some wrong ways, and you can be sure that none of our five advisers would have suggested sinking all (or perhaps any) of your money into Periwigs*.

10　So what should you do? We'll assume that you have sorted out the basics—like mortgages, pensions, insurance and access to sufficient cash reserves. You should then establish your own individual aims. These are partly a matter of personal circumstances, partly a matter of psychology.

For instance, if you are older you have less time to recover from any major losses, and you may well wish to boost your pension income. So preserving your capital and generating extra income are your main
15　priorities. In this case, you'd probably construct a portfolio with some shares (but not high risk ones), along with gilts, cash deposits, and perhaps convertibles or the income shares of split capital investment trusts.

If you are younger, and in a solid financial position, you may decide to take an aggressive approach—but only if you're blessed with a sanguine disposition and won't suffer sleepless nights over share prices. If you recognize yourself in this description, you might include a couple of heady growth stocks in your
20　portfolio, alongside your more pedestrian investments. Once you have decided on your investment aims, you can then decide where to put your money. The golden rule here is spread your risk—if you put all of your money into Periwigs International, you're setting yourself up as a hostage to fortune.

* 'Periwigs' is the name of a fictitious company.

INVESTOR'S CHRONICLE, March 23 1990

New words and expressions 生词和短语

portfolio (title) /ˌpɔːtˈfəʊliəʊ/ *n.* 投资组合
tipster (1.1) /ˈtɪpstə/ *n.* （以提供证券投机等内部消息为生的）情报贩子
Las Vegas (1.2) /ˌlɑːsˈveɪgəs/ *n.* 拉斯维加斯
fritter (1.2) /ˈfrɪtə/ *v.* 挥霍，浪费
reputable (1.5) /ˈrepjʊtəbəl/ *adj.* 享有声望的
broker (1.5) /ˈbrəʊkə/ *n.* 经纪人
finance (1.7) /faɪˈnæns/ *n.* 资金，财源
mortgage (1.10) /ˈmɔːgɪdʒ/ *n.* 抵押贷款
pension (1.10) /ˈpenʃən/ *n.* 养老金

priority (ll.14-15) /praɪˈɒrəti/ *n.* 优先权
gilt (1.16) /gɪlt/ *n.* 金边证券（高度可靠的证券）
convertible (1.16) /kənˈvɜːtəbəl/ *n.* 可换证券
sanguine (1.18) /ˈsæŋgwɪn/ *adj.* 乐观的
heady (1.19) /ˈhedi/ *adj.* 令人陶醉的
alongside (1.20) /əˌlɒŋˈsaɪd/ *prep.* 在 …… 旁边，和 …… 一起
pedestrian (1.20) /pɪˈdestriən/ *adj.* 平淡无奇的，乏味的

The Stock Exchange, Tokyo 1994

Notes on the text 课文注释

1　go about, 从事, 做 。

2　Periwigs, 是一个假想中公司的名字 。

3　the basics, 这里指基本情况, 基本要素 。

4　If you recognize yourself in this description, 如果你觉得你的情况是这样的话 。

参考译文

我们周围不乏情报贩子, 向人们提供迅速发财致富的机遇 。但是, 如果你是一个认真的私人投资者, 就把拉斯维加斯的心态留给那些有钱可供挥霍的人 。认真的投资者需要一份正规的投资组合表——一种计划很周密的投资选择, 结构明确, 目标清晰 。但是, 一个股票市场的新手又如何能做到这一点呢?

如果你去向 5 位有威望的股票经纪人咨询, 询问你应该如何使用你的资金, 你很可能得到 5 种不同的答复, 即便你提供了所有关于你的年龄 、家庭 、财源和你想从投资中获得的好处的信息 。这是个道德问题吗? 没有一种完全 "正确" 的方法来排列这种投资组合, 然而, 却毫无疑问地有几种错误的方法 。可以相信 5 位经纪人中不会有人建议你把全部 (或一部分) 资金投入佩里威格斯公司 。

那么你该怎么做呢? 我们假定你已把基本情况弄清楚了, 如抵押贷款 、养老金 、保险金和动用现金储备的机会 。然后, 你一定要建立起自己的目标 。这里一方面是个人所处的环境, 另一方面是个心理学的问题 。

比如说, 如果你年纪较大, 你从重大投资损失中恢复过来的时间就较少, 你就很希望能够提高你的养老金收入 。因此, 你的首要任务就是保护你的资金和引发额外的收入 。在这种情况下, 你大概想制定出一份包括某些股份 (但不是风险很大的股份) 的投资组合, 同时还有高度可靠的证券 、现金储蓄, 可能还有可换证券, 或分割资本投资信托公司的所得股 。

如果你年轻一些, 并且经济状况可靠, 你可能会采取一种积极进取的方式——你必须性格开朗, 不会因股票价格的浮动而夜不能眠 。如果你觉得你的情况是这样的话, 你可在投资组合中包括几项有令人陶醉的增值前景的增长股, 和其他比较平淡的投资项目放在一起 。一旦你的投资目标确立以后, 你就可以决定你的钱投向何处 。这里的指导原则是: 分散你的投资风险 。如果你把所有资金投入佩里威格斯国际公司, 你就把自己当成了命运的人质 。

Unit 6   Lesson 48

Comprehension 理解

Answer these questions:

1 What kind of portfolio should a serious investor have?
2 How do we know there's no 'right way' to invest money?
3 What's one of the worst things you can do if you're investing money?
4 What arrangements should you have in place before you can think of investing money?
5 What would you probably want to achieve if you were an older investor?
6 What can you afford to do if you are a younger investor?
7 What's the main thing you have to do, whatever your age, when investing money?

Vocabulary 词汇

Refer to the text to see how the following words have been used, then write sentences of your own using these words: shortage (1.1); tipsters (1.1); fritter (1.2); structure a portfolio (ll.7-8); undoubtedly (1.8); sinking (1.9); sufficient cash reserves (1.11); personal circumstances (1.12); preserving your capital (1.14); pedestrian (1.20).

Summary 摘要

Drawing your information from the whole passage, give advice to a new investor (young or old). Do not write more than 100 words. Use your own words as far as possible. Your answer should be in one paragraph.

Composition 作文

Write a composition on one of the following subjects:

1 Saving and spending.
2 'Fear and greed are the driving forces of those who invest in stocks and shares.' Discuss.
3 Many people get hurt in a capitalist system.

Key structures 关键句型

A Supply *a* or *the* only where necessary in the following piece. Do not refer to the passage until you have finished the exercise:

There is no shortage of tipsters around offering _____ 'get-rich-quick' opportunities. But if you are _____ serious private investor, leave _____ Las Vegas mentality to those with _____ money to fritter. _____ serious investor needs_____ proper 'portfolio'— _____ well-planned selection of investments with _____ definite structure and _____ clear aim. But exactly how does _____ newcomer to _____ stock market go about achieving that?

   Well, if you go to five reputable stock brokers and ask them what you should do with your money, you're likely to get _____ five different answers—even if you give all _____ the relevant information about your age, _____ finances and what you want from your investments. Moral? There is no one 'right' way to structure _____ portfolio. However, there are undoubtedly some wrong ways, and you can be sure that none of our five advisers would have suggested sinking all (or perhaps any) of your money in Periwigs. (ll.1-9)

282

B   Complete these sentences. Do not refer to the passage until you have finished the exercise.

1   But if you are a serious private investor _____ (ll.1-2)

2   If you go to five reputable stock brokers _____ (l.5)

3   You're likely to get five different answers—even if _____ (ll.5-6)

4   If you are older _____ (l.13)

5   If you are younger _____ (l.17)

6   If you recognize yourself in this description _____ (ll.18-19)

7   If you put all of your money into Periwigs International _____ (ll.21-22)

Special difficulties 难点

Supply *any, some* or *no* in the following sentences. Do not refer to the passage until you have finished the exercise:

1   There is _____ shortage of tipsters around offering 'get-rich-quick' opportunities. (l.1)

2   There is _____ one 'right' way to structure a portfolio. (ll.7-8)

3   There are undoubtedly _____ wrong ways (to structure a portfolio). (l.8)

4   If you are older, you have less time to recover from _____ major losses. (l.13)

5   You'd probably construct a portfolio with _____ shares along with gilts. (ll.15-16)

Multiple choice questions 选择题

Choose the correct answers to the following questions.

Comprehension 理解

1 The writer distinguishes between serious investors and _____ .

(*a*) people who gamble at Las Vegas

(*b*) private investors

(*c*) those who want to make money fast

(*d*) newcomers to the stock market

2 If you want to invest money seriously, you _____ .

(*a*) should get at least five opinions

(*b*) should put all your money into a young company

(*c*) won't find it easy to decide, even with good advice

(*d*) should make sure you have sufficient funds after meeting all your other expenses

3 Priorities for investment largely depend on _____ .

(*a*) how quickly you want to make a lot of money

(*b*) your age and circumstances

(*c*) how much money you have available for investment

(*d*) how much income you expect from your investments

4 According to the writer, different financial advisers would probably agree that you _____ .

(*a*) should select stocks that will grow in value

(*b*) will have sleepless nights whatever you decide

(*c*) shouldn't 'put all your eggs in one basket'

(*d*) should understand your personality very well

Unit 6 Lesson 48

Structure 句型

5 There are _____ tipsters around offering 'get-rich-quick' opportunities. (l.1)

(a) many of   (b) a lot   (c) plenty of   (d) much

6 If you _____ them, none of our five advisers would have suggested sinking all your money into Periwigs. (ll.8-9)

(a) would ask   (b) ask   (c) had asked   (d) will ask

7 The younger you are _____ time you have to recover ... (l.13)

(a) the extra   (b) more   (c) the more   (d) the less

8 You might include a couple of heady growth stocks _____ with your more pedestrian investments. (l.20)

(a) apart   (b) beside   (c) as well as   (d) side by side

Vocabulary 词汇

9 Leave the Las Vegas mentality to those with money to _____ . (l.1)

(a) scatter   (b) waste   (c) invest   (d) gamble

10 We'll assume that you've _____ of the basics. (l.10)

(a) taken care of   (b) ordered   (c) discharged   (d) differentiated

11 You may well wish to _____ your pension income. (ll.13-14)

(a) increase   (b) facilitate   (c) establish   (d) replace

12 If you're blessed with a more _____ disposition ... (l.18)

(a) reckless   (b) confident   (c) bloody   (d) adventurous

Appendix 1:Personal names 附录 1：人名中英文对照表

英文（课）	译文	英文（课）	译文
Alex Au (10)	亚历克斯·奥	James Clark Ross (30)	詹姆斯·克拉克·罗斯
Alfred (9)	阿尔弗雷德	John Dewey (44)	约翰·杜威
Aristotle (32)	亚里士多德	John Wayne (21)	约翰·韦恩
Bertrand Russel (8) (11)	伯特兰·罗素	Julius E. Lips (33)	路易斯·E.利普斯
C. Clark (35)	C.克拉克	N. Damodar Reddy (10)	N.达蒙达·雷迪
Carver Mead (10)	卡弗·米德	Ptolemy (32)	托勒密
Christopher Cockerell (29)	克里斯托弗·科克雷尔	Ronald Bracewell (43)	罗纳德·布雷斯韦尔
Doris Odlum (34)	多丽丝·奥德伦	Rosse (32)	罗斯
Galileo (32)	伽利略	Thomas Carlyle (28)	托马斯·卡莱尔
Gary Cooper (21)	加里·古柏	Vera Petrova (4)	维拉·佩特瓦
Gustavus Adolphus (27)	古斯塔夫斯·阿道弗斯	Walter Sullivan (43)	沃尔特·沙利文
Guthrum (9)	格斯罗姆	William S. Hart (21)	威廉·S.哈特
Henry Taylor (28)	亨利·泰勒		

Appendix 2:Geographical names 附录 2：地名中英文对照表

英文（课）	译文	英文（课）	译文
Africa (29)	非洲	Los Angeles (26)	洛杉矶
Alps, the (3)	阿尔卑斯山脉	Matterhorn (3)	马特峰
Antipodes (17)	新西兰和澳大利亚	Missouri (10)	密苏里州
Athelney (9)	阿塞尔纳	Morocco (45)	摩洛哥
Atlantic, the (29)	大西洋	New Jersey (14)	新泽西州
Australia (17) (29)	澳大利亚	Norfolk (29)	诺福克
Baltic (27)	波罗的海	Pacific, the (23)	太平洋
Britain (9)	英国	Petersburg (26)	彼得堡
California (10) (32)	加利福尼亚	Pisa (32)	比萨
Chamonix (3)	夏蒙尼	Princeton (14)	普林斯顿
Cheshire (15)	柴郡	Qomolangma (35)	珠穆朗玛峰
Chippenham (9)	奇彭纳姆	Rancho la Brea (26)	兰桥·拉·布里
England (33)	英格兰	Russia (4)	俄罗斯
France (17) (33)	法国	Salem (43)	塞勒姆
Germany (23) (47)	德国	Scottish Highlands (39)	苏格兰高地
Grand Canyon (35)	大峡谷	Skeppsbron (27)	斯开波斯布朗
Hong Kong (10)	香港	Solent, the (29)	索伦特海峡
India (10)	印度	Sweden (27)	瑞典
Japan (10)	日本	Taiwan (10)	台湾
Kansas City (10)	堪萨斯城	Ulyanovsk (4)	乌里扬诺夫斯克
Kashmir (39)	克什米尔	U.S., the (10)	美国
Las Vegas (48)	拉斯维加斯	Zermatt (3)	采尔马特

新概念英语系列·全套产品目录

教材及教学辅导用书	书号 *
新概念英语 1（另配录音带 2 盒）	1346-6 (01)
新概念英语 2（另配录音带 3 盒）	1347-3 (01)
新概念英语 3（另配录音带 3 盒）	1348-0 (01)
新概念英语 4（另配录音带 3 盒）	1349-7 (01)
新概念英语 教师用书 1（另配录音带 4 盒）	1350-3
新概念英语 教师用书 2（另配录音带 4 盒）	1351-0
新概念英语 教师用书 3（另配录音带 4 盒）	1771-6
新概念英语 教师用书 4（另配录音带 4 盒）	1841-6
新概念英语 练习册 1	1840-9
新概念英语 练习册 2	1723-5
新概念英语 练习册 3	2482-0
新概念英语 练习册 4	2775-3
新概念英语 自学导读 1	1799-0
新概念英语 自学导读 2	1733-4
新概念英语 自学导读 3	1940-6
新概念英语 自学导读 4	2512-4
新概念英语 练习详解 1	2225-3
新概念英语 练习详解 2	1812-6
新概念英语 练习详解 3	1873-7
新概念英语 练习详解 4	2329-8
新概念英语 词汇随身听速记手册 1（另配录音带 4 盒）	3063-0
新概念英语 词汇随身听速记手册 2（另配录音带 4 盒）	3150-7
新概念英语 词汇随身听速记手册 3（另配录音带 7 盒）	3151-X
新概念英语 词汇练习 1	4208-4
新概念英语 词汇练习 2	5632-6
新概念英语 词汇练习 3	4390-6
新概念英语 词汇练习 4	5633-4
新概念英语 语法练习 1	3304-4
新概念英语 语法练习 2	4591-X
新概念英语 语法练习 3	4308-1
新概念英语 口语练习 1	4391-3
新概念英语 口语练习 2	4573-3
新概念英语 口语练习 3	4752-2
新概念英语 口语练习 4	4792-8

教材及教学辅导用书	书号 *
新概念英语 词汇大全	1727-3
新概念英语 语法手册	4230-5
新概念英语（1）课本同步讲解辅导 VCD	
新概念英语（2）课本同步讲解辅导 VCD	
新概念英语（3）课本同步讲解辅导 VCD	
新概念英语（4）课本同步讲解辅导 VCD	
新概念英语（课堂教学版）	
新概念英语 1A（含 mp3）	7454-2
新概念英语 1B（含 mp3）	7455-9
新概念英语 2A（含 mp3）	7456-6
新概念英语 2B（含 mp3）	7457-3
新概念英语 3（含 mp3）	7458-0
新概念英语 4（含 mp3）	7459-7
新概念英语青少版	
新概念英语青少版 学生用书 1A（含 mp3 和动画 DVD）	7354-5
新概念英语青少版 学生用书 1B（含 mp3 和动画 DVD）	7356-9
新概念英语青少版 学生用书 2A（含 mp3 和动画 DVD）	7371-2
新概念英语青少版 学生用书 2B（含 mp3 和动画 DVD）	7372-9
新概念英语青少版 学生用书 3A（含 mp3 和动画 DVD）	7373-6
新概念英语青少版 学生用书 3B（含 mp3 和动画 DVD）	7374-3
新概念英语青少版 练习册 1A	7355-2
新概念英语青少版 练习册 1B	7357-6
新概念英语青少版 练习册 2A	7375-0
新概念英语青少版 练习册 2B	7376-7
新概念英语青少版 练习册 3A	7377-4
新概念英语青少版 练习册 3B	7378-1
新概念英语青少版 教师用书 1（含 mp3）（另配录音带）	7368-2
新概念英语青少版 教师用书 2（含 mp3）（另配录音带）	7369-9
新概念英语青少版 教师用书 3（含 mp3）（另配录音带）	7370-5

* 本产品目录中书号为完整书号的后 5 位；如订书，请在前面加 978-7-5600-。

上述图书和音像产品全国各大书店均有销售。欢迎登录新概念英语官方教学网站 **www.ncehome.com** 查询具体信息。